Ex Libris

Jess Guth

EUROPEAN ECONOMIC AND SOCIAL CONSTITUTIONALISM AFTER THE TREATY OF LISBON

European studies frequently regard the economic and social dimensions of EU integration as diametrically opposed, maintaining that this state of affairs is beyond change. This edited collection challenges this perceived wisdom, focusing on the post-Lisbon constitutional landscape. Taking the multilayered polity that is Europe today as its central organising theme, it examines how the social and the economic might be reconciled under the Union's different forms of governance. The collection opens with a theoretical appraisal of its theme, before considering three specific policy fields: migration policy and civic integration; company law and corporate social responsibility; and the role of third-sector providers in public healthcare. It concludes with three case studies in these fields, illustrating how the argument can be practically applied. Insightful and topical, with a unique interdisciplinary perspective, this is an important contribution to European Union law and politics after the Treaty of Lisbon.

DAGMAR SCHIEK is Chair in European Law, Director of the Centre of European Law and Legal Studies and Jean Monnet Chair in Law at the University of Leeds. She has worked extensively on European labour law and non-discrimination law, and published in leading academic publications on the German constitution and German collective agreement act.

ULRIKE LIEBERT is Professor of Political Science, Jean Monnet Professor for European Politics, director of the Jean Monnet Centre for European Studies and co-director of the section 'European integration' of the Bremen International Graduate School for Social Sciences.

HILDEGARD SCHNEIDER is Professor of European Law at Maastricht University, the Netherlands and at Universiteit Hasselt, Belgium, and Jean Monnet Chair for European Migration Law at Maastricht University.

EUROPEAN ECONOMIC AND SOCIAL CONSTITUTIONALISM AFTER THE TREATY OF LISBON

Edited by

DAGMAR SCHIEK

ULRIKE LIEBERT

HILDEGARD SCHNEIDER

CAMBRIDGE
UNIVERSITY PRESS

CAMBRIDGE UNIVERSITY PRESS
Cambridge, New York, Melbourne, Madrid, Cape Town,
Singapore, São Paulo, Delhi, Tokyo, Mexico City

Cambridge University Press
The Edinburgh Building, Cambridge CB2 8RU, UK

Published in the United States of America by Cambridge University Press, New York

www.cambridge.org
Information on this title: www.cambridge.org/9781107006812

First published 2011

Printed in the United Kingdom at the University Press, Cambridge

A catalogue record for this publication is available from the British Library

Library of Congress Cataloguing in Publication data
European economic and social constitutionalism after the Treaty of Lisbon / edited by Dagmar
Schiek, Ulrike Liebert and Hildegard Schneider.
p. cm.
Includes bibliographical references and index.
ISBN 978-1-107-00681-2
1. Constitutional law – European Union countries.   2. Law – European Union countries –
International unification.   3. Law – Economic aspects – European Union
countries.   4. European Union countries – Economic policy.   5. Social integration – European
Union countries.   I. Schiek, Dagmar.   II. Liebert, Ulrike.   III. Schneider,
Hildegard.   IV. Title.
KJE5076.E93   2011
343.24′07–dc22
2010051574

ISBN 978-1-107-00681-2 Hardback

CONTENTS

CONTRIBUTORS

THOMAS BIERMEYER, LL.M., is a PhD researcher at the Maastricht University and a paralegal at Paulussen NV in Maastricht. His research interests lie in the field of company law and competition law. He is a section editor of the Maastricht Journal of Comparative and European Law.

DR SERGIO CARRERA is the Head of Section & Research Fellow at the Centre for European Policy Studies (CEPS), Brussels, and researcher at the Maastricht University. His main research interests include EU legal frames on immigration, integration and citizenship, and he is researching in the field of Justice and Home Affairs at CEPS.

PIETER VAN CLEYNENBREUGEL, LL.M., is a Research Fellow of the Fund for Scientific Research – Flanders and a PhD candidate at the Leuven Centre for a Common Law of Europe (Katholieke Universiteit Leuven). His research interests lie in the field of European economic law.

PROFESSOR DR WOUTER DEVROE, is a fully tenured law professor at the Katholieke Universiteit Leuven and at Maastricht University. He teaches comparative, EU and competition law. As an attorney and member of the Brussels Bar, he regularly appears before national courts and authorities and before the European Court of Justice (ECJ). Previously, he clerked at the ECJ (Chambers of Advocate General van Gerven and Judge Sevón, 1992–5) and he was a member of the Belgian competition authority (2000–7). He received a PhD on privatisation and corporatisation. His research focus is on EU and national economic law.

ANDREA GIDEON, LL.M., is a Research Officer supporting the Jean Monnet Multilateral Research Group 'European Economic and Social Constitutionalism after the Treaty of Lisbon' and a PhD researcher at the University of Leeds (Centre of European Law and Legal Studies). Her main research interests include EU law constraints on national welfare policies and human rights law.

DR SANDRA KRÖGER is a senior lecturer at the Jean Monnet Centre for European Studies (CEuS) at the Universität Bremen. Her main research interests include steering through soft law on which she has widely published and non-electoral forms of representation via civil society organisations in the EU, with a focus on social and agricultural policies. She is an associate of the research project 'Reconstituting Democracy in Europe' (RECON) and of the Observatoire Social Européen (OSE) and a member of the Consortium for the evaluation of the OMC.

PROFESSOR DR ULRIKE LIEBERT is Professor of Political Science at the Universität Bremen, Jean Monnet Professor for European Politics, director of the Jean Monnet Centre for European Studies (CeuS) and co-director of the section 'European integration' of the Bremen International Graduate School for Social Sciences (BiGSSS). She has held various visiting professorships, for example at RGGU and PFUR (Moscow), the Universitat Autonomà de Barcelona and the EUI (Florence). She holds leading roles in the research project 'Reconstituting Democracy in Europe' (RECON, coordinated by ARENA, Oslo 2007–11) and 'Citizenship and Constitutionalisation: Transforming the Public Sphere in the New Europe' (funded by Volkswagen Foundation).

DR NICOLE LINDSTROM researches and teaches in the areas of international relations and comparative political economy at the University of York. She has held visiting positions in the Graduate Programme of International Affairs at The New School for Social Research and the Centre for the Study of Globalisation and Regionalisation at the University of Warwick. Her research interests lie in the dynamic interactions between transnational actors and domestic change, with a regional focus on Central and East Europe and the Balkans. Other ongoing research considers political debates over liberalisation of services in the newly enlarged European Union.

PROFESSOR DR ULLA NEERGAARD is Professor of EU law at the Law Faculty, Københavns Universitet, and an expert member of the Danish Council of Competition and of the Danish Energy Regulatory Authority. She has been a principle investigator in the research project 'Blurring Boundaries' on the relationship between national welfare states and EU law, and has been involved in the research group 'TOMAS' (Transformation of Markets and States). Her research interests include EU competition law, European legal methods, healthcare and EU law and social services of general interest.

PROFESSOR DR DAGMAR SCHIEK, of the University of Leeds, is Chair for European Law, Jean Monnet Professor and Director of the Centre of European Law and Legal Studies. She has been a visiting professor and guest lecturer at various universities, including London School of Economics and Maastricht University. Her research interests lie in the field of European Economic and Social constitutionalism, new forms of governance in the EU involving civil society and European and international equality law. She is on the editorial board of the Maastricht Journal for Comparative and European Law and of Kritische Justiz (Critical Legal Studies, Germany).

PROFESSOR DR HILDEGARD SCHNEIDER is Professor of European Law at Maastricht University, the Netherlands and at Universiteit Hasselt, Belgium, and Jean Monnet Chair for European Migration Law at Maastricht University. She has been a visiting professor and guest lecturer at various universities and institutions abroad including Peking University in 2006 and 2007. Her research interests lie in the fields of European substantive law, migration and non-discrimination law and European competition and company law. Furthermore she publishes in the area of art law and cultural property law. She is involved in several international research networks and member of the research school Ius Commune.

DR IDA WENDT is a lecturer in European Law at the Erasmus Universiteit Rotterdam and a legal specialist for the Dutch Competition Authority. Her main research interests include EU competition law, and the laws that govern the liberal professions. She served on the editorial committee of the Maastricht Journal of European and Comparative Law (2006–10).

DR ANJA WIESBROCK is a lecturer in European Law at the law faculty of the Maastricht University. Her main research interests include EU substantive law, European migration and nationality law and European criminal law. She is currently working as a Visiting Lecturer at Eylül University, Izmir.

PREFACE

This book results from a 'Multilateral Jean Monnet Research Group' called 'European Economic and Social Constitutionalism after the Treaty of Lisbon: an Interdisciplinary Perspective', which took up its work in September 2008. The idea for the group originated in collaborations between Hildegard Schneider and Dagmar Schiek within the framework of the IUS COMMUNE research school, where both had attempted to establish a research focus 'Economic and Social Constitutionalism', as well as in the contacts between Ulrike Liebert and Dagmar Schiek, who had been working at neighbouring universities for quite a while, often noticing that they had some overlap in research interests, but not succeeding in teaming up for research.

The Jean Monnet Programme offered an ideal opportunity to acquire the funds necessary to intensify these exchanges. When we wrote the application in February 2008, the fate of the Treaty of Lisbon was not yet decided. However, we bravely assumed that the eternal issue of tensions between the economic and social dimensions inherent in the European integration project would remain of prominent importance, and that there was not a sufficient amount of research concerning their interrelation at different levels and with modes of EU governance. Moreover, we supposed that neither stylising the *Laval* and *Viking* cases as a conflict between the ECJ and the Member States nor to newly suggest purely procedural solutions to ameliorate the perceived subordination of the social to the economic dimension of European integration would suffice. Of course, we have been immensely fortunate to receive funding from our main sponsor, the European Commission, based on those ideas. We also acknowledge Leeds University School of Law for having provided some additional funds during the project's lifetime, as well as the research support structures at Leeds, the home base where the leadership and organisation of the project resided.

We are deeply appreciative of the participants to a conference in Leeds in September 2009 for discussing our ideas and framework, among them several who later turned their contributions into book chapters, while other contributors joined in later. Our greatest thanks, however, go to our research team, which initially consisted of three research officers (Stephie Fehr (LL.M) at Leeds, Dr Sandra Kröger at Bremen and Dr Sergio Carrera at Maastricht). Sergio Carrera was subsequently joined by Dr Anja Wiesbrock in Maastricht, while Andrea Gideon (LL.M) took over the role of the Leeds research officer when Stephie Fehr went on maternity leave. She was joined by Sadana Perera, combining project administration and research assistance; Dr Ida Wendt, authoring the Leeds case study; and Dr Wendy Guns and Richard Butterworth (MA), acting as editorial assistants in the preparation of the publication. All of them have tremendously contributed to the project and the results would not have been possible without their engagement.

Final thanks go to Sinéad Moloney at Cambridge University Press, who supported our publishing proposal from the start and, together with Elizabeth Spicer, provided smooth editorial support for this project.

ABBREVIATIONS

ACVZ	Adviescommissie voor Vreemdelingenzaken (Committee for Advice on Foreigners' Affairs, the Netherlands)
AIRAANZ	Association of Industrial Relations Academics of Australia and New Zealand
AOF	Annual Operation Framework
AWBZ	Algemene Wet Bijzondere Ziektekosten (General Act on Special Health Expenses, the Netherlands)
BITC	Business in the Community
CAI	Contrat d'Accueil et d'Intégration (Welcome and Integration Contract, France)
CAIF	Contrat d'Accueil et d'Intégration pour la Famille (Family Welcome and Integration Contract, France)
CBPs	Common Basic Principles of Immigrant and Integration Policy
CCP	Common Commercial Policy (EU)
CEEP	European Centre of Employers and Enterprises Providing Public Services
CEPS	Centre for European Policy Studies
CESEDA	Code de l'Entrée et de Séjour des Estrangers e du Droit d'Asile (Code on Admission and Residence of Foreigners and on Right to Asylum, France)
CFI	Court of First Instance (EU until Nov. 2009, now: General Court)
CiMU	Committee on Circular Migration and Development (Kommittèn för cirkulär migration och utveckling)
CME	Co-ordinated Market Economies
CMLRev	*Common Market Law Review*
Columbia JEL	*Columbia Journal of European Law*
Columbia JTL	*Columbia Journal of Transnational Law*
CompEurPolit	*Comparative European Politics*
CPB	Centraal Plan Bureau (Central Planning Office, the Netherlands)
CQC	Care Quality Commission
CSO	Civil Society Organisation
CSR	Corporate Social Responsibility

DGB	Deutscher Gewerkschaftsbund (Trade Union Congress, Germany)
DGIS	Directoraat-Generaal Internationale Samenwerking (General Office for International Co-operation, the Netherlands)
DVBl	*Deutsches Verwaltungsblatt*
EC	European Community (also used as abbreviation of the EC Treaty)
ECB	European Central Bank (EU)
ECJ	Court of Justice of the European Union (EU)
ECOFIN	Economic and Financial Ministers Council (EU)
ECR	European Court Reports (EU)
ECSC	European Coal and Steel Community
ECtHR	European Court of Human Rights (Council of Europe)
EC Treaty	European Community Treaty
EEA	European Economic Area
EEC	European Economic Community
EIOP	*European Integration Online Papers*
EIRonline	*European Industrial Relations Observatory Online*
EITI	Extractive Industries Transparency Initiative
ELJ	*European Law Journal*
ELRev	*European Law Review*
EMMI	European Modules for Migrants Integration
EMS CSR Forum	EU Multi-stake Forum on Corporate Social Responsibility
EMU	European and Monetary Union (EU)
EPL	*European Public Law*
EPP-ED Group	Group of the European People's Party (Christian Democrats) and European Democrats in the European Parliament
EPS	*European Political Science*
ERT	European Round Table of Industrialists (EU)
ESM	European Social Model
ETUC	European Trade Union Congress
ETUI	European Trade Union Institute
EU	European Union
FOC	Flags of Convenience
FOII	Office Français de l' Immigration et de l'Intégration (French Office of Immigration and Integration)
FSU	Finnish Seamen Union
FTSE	Financial Times Stock Exchange
GCIM	Global Commission on International Migration (UN)
GDP	Gross Domestic Product

GP	General Practitioner (England, Wales)
IJGLS	*Indiana Journal of Global Legal Studies*
ILJ	*Industrial Law Journal*
ILO	International Labour Organisation
IMI	International Migration Institute
IND	Immigratie-en Naturalisatie Dienst (Immigration and Naturalisation Service, the Netherlands)
InfAuslR	*Informationsbrief Ausländerrecht*
IOM	International Organisation for Migration
ISTC	Independent Sector Treatment Centre (England, Wales)
ITF	International Transport Worker's Federation
JCMS	*Journal of Common Market Studies*
JEPP	*Journal of European Public Policy*
J Law&Soc	*Journal of Law and Society*
Jnl Soc. Pol.	*Journal of Social Policy*
LHB	Local Health Boards (England, Wales)
LME	Liberal Market Economies
LS	*Legal Studies*
LSI	*Law & Social Inquiry*
MEP	Member of the European Parliament
MIDA	Migration and Development in Africa (IOM capacity-building programme)
MLR	*Modern Law Review*
MOIA	Ministry of Overseas Indian Affairs
MPI	Migration Policy Institute
MPIfG	Max-Planck Institut für Geschellschaftsforschung (Max Planck Institute for the Study of Societies, Cologne)
MS	Member State(s) (EU)
MVV	Machtiging tot voorlopig verblijf (Provisional Leave to Remain, the Netherlands)
NCP	National Contact Point
NGO	Non-governmental Organisation
NHS	National Health Service (England, Wales)
Nma	Nederlandse Mededingsautoriteit (Competition Authority, the Netherlands)
NTER	*Nederlands tijdschrift voor Europees recht*
Nza	Nederlandse Zorgautoriteit (Authority supervising the care sector, the Netherlands)
OCI	Overseas Citizenship of India
OECD	Organisation for Economic Co-operation and Development (UN)
OFT	Office of Fair Trading (UK)

OJ	Official Journal of the European Union
OJLS	*Oxford Journal of Legal Studies*
OMC	Open Method of Co-ordination (EU)
PbR	Payment by Result
PCT	Primary Care Trusts (England, Wales)
PWD	Directive 96/71/EC of the European Parliament and of the Council of 16 December 1996 concerning the posting of workers in the framework of the provision of services (Posting of Workers Directive)
QMV	Qualified Majority Voting (EU)
Qual Saf Health Care	*Quality and Safety in Health Care*
RTDE	*Revue trimestrielle de droit européen*
SE	Societas Europaea
SER	Sociaal Economische Raad (Social and Economic Council, the Netherlands)
SEW	*Sociaal-Economische Wetgeving – Tijdschrift voor Europees en Economisch Recht*
SGEI	Services of General Economic Interest (EU)
SME	Social Market Economy
TCN	Third-country National
TEU	Treaty on European Union
TFEU	Treaty on the Functioning of the European Union
ToL	Treaty of Lisbon
UK	United Kingdom
UN	United Nations
US	United States
VoC	Varieties of Capitalism
WAG	Welsh Assembly Government
WIB	Wet inburgering in het Buitenland (Integration Abroad Act, the Netherlands)
WMG	Wet Marktordening Gezondheidszorg (Act on creating a Market in Healthcare, the Netherlands)
WWII	World War II

I   Court of Justice of the European Union and General Court: Numerical Order

II Court of Justice of the European Union and General Court: Alphabetical Order

III   European Court of Human Rights: Numerical Order

IV   European Court of Human Rights: Alphabetical Order

V   National Cases

~

Introduction

DAGMAR SCHIEK, ULRIKE LIEBERT AND
HILDEGARD SCHNEIDER

This introduction contextualises the hypothesis of the two-year research
project on which this book is based, and explains how the single chapters
relate to this hypothesis. The reader will see that we are opening a new
debate with new questions, which still await definite answers.

I The context of the book

Over the past decade tensions between 'Social Europe' and 'European
economic integration' have surged at manifold sites.[1] Frequently, these
tensions were perceived as dissonances between the European economic
integration project and social policies at national level. Once the Court of
Justice delivered its judgments in the *Laval* and *Viking* cases,[2] clashes
between the EU market freedoms of services and establishment with
industrial action at national and transnational level have been discussed
widely.[3] These spectacular cases have prompted authors who were
alien to debates on European labour law to position themselves in this

---

[1] F. Scharpf, 'The European Social Model: Coping with the challenges of diversity', *JCMS*
40 (2002), 645; W. Streeck, 'Competitive solidarity: Re-thinking the European Social
Model', MPIfG Working Paper 8 (September 1999); A. Giddens, P. Diamond and
R. Liddle (eds.), *Global Europe, Social Europe* (Cambridge: Polity Press, 2006);
U. Neergaard, R. Nielsen and L. Roseberry (eds.), *Integrating Welfare Functions into
EU Law: From Rome to Lisbon* (Copenhagen: DJØF, 2009); J. Trachtman, *The
International Law of Economic Migration: Toward the fourth freedom* (Kalamazoo:
W. E. Upjohn Institute for Employment Research, 2009).

[2] C-341/05 *Laval* [2007] ECR I-11767 and C-438/05 *ITWU, FSU* v. *Viking Line ABP, OÜ
Viking Line Eesti* [2007] ECR I-10779.

[3] See R. Blanpain, A. Świątkowski (eds.), *The Laval and Viking Cases: Freedom of Services
Establishment* v. *Industrial Conflict in the European Economic Area and Russia*
(Deventer: Kluwer, 2009); for more references see chs. 1 (Schiek) and 3 (Lindstrom).

field,[4] as well as giving those who had foreseen these conflicts for a long time the dubious satisfaction of seeing their predictions realised.[5] Conflicts between EU market freedoms and competition law on the one hand and national social policies on the other not only exist in relation to (national) labour standards,[6] but also to national social security systems,[7] in particular healthcare systems.[8] Some of this debate focused on the judicial activism of the Court of Justice,[9] but it also became acute through legislative endeavours initiated by the European Commission, such as the services directive,[10] or the port directive,[11] which were seen as pushing neoliberalism

---

[4] C. Joerges and F. Rödl, 'Informal politics, formalized law and the 'social deficit' of European integration: Reflections after the judgments of the ECJ in *Viking* and *Laval*', *ELJ* 15 (2009), 1.

[5] After the ECJ held that France's omission to take a tough stance on French farmers' collective action against the Common Market constituted a breach of free movement of goods (C-265/95 *Commission* v. *France* [1997] ECR I-6959), future impact on industrial relations was widely foreseen (e.g. J. Kühling, 'Staatliche Handlungspflicht zur Sicherung der Grundfreiheiten', *NJW* (1999), 403; P. Szczekalla, 'Grundfreiheitliche Schutzpflichten', *Deutsches Verwaltungsblatt* (1998), 219; K. Muylle, 'Angry farmers and passive policemen: Private conduct and the free movement of goods', *ELRev* 23 (1998), 467; and G. Orlandini, 'The free movement of goods as a possible "Community" limitation on industrial conflict', *ELJ* 6 (2000), 341. Orlandini drew the line from *Commission* v. *France* to *Viking* in 'Trade union rights and market freedoms: The European Court of Justice sets out the rules', *Comparative Labor Law & Policy Journal* 29 (2008), 573.

[6] See N. Bruun and B. Hepple, 'Economic policy and labour law' in B. Hepple and B. Veneziani (eds.), *The Transformation of Labour Law in Europe* (Oxford and Portland: Hart Publishing, 2009), pp. 31–57; B. Bercusson, *European Labour Law* (Cambridge: Cambridge University Press, 2009).

[7] G. de Búrca (ed.), *EU Law and the Welfare State* (Oxford: Oxford University Press, 2005); B. von Maydell *et al.* (eds.), *Enabling Social Europe* (Berlin: Springer, 2006); U. Neergaard *et al.* (n. 1 above).

[8] E. Mossialos *et al.* (eds.), *Health Systems Governance in Europe: The role of EU law and policy* (Cambridge: Cambridge University Press, 2010).

[9] e.g. J. Monks, 'European Court of Justice and Social Europe: A divorce based on irreconcilable differences?', *Social Europe Journal* 4 (2008), 22.

[10] U. Neergaard, R. Nielsen and L. Roseberry, *The Services Directive: Consequences for the welfare state and the European Social Model* (Copenhagen: DJØF, 2008).

[11] COM (2004) 654 Final. The draft inter alia contained the principle of self-hauling of cargo in its attempt to liberalise port services. This would exclude legislating providing dock workers with stable employment locally. (For a successful legal challenge of such legislation see C-179/90 *Merci Convenzionali Porto di Genova* v. *Siderurgica Gabrielli* [1991] ECR I-5889.) Self-haulage of cargo was the main concern of European trade unions (P. Turnbull, 'The war on Europe's waterfront – Repertoires of power in the port transport industry', *British Journal of Industrial Relations* 44 (2005), 305), but the draft was also opposed by some Member States and business representatives on other grounds (see A. Pallis and G. Tsiotsis, 'Maritime interests and the EU port services directive', *European Transport* 38 (2008), 17).

with undue emphasis. Opposition to these legislative proposals com-
manded one of the first 'Euro-demonstrations' in front of the European
Parliament, which in turn led to the withdrawal of one proposal and the
thorough overhaul of another. Against this background, debates about
Social Europe were pursued in the Convention debates about a
Constitution for Europe and also subsequently in negotiating the Treaty
of Lisbon (ToL). During both processes, the EU was widely perceived as
threatening social policy by favouring economic integration. This perception arguably contributed to the demise of the Constitutional Treaty and
the initial Irish rejection of the ToL.[12]

While these debates raged, notions of 'social integration' were increasingly used in EU immigration law and policy. Originally, 'social integration' was meant to enhance social inclusion of those migrating into the
EU, which could have been perceived as an increasing acknowledgement
of an emerging European society. More recently, social integration has
been re-conceptualised as a requirement for third-country nationals
(TCNs) to fulfil, partly before coming to the EU. This can be understood
as a perversion of integration into an instrument of social exclusion.[13]

Recently, conflict about Social Europe has intensified again as a consequence of the mid-term review of the Lisbon process. This process had been
launched in 2000 in order to inter alia reconcile economic and social
objectives of the European Union. However, the Commission's strategy
'Europe 2020'[14] has again attracted criticism for not enabling the EU to
develop a sustainable social policy.[15] Last but not least, ever since the Lisbon

---

[12] According to the post-referendum surveys by Eurobarometer in France, the Netherlands
   and Luxembourg in 2005, 31% of French, 7% of Dutch and 37% of Luxembourg 'no-
   voters' feared negative effects on the employment situation in their country; 19% of
   French, 6% of Dutch and 11% of Luxembourg 'no-voters' found the Constitutional
   Treaty too liberal; while 16% of the French, 2% of the Dutch and 22% of the Luxembourg
   no-voters missed emanations of 'social Europe'. ('Flash Eurobarometers' 171–2, available from http://ec.europa.eu/public_opinion/index_en.htm. These questions were not
   asked for Flash Eurobarometers 168 and 245 on the Spanish Referendum on the
   Constitutional Treaty and the Irish referendum on the Lisbon Treaty.)
[13] For critical appraisals of EU immigration policy see S. Carrera, *In Search of the Perfect
   Citizen? The intersection between integration, immigration and nationality in the EU* (Leiden:
   Martinus Nijhoff, 2009); E. Guild, K. Groenendijk and S. Carrera (eds.), *Illiberal Liberal
   States: Immigration, citizenship and integration in the EU* (Aldershot: Ashgate, 2009).
[14] COM (2010) 2020 of 3 March 2010.
[15] L. Magnusson, *After Lisbon: Social Europe at the crossroads?* (Brussels: ETUI, 2010), on
   earlier versions of the 'Lisbon process' see U. Liebert, 'The politics for a Social Europe
   and the Lisbon process' in L. Magnusson and B. Strath (eds.), *European Solidarities:
   Tensions and contentions of a concept* (Frankfurt a M: Peter Lang, 2007), p. 267.

Treaty reform has entered into force in December 2009,[16] the social repercussions of the global financial and economic crisis have aggravated the EU's search for a stable normative and institutional order. Thus, researching how the norms of economic and social constitutionalism perform in the practices of European Union governance is a highly topical endeavour.

Accordingly, more has been written on these issues in parallel to the research leading to this book. Some contributions within the framework of the RECON project[17] have investigated the impact of EU law on national law, emphasising social and environmental issues,[18] and contributed to the debate on European constitutionalism.[19] The 'Blurring Boundaries' project[20] too investigated clashes between market access justice at European level and distributive justice at national levels, ultimately demanding a 'constitutionalisation of the European Social Model'. A 2010 edited collection assembles more sceptical views:[21] on the one hand, political science analysis is said to conclude that European social policy is a practical impossibility, on the other hand, legal scholars demand developing solidarity as a new EU constitutional principle, capable of supporting the development of 'new, potentially European, solidarities'.[22] Recent analysis of the ToL seems to concur with part of our deliberations in concluding that a number of imbalances remain in place after the Lisbon Treaty, among which the imbalance between opening internal borders to a free flow of goods, services, capital and workers on the one hand and maintaining differences between social and fiscal national laws, while pretending that these are not distortions of competition, on the other, features prominently.[23] This seems

---

[16] The ToL entered into force on 1 December 2009 with its ratification by the Czech Republic; see for consolidated versions of the Treaties OJ C 83/1–404 of 31 March 2010.

[17] For an overview of the project's results see www.reconproject.eu/projectweb/portalproject/ Index.html.

[18] C. Joerges and F. Rödl, 'On the "social deficit" of the European integration project and its perpetuation through the ECJ-judgements in *Viking* and *Laval*', RECON Online Working Paper 6 (2008), published in *ELJ* 2009 (n. 4 above).

[19] N. Walker, 'Constitutionalism and pluralism in a global context', RECON Online Working Paper 3 (2010).

[20] See U. Neergaard and R. Nielsen, 'Blurring boundaries: From the Danish welfare state to the European Social Model?' (Copenhagen 2010), http://papers.ssrn.com/sol3/papers. cfm?abstract_id=1618758; and U. Neergaard *et al.* (nn. 1 and 10 above) and *The Role of Courts in Developing a European Social Model* (Copenhagen: DJØF, 2010).

[21] M. Ross and Y. Borgmann-Prebil (eds.), *Promoting Solidarity in the European Union* (Oxford: Oxford University Press, 2010).

[22] *Ibid.*, pp. 20–1.

[23] J.-C. Piris, *The Lisbon Treaty. A legal and political analysis* (Cambridge: Cambridge University Press, 2010), p. 334.

to suggest – as do the conclusions of the Blurring Boundaries project – that EU-level solutions to social imbalances resulting from European economic integration need to be sought.

II   The specific contribution of this book

This book aims at presenting a new vision of reconciling economic and social dimensions of European integration under perspectives of constitutionalism and different forms of governance, reflecting on the impact generated by the ToL. It relates to intense debates having been conducted in different quarters of European studies, particularly in political science, sociology and legal studies.

In doing so, we depart from a two-part hypothesis. First, we assume that economic and social dimensions of European integration have been decoupled in the historic reality of the European integration process. Economic integration has been constitutionalised at EU level through individual rights. The ensuing juridification has advanced a rights-based promotion of commodification and market liberalisation, which in turn 'protected' European economic integration from political discourse. Merely judicial enforcement of fundamental freedoms and EU competition law tended to destabilise national institutions contributing to social integration. Concurrently, the European integration process failed to develop a hard-and-fast social dimension. As a result, EU-level institutions favouring social integration or safeguarding the functioning of national or sub-national institutions in nested systems of welfare[24] have not developed beyond some pin-pointed social policy initiatives, partly resulting in legally binding rules (e.g. through directives on equality or workers' protection and participation in cases of restructuring enterprises), but mainly focused on co-ordinating different national models of social law and policy. Thus, social integration is still a field for national level political discourse, although its reconfiguration is partly inhibited by the constitutionalised norms of European economic integration.

The second part of the hypothesis suggests that this state of affairs is neither sustainable nor an inevitable consequence of European integration. As a consequence of successful European integration processes, EU law and politics impact to an ever more discernible degree on social

---

[24] The image of nesting is owed to M. Ferrera, *The Boundaries of Welfare* (Oxford: Oxford University Press, 2005).

institutions which – at national level – mirror the provisional outcome of social struggles between antagonist forces. Such sites of conflict relate to industrial relations, the level of protection of the un-propertied populace against typical risks and ultimately poverty, or the division of reproductive work between families and more public spheres. As the EU increasingly influences and destabilises these compromises, its success becomes ever more contingent upon offering ways to provide equivalents. The EU discourse on equality and immigration – even if partly perverting the notion of social inclusion – is symptomatic for this need and thus warrants special attention.

Yet, we are not convinced by the increasingly popular proposition of maintaining mainly national responsibility for social policy while proceeding with economic integration at European levels in order to solve these problems.[25] Contrasting these trends, we aim to explore whether and how the economic and the social can be – and are being – reconciled within the EU multilayered polity. Any hard-and-fast separation of national and EU-level policy is increasingly untenable, as their interdependencies grow. EU policy and law impact upon national policy and law, enabling the development of sub-national spheres, as much as they are shaped by national law and policy. The interrelation of economic and social dimensions of European integration thus needs to be comprehended as a succession of dynamic interactions across different levels.

The success of any strategy in this direction will depend on different forms of governance. A common thread running through the book's chapters is the assumption that governance needs to be incorporated as an element of constitutionalism. This implies that different forms of governance are also considered in their relationship to and relevance for economic and social integration. As three archetypical modes of governance, we consider judicial enforcement of directly applicable Treaty norms (hard law), implementation of secondary Community legislation (harmonising law) and so-called soft-law mechanisms such as the open method of co-ordination (OMC). Here is another aspect in which this book deviates from received wisdom. We do not assume that a certain governance style is necessarily better suited to enhance economic or social aspects of European integration. Often, the implicit or even

---

[25] See e.g. F. Scharpf, 'The double asymmetry of European integration', MPIfG Working Paper 12 (2009); P. Syrpis, *EU Intervention in Domestic Labour Law* (Oxford: Oxford University Press, 2007); and G. Majone, *Dilemmas of European Integration: The ambiguities and pitfalls of integration by stealth* (Oxford: Oxford University Press, 2005), ch. 6.

explicit[26] assumption is that economic integration and hard law go hand in hand. Hard EU law, when applied directly by courts reacting to challenges by economic actors, engenders 'negative integration', i.e. the eradication of national rules conflicting with EU rules. Mainly, this form of integration results from applying economic market freedoms and competition law. However, application of the equal pay clause (Article 157 TFEU) may also lead to negative integration in that it may invalidate national legislation or collective agreements. Similarly, positive integration has been identified with social policies (or environmental, consumer or other policies). And indeed, harmonising legislation has been used to establish an EU level of social values. However, it has also been used to support economic integration, for example through the services directive, a number of directives regulating the European insurance market or establishing common bases for company law in the Member States. Thus, both economic integration and its social dimensions depend on positive integration. Even soft law is used in both realms – and indeed, the base of the European OMC has been laid initially in the Treaty chapter on economic and monetary union.

III The structure and common threads of the chapters

This book takes stock of ways of achieving sustained interaction between social and economic dimensions of European integration, by assessing norms and practices of European integration in fields where issues of economic and social imbalances are at stake. This is pursued in the following structure.

Part I of the book contributes different theoretical perspectives on European economic and social constitutionalism. It offers a theoretical appraisal of the balance of economic and social values within the EU integration project.

The first chapter in this part develops a normative perspective on re-embedding economic and social constitutionalism. Dagmar Schiek applies the 'Polanyian'[27] metaphor of social embedding to EU constitutionalism, countering a merely neoliberal notion of EU economic constitutionalism. As a first step, she develops a multidisciplinary societal perspective on European integration. In a second step, she recounts the

---

[26] F. Scharpf, 'Reflections on multi-level legitimacy', MPIfG Working Paper 7 (2003), esp. pp. 10–16.

[27] K. Polanyi, *The Great Transformation* (Boston: Beacon Press, 1957).

incremental constitutionalisation of economic and social dimensions of European integration from the Treaty of Rome to the Treaty of Lisbon. While the familiar imbalance between fundamental freedoms and competition law on the one hand and the social and employment law on the other hand still persists, Schiek finds that the Treaties increasingly stress the normative intertwinement of economic and social dimensions of European integration. She demonstrates that this contradiction in values has increased considerably, and that the ToL has contributed a number of new social values in this regard. Socially embedded EU constitutionalism emerges as a way to overcome the discrepancy between the normative commitment and the familiar imbalance. Conceptualising law and constitutionalism as social practices, Schiek demands to embrace the potential of incrementally developing EU constitutional law as an instrument in the hands of civil society actors, who can use it to establish and support the social dimensions of European integration.

In chapter 2 Ulrike Liebert approaches the tensions between market integration and Social Europe from a political science and institutionalist perspective. Considering substantive changes by the ToL, she highlights inter alia the governance of globalisation, changes in relation to economic governance and monetary union, as well as changes in institutional matters, which in her account 'redefine' the inter-institutional balance of power. Enhancing the powers of the European Parliament and – through establishing a written catalogue of fundamental rights – also the importance of the Court of Justice, the ToL will, in Liebert's view, provide a multilayered playing field for solving collective-action problems. Further, she highlights the creation of new constituencies for Social Europe via expanded rights of citizens and TCNs. Taking a theoretical stance based on institutional political economy and social constructivism, Liebert suggests that scepticism based on the alleged 'decoupling' of economic and social dimensions of European integration disregards important aspects, such as 'new clues' for protecting the 'acquis communautaire social' or new tools such as the citizens' legislative initiative and other forms of civil society participation. In conclusion, she suggests that provided they will use these formal rules as tools in practice, social constituents will eventually transform the model of social capitalism – widely viewed as defining Europe – in a more sustainable way.

In chapter 3, Nicole Lindstrom takes up the discussion of the *Viking* and *Laval* cases, using these to reconsider tensions between market liberalisation and social protection against the background of EU enlargement. She considers the potential to socially re-embed EU market liberalisation, stressing that market liberalisation will always lead to counter-moves re-embedding markets into society. She also investigates how re-embedding transnational markets in transnational societies may succeed. Lindstrom finds contradicting claims in this regard. On the one hand, the transnational legal procedures before the Court of Justice open discursive arenas for actors supporting market liberalisation as well as those seeking to re-embed markets. On the other hand, in the wake of these two judgments pushing market liberalisation, national and transnational actors find themselves under pressure to initiate countermoves. On the whole, this process of moves and countermoves may well contribute to transnational re-embedding of market liberalising moves between east and west.

In the final chapter of this part, Wouter Devroe and Pieter van Cleynenbreugel focus on EU economic constitution. From the start of their chapter, they stress that this economic constitution was always interwoven with non-economic, including social, overarching aims. They criticise the limited ambition of much of the EU economic constitutionalism scholarship, demanding to look beyond fundamental freedoms and competition law in a normative approach to EU economic constitutionalism. They propose to consider values, principles of governance, methods for balancing contradicting values, division of competences, mechanisms of decision-making and enforcement as well as foreign economic relations principles and constitutional modification works as necessary elements of any economic constitution. Evaluated against this yardstick, the EU Treaties after Lisbon emerge as a still incomplete economic constitution. Accordingly, the authors consider that the chosen mode of economic governance will be decisive for EU economic policies. They find the concept of economic governance to be rooted in 'corporate governance', which they consider as 'best served by voluntarily, non-binding codes'. They recommend developing more smoothly functioning ways of economic governance in order to make choices for and against certain values transparent. They conclude that the EU's economic constitution is at best an open one, which does not justify shortcomings in the realisation of social dimensions of EU integration.

The common cognisance of the four theoretical chapters in this foundational part lies in acknowledging the 'flux' (Liebert) of EU social and economic constitutionalisation. Between diverse and contradicting values without clear hierarchies, EU constitutionalism is constructed by

social actors. This conceptual framework also captures adaptive developments towards a more adequate and better balancing of European
economic and social constitutionalism after the ToL.

Part II of the book assembles three chapters that exemplify conceptions of social and economic constitutionalisation for specific substantive policy fields.

Hildegard Schneider and Anja Wiesbrock open this part with a chapter on circular migration of TCNs to the EU. As one of the parameters of
globalisation, international migration interrelates with other parameters, including the free movement of goods and services. From an
economic perspective, liberalisation of migration might achieve greater
welfare gains than liberalisation of international trade. The EU
Commission encourages now circular migration as a positive tool to
liberalise migration globally. Schneider and Wiesbrock critically analyse
whether circular migration as practised within the EU realises the
potential of generating 'triple win situations' for countries of origin,
home countries and the migrants themselves. They compare three
national varieties of this kind of migration policy, tracing 'circular
migration' to its less progressive predecessor, the 'guest-worker model'.
They find that circular migration in practice constitutes a tool for limiting migration rather than contributing to economic development in the
migrants' home countries and the migrant's welfare. They conclude that
the EU and its Member States should further develop circular migration
as a sustainable form of migration policy, which enables TCNs to truly
socially integrate into their host countries and to return to their countries of origin without losing acquired rights. In this way, they argue that
EU migration policy could become an example of a globally responsible
EU social policy.

In chapter 6 Thomas Biermeyer returns to the theme of tensions
between economic and noneconomic dimensions of European integration, using the field of company law as an example. This field has been
the subject of EU harmonising legislation from the 1960s and of a series
of cases in the Court of Justice of the European Union (ECJ) concerning
company mobility since the 1980s, thus offering an illustration of the
interplay of these two archetypes of governance. Given the central
relevance of companies for capitalist economies, it also provokes comparison between different types of capitalism in Europe. Biermeyer
perceives the company as a compromise between different constituencies establishing a long-term relationship. The company's relationship
with government depends much on the style of capitalism. Both the

differences in style of capitalism and the changing strength of diverging interests around company law have prevented positive integration by harmonisation at EU level. This again invited incremental case law dismantling elements of national company law that were perceived as inhibiting companies' freedom of establishment. Biermeyer concludes that this situation has led to mainly economic constitutionalisation of EU company law, without any serious social dimensions. He also perceives opportunities to change this imbalance, inter alia by incorporating a choice of social values in EU-level secondary legislation, which then can pre-empt challenges against these values in reliance on market freedoms.

Closing this part, in chapter 7 Ulla Neergaard discusses EU law constraints on services of general economic interest (SGEIs). She focuses on the interplay of Treaty law and ECJ case law in relation to antagonisms between market liberalisation and the welfare advanced (nationally) by SGEIs. This is one of the fields where the ToL fits the final stone onto a building that has been progressing since the Treaty of Amsterdam (1997), and in which tensions between programmatic and specific Treaty norms have evolved. Today, Article 14 TFEU establishes a strong normative commitment to SGEIs, which is also supported by Article 36 of the Charter of Fundamental Rights of the European Union. At the same time, Article 106(3) TFEU only acknowledges the role of SGEIs to a limited extent, allowing only exceptionally for them to escape the market-liberalising discipline of EU competition law. Neergaard finds that this tension is the source of complexity in this field with an increasing involvement of the EU. As in the ECJ case law on SGEIs – the 'market element weighs heavier than the social element' – Neergaard demands for the EU legislator to further limit the application of EU competition law, which she perceives as a severe inhibition of the SGEIs' social function.

The chapters on more specific fields of EU social and economic constitutionalisation in Part II have paved the way for the three case studies in Part III. These take up concrete law and policy perspectives to explore tensions between market liberalism and social policy. At the same time each case study concentrates on one of the three 'archetypes of governance' introduced above ('directly enforceable Treaty law', 'harmonising secondary legislation' and 'soft modes of governance').

Chapter 8, by Sergio Carrera and Anja Wiesbrock, opens this part with a case study on civic integration of immigrants into the EU. The authors establish how integration, as used within the EU Immigration

Framework, has evolved from furthering stable social integration of migrants into societies towards an immigration rule utilised for social exclusion. This process was formally based on binding legislation, which is often associated with positive integration through defining common EU-level values. However, secondary legislation was used in a different way here: the legal framework enables Member States to impose integration conditions on migrants, but does not provide a common concept. Thus, secondary legislation initiated the development of common notions of civic integration through exchange of practices. Learning from best practices is usually seen as constitutive for the OMC. The chapter's comparative part traces the incremental development of the systematic exclusion of non-Western migrants in three Member States (Germany, France and the Netherlands), critically evaluating the extent to which the equivalent reduction of free movement rights of migrants satisfies the requirements of non-discrimination and proportionality. In conclusion, the authors plead for a principle of social integration defined as 'social inclusion' to be reintroduced into EU immigration law and policy.

In chapter 9, Sandra Kröger investigates EU policies on corporate social responsibility (CSR) as an example of whether and how the social dimensions of European integration can be supported by non-legally binding policy strategies. In contrast to Thomas Biermeyer, but concurring with Devroe and Cleynenbreugel, Kröger cannot perceive of any role for hard law in the field of corporate governance. Relying on the theoretical framework offered by the 'varieties of capitalism' approach, Kröger doubts whether there can ever be a successful EU-level CSR strategy, given the diversity of capitalisms among the Member States. Comparing the United Kingdom – as representative of liberal market economies – and Germany – as representative of social market economies – she finds that CSR plays a fundamentally different role in these countries. This is followed by an analysis of the EU CSR strategy that culminates in the conclusion that CSR is inevitably wedded to 'the uncertain world of soft law' and thus cannot provide an adequate strategy to foster the social dimensions of European integration.

In chapter 10, the final case study, Ida Wendt and Andrea Gideon approach the tensions between public healthcare and EU internal market rules from a novel angle. They focus on the situation of third-sector providers and the impact of EU competition law (as an example of EU hard law) upon it. Transcending the level of nation states, the chapter compares the healthcare systems of England, Wales and the

Netherlands. The role of third-sector providers differs vastly: while their position is quite established in the Netherlands, in England and Wales they have only more recently established a position in which to compete with traditionally public providers. Wendt and Gideon value the impact of EU competition law as fundamentally positive here, as it enables third-sector providers to challenge established market structures or inequitable distribution of state aid. Yet, they also detect some detriment in the adverse position of EU competition law towards co-operative structures and in the chilling effect of state aid rules on cross-subsidising activities. Co-operative structures have a long tradition in the third sector, and cross-subsidising is seen as an instrument to maintain ethical commitment. This contrasts with Neergaard's approach, which exposes possible frictions between the provision of services of general economic interest and a liberal market competition law regime.

IV Common findings and open questions

From these chapters, a number of novel common findings emerge. As regards the operation of different modes of governance, several chapters find the stark distinction between three archetypes (hard law, harmonised binding law and soft law) to have become increasingly blurred. Accordingly, both Biermeyer's chapter on company law as well as Carrera's and Wiesbrock's chapter on immigration law, found a tendency to use binding secondary legislation for establishing options of choice and processes of best practice comparison in contested policy fields such as employee co-determination and immigration of non-Western migrants.

Also, there is no clear association of hard law (and associated negative integration) with economic dimensions of integration or with harmonisation (and associated positive integration), and a correlation of soft law with social dimensions of European integration. Rather, positive impacts of hard law such as competition law on social dimensions of integration have been identified as well as negative impacts of OMC-like varieties of corporate governance on social integration.

As regards the tensions between economic and social dimensions of European integration, several chapters support the view that these dimensions necessarily interrelate, and that social actors use enhanced scope of action to liberalise – or to socially 'embed' – markets, depending on their inherent interests. Finally, the ToL does not merely rephrase economic EU integration, but rather enhances social elements in the value base of the EU and, what may be even more important, it restructures the potential for collective action both institutionally and in societal perspectives.

Some questions still await answers. These include whether and how far transnational social actors will truly emerge in practice and make use of novel norms and procedures, building on the socio-political dynamics engendered by the increasing politicisation of European integration.

PART I

European economic and social constitutionalism
between norms and practices

1

Re-embedding economic and social constitutionalism: Normative perspectives for the EU

DAGMAR SCHIEK

I Introduction

Tensions between the economic and the social dimensions of European integration are being perceived as increasing, and so is the potential for conflict between national and European levels of policy-making. Both are well illustrated by a highly controversial line of Court of Justice of the European Union (ECJ) cases on industrial relations: *Viking* and *Laval* have become symbols for the continuing dominance of the economic over the social dimension of European integration and for an increasing tendency of the EU to diminish national autonomy.[1] As one consequence, demands to protect Member States' social policy choices from EU law pressures arise.[2] For such demands to be tenable, isolation of

---

[1] C-341/05 *Laval* [2007] ECR I-11767 and C-438/05 *Viking* [2007] ECR I-10779. See for a selection of reviews *The Cambridge Yearbook of European Legal Studies* 10 (2007–2008) (Oxford: Hart, 2009) (Introduction by Barnard (pp. 463–92), followed by a number of articles) and the special issue *Comparative Labor Law and Policy Journal* 29 (2008) (editorial introduction and articles by Eklund and Orlandini). See also B. Bercusson 'The trade union movement and the European Union: judgment day', *ELJ* 13 (2007), 279.

[2] e.g. F. Scharpf, 'The double asymmetry of European integration', MPIfG Working Paper 12 (2009) (demanding an option for Member States to reject specific judgments); C. Joerges, 'Rethinking European law's supremacy: A plea for a supranational conflict of laws' in B. Kohler-Koch and B. Rittberger (eds.), *Debating the Democratic Legitimacy of the European Union* (Lanham, MD: Rowman & Littlefield Publishers, 2007), pp. 311–27 (proposing to replace supranationality by a conflicts of law approach). The German Constitutional Court, too, demands that the EU should not interfere with national social policies (Judgment of 30 June 2009 – 2 BvE 2/08 *et al.*, www.bundesverfassungsgericht. de/entscheidungen/es20090630_2bve000208en.html, paras. 256–9).

national and EU policy-making and of economic and social dimensions of European integration would have to be possible. This is arguably not the case. Economic and social dimensions of integration will thus have to be reconciled across EU and national levels, if the EU and its Member States are to maintain the ability of enhancing social justice against the pulls of economic globalisation.

Achieving such reconciliation will also require a re-embedding of EU constitutionalism. It is true that the Treaty of Lisbon (ToL) has abandoned all constitutional rhetoric after the demise of the Constitutional Treaty. However, EU constitutionalism does not require constitutional rhetoric or any written constitutional document. As a dynamic process for a post-national entity it is necessarily open-ended,[3] beyond positive law.[4] As tensions between social and economic interest tend to be reformulated as legal issues, their reconciliation can only be achieved through (re-conceptualised) constitutionalism.

This chapter develops an EU Treaty-based normative perspective for this reconciliation. The concept of socially embedded constitutionalism rests on three normative assumptions: first, the European integration project needs to be considered from a societal perspective rather than one transfixed on state and post-state institutions; secondly, the legal framework for European integration should not (and does not) juxtapose economic and social dimensions of social and economic integration; thirdly, constitutionalism as a dynamic concept can sensibly contribute to reconcile the tensions between economic and social dimensions of European integration and thus to engendering a European society based on social justice.

The chapter starts with a sketch of a societal as opposed to a state-centred notion of European integration, and highlights social and economic dimensions of European integration under normative perspectives. It then contextualises current debates on constitutionalism beyond states. Finally, it proposes further steps to pursue the concept of socially embedded EU constitutionalism with a view to offering new modes of reconciling economic and social dimensions of European integration.

---

[3] J. Shaw, 'Process, responsibility and inclusion in EU constitutionalism', *ELJ* 9 (2003), 45.

[4] J. Wouters, L. Verhey and P. Kiiver, *European Constitutionalism beyond Lisbon* (Antwerp: Intersentia, 2009); M. Dani, 'Constitutionalism and dissonances: Has Europe paid off its debt to functionalism?', *ELJ* 15 (2009), 324.

II Towards a societal perspective on European integration

Any concept of EU constitutionalism presupposes a perspective on European integration.[5] Pursuing the project to establish a socially embedded EU constitutionalism, this chapter needs to approach European integration from a perspective that relates to socio-economic reality. After all, the European integration project has been most successful in integrating economies, and it is as a consequence of this that tensions between the social and the economic have been experienced with increasing intensity recently. The subsequent overview considers what European integration theory has to offer in this vein, distinguishing state-centred from society-centred approaches.

A The notion of European integration

If taken literally,[6] the word integration has two potential meanings: on the one hand, 'integration' can capture a process from 'mere cooperation to … complete unification'.[7] This first meaning of integration is frequently used in the *state-centred perspective* of the endeavour, which focuses on the activities of states aiming at converging towards a European Union – or as maintaining their sovereignty and co-operating within an international organisation. The object of research in this regard consists of state institutions, and their replication at EU level.

On the other hand, integration can refer to combining individual elements into smaller political units, such as cities, inner-state regions and states. In this perspective, integration may relate to integrating individuals into a coherent society – which may nevertheless be diverse – or to integrating different groups of individuals into a multi-levelled community interacting with each other. This second meaning of integration can support *a societal perspective*. From this perspective,

---

[5] J. Shaw, 'Post-national constitutionalism in the European Union', *JEPP* 6 (1999), 579, 586; see also the contributions by Weiler and Maduro in J. Weiler and M. Wind (eds.), *European Constitutionalism beyond the State* (Cambridge: Cambridge University Press, 2003).

[6] The series *Integration through Law* actually commenced its deliberations with a reference to the Oxford English Dictionary's entry on 'to integrate': M. Cappelletti, M. Seccombe and J. Weiler (eds.), *Integration through Law: Europe and the American federal experience*, vol. I(1) (Berlin and New York: Walter de Gruyter, 1985), p. 12.

[7] D. Curtin, 'European legal integration: Paradise lost' in D. Curtin (ed.), *European Integration and Law* (Antwerp and Oxford: Intersentia, 2006), p. 8.

research would focus on actors within states and the EU, such as trade unions, consumer associations, churches and social policy initiatives.

B State-centred perspectives on European integration

European integration has been approached as a state-centred endeavour from a number of disciplines.

Liberal intergovernmentalism[8] is a prominent example from political science. Perceiving the European integration process as a result of bargaining between nation states (represented by their governments), it analyses supranational institutions, such as the ECJ, or the European Commission in their role as functional agents of states. Often, such researchers conclude that governmental bargaining will result in entrusting European institutions with (less popular) powers to take measures to 'modernise' the economy, while social policy will be defended as national terrain. Federalism, as another political science approach to European integration theory,[9] too, is focused on states' activities. The co-operation of states may, in the view of federalism, result in amalgamating states into larger federations.

Scholars of international law have tended to analyse the legal framework of European integration from the perspective of inter-state co-operation. Early studies of European law have been characterised as being steeped in positivist doctrinarism of international lawyers paired with the excitement of the same international lawyers observing how international law could actually become adhered to and a viable instrument of governance.[10] Introducing a more interdisciplinary approach to legal studies,[11] the 'integration through law' scholarship[12] evolved

---

[8] A. Moravcsik and F. Schimmelfenning, 'Liberal intergovernmentalism' in A. Wiener and T. Diez (eds.), *European Integration Theory*, 2nd edn (Oxford: Oxford University Press, 2009).

[9] D. Chryssochoou, *Theorizing European Integration*, 2nd edn (Abingdon: Routledge, 2008), p. 57 *et seq.*

[10] A. Arnull, 'The Americanization of EU law scholarship' in A. Arnull, P. Eackhout and T. Tridimas (eds.), *Continuity and Change in EU Law: Essays in honour of Sir Francis Jacobs* (Oxford: Oxford University Press, 2008), pp. 416–17.

[11] 'Legal studies' are works by legal scholars who integrate methods and deliberations from other social sciences such as political science, sociology and political economy (see J. Shaw, 'Introduction' in J. Shaw and G. More (eds.), *New Legal Dynamics of European Union* (Oxford: Clarendon Press, 1995) p. 4).

[12] For a summary beyond the founding volume see U. Haltern, 'Integration through law' in A. Wiener and T. Diez (eds.), *European Integration Theory*, 1st edn (Oxford: Oxford

around the question as to how the ECJ could through some pivotal judgments create the supranational nature of today's EU law and equip this new entity with the capacity to govern through law. These attempts are state-centred in that they explain why nation states have surrendered part of their sovereignty to the European Union.

C Societal perspectives on European integration

There are also numerous societal perspectives on European integration. In political science, transaction-analytical approaches are an early example of this perspective. Its founder, E. Deutsch, defined the end-state of an integrated entity as 'attainment within a territory of a sense of community and of institutions and practices strong enough and widespread enough to assure for a long time dependable expectations of peaceful change among its population'.[13] Transactionalism re-focused international relations theory on societal (non-state) actors, and the community of human beings.[14] Ernst Haas' neo-functionalism, often considered the origin of European integration theory,[15] also allows a societal perspective on European integration. Its original definition of integration envisages the end-state of European integration through the prism of political community, which clearly refers to societal actors.[16]

University Press, 2004), pp. 177–96, discontinued in 2nd edn (n. 8 above). Some contributions from political science are said to overlook the richness of legal argument by D. Curtin (n. 7 above), p. 5. Approaches that integrate both disciplines include G. de Búrca, 'Rethinking law in neofunctionalist theory', *JEPP* 12 (2005), 310, 310–12; B. Rehder, 'What is political about jurisprudence? Courts, politics and political science in Europe and the United States', MPIfG Discussion Paper 5 (2007); and K. Alter, *The European Court's Political Power: Selected essays* (Oxford: Oxford University Press, 2009).

[13] Cited from F. Laursen, *Comparative Regional Integration* (Aldershot: Ashgate, 2003), p. 4, referring to K. W. Deutsch, *The Analysis of International Relations* (Englewood Cliffs, NJ: Prentice Hall, 1971).

[14] Transactionalism is partly deemed a dead theory (A. Wiener and T. Diez, 'Introducing the mosaic of integration theory' in Wiener and Diez (n. 8 above), p. 13, partly as the root of more current approaches (Chryssochoou, n. 9 above, pp. 25–7). It is also a starting point for European sociology (N. Fligstein, *Euroclash: The EU, European identity, and the future of Europe* (Oxford: Oxford University Press, 2008); W. Outhwaite, *European Society* (Oxford: Oxford University Press, 2008)).

[15] E. B. Haas and D. Dinan (eds.), *The Uniting of Europe: Political, social and economic forces 1950–1957* (Indiana: University of Notre Dame Press, 2004).

[16] 'Political community ... is a condition in which specific groups and individuals show more loyalty to their central political institutions than to any other political authority in a specific period of time and in a definable geographic space' (*ibid.* p. 5). See also Haas' own introduction, p. xiv, where he also maintains that social actors are in the centre.

Even after considerable reframing,[17] the focus on social actors as partly autonomous from states and supranational institutions remained characteristic for neo-functionalism. Social constructivism,[18] which has been hailed as the new school of European integration theory[19] and as the logical route to update neo-functionalism,[20] also focuses on human beings and their interactions – i.e. it is based on a societal perspective.[21] From a social constructivist view, social actors construct social reality – with slight variations depending on whether this happens independently from or in interaction with the material base of social reality.[22] Also, theories focusing on governance[23] beyond the state display societal perspectives on European integration, when they analyse the interaction of public institutions beyond state borders and the involvement of non-state actors at different levels of the polity. While often focused on analysing the interaction of public institutions across levels, they are bound to consider the relevance of actors beyond the public realm, such as undertakings, trade unions and other emanations of civil society.

Analysing European integration as a societal phenomenon is also the aim of the recently emerged sociology of European integration.[24] Asking the question whether and how far societal integration occurs at

[17] A. Niemann and P. Schmitter, 'Neo-functionalism' in Wiener and Diez (n. 8 above), pp. 45–6.

[18] See the theory-founding T. Christiansen, K. Jorgensen and A. Wiener, *The Social Construction of Europe* (London et al.: Sage, 1999); and T. Risse, 'Social constructivism and European integration' in A. Wiener and T. Diez (eds.), *European Integration Theory* (Oxford: Oxford University Press, 2004); Moravcsik and Schimmelfenning (n. 8 above), pp. 144–61.

[19] See A. Wiener and T. Diez, 'Taking stock of integration theory' in Wiener and Diez (n. 8 above), pp. 245–6.

[20] Haas and Dinan (n. 15 above), p. xvii: 'Our job is to see how NF [neo-functionalism] as amended by these challengers, can become part of a respectable constructivism.'

[21] Thus, it is also viewed as a sociological perspective on European integration (see J. Checkel, 'Social construction and integration', *JEPP* 6(4) (1999) 545–60).

[22] See Chryssochoou (n. 9 above), pp. 110–13.

[23] M. Jachtenfuss and B. Kohler-Koch, 'Multi-level governance' in Wiener and Diez, 1st edn (n. 12 above), pp. 97–115, discontinued in the 2nd edn (n. 8 above); Chryssochoou (n. 9 above), pp. 59–64. See also A. Stone Sweet and W. Sandelholtz, 'Integration, supranational governance and institutionalization of the European polity' in A. Stone Sweet and W. Sandelholtz (eds.), *European Integration and Supranational Governance* (Oxford: Oxford University Press, 1998), pp. 1–26.

[24] J. Delhey, 'European social integration: From convergence of countries to transnational relations between people', WZB Discussion Paper (Berlin, February 2004); R. Münch, 'Constructing a European society by jurisdiction', *ELJ* 14 (2008), 519–41; Fligstein (n. 14 above); Outhwaite (n. 14 above); H.-J. Trenz, 'Elements of a sociology of European integration', ARENA Working Paper 11 (2008).

transnational and even EU levels[25] presupposes a conception of the EU as a social space and not as a mere political (co-operation) project.[26] Some have endeavoured to develop a special notion of societal integration in transnational spaces, whose indicators would include transactions between people at transnational levels.[27] Others would define the sociological perspective of European integration as one concerned with deeper structural changes in relation to solidarity and justice within national society and an emerging European society.[28]

Legal studies are also able to approach European integration from a societal angle. The need to integrate a diverse society also emerges at national level. Accordingly, national constitutions are being measured against their potential of contributing to social integration.[29] As the European Union attains more and more competences that have traditionally been taken upon by national states, Grimm has proposed to extend such constitutional law approaches to the EU.[30] In his view, the influence of law upon (societal) integration is dependent on social preconditions, such as common values imbued by education, which are lacking at European level.

D   Focus on the interplay between societal actors of European integration

The above demonstrates that there exists a variety of approaches enabling us to consider European integration from a societal perspective. Theories from various disciplines allow a focus on the interaction between socio-economic actors engaged with economic and social integration at a European or national level. Such approaches, it is submitted, are pivotal to understanding European integration, because its success depends on socio-economic actors just as much (possibly more) than on state and supranational actors.

---

[25] Trenz (n. 24 above), p. 14 ('EU as laboratory of new forms of social integration'); Delhey (n. 24 above), pp. 14–22.
[26] Delhey (n. 24 above), p. 6.
[27] Outhwaite refers rather unspecifically to 'transborder interaction' (p. 128) as well as very specifically to increases in migration (p. 140), Delhey mentions marriages, travel, friendship and migration (p. 18) and Fligstein considers changed patterns of interaction that increase transnational social fields (pp. 121, 165) (all quoted in n. 24 above).
[28] Münch (n. 24 above), p. 519.
[29] See on different perspectives G. Schaal, *Integration durch Verfassung und Verfassungsrechtsprechung?* (Berlin: Duncker & Humblot, 2000).
[30] D. Grimm, 'Integration by constitution', *I-CON* 3 (2005), pp. 193–208.

This derives from the initial focus of EU integration on market integration. In the EU Member States, markets are not public, but rather societal realms. Accordingly, EU integration affects societies, in that its economic dimension tends to liberate individual (economic) actors from restrictive public policies. Analysing such processes requires a societal perspective, that visualises the interplay of economic and social actors at different levels within the EU integration process instead of imagining all these as interplay between the European Union and its Member States.

III   Economic and social dimensions of European integration

If we consider European integration from a societal perspective, its economic and social dimensions attain centre stage. Both dimensions have been constitutionalised, i.e. defined in legally enforceable terms, to different degrees.

A   Economic dimensions

If integration consists of combining formerly separate entities into a consistent whole, its economic dimensions aim at combining national markets into a larger market. The initially predominant economic impetus of the EEC aimed at amalgamating the national economies of the then six Member States into a Common Market. Going beyond a free trade area (in which goods and possibly services flow freely), it also provided for factor mobility (i.e. free movement of labour and capital). Only in 1993, with the Treaty of Maastricht, did the renamed EU proceed towards economic and monetary union. It remains restricted to co-ordination in the field of economic union though (Articles 121 and 126 TFEU), and a full union is not yet accomplished.[31]

---

[31] The implied picture of developing economic integration in necessarily successive stages – from a free trade area, via a customs union, towards a Common Market (including factor mobility), to economic and monetary union, followed by a full union – has been a recurrent theme in political economy (see initially J. Tinbergen, *International Economic Integration* (Amsterdam: Elsevier, 1954) and B. Balassa, *The Theory of Economic Integration* (Homewood, IL: R. D. Irwin, 1961); now W. Molle, *The Economics of European Integration: Theory, practice, policy*, 5th edn (Aldershot: Ashgate, 2006)). The quasi-natural consequence has been criticised because even the initial stages are ultimately dependent on political integration (S. Nello, *The European Union: Economics, policies and history*, 2 edn (London *et al.*: McGraw Hill, 2009), p. 6).

The Treaty of Rome emphasised economic dimensions of European integration by enshrining the Common Market into a fixed legal frame, consisting mainly of guarantees of four fundamental freedoms (free movement of goods, services, persons – freedom of establishment and free movement of workers – and capital). Free movement of goods was fortified by a prohibition to establish protective or discriminatory taxes. At the same time the Treaty of Rome established a European-level competition law regime which prohibited cartels between, and abuses of a dominant market position by, private economic actors and subjected any state aid to prior approval by the EU Commission. Mainly, these provisions have remained unchanged and are now part of the Treaty on the Functioning of the European Union (TFEU)[32] as established by the ToL.[33]

It will never be known whether the founding states intended these provisions to become directly effective within their borders.[34] In the 1960s, the ECJ held in two pivotal judgments on free movement of goods that the EEC Treaty was not just any international Treaty, but rather constituted a new form of (international) law in that it enjoyed primacy over national law[35] and in that individuals could rely on its provisions before national courts (direct effect).[36] Together, primacy and direct effect of Treaty Articles were the cornerstones of the

---

[32] With the coming into force of the ToL, the EC Treaty has mainly been superseded by the Treaty on the Functioning of the European Union (Art. 1(10) ToL).

[33] Under Art. 26 TFEU (ex Art. 14 EC), the internal market comprises an area without internal frontiers where the free movement of goods, persons, services and capital is ensured. Art. 30 prohibits internal custom duties; Arts. 34–5 (ex Arts. 28–9 EC) prohibit quantitative restrictions on imports and exports and measures having equivalent effect, with some exceptions in Arts. 36–7. Art. 45 (ex Art. 39 EC) guarantees free movement of workers, Art. 49 (ex Art. 43 EC) contains freedom of establishment for natural persons as well as for companies, and Art. 56 (ex Art. 49 EC) guarantees freedom to provide services. Free movement of capital and payments, which was only mentioned in outline in the original EEC Treaty, is now guaranteed in Art. 63 TFEU (ex Art. 56 EC). Art. 55 TFEU (ex Art. 294 EC), now contained in the chapter on freedom of establishment, clarifies that freedom of establishment for companies also entails freedom to invest in foreign companies. As regards competition law, prohibitions of cartels and abuse of dominant market powers (applying to undertakings) are now to be found in Arts. 101–6 TFEU (ex Arts. 81–6 EC), and rules preventing Member States from granting state aid without the EU Commission's approval in Arts. 107–9 (ex Arts. 87–9 EC).

[34] T.C. Hartley criticises the doctrine of primacy as blatant judicial lawmaking, as the natural meaning of these norms would not suggest direct effect (*EU Law in a Global Context* (Cambridge: Cambridge University Press, 2004), p. 150). For a more recent account see A. Vauchez, 'The transnational politics of judicialization: Van Gend en Loos and the making of EU polity', *ELJ* 16 (2010), 1.

[35] 6/64 *Flaminio Costa* v. *ENEL* [1964] ECR 585.

[36] 26/62 *NV van Gend en Loos* [1963] ECR 3.

supranationality of today's EU law. While national courts have not wholeheartedly accepted the supranational character of EU law,[37] in practice its demands are frequently complied with.

These doctrines imply that any directly effective Treaty Article can be relied upon by any economic actor before national courts, with the potential of the ECJ acting as ultimate arbitrator.[38] Over time, the ECJ has acknowledged direct effect[39] for all four fundamental freedoms. All these, except free movement of goods, are considered as horizontally effective, i.e. they can be wielded against any state and any socio-economic actor who is perceived as inhibiting transnational economic activity. The same applies to the prohibition of cartels and abuse of a dominant market position. All in all, this means that the cornerstones of economic integration have also been enshrined as legal norms, which has led to them being referred to as an 'Economic Constitution'.[40]

Expansive judicial activity has added efficiency to this legal frame-work. In relation to free movement of goods, the ECJ has read the prohibition of quantitative restrictions and measures of equivalent effects to capture any (i.e. also non-discriminatory) 'rules enacted by Member States which are capable of hindering, directly or indirectly, actually or potentially, intra-Community trade'.[41] In the seminal *Cassis de Dijon* case, the Court established a presumption that any good considered as tradable in any Member State is free to circulate through-out the Common Market,[42] forcing Member States to justify any

---

[37] See K. Alter, 'The European Union's legal system and domestic policy: Spillover or backlash' (2009) and 'Who are the masters of the Treaty? European governments and the European Court of Justice' (1998), both repr. in Alter (n. 12 above).

[38] This derives from Art. 267 TFEU, according to which any court in the EU can refer a case to the ECJ, while courts of last instance can even be under an obligation to refer. Also, the Commission or another Member State can raise infringement procedures before the ECJ to review the legality of Member States' legislation (Arts. 258–9 TFEU). See on these D. Chalmers, G. Davies and G. Monti, *European Union Law*, 2nd edn (Cambridge: Cambridge University Press 2010), pp. 149–67, 315 *et seq.*

[39] On the notion of direct effect see Chalmers, Davies and Monti, *ibid.* pp. 267 *et seq.*

[40] See for a summary in English (of this Germanised line of thought), M. Streit and W. Mussler, 'The economic constitution of the European Community', *ELJ* 1 (1995), 5; for a critique see J. Baquero Cruz, *Between Competition and Free Movement* (Oxford: Hart, 2002), ch. 3.2, pp. 26–9.

[41] 8/74 *Dassonville* [1974] ECR, para 5.

[42] 120/78 *Rewe-Zentral AG (Cassis de Dijon)* [1979] ECR 649. That case stated that there was 'no valid reason why, provided that they have been lawfully produced and marketed in one of the Member States, alcoholic beverages should not be introduced into any other Member State'.

incidental impact of their national legislation on cross-border trade before the Court. From 1991, the Court applied the same principles to the other market freedoms.[43] Combined with their horizontal effect, this means that any piece of legislation or any rule or practice engendered by non-state actors 'liable to hinder or make less attractive the exercise of the fundamental freedoms guaranteed by the Treaty'[44] will be subject to ECJ scrutiny. This is the judicial mechanism which prompts social scientists to state that it is 'virtually impossible to justify exceptions to the four fundamental freedoms ... for the sake of social policy objectives'.[45] Some far-sighted legal scholars criticised its potential effects on industrial relations from the late 1990s,[46] while only the recent cases referred to above[47] led to widespread discontent.

It would be naïve to assume that even seminal cases such as *Cassis* would shape EU economic policy in isolation.[48] While the Commission initially purported that after this judgment the principle of mutual recognition had to be accepted as a principle of primary Community law,[49] soon political action was taken, first by a Council resolution on free movement of goods and services, a legally non-binding act (Article 288 TFEU = ex Article 249 EC).[50] Today, the principle of mutual recognition of goods is laid down by regulation,[51] while the Commission's attempt to achieve the same for the freedom to provide services failed.[52]

---

[43] Usually, the *Säger* case (C-76/90 *Säger* [1991] ECR I-4221) is quoted as the starting point (see C. Barnard, *The Substantive Law of the EU*, 2nd edn (Oxford: Oxford University Press, 2007), pp. 19, 273–9.

[44] C-55/94 *Gebhard* [1995] I-4165.

[45] See A. Schäfer and S. Leiber, 'The double voluntarism in EU social dialogue and employment policy', *EIOP* 13 (2009), Article 9, p. 3.

[46] e.g. G. Orlandini, 'The free movement of goods as a possible 'Community' limitation on industrial conflict', *ELJ* 6 (2000), 341; see also Introduction (in this volume), n. 5.

[47] See n. 1 above.

[48] Alter and Meunier-Atsahalia have shown that the Commission's efforts to capitalise on the ECJ *Cassis* jurisprudence triggered interest-group activity and more policy-making ('Judicial politics in the European Community' repr. in Alter (n. 12 above)).

[49] Communication from the Commission concerning the consequences of the judgment given by the Court of Justice on 20 February 1979 in Case 120/78 (*Cassis de Dijon*), 1980 OJ C256/2; Communication from the Commission on the mutual recognition in the context of the follow-up to the Action Plan for the Single Market, COM 1999 (299), which argues that the same principle must apply to goods and services alike.

[50] Council Resolution 2000 C-141/02 (2000) OJ C 141/5.

[51] Regulation (EC) No. 764/2008, OJ 2008 No. L218/21 (repealing Commission Decision No. 3052/95/EC).

[52] Directive 2006/123/EC is fundamentally different from the Commission's original proposal of the 'Services Directive' (on this U. Neergard, R. Nielsen and L. M.

Legal studies view the principle of mutual recognition as encouraging competitive federalism[53] as a method of governing the internal market: regulators from public and private realms generate competing sets of norms. In political science, this has been seen as 'new governance',[54] because it may render EU-level rules protecting values such as consumer health, workplace safety or sustainable wages as superfluous. National regulators and non-state rule-makers were free to establish whatever regime they saw fit. Only if this was a potential hindrance to cross-border movement of products and factors[55] would the need to justify the policy choice arise. The Commission and the Council used the *Cassis* doctrine to justify a 'new approach' to harmonisation from 1987.[56] Under this approach, EU legislation will only set loosely specified standards with which goods must comply, delegating the setting of 'technical rules' to expert committees.[57] While encouraging a certain degree of 'expertocracy', this regulatory technique also empowered economic actors to autonomously develop procedures to achieve the legislative standards, which is certainly one of its innovative facets.[58]

Embarking on active economic policy-making from 1993, the EU developed new forms of governance beyond traditional models of hierarchical rule. According to Article 121(1) and (2) TFEU (ex Article 99 EC), the Council develops broad economic guidelines in order to achieve co-ordination of national economic policies, rather than binding legislation. This can be regarded as the prototype of co-ordinating policies without binding legislation, which is at the same time characteristic of

Roseberry (eds.), *The Services Directive: Consequences for the welfare state and the European Social Model* (Copenhagen: DJØF, 2008).

[53] On the notion Barnard (n. 43 above), pp. 17–23 with references from different disciplines.

[54] See S. Schmidt, 'Mutual recognition as a new mode of governance', *JEPP* 14 (2007), 667. On the debate of 'new governance' see e.g. G. de Búrca and J. Scott (eds.), *Law and new Governance in the EU and the US* (Oxford et al.: Hart Publishing, 2006).

[55] See, however, the analysis of ECJ case law relating to free movement of workers on the one hand and free movement of services on the other hand by S. Deakin, which exposes that the ECJ leans towards regime portability in favour of enterprises, but not in favour of workers ('Regulatory competition after *Laval*' in *Cambridge Yearbook* (n. 1 above), pp. 581–609).

[56] Initiated by Council Resolution of 7 May 1985 on a new approach to technical harmonisation and standards, OJ 1985 No. C136/1.

[57] It is impossible here to recount all publications on this. See Ch. Joerges and E. Vos (eds.), *EU Committees: Social regulation, law and politics* (Oxford: Hart, 1999) for an initial appraisal.

[58] On this see H. Schepel, *The Constitution of Private Governance: Product standards in the regulation of integrating markets* (Oxford: Hart, 2005).

the 'open method of co-ordination' (OMC). Thus, alongside traditional forms of legislation, soft-law mechanisms are at work in the field of economic integration.

Changes instigated by the ToL in the field of economic integration are minimal; in particular fundamental freedoms and competition law remain unchanged substantively. Though the explicit connection between establishing the internal market and free and undistorted competition was excluded from the TEU, Article 3 TFEU clarifies that competition rules are necessary for the functioning of the internal market. Protocol No. 27 on internal market and competition was thus arguably superfluous.[59] Provisions relating to economic and monetary union and in particular regarding the Eurozone have been streamlined: the Council can now strengthen co-ordination and surveillance of budgets in Member States whose currency is the Euro, and also set out specific economic guidelines for them. In these decisions, only Council members representing states whose currency is the Euro can vote (Articles 133, 136 TFEU). Beyond the 'Eurozone', co-ordination of national policies remains the main mode of governance, and the Council will in most cases continue to act only on recommendation by the Commission. Such a recommendation can be rejected by a majority in the Council. There is an exception in cases of excessive budgetary deficit, where the Council acts on a proposal by the Commission (Article 126 TFEU). Such a proposal can only be rejected unanimously by the Council (Article 293(1) TFEU).

B   Social dimensions

If integration consists of combining formerly separate entities into a consistent whole, its social dimensions would relate to combining national policies and societal activities referred to under the notion of 'welfare' or 'social state' into a European endeavour. If successful, this would engender European dimensions of solidarity and social justice.

The social dimension of European integration is generally approached with more caution than its economic counterpart. Social integration as pursued on national levels is widely considered as being based on ideals of social justice.[60] Social justice will encompass the goals of enhancing

---

[59] J.-C. Piris, *The Lisbon Treaty: A legal and political analysis* (Cambridge: Cambridge University Press, 2010), p. 308.

[60] United Nations Research Institute for Social Development, *Social Integration: Approaches and Issues*, March 1994.

social equality and enabling individuals to participate actively in society
and to fulfil their personal potential (micro-level integration) as well as
balancing social tensions at the macro level of society.[61] 'Classical fields'
of national welfarism comprise solidarity regimes for those (temporarily) threatened by social exclusion, due to an inability to market their
labour (old age pensions, healthcare, specific services for the elderly,
persons with disabilities and the very young).[62] These systems are being
'modernised' since the 1980s by enhancing individual responsibility and
capability and reducing patronising welfarism.[63] From a wider perspective, social policy encompasses any activity – by states or social actors,
including civil society – aimed at enabling persons to become at least a
co-agent of their destiny rather than being the object of decisions made
by economic actors such as employers, landlords or financial managers.[64] From this perspective, national welfarism encompasses rules
enhancing industrial democracy and social justice in the work place[65]
as well as consumer law,[66] alongside the classical solidarity regimes.[67]
The modernisation of social policy from this wider perspective demands
a focus on capabilities to cope with increasing insecurities.[68]

[61] D. Schiek, 'Artikel 20 Abs. 1–3 V: Sozialstaat' in E. Denninger et al. (eds.),
Alternativkommentar zum Grundgesetz, vol. II (Neuwied et al.: Luchterhand, 2001),
paras. 75 et seq. with examples from the German national background.
[62] For an example of this conception of EU social policy see B. V. Maydell et al., Enabling
Social Europe (Vienna: Springer, 2006).
[63] Ibid. propagating the enabling welfare state (pp. 73–89). Modernising the welfare state is
also a theme of A. Giddens' programmatic writings (The Third Way and its Critics
(Cambridge: Polity, 2000)); for a condensed version adapted to the EU level see
A. Giddens, 'Social model for Europe?' in A. Giddens, P. Diamond and R. Liddle
(eds.), Global Europe Social Europe (Cambridge: Polity, 2006), p. 14.
[64] Also termed as de-commodification as main aim of welfare states (G. Esping-Andersen,
Social Foundations of Post-Industrial Economies (Oxford: Oxford University Press, 1999)).
[65] See C. Barnard, EC Employment Law, 2nd edn (Oxford: Oxford University Press, 2007), p. 1;
contributions to J. Shaw (ed.), Social Law and Policy in an Evolving European Union (Oxford:
Hart, 2000); and S. Guibboni, Social Rights and Market Freedom in the European Constitution
(Cambridge: Cambridge University Press, 2006) – all referring mainly to employment law,
workplace democracy and social protection in discussing EU social policy.
[66] On the impact on consumer law see A. Maurer, 'Consumer protection and social models
of Continental and Anglo-American contract law and the transnational outlook', IJGLS
14 (2007), 353.
[67] For a more elaborate development of this see Schiek (n. 61 above).
[68] J. Browne, S. Deakin and F. Wilkinson, Social Rights and European Market Integration
(University of Cambridge, CBR WP 253 December 2002) inaugurated a research design
on the capabilities approach. S. Deakin ('The capability concept and the evolution of the
European Social Model' in M. Dougan and E. Spaventa (eds.), Social Welfare and EU
Law (Oxford: Hart, 2005), p. 3) elaborates the concept in relation to EU social policy,

Whether, and if so in which fields, EU-level policy-making should contribute remains disputed, partly corresponding to the width of the notion adopted. Those focusing on the classical fields tend to see no legitimate scope for autonomous EU social policy,[69] while those ascribing to wider notions tend to concede that the EU has a legitimate role in regulation of employment and consumer law, for example. Both 'camps' agree that traditional redistributive policies are not suitable candidates for hard European legislation[70] and that EU social policy-making needs to develop beyond 'command and control governance' and enhance capability and flexibility.[71]

The legal frames for social dimensions of EU integration are weaker than for its economic dimension. From the founding of the EEC, the principle of equal pay for equal work for women and men (Article 157 TFEU = ex Article 141 EC) was the exception to the rule that there were no binding commitments in the social policy field. This provision has been the source of a wealth of case law, mainly initiated by a limited number of strategic litigators.[72] The expansion of the European integration project beyond economic dimensions post 1993 was partly achieved by introducing rights for EU citizens independently of their market activities (now Articles 20–5 TFEU = ex Articles 17–22 EC; see also Article 9–11 EU, these last provisions are unprecedented). While the provisions on citizenship were deemed to be merely symbolic initially, ECJ case law developed these, taken together with

and the contributions in S. Deakin and A. Supiot (eds.), *Capacitas* (Oxford: Oxford University Press, 2009) apply it to contract law.

[69] T. Atkinson *et al.*, *The EU and Social Inclusion* (Oxford: Oxford University Press, 2002), p. 5 (while conceding 'the evolution of the European Union will ... lead us ... to ask about the social cohesion of the European Union as a whole': p. 186). See similarly Maydell *et al.* (n. 63 above), p. 140 (stating that social policy currently remains a national matter) and executive summary pp. xxvi and 19–28 (explaining that diversity of national welfare state expectations is too pronounced to provide a single European Social Model).

[70] D. Damjanovic and B. de Witte, 'Welfare integration through EU law: The overall picture in the light of the Lisbon Treaty' in U. Neergard, R. Nielsen and L. Roseberry (eds.), *Integrating Welfare Functions into EU Law: From Rome to Lisbon* (Copenhagen: DJØF, 2009). See also M. Ferrera, *The Boundaries of Welfare* (Oxford: Oxford University Press, 2005).

[71] See those cited in nn. 66 and 69 above; see also M. Maduro, 'European constitutionalism and three models of Social Europe' in M. Hesselink (ed.), *The Politics of a European Civil Code* (Kluwer International, 2006), p. 125.

[72] See K. Alter and J. Vargas, 'Explaining variation in the use of European litigation strategies: European Community Law and British gender equality policy' in Alter (n. 12 above), pp. 159–82; see also U. Liebert, with S. Sifft (eds.), *Gendering Europeanization (Public Discourses on EC Equal Treatment and Equal Opportunity Norms in Six Member States)* (Brussels: Peter Lang, 2003).

the non-discrimination principle (Article 18 TFEU = ex Article 12 EC), into constitutionalised social rights.[73]

Social policy-making at EU level too remains restricted. The EEC had very limited competences in this field, comprising of providing a European social fund and some legislative competences relating to free movement of workers. Still, European social policy also took legal forms from the late 1970s, when altogether eight directives on protecting interests of workers in cases of economic concentration processes and on equal treatment of women and men in the labour market were passed. Subsequent Treaty reforms led to the inclusion of a comprehensive social chapter into the EC Treaty in 1998, with regulatory competences in employment law. However, core welfare state policies remained safely within national competence. Co-ordination rather than harmonisation was used where necessary to facilitate free movement of workers and self-employed persons.

The Treaty of Amsterdam (1997) introduced a special title on employment policy into the then EC Treaty (now: Articles 145–50 TFEU), meant to counterbalance the title on economic and monetary policy inserted by the Treaty of Maastricht (1993). This chapter introduced the OMC in the field of employment. This mode of governance leaves the primary responsibility with the Member States, but introduces processes of benchmarking and comparative policy development that have proven surprisingly effective.[74] With the Treaty of Nice, this policy method was elevated to the main instrument not only in the field of employment policy, but also of social policy at large.[75] The ToL elevates social policy, social cohesion, consumer protection and public health to shared competences, and expands the EU's competences regarding services of general interest and public health (Articles 4, 14 and 168(4) TFEU).

Directly binding EU Treaty law and secondary legislation are considerably scarcer in the social than in the economic field. Accordingly, 'new governance modes' beyond binding law seem of heightened practical relevance here. The OMC, while originating in the economic policy chapter, is widely used to integrate civil society actors into transnational governance

---

[73] For a concise overview see D. Kostakopoulou, 'The evolution of European Union citizenship', *EPS* 7 (2008), 285, 293. See also E. Spaventa, 'Seeing the wood despite the trees? On the scope of Union citizenship and its constitutional effectiveness', *CMLRev* 45 (2008), 13; and the articles in S. Besson (ed.), 'Special issue on citizenship', *ELJ* 13 (2007), 573.

[74] See for an overview of these S Kröger, 'What we have learnt: Advances, pitfalls and remaining questions in OMC research', *EIOP 13* (2009), Special Issue 1.

[75] See the critical résumé in Barnard (n. 65 above), p. 71.

processes.[76] Despite all justified criticism on how exactly this is done,[77] this also demonstrates the chance to further the transnationalisation of society through non-legally binding policies. However, as long as no binding law supports the social dimension of European integration, economic elites have more opportunities for developing a European identity than the economically less fortunate through direct legal action.[78]

C   Interrelation of economic and social dimensions of European integration

So far economic and social dimensions of European integration have been described as separate spheres. Such separation has long been characterised as not sustainable.[79] This is also mirrored in the Treaties as a normative framework of EU integration.

From the founding of the European Economic Community, social and economic dimensions of European integration were meant to interrelate normatively. The original version of Article 2 EEC reads:

> The Community shall have as its task, by establishing a Common Market and progressively approximating the economic policies of Member States, to promote throughout the Community . . . an accelerated raising of the standard of living . . .

Market integration appears as merely a secondary measure, meant to serve social policy aims such as the raising of the standard of living.

Steps enhancing the economic liberal thrust of the Treaties have often been taken in parallel with endeavours to enhance social regulation. The Treaty of Maastricht introduced the 'market economy clause' (ex Article 4 EC), requiring:

> the adoption of an economic policy which is based on the close co-ordination of Member States' economic policies, on the Internal Market and on the definition of common objectives, and conducted in accordance with the principle of an open market economy with free competition.

---

[76] See C. Kilpatrick, 'New EU employment governance and constitutionalism' in G. de Búrca and J. Scott (eds.), *Law and Governance in the EU and the US* (Oxford: Hart Publishing, 2006), pp. 134–41.

[77] D. Ashiagbor, *The European Employment Strategy* (Oxford: Oxford University Press, 2005) esp. pp. 226–33.

[78] Fligstein (n. 14 above), esp. ch. 6 (Conclusions, pp. 206–7).

[79] See already B. de Sousa Santos, *Towards a New Legal Common Sense*, 2nd edn (Reed: Elsevier, 2002), pp. 204 *et seq.*

The same Treaty also introduced a sea change in ex Article 2 EC, hidden between two commas in the beginning of the sentence. The Community was now to achieve its aims by 'establishing a Common Market and an economic and monetary union *and by implementing the common policies and activities referred to in Article 3*' (author's emphasis). Instead of relying on effects of economic integration, regulatory activity at EU level was now seen as essential. This change has legal implications. Earlier, the Court had confirmed that social aims stated in ex Article 2 EEC would be furthered by establishing the Common Market, while regulatory social policy remained the sole competence of the Member States.[80] The new Article 2 EC rendered this case law obsolete. The instrumental character of the internal market remained in place until the Treaty of Nice. Also, aims contained in Article 2 EC were increased with each Treaty reform. These aims are not merely moral imperatives, but have been acknowledged as legally binding. For example, in the *Viking* and *Laval* judgments, the Court relied on Articles 2 and 3 EC in concluding that free movement of services and freedom of establishment respectively must be 'balanced against objectives pursued by social policy'.[81]

Under the ToL, the values of the European Union are specified in Article 2 TEU. In addition to values already contained in Article 6 EU (before Lisbon),[82] this provision lists human dignity, equality and the rights of persons belonging to a minority. These are then qualified as being common to Member States 'in a society in which pluralism, non-discrimination, tolerance, justice, solidarity and equality between women and men prevail' (Article 2 EU). This seems to imply that social policy values such as justice and solidarity are left for Member States to pursue. Article 3 TEU paragraph 3, however, states further aims of the EU which include 'work[ing] for sustainable development ... based on balanced economic growth, a highly competitive social market economy, aiming at full employment and social progress, and a high level of protection and improvement of the environment' and 'combat[ing] social exclusion and discrimination' as well as 'promot[ing] social justice'. In addition, the gender mainstreaming clause (Article 8 TFEU = ex Article 3(2) EC) and environmental sustainability clause (Article 11

---

[80]   126/86 *Zaera* [1987] ECR 3697, paras. 10–11; C-339/89 *Alsthom Atlantique* [1991] ECR I-17, para. 8.

[81]   ECJ *Viking*, paras. 78–9; and ECJ *Laval*, paras. 104–5 (both n. 1 above).

[82]   Liberty, democracy, respect for human rights and fundamental freedoms and the rule of law.

TFEU= ex Article 6 EC) are complemented by new mainstreaming clauses, among others obliging the EU to take into account 'the guarantee of adequate social protection' and 'the fight against social exclusion' (Article 9 TFEU). Although possibly a little imprecise,[83] the addition signals the enhanced relevance of social policy.

As regards economic integration, the ToL upgrades the internal market from a secondary to a primary aim (Article 3 EU). At the same time, the 'open market economy with free competition' (ex Article 4 EC) is transformed towards a 'highly competitive social market economy' (Article 3 TEU, Article 119 TFEU). While this has been read as a step backwards,[84] overall the market economy is now connected to social policy, while open markets are no longer endorsed.

The development of Treaty aims, and the consistent expansion of social policy aims, seems to imply a normative case for reconciling the social and the economic in the endeavour of EU integration.

This normative case illustrates that the dominant views at the time of founding the European Economic Community[85] are no longer the basis of the Treaties. In the 1950s, it was seriously believed that market integration would lead to increased stability, enhanced living standards[86] and accelerated development of production methods, which would in turn lead to lower consumer prices, higher wages, currency stability, expansion of production and social progress.[87] In 1993, the makers of the Treaty of Maastricht acknowledged that this was not realistic and introduced the principle of a regulatory European integration process. This resonates with more recent critical voices from the field of political economy, according to whom the present crisis of European integration could be counteracted by 'deepening political integration and substantive solidarity'.[88] Moreover, the interrelation of the rather efficient implementation of 'constitutionalised' fundamental freedoms and competition law rules with national social policies and institutions may have

---

[83] See B. Bercusson, 'The Lisbon Treaty and Social Europe', ERA Forum 10 (2009), 87, 101.

[84] C. Joerges, 'The social market economy as Europe's social model?' in L. Magnusson and B. Strath (eds.), *A European Social Citizenship? Pre-conditions for future policies in historical light* (Brussels: Peter Lang, 2005), p. 125.

[85] As expressed in the 'Spaak report', drafted in support of founding the Community (Rapport des chefs de délégation aux ministres des affaires étrangères, Brussels: 21 April 1956).

[86] *Ibid.*, p. 13.

[87] *Ibid.*, p. 14; R. Baldwin and C. Wyplosz, *The Economics of European Integration* (Maidenhead: McGraw Hill, 2009), still maintain this view.

[88] A. Cafruny and J. Ryner, 'Critical political economy' in Wiener and Diez (eds.) (n. 8 above), quotes from pp. 233 and 238.

devastating effects. Economic and monetary union is said to support neoliberal welfare politics[89] while implementation of legally enshrined market integration has been shown to deconstruct traditional pillars of national welfare states.[90] Even from more moderate positions European redistribution *and* regulatory policies are deemed a necessary complement to enhanced efficiency of competitive markets.[91]

Pressures towards neoliberal welfare politics and dismantling of social security at national level are also a consequence of globalisation of markets.[92] This would suggest that nation states are increasingly unable individually to develop social policy counterbalancing poverty, unemployment and social disintegration. Accordingly, a European dimension of efforts to enhance social justice is necessary, if social justice should be a realistic option.[93]

IV   EU constitutionalism – socially embedded rights?

Enhancing justice is not merely a political programme, but also a normative aim. This part considers how far EU constitutionalism can contribute to achieving it. It is submitted that constitutionalism for a supranational polity with increasing social, economic and cultural competences and diversity, but without a strong symbolic constitution for the foreseeable future,[94] should be socially embedded. Obviously, this is not meant to close the wide debate about EU constitutionalism,[95] but rather to open it for a different argument.

---

[89] T. Bolukbasi, 'On consensus, constraint and choice: Economic and monetary integration and Europe's welfare states', *JEPP* 16 (2009), 527.

[90] For employment law see P. Syrpis, *EU Intervention in Domestic Labour Law* (Oxford: Oxford University Press, 2007), esp. pp. 103–44; for welfarist solidarity regimes see Ferrera (n. 70 above).

[91] Molle (n. 31 above), p. 290–311; see also Nello (n. 31 above), p. 123.

[92] J. Habermas, 'The postnational constellation and the future of democracy' in J. Habermas (ed.), *The Postnational Constellation: Political essays* (Cambridge, MA and London: MIT Press, 2001), pp. 99–103. On the EU's active involvement in establishing these 'external forces', A. Antoniadis, 'Social Europe and/or global Europe? Globalisation and flexicurity as debates on the future of Europe', *Cambridge Review of International Affairs* 21 (2008), 327.

[93] See J. Habermas, 'Learning from catastrophe? A look back at the short twentieth century' in Habermas (n. 92 above), pp. 52–9.

[94] C. Reh, 'The Convention on the Future of Europe and the Development of Integration Theory: A lasting impact?', *JEPP* 15 (2008), 781.

[95] Legal studies contributions to this include Weiler and Wind (n. 5 above); Wouters, Verhey and Kiiver (n. 4 above); Shaw (nn. 3 and 5 above); N. Tsagourias, *Transnational*

A   Constitutions – within states

Constitutionalism as a legal or political theory obviously has its origin within nation states.[96]

1   Conventional constitutionalism: liberal rights and market freedoms

While pre-modern constitutions were content with fixing a set of rules capable of formally justifying territorial sovereignty, constitutions of modern states find the legitimacy of public rule in democracy as a principle. Democratic constitutions tend to follow two different models. In majoritarian democracies, constitutions are mainly procedural and justify rule through parliamentary majority. Constitutional democracies use a set of legal endowments protected by independent courts as a complementary justification of majority rule.[97]

Beyond the differences between these traditions, democratic constitutionalism aims to constrain arbitrary rule. Traditionally, national constitutions were based on the assumption that such arbitrariness emanates from public actors. Early democracy constrained arbitrary power of the monarch and/or other traditional rulers, and modern democracy has constrained arbitrary power emanating from the state. This has happened through rights endowments, procedural rules, checks and balances of public powers or a combination of all three. The conventional departure for constitutionalism has thus been sketched:

Constitutionalism (Cambridge: Cambridge University Press, 2007). Political science approaches include Reh (n. 94 above); A. Wiener, 'Contested meanings of norms', CompEurPolit 5 (2007), 1; U. Liebert, J. Falke and A. Maurer (eds.), Postnational Constitutionalism in the New Europe (Baden-Baden: Nomos, 2006).

[96]   See Tsagourias, 'Introduction' in Transnational Constitutionalism (n. 95 above), p. 4.

[97]   On these different traditions R. Dworkin, Freedoms Law: The moral reading of the American Constitution (Oxford: Oxford University Press, 1996) (developing the dichotomy of majoritarian democracy and his moral reading, consisting of constitutional democracy in the introduction, pp. 1–38); T. Ginsburg, Judicial Review in New Democracies (Cambridge: Cambridge University Press, 2003), pp. 1–19 (juxtaposing the British majoritarian principle of parliamentary supremacy to the US idea of constitutional democracy). For European voices, see E. U. Petersmann, 'Multilevel trade requires multilevel constitutionalism' in C. Joerges and E. U. Petersmann (eds.), Constitutionalism, Multilevel Trade Governance and Social Regulation (Oxford et al.: Hart, 2006), p. 7 (portraying the dichotomy as between rights-based constitutions – examples being Germany, South Africa and India – process-based or popular democracies – examples being the UK and the US) and p. 28. There is also a perceived rift between the Nordic states and the EU (J. Nergelius, 'Between collectivism and constitutionalism: The Nordic countries and constitutionalism' in J. Nergelius (ed.), Constitutionalism: New challenges (Leiden/Boston: Martinus Nijhoff, 2008), pp. 119–54).

parliamentary rule is complemented by inalienable rights bestowed on individuals, who are also enabled to enforce these rights judicially.

In debates about national citizenship, different layers of constitutional rights have been distinguished, following T. H. Marshall. The first layer is described as the protection of personal liberties (e.g. property, free movement and economic activity). The second layer provides the institutional base for democracy, again also endowing individuals with rights such as the right to participate in elections, publicly declare their opinion and to organise themselves in political parties. The third layer provides for a minimum level of social equality and the practical opportunity for all citizens to participate in democratic and socio-economic life. It comprises financial endowments from state sources and proceeds to rights of workers to combine in trade unions and to participate in corporate governance through codetermination in enterprises.[98] Conventional constitutionalism tends to focus on the first two layers of rights. Widespread scepticism towards the juridification of social rights[99] frequently leads to a narrow conception of constitutional rights as individual and negative, under which any constitutionalisation of the third layer seems unattainable.

In this traditional vision, the rule of law is constructed as an instrument to safeguard individual liberties, strengthening citizens who are sufficiently autonomous in relying on their personal wealth to be able to fend for their own wellbeing. Unsurprisingly, this conventional constitutionalism is closely related to market-based societies.

2   Socially embedded constitutionalism

However, constitutionalism is capable of embracing social rights. If a constitution aims at integrating a society,[100] and the constitution is at the same time rights-based, rights must be interpreted in ways that hold out their promise to the majority of the population. Accordingly, the endeavour to guarantee rights beyond hollow formulas is a common

[98] See M. Everson, 'The legacy of the market citizen' in Shaw and More (n. 11 above), pp. 73–90 (at 82), with ample reference to T. H. Marshall ('Citizenship and social class' (Oxford: Oxford University Press, 1950) repr. in T. H. Marshall and T. Bottomore, *Citizenship and Social Class* (London *et al.*: Pluto Press, 1992), pp. 1–47).

[99] For a criticism of such narrow perspectives see D. Bilchitz, *Poverty and Fundamental Rights: The justification and enforcement of socio-economic rights* (Oxford: Oxford University Press, 2007), using the term 'socio-economic' as used in UN Convention on Social, Economic and Cultural Rights for what is referred to as social rights in constitutional (national) theory.

[100] See above text accompanying n. 29.

endeavour of constitutional courts. Guaranteeing socio-economic rights explicitly,[101] embracing a social state principle which informs the content of rights[102] or interpreting rights as enabling rather than liberating[103] are ways of making human rights meaningful for all factions of society.

Making human rights significant in the reality of many (rather than protecting the privileges of a few) ultimately aims at creating conditions where all human beings are capable of governing their own lives, if necessary collectively or co-operatively. Such self governance can be endangered by states and their conglomerates, and accordingly protection of rights and liberties against public appropriation remains important. However, self-governance is increasingly threatened by economically powerful actors outside public realms. This results inter alia from the tendency of markets to reinforce existing social stratification and to work to the advantage of frequent players. A substantive rather than a merely formal notion of rights thus is traditionally safeguarded by state action (or state intervention in markets). For example, rights to protect personal data are increasingly protected against impositions by employers as well as against the states' insatiable hunger for information.

Socially embedded constitutionalism as proposed here should not merely rely on substantive rights enforced by states. Transgressing the boundaries of the state–citizen relationship, it has extended its reach towards relations that are predominantly perceived as belonging to societal realms beyond state governance. Examples include markets, families and other realms of non-state community. In order to imbue these spheres with substantive human rights, rights become relational, opening adequate procedures to pursue self-governance in horizontal relationships. These include rights to develop counter-powers by collectivisation in order to overcome ingrained imbalances of market participants. Constitutionalised labour relations[104] certainly have the longest practical tradition among such rights. However,

---

[101] The South African constitution is one of the most prominent examples; see D. Davis, 'Socioeconomic rights: Do they deliver the goods?', *ICON* 6 (2008), 687–711; S. Koutnatzis, 'Social rights as a constitutional compromise: Lessons from comparative experience', *Columbia JTL* 44 (2005), 74.

[102] See for an English-language overview on such effects of the German constitutional social state principle, Koutnatzis (n. 101 above); see also Schiek (n. 61 above).

[103] K. Moeller, 'Two conceptions of positive liberty: Towards an autonomy-based theory of constitutional rights', *OJLS* 29 (2009), 757–86.

[104] On the concept of constitutionalising labour relations through guaranteeing procedural fundamental rights see M. Kittner and D. Schiek, 'Artikel 9 Abs. 3 Koalitionsfreiheit' in Denninger *et al.* (n. 61 above) and R. Dukes, 'Constitutionalising employment relations: Sinzheimer, Kahn-Freund, and the role of labour law', *J Law&Soc* 35 (2008), 341.

the employment relationship is certainly not the only sphere where private power needs to be contained. Also, practices developed in the late nineteenth century may well be in need of refurbishment if they are to meet challenges of a post-national age. The ongoing relevance of these early forms of societal constitutionalism lies in their capacity to create an alternative to competitive markets as well as to paternalistic state rule. This alternative lies in co-operative forms of governance, in other words through collective action. Collective action can be realised through self-organisation in a number of ways, be it through housing associations, the economic sociale, or self-organised care for old people.

It is nearly commonplace to state that the age of national constitutions has come to an end. The powers that threaten individual liberties that have been the traditional focus of these constitutions no longer emanate from state actors alone. States are vastly dependent on each other if they are to maintain any order at all. Furthermore, private ordering has increased immensely. This may render state legislation as dysfunctional, and the same may be true for legislation issued by a conglomerate of states. Accordingly, constitutionalism is now being developed beyond national borders. European constitutionalism is only one example for this, on which the following will focus.

B   EU constitutionalism beyond states

1   Conventional constitutionalism: liberal rights and market freedoms

While the forerunners of the EU, and especially the EEC, have not been overly concerned with establishing procedural preconditions for democratic rule, its early constitutionalism has been successful in guaranteeing judicially enforceable rights. This form of constitutionalism is well suited to be employed beyond the nation state. Individual rights, such as those protected by the fundamental freedoms, and any protection of traditional liberties connected to property, exercising one's economic preferences and free trade can easily be guaranteed beyond states. Beyond the EU, such 'new constitutionalism' has been criticised as 'institutionalising neo-liberal reforms'[105] and 'removing key aspects of economic life from the influence of domestic politics within states'.[106]

---

[105] S. Gill, 'New constitutionalism, democratisation and global political economy', *Pacifica Review: Peace, Security & Global Change* 10 (1998), 23.

[106] D. Schneidermann, 'Investment rules and the new constitutionalism', *LSI* (2000) 757, 762.

The critique resonates with the findings of legal sociologists that rights-based constitutionalism tends to empower 'pro-constitutionalisation elites'.[107]

This critique also resonates with the negative voices on the practical functioning of the EU market freedoms. Clearly, there is still a good measure of conventional constitutionalism in the EU. The ToL continues to stress economic liberties. The TFEU guarantees the old fundamental freedoms and competition norms, which remain individually enforceable. Accordingly, the EU Treaties, as currently interpreted by the Court's case law, may well appear as imposing new constitutionalism on the EU based on market-liberal values.

2 Socially embedded EU constitutionalism?

Doubts whether the successes of socially embedding constitutionalism can be expanded beyond the nation states abound. A recent analysis of the ToL concludes that the imbalance between the internal market at EU level and the powers to rein in any overbearing market forces remaining at national level is 'not easy to correct'.[108] The underlying asymmetry is said to make an EU social market economy eternally untenable.[109] If the fundamental freedoms' rudimentary form of liberal rights constitutionalism was to prevail in the EU, permanent decoupling of social and economic dimensions of integration would seem inevitable.

We have also seen, that the normative base of EU economic and social constitutionalism would contradict such a result. Ever since 1957, and even more so since the ToL, the Founding Treaties embrace policy aims going beyond the economic sphere. These include social inclusion, combating inequality and poverty, diminishing unemployment, and environmental and economic sustainability, to name only a few cornerstones for a truly EU-level social policy. The TFEU after Lisbon now sports a new horizontal social clause. According to its Article 9 the EU must take into account in the definition and implementation of all its policies the 'requirements linked to the promotion of a high level of employment, the guarantee of adequate social protection, the fight against social exclusion, and a high level of education, training and

---

[107] R. Hirschl, *Towards Juristocracy* (Cambridge, MA: Harvard University Press, 2004), p. 44; see for the EU, Münch (n. 24 above).

[108] Piris (n. 59 above), p. 334.

[109] F. Scharpf, 'The asymmetry of European integration, or why the EU cannot be a "social market economy"', *Socio-Economic Review* 8 (2010), 211.

protection of human health'. The Treaties thus presuppose an interrelation of economic and social integration, within which the ToL strengthens the social element by adding considerably to the list of social Treaty aims.

However, the Treaties also provide a fixed legal framework mainly for establishing the internal market and protecting competition from distortions and national protectionism. As regards social dimensions of European integration, they are content with rather open norms and procedural provisions. Their normative impetus thus appears as unattainable, if we only regard positive Treaty law. This would constitute an inherent contradiction in EU (constitutional) law.

(a) **EU constitutionalism as social practice**   However, EU constitutionalism is not necessarily restricted to such a positivistic approach. If we consider law as a social practice,[110] it consists of an open-ended process of actions and interactions between social actors who are abiding by the law, calculating the costs of violating the law and generally exhibiting and subjecting themselves to normative expectations. Positive law is only a written expression of a web of social practices ultimately resisting complete articulation,[111] and is thus necessarily less than law as a social practice. The limited degree to which social dimensions of European integration are constitutionalised in positive Treaty law does not thus unavoidably limit socially embedded EU constitutionalism. Indeed, the ECJ has hardly been held back by positive law when developing EU market constitutionalism.[112]

Moreover, constitutional law must be considered as even less positivistic than other law. It is characterised by a heightened degree of durability. It is higher law, on which all other law rests, after all. At the same time, it encompasses the most important substantive and procedural values of a given polity, or in the case of post-national law, of webbed cells of polities. Accordingly, constitutional law is in even more need of being flexible and adaptable to changes in reality.[113] This applies

---

[110] See for this concept de Búrca and Haltern (both n. 12 above) and Wiener (n. 95 above).

[111] Even from a positivist perspective on law, this concept of the 'open texture of law' is acknowledged (see H. L. A. Hart, *The Concept of Law*, 2nd edn (Oxford: Clarendon Press, 1994), pp. 124–36).

[112] See text accompanying n. 34 above for the limited degree of textual base for the supranational character of EU law.

[113] See from national perspectives E. Stein, *Einleitung II* in E. Denninger *et al.* (n. 61 above), paras. 28–9.

even more to EU constitutionalism, which is post-national and based on processes and procedures open to contestation, change and development.[114]

EU constitutionalism will have to offer modes of adapting open norms to ever changing and developing societal realities within and beyond the EU. Their complexity is beyond the grasp of positive legislation. The inertia imbued upon the EU legislative process by the necessity to achieve agreement between twenty-seven Member States, the diversity between which has increased considerably since 1957, has been lamented by authors from vastly different angles. Intergovernmentalists have proposed relying on authoritative institutions or expertocracy instead of cumbersome democratic institutions in order to produce outcome legitimacy;[115] pro-Europeans have proposed leaving complex social policy decisions to nation states rather than to the EU.[116] 'New governance' within the EU has been assessed as leading to the inclusion of civil society actors in lawmaking processes beyond traditional structures of representative democracy.[117] Accordingly, European constitutionalism, if it is to be relevant not only for enhancing economic liberalism but also in social terms of increasing citizens' self-governance irrespective of personal wealth, must encompass a variety of realms.[118]

(b) EU constitutionalism in societal realms   If we consider constitutionalism as a mode of guaranteeing a realistic opportunity to self-govern for all, its concepts cannot be meant to protect against being ruled by states or any other actors emanating from the public sphere. This would be inadequate in any post-national constellation, where power and domination does not necessarily emanate from states or the public sphere. Indeed, with the diminishing relevance of the Westphalian state, private actors and networks are said to attain ever more substantive power to govern.[119] An adequate conceptualisation of

---

[114] Shaw (nn. 3 and 5 above).
[115] G. Majone, *Dilemmas of European Integration: The ambiguities and pitfalls of integration by stealth* (Oxford: Oxford University Press, 2005).
[116] See those quoted above in n. 2 above.
[117] Schepel (n. 58 above); D. Schiek, 'Private rule-making and European governance: Issues of legitimacy', *ELRev* 32 (2007), 443. This resonates with G. Bronzini's suggestion to combine OMC methodology with effective administrative control ('The social dilemma of European integration', *Law and Critique* 19 (2008), 255).
[118] On the notion see N. Walker, 'The idea of constitutional pluralism', *MLR* 65 (2002), 317.
[119] e.g. C. Cutler, *Private Power and Public Authority* (Cambridge: Cambridge University Press, 2003).

constitutionalism beyond the state would thus also include domination
and rule by private actors such as multinational corporations. In the
realm of individual rights against states and supranational entities, such
constitutionalism leads to demands for constitutionalisation of private
law.[120] In the realm of procedural guarantees, democratic procedures for
public institutions must be complemented by democratic rights in presumably private realms.[121]

EU constitutionalism, as shaped through ECJ case law, has in the past
already enhanced the agency of civil actors – mainly of economic undertakings[122] driving a market integration project beyond national borders.
It has failed to develop aspects of constitutionalising agency of those who
are subject to being governed by those owning these undertakings. Trade
unionism is obviously only one – possibly dated – strategy to overcome
such heteronomous structuring of social reality. Any evolution of transnational trade unionism in action within the EU internal market would,
however, be a further step towards developing the transnational society
so dearly needed to make EU integration a reality. Other socio-political
fields where social agency is threatened without constitutionalising societal spheres include economic relations between professionals and their
clients, for example in banking, healthcare and legal advice. In addition,
the field of obtaining housing shelter can be named. Though functionally
tied to the soil of states, access to living space is dependent on a web of
contractual relations granting access to credit or rented accommodation,
which are capable of being constitutionalised beyond the state. If it is
to attain its normative goals, EU constitutionalism should be able to
embrace the development of transnational interest coalitions of the
weaker parts in these relations rather than defeat them, as happened in
Viking and *Laval*.

For EU constitutionalism to embrace civic realms more comprehen-
sively, individual and collective rights conferred by the EU polity must
go beyond rights guaranteed against intrusion by states and the EU itself.
As human rights in their substantive dimension are mainly threatened

---

[120] See T. Barkhuysen and S. Lindenbergh (eds.), *Constitutionalisation of Private Law*
(Leiden, Boston: Martinus Nijhoff, 2006); and C. Joerges, 'European challenges to
private law: On false dichotomies, true conflicts and the need for a constitutional
perspective', *LS* 18 (2006), 146.

[121] D. Schiek, 'Autonomous collective agreements as a regulatory device in European
Labour Law: How to read Article 139 EC', *ILJ* 34 (2005), 23.

[122] See again the results achieved by Fligstein (n. 14 above), pp. 121, 165.

by non-state actors,[123] EU constitutionalism must also include socially embedded rights furthering capability for self-governance of all.

V   Conclusion: European economic and social constitutionalism after the Treaty of Lisbon

Having outlined a potential further development for European constitutionalism, a logical next step would be to develop a mode of reasoning which could bring such constitutionalism to life within the EU. This next step lies beyond this chapter though, which has only pursued the aim of outlining a framework for undertaking these next steps.

As we have seen above, the Founding Treaties after the ToL do not support an alleged dominance of economic dimensions of European integration over its social dimensions, although they constitutionalise economic dimensions of integration more efficiently than their social counterparts. Re-conceptualising EU constitutionalism on the base of its open-textured norms and with regard to empowering transnational civil society will enable European scholars to contribute to reconciling perceived tensions between the social and economic dimensions of European integration.

The next steps for legal studies – lying beyond this book, though – will encompass offering new ways of interpreting rights vested in individuals and at the same time suggesting modes of governance suitable to engender European societal integration. Those constitutional rights of a new quality must also bar any reading of the directly effective economic freedoms and competition law rules in such a way as to inhibit national[124] and transnational solutions to deprivation from self-governance.

These steps towards creating a constitutional realignment of economic and social dimensions of European integration will have to consider interactions between the European and the national level, as well as different effects of different modes of governance. While it may very well

---

[123]   B. de Witte, 'The past and future role of the European Court of Justice in the protection of human rights' in P. Alston (ed.), *The EU and Human Rights* (Oxford: Oxford University Press, 1999), p. 874. For responses in international human rights law, see the contributions in P. Alston (ed.), *Non-State Actors and Human Rights* (Oxford: Oxford University Press, 2005).

[124]   For more detailed arguments to protect the national status quo in fields where no social dimension of EU integration at European level can be offered yet see D. Schiek, 'The European Social Model and the Services Directive' in Neergard, Nielsen and Roseberry (n. 52 above), pp. 45–51.

be the case that enforcing EU 'hard economic law' will unduly impinge on national social state arrangements, hard law may not always be the most efficient method to establish new forms of interaction. Socially and economically embedded constitutionalism for the European multilevel polity will have a pivotal role in supporting the social agency of those unable to avail themselves of individual rights to wealth.

2

Reconciling market with Social Europe? The EU under the Lisbon Treaty

ULRIKE LIEBERT

I Introduction

Since many of the goods and services desired in a modern economy are not pure private goods, this leads to the prescription that the State – in the singular – should provide and produce all the goods and services where markets fail. Showing that one institutional arrangement leads to sub-optimal performance is not equivalent, however, to showing that another institutional arrangement will perform better.[1]

The most recent global financial and economic crisis has accelerated the European Union to a crossroads where it can either strengthen or fall apart. Amidst the contemporary capitalist constellation, achievements of several decades of economic and social integration are at stake.[2] Hence, after a decade-long contentious EU Treaty reform, the newly enacted Lisbon Treaty has to prove itself under quite unfavourable conditions. Faced with failing markets and states, many suspect the EU under the new Lisbon rules of seeking to further empower 'Market Europe' while others are concerned it might unduly advance a burdensome supranational 'European social polity'. As a matter of fact, European integration has been shaped by the 'competitive fight for survival' between these two paradigms of a legitimate social and economic order at least since the

---

[1] E. Ostrom, 'The comparative study of public economies', Acceptance paper for the Frank E. Seidman Distinguished Award in Political Economy, *The American Economist* 42 (1998), 3.

[2] See L. Magnusson, 'After Lisbon? Social Europe at the crossroads', ETUI Working Paper 1 (2010): 'the global crisis has accelerated previous trends from tax competition to social race to the bottom'; J.-P. Fitoussi and F. K. Padoa Schioppa (eds.), *Report on the State of the European Union*, vol. I (London: Palgrave Macmillan, 2005), pp. 207 et seq.

1980s.[3] While the economic liberalistic project has been striving for monetary unification and financial rigidity, the social solidarity venture has sought to promote a 'Social Europe' with redistributive ambitions, albeit 'less in financial terms than in terms of equal standards and political co-ordination'.[4] Moreover, in the complex multilayered EU, tensions between national and EU levels have grown over the years, 'as economic decision-making has increasingly moved upwards towards the EU level while social politics and identity have largely remained national, along with the mechanisms of electoral sanctions'.[5]

Yet, in EU politics and policy-making, the struggles along these two conflict lines have not necessarily led to disjuncture and stalemate. Economic liberties have not always been played out at the disadvantage of social justice, as the economic liberal doctrine would have it,[6] or vice versa, as socialist ideologues would suspect. As a matter of fact, the evolving European constitutionalism has paved some ways for making economic and social rationalities mutually constitutive, albeit with varying success in practice: While the 1987 'Single Market' and the 'Delors Report' succeeded in coupling social and economic dimensions of European integration through the political regulation of markets, the 2000 Lisbon process could not help but assist a growing divide between 'Market Europe' and the would-be 'social European polity'; between the 'hard legal framework' aimed at fostering the EU's global economic competitiveness, on the one hand, and the 'soft law' or less legalised framework on which the promoting of social cohesion relied, on the other.[7]

---

[3] B. Strath, 'The monetary issue and European economic policy in historical perspective' in C. Joerges, B. Strath and P. Wagner (eds.), *The Economy as a Polity: The political constitution of contemporary capitalism* (London et al.: UCL Press, 2005), p. 70.

[4] *Ibid.* at p. 70. While the 'Growth and Stability Pact' is the most distinctive outcome of 'Market Europe', imposing budgetary discipline on EMU Member States while enhancing individual market flexibility, 'Social Europe' has taken shape through successive European Council decisions (Maastricht 1992, Essen 1994, Luxembourg and Amsterdam 1997, Köln 1999 and Lisbon 2000).

[5] V. Schmidt, 'EU economic solidarity: A great leap forward or a bridge too far?' *Neue Gesellschaft - Frankfurter Hefte* 7 (2010), 18.

[6] Friedrich Hayek's contributions to economics, philosophy and politics include a study of the relations between law and liberty where Hayek expounded his conviction that the continued unexamined pursuit of 'social justice' will contribute to the erosion of personal liberties and encourage the advent of totalitarianism. See F. Hayek, *The Constitution of Liberty* (London: Routledge & Kegan Paul PCL, 1960); and *Law, Legislation, and Liberty*, I: *Rules and Order* (London: Routledge & Kegan Paul PCL, 1973).

[7] The Lisbon process failed its ambitious aims, namely to turn the EU during the first decade of the twenty-first century into 'the most competitive and socially cohesive region

To sum up, the issue of whether and how to bring the social and economic dimensions of European integration in sync that have drifted apart is a contentious question that remains historically, politically and institutionally to be resolved: 'the EU seems to be more than just market integration, but what more and how much more is an open issue'.[8] In this context, the 2009 Lisbon Treaty (ToL) is but the most recent and arguably most important test case for examining this issue. In the evolving practices of EU politics and policy-making, will the ToL help develop a socially embedded European constitutionalism that can guide the European Union in its search for legitimate governance?

Political science and legal scholarly debates are deeply divided as regards the answer to this question. On the one hand, there is the account by European political scientists and lawyers who subsume the EU's 'social dimension' under the achievements of the Continental and social democratic welfare state that European economic integration progressively undermines. From this sceptical angle, the ToL presents another case of 'cheap talk' about 'Social Europe' that cannot cope with the 'hard' facts of liberal market expansion. On the other hand, normative and social constructivist perspectives focus on socially embedded, post-, trans- or supranational varieties of 'constitutionalisation'. Following these approaches, the EU is believed to be capable of responding to economic challenges in socially solidaristic ways. More than its predecessors, the ToL is valued in terms of rules as tools for reconciling tensions between economic and social dimensions of European integration.

Thus, whether the ToL will further empower 'Market Europe' or enhance a 'Social Europe' capable of coping with failures of markets and states, depends on several empirical questions, including the following: first of all, regarding formal norms, what is in the Treaty for reconciling Social and Market Europe; moreover, regarding rules in use, how will the EU under the ToL cope with the challenges of failing markets or states (i.e. with tensions between economic freedoms and social values) or dilemmas of providing social welfare efficiently and equitably; and, finally, will the EU under the ToL empower only market citizenship or also social citizenship, and the EU's social constituencies, at large?

---

of the world'. For criticisms and an overview of the debate on the 'Lisbon Process' and the politics for a 'Social Europe' that it entailed, see U. Liebert, 'The politics for a Social Europe and the Lisbon process' in L. Magnusson and B. Strath (eds.), *European Solidarities: Tensions and contentions of a concept* (Bruxelles: Peter Lang, 2007), p. 267.

[8] Strath (n. 3 above), p. 70.

In the following, addressing these questions, I develop an argument in three steps: (1) the first establishes how far what is in the ToL matters for 'Social Europe'; (2) in the second, propositions are developed about whether the EU under the ToL constitutes itself as a polycentric system of self-governance using institutional rules as 'tools in use' for coping with problems of migration, failing markets and state dilemmas; (3) and in the conclusion, I discuss social, political and institutional requirements for the EU under the ToL not to dismantle national social welfare systems by a European market order, but to renew a social European polity that transcends the divide between 'markets' and 'states' that has characterised the contested political space of European constitutionalisation.

II   What is in the Lisbon Treaty for reconciling Market and Social Europe?

The EU's ToL is the most recent chapter in a continuous process of transformations since the second half of the twentieth century. It has furthered the process whereby state legal systems are tailored to European law, national citizenship is extended to include international human and European citizenship rights, and constitutionalism is evolving into a post-national economic,[9] contentious social[10] and arguably also democratic order[11] that transcends the borders of the nation state. The ToL provides changed rules for governing the social dimensions of the European Union and thus further develops the framework of 'socially embedded constitutionalism'.[12] The constitutional choices introduced by it have the potential to reshape the EU's practices of

---

[9] For the conception of European economic constitutionalism in the tradition of liberal economic philosophers, namely F. Hayek, see J. Buchanan, 'Europe's constitutional opportunity' in J. Buchanan, K. Otto Pöhl, V. Curzon Price and F. Vibert (eds.), *Europe's Constitutional Future* (London: The Institute of Economic Affairs, 1990), p. 1.

[10] For the conception of European social constitutionalism, designed to 'conserve the great democratic achievements of the European nation-state', including 'not only formal guarantees of civil rights, but levels of social welfare, education and leisure that are the precondition of both an effective private autonomy and of democratic citizenship', see J. Habermas, 'Why Europe needs a constitution', *New Left Review* 11(2001), 5, 6.

[11] For an overview and discussion of the foundations, procedures, and legitimacy of European democratic constitutionalism and its prospects, see U. Liebert, J. Falke and A. Maurer (eds.), *Postnational Constitutionalisation in the New Europe* (Baden-Baden: Nomos, 2006).

[12] The concept and framework of 'socially embedded constitutionalism' is discussed in more detail by Schiek, ch. 1 in this volume.

socio-economic governance.[13] Which of the ToL provisions will affect the EU's capabilities of coping with tensions between economic and social integration? Are they only 'rules in form' or are they also likely to affect the EU's practices of governance – that is, solve collective-action problems better and enhance socially beneficial co-operative behaviour that is based on social norms? Before addressing these questions in part III, in this section a close constitutionalist reading of the ToL is proposed to establish what formal norms and rules have changed or have been newly introduced and which define the EU's type of socio-economic order.

To anticipate my findings: the ToL does not fundamentally reconstitute the European order in terms of shifting between an economic and a social type of constitutionalism, but it better balances both. Also, the Treaty strengthens some elements of 'socially embedded constitutionalism', namely by empowering the EU's social constituency's or stakeholders' fundamental rights. Moreover, it changes little in the vertical distribution of powers and competences in socio-economic policy-making between the Member States and the EU institutions. Yet, it develops the bases for a 'would-be' European polycentric social polity, by redesigning vertical and horizontal inter-institutional relations between EU and Member State institutions, decentralising within the EU's polycentric system of governance and also by stepping up non-judicial conflict-resolution mechanisms and nesting rules. Finally, the ToL norms help rationalise European polycentric governance by balancing economic and market with social values.

A   Balancing social and economic dimensions of European integration

Does the ToL reconstitute the European order and significantly shift the balance between economic and social constitutionalism?[14] Admittedly, there are very few modified or newly introduced provisions – notably the

---

[13] During the Convention on the Future of Europe, tasked with the drafting of the ToL's predecessor, the Treaty establishing a Constitution for Europe, a major group of members self-organised and put pressure on the Convention president to establish a Working Group 'Social Europe' which initially had not been planned for, since it was expected to create contentions and impede the necessary consensus. Yet, despite this initial reluctance, the Working Group achieved a range of innovative results; see M. O'Neill, *The Struggle for the European Constitution: A past and future history* (London and New York: Routledge, 2008).

[14] Socially embedded constitutionalism is discussed in more detail by Schiek, ch. 1 in this volume.

horizontal 'social clause' – with a potential to affect the distribution of powers and competences in social policy-making between the Member States and the EU institutions. The ToL basically continues the path of former Treaty reforms to advance supranational market integration by expanding community competences, for instance in the domain of economic governance, yet with some discontinuities. For instance, it replaces the concept of 'Community', depicting European supranationality by the apparently intergovernmental notion 'European Union'. 'Regarding the established meanings this is normatively misleading since the renamed European organisation with proper legal personality continues basically the tradition of the supranational community, but not that of the intergovernmental union pillars.'[15] More importantly, however, the ToL reframes EU values and objectives in ways that seek to bridge the gap between economic and social dimensions of European integration. Thus, the ToL contributes to socially re-embedding the European order in several ways: first, through a restatement of the EU's objectives and values (Articles 2–3 TEU) as well as a new horizontal 'social clause' (Article 9 TFEU);[16] secondly, the reappraisal of services of general interest by a new EU competence, and enhanced emphasis on the Union's values and the TFEU's horizontal clauses and a specific protocol reacting to the initial Irish reaction of the Treaty[17] contribute to improved co-ordination between EU economic integration and European social models across levels.[18] Moreover, by coupling economic and social dimensions of its external actions, the ToL aims at a socially embedded governance of globalisation. In addition, it seeks to strengthen the underdeveloped economic dimension of economic and

---

[15] 'Dies ist nach dem bislang eingeschliffenen Verständnis normkategorial missverständlich, weil die umbenannte rechtspersonale europäische Organisation in ihrem Kern die Linie der supranationalen Gemeinschaft, nicht aber der intergouvernementalen Unionssäulen tradiert ...' (P. C. Müller-Graff, 'Der Vertrag von Lissabon auf der Systemspur des Europäischen Primärrechts', *Integration* 31 (2008), 123 (author's translation).

[16] For more detail see Schiek, ch. 1 in this volume.

[17] The 'statement of the concerns of the Irish People on the Lisbon Treaty' as set out by the Taoiseach, 11–12 December 2008, referred explicitly (among others) to 'the essential role and wide discretion of national, regional and local Governments in providing, commissioning and organising non-economic services of general interest which is not affected by any provision of the Treaty of Lisbon, including those relating to the common commercial policy'; see J.-P. Piris, *The Lisbon Treaty: A legal and political analysis* (Cambridge: Cambridge University Press, 2010), p. 55.

[18] More detail on this field is provided by Neergaard in ch. 7 below.

monetary union. And, finally, it balances EU and Member State competences in the multilayered European social polity.

1   Coupling economic and social dimensions in the governance of globalisation[19]

Some advances towards the re-coupling of economic and social policy-making can be found in the provisions concerning the EU's external actions. Aimed at furthering the EU's global ambitions – namely, not to become reduced to push through G20 decisions but to actively help govern globalisation – the TFEU (Part V) provides a new framework for a more closely intertwined economic and foreign diplomacy. This includes tools for strengthening the coherence among economic and social activities, such as: open trade policy; liberalisation and facilitation of trade for developing countries; development co-operation; economic, financial and technical co-operation with third countries; and humanitarian aid, among others. Notably, 'common principles' are established for all external policies that encompass the promotion of democracy, rule of law and human rights (Article 21 TEU). Thus, the coherence of economic and social dimensions of EU external action is enhanced substantially. But whether and to what extent the Member States and the EU institutions will fill the new framework with life remains to be seen. The European Treaty framers did address the EU's responsibilities in the governance of globalisation – but much remains to be done.[20]

2   Matching monetary union with economic governance

Within monetary union, sixteen EU Member States have merged monetary policies, albeit without matching it with an equally strong political economic union. Against EMU-sceptical claims calling for the dismantling of the entire project,[21] Commission President J. M. Barroso calls for EU leaders to engage in 'building a political Europe' and to 'enforce economic governance', as Member States ought to acknowledge their interdependence and the collapse of confidence in markets. Whether the ToL will foster community decision-making for governing the economy,

---

[19] Oral communication by Karel De Gucht: International Trade Commissioner, Global Jean-Monnet – ECSA conference, Brussels, May 2010.

[20] As a conditionality of development co-operation, the observation of human rights is no longer specified by the ToL. Therefore, it remains less clear and it is to be seen in practice whether the ECJ will make use of the 'common principles'.

[21] See A. Verdun, 'Ten years EMU: An assessment of ten critical claims', *International Journal of Economics and Business Research* 2 (2010), 144.

thus reinforcing EU institutions and provide for more coherence, effectiveness and legitimacy, will depend on how new procedural rules will be
used in practice. The toolbox provides for qualified majority rule in
combination with the enhanced role of the European Parliament; the
upgrading of Commission competences in economic and monetary
union and external affairs; a new permanent European Council enabling
more continuity, coherence and leadership, in particular if following a
Community approach based on co-operation between Member States
and EU institutions. Thus, the ToL promises to strengthen the economic
dimension of EMU in four respects. First, the European Central Bank
(ECB) becomes a fully fledged institution (Article 13 TEU) and the rules
of the Eurozone are incorporated into the Treaty (see Title VIII TFEU).
Secondly, sanction rules are stepped up, strengthening the Commission's
powers to warn Member States (Article 121(4) TFEU, ex Article 99 EC),
and the Council to take decisions without the vote of the respective
Member State with the European Parliament. Thirdly, the Council is
empowered to set out economic policy guidelines, the discipline of
Eurozone members strengthened (Article 136 TFEU). Finally, the
Commission gains the power to represent the EU in the IMF.

The global economic crisis has pushed the EU into a period of
stagnation. In this existential crisis, the traditional model of quantitative
economic growth is put into question and a new European model,
beyond quantitative change, is searched for. For coping with financial
and economic crises, not only a legal framework but the appropriate
political will and sufficient economic resources are needed. In practice,
the EU – since December 2009 under the ToL – has started proving that
it is able to make effective use of the new Treaty framework for enhancing the economic governance of the EU.[22]

3   Balancing EU and Member State competences in
multilayered social policy

In the post-enlargement EU-27, social inequities have been on the rise,
aggravated by transformation strategies and global competition, and
indicated by growing nominal income differences and contradictory
trends in real consumption. Present social security systems appear

---

[22] An example for the improvement of EU economic governance is the ECOFIN decision
of 10 May 2010 enforcing the co-ordination of economic policies adopted in July 2010.
See E. Barón Crespo, 'Economic governance and the Treaty of Lisbon', Contribution to
Global Jean Monnet – ECSA-World Conference (Brussels, 25–6 May 2010), pp. 2–6.

inefficient and are in need of being adapted if they are to become sustainable. In this context, the EU under the ToL strengthens its commitment to social progress and to social rights. At the same time, it defines European social policy as a competence that is shared between the EU and its Member States:

> However, the fact remains that ... the EU has only a small share of that competence ... The few cases in which progress has been made, such as the horizontal social clause and a very limited switch to QMV [qualified majority voting] in the Council, should not hide the fact that social policy remains, essentially, within the competences of the MSs. This corresponds to the political will of the majority of them.[23]

Acknowledging these basic constraints, the ToL brings nevertheless a few changes, including the following:[24]

- Measures in the field of social security (Article 48 TFEU) which are necessary to bring about freedom of movement for migrant workers and their dependants have been switched to QMV and co-decision, and their scope has been extended to cover also self-employed workers.[25]
- QMV is established as the rule 'in principle', where a Member State may obtain a right of veto, only if the government brings the matter to the EC. This is in case of serious problems.
- The provision that 'the definition of the rights of third-country nationals residing legally in a Member State' can be regulated by QMV and co-decision.[26]
- A special reference to the role of the social partners at the level of the EU, committing the EU to facilitate dialogue between the social partners and referring to that the 'Tripartite Summit for Growth and Employment' shall contribute to this social dialogue.[27]

Apart from these new rules, the provisions on social policy continue to be broadly the same as before the ToL, notably:[28]

---

[23] Piris (n. 17 above), p. 313.   [24] *Ibid.*, pp. 310 *et seq.*
[25] In this case, however, the so-called 'emergency brake' procedure applies (Art. 48, second subpara., TFEU); see Piris (n. 17 above), p. 311.
[26] Art. 79(2) TFEU (ex Art. 63 EC).
[27] Art. 152 TFEU. The TSGE takes place once a year, before the Spring Council, as established by the Decision of the Council 2003/174/EC of 6 March 2003 (OJ No. L70, 14.3.2003, 31–3); Piris (n. 17 above), p. 312.
[28] Art. 153 TFEU on social policy is identical to Art. 137 EC.

- The European Parliament and Council continue to adopt legislation in co-decision, the Council using QMV, in areas regarding minimum requirements for certain matters, namely the protection of workers' health and safety, working conditions, information and consultation of workers, integration of persons excluded from the labour market and equality between men and women with regard to labour market opportunities and treatment at work.
- As before, unanimity is applicable in the Council for the adoption of minimum requirements in sensitive matters, such as social security and social protection for workers; protection of workers where their employment contract is terminated; the representation and collective defence of the interests of workers and employers; and conditions of employment of third-country nationals (TCNs).[29]
- Minimum requirements shall not affect the right of Member States to define the funding principles of their social security systems and they must not affect the financial equilibrium of such systems and shall not prevent any Member State from maintaining or introducing more stringent or protective measures compatible with the Treaties.[30]
- As before, 'pay, the right of association, the right to strike or the right to impose lockouts' continue to be excluded from EU competence and remain exclusively national prerogatives.[31]

B   Resolving collective-action problems: how inter-institutional relations matter

Whether the ToL will make a difference for reconciling economic with social dimensions of European integration is, arguably, a question of political will. It is a collective-action problem that depends on whether these problems are exacerbated or solved by appropriate inter-institutional relations. If European integration is about solving collective-action problems, different institutions will matter differently.[32] As trans-governmental co-operation alone cannot lead to efficient problem-solving, institutional choices from Messina to Maastricht have pooled sovereignty and delegated powers to create 'credible commitments'.[33] The EU, from Laeken to Lisbon,

---

[29] Piris (n. 17 above), p. 311.   [30] Art. 153(4) TFEU (ex Art. 137 EC).
[31] Art. 153(5) TFEU (ex Art. 137 EC).
[32] See F. Laursen, *Comparative Regional Integration: Europe and beyond* (Aldershot: Ashgate, 2010), p. 286.
[33] A. Moravcsik, *The Choice for Europe: Social purpose and state power from Messina to Maastricht* (Ithaca: Cornell University Press, 1998), p. 24.

has continued in the same vein, seeking to improve the efficiency of EU decision-making. In legal terms, the ToL amounts to a re-foundation of a new Union. But politically, it is just another step in a successive process of Treaty reforms over the EU's past development. It contributes by a series of incremental changes – further evolution towards more efficiency and democratic accountability, namely by using more QMV in the Council, and increased legitimacy by empowering the European Parliament:

- The ToL has strengthened the role of the European Parliament in EU decision-making by extending co-decision in primary legislative and budgetary powers to cover forty new fields, including agriculture, energy, immigration and structural funds. In total, eighty-six legal subjects are subsumed under the ordinary legislative procedure.[34]
- The influence of the Commission is weakened, as the European Parliament deals more directly with the Council.
- The EU Council is strengthened, by gaining direct impact on legislative processes under the referral clauses in police, in judicial co-operation, and in emergency decision-making in response to international developments.

The institutional provisions of the ToL redefine the relationship between larger and smaller, old and new Member States, primarily indirectly by reshaping the inter-institutional balance of power and the relationship between the EU institutions and European citizenship. As a result of successive Treaty reforms from Rome to Lisbon, the original institutional system constituted after 1958 by Commission, Court and Council mutated into a polycentric system of inter-institutional balance, with a European Parliament and a European Council in addition to these, enriched by a legally operative Union citizenship.[35]

In this new configuration, most significantly the position of the European Parliament and that of the European Council are reinforced, while the role of the Commission has been weakened and that of the Council downgraded. The Court of Justice of the European Union (ECJ), last but not least, increased its constitutional role due to the effect of the

---

[34] In the fields of education, innovation, mobility and research the EU restricts itself to complementing, promoting or soliciting national policies.

[35] J. Monar, conceiving of the EU's 'institutional balance and inter-institutional cooperation', in the terms of a 'hybrid quadric-polar system', yet omitting the ECJ as well as Union citizenship; see 'The institutional balance after the Treaty of Lisbon', Global Jean Monnet – ECSA-World Conference 2010, Brussels, 25–6 May 2010, http://ec.europa.eu/education/jean-monnet/doc/ecsa10/monar_en.pdf.

Charter of Fundamental Rights. It will have jurisdiction over the acts of the European Council, bodies, offices or agencies; it will conduct legal review of acts intended to produce legal effects vis-à-vis third parties and failures to act; and it will give preliminary rulings. Formally, its role as the last arbiter has not changed. But in practice, a number of foreseeable changes have been noted:[36]

- The importance of fundamental rights litigation in the case law of the Court is expected to grow as a consequence of three developments: first, increased EU legislation expanding the scope of an EU fundamental rights policy, such as non-discrimination legislation adopted under Article 19 TFEU; secondly, the increased visibility of EU fundamental rights due to the Charter of Fundamental Rights; and thirdly, increased EU legislation with the potential to enter into conflict with fundamental rights (justice and internal affairs).
- These developments are expected to require the Court to progressively articulate a theory of fundamental rights review.
- As a consequence of the ToL, EU competences will be extended as well as majoritarian decision-making. This will require the Court to increasingly control how and when the Union exercises its competences.

Poiares Maduro expects even more profound transformations regarding the type of 'activism' of the ECJ, namely a progressive shift from an unconventional majoritarian to a more conventional counter-majoritarian approach:

> While the competences of the Union were relatively limited and controllable by the states through unanimous decision making, it made sense for the Court to concentrate its judicial scrutiny on the risks of state evasions from the broader collective interests of the Union (which, using traditional constitutional jargon, we could qualify as a majoritarian judicial approach). However, the increased scope of EU powers and its majoritarian character will increasingly plead for the Court to also develop a more traditional counter-majoritarian approach in reviewing the actions of the EU political process.[37]

Regarding social policy, however, the new institutional framework as designed by the ToL appears not wholly satisfying. It seems too feeble

---

[36] M. Poiares Maduro and L. Azoulai (eds.), *Past and Future of European Law: The classics of EU law revisited on the 50th anniversary of the Rome Treaty* (Portland: Hart Publishing, 2010).

[37] *Ibid.*, Introduction, p. xix.

to address any severe crisis, to the degree to which unanimity is needed. It hardly offers new ground and instruments to cope with Member States that resist co-ordination. While the ToL codifies exclusive external competences of the EU and advances its Common Commercial Policy (CCP),[38] it will benefit multilayered European social policy only to a very limited degree. Its failure to extend institutional pooling and delegation – that is, the Community method – to European social policy will limit the EU's capability of joint decision-making in this field. Two collective-action problems hamper EU social policy: how to establish efficient solutions as well as equitable solutions. Solutions will depend on national governments and parliaments rather than on the European Parliament or the European Council to provide leadership and more coherence in social policy. The 'open method of co-ordination' (OMC) is allegedly ill-suited to cope with two key problems: how to bring the components of social and economic policy in sync, on the one hand, and, on the other hand, how to identify common interests by unanimity, with the possibility of constructive abstention. Institutional learning processes, actor socialisation that may lead to collective identity formation and the convergence of interests notwithstanding, the German Constitutional Court in its June 2009 Lisbon ruling has defined the red line for the German jurisdiction, stipulating that 'the essential decisions in social policy must be made by the German legislative bodies'.[39]

C   Re-constituting the EU's social constituencies: Union citizenship and fundamental rights

Finally, the ToL does not only provide general values, objectives and clauses aimed at balancing economic and social dimensions of integration; it goes beyond the reconfiguring of social and economic policies and of inter-institutional relations in the multilayered EU. Most importantly, regarding the issue of embedding 'Market Europe' within a 'Social Union', the ToL reconstitutes the EU's social constituencies. Until the establishment and incorporation of the Charter of Fundamental Rights

[38] The ToL provisions relating to the CCP cover the entire WTO agenda (except transport). CCP involves the European Parliament on an equal footing with the Council, under the ordinary legislative procedure (Art. 207(2) TFEU (ex Art. 133 EC)), where the consent of European Parliament is necessary for concluding an agreement (Art. 218(6) TFEU (ex Art. 300 EC)), including association agreements.

[39] Judgment of 30 June 2009 – 2 bve 2/08 et al., www.bundesverfassungsgericht.de/entscheidungen/es20090630_2bve000208en.html, para. 259.

in the ToL, fundamental rights belonged to national constitutions or to international treaties and were determined by national authorities. Yet, the EU's Convention of 1999, presided over by Roman Herzog, drafted the Charter of Fundamental Rights 'as if' it would be legally binding, based on the premise that the EU was more than a single market, namely also a political project that needed to have shared principles and values.[40] Adopted as part of the ToL, the Charter provides a new source of rights which cannot be modified except by Treaty revision procedures. Although the Charter is neither a constitution nor an international treaty, it transforms the relations between individuals and the EU polity significantly. As EU law engages in areas where citizens are directly affected, it establishes the necessary safeguards so that there cannot be a creeping empowerment of the supranational institutions of the EU. In addition to incorporating into the Union a fundamental rights foundation, the ToL introduces two more layers to make part of the construction of democratic life in the Union: participatory democracy based on civil society, and the citizens' legislative initiative.

First, knowledgeable analysts claim that 'It is difficult to over-estimate the importance, and in the fullness of time, the impact which the Lisbon Treaty has and will have regarding fundamental rights and citizens of the Union', as European citizenship has finally acquired its bill of rights, the skeleton of European citizenship, the 'Charter of Fundamental Rights'.[41] The Charter defines who is entitled to enjoy what kinds of rights.[42] More especially, the 'Charter' expands the EU's social constituency by extending the scope of Union citizens as rights holders to TCNs.[43] The entitlement to rights no longer depends on national authorities nor international organisations, but is in the hands of the individuals.[44]

---

[40] I. Méndez de Vigo, 'La Unión Europea después del Tratado de Lisboa y los Derechos Fundamentales de la Unión Europea', Contribution to Global Jean Monnet – ESCA-World Conference 2010, Brussels, 25–6 May 2010, http://ec.europa.eu/education/jean-monnet/doc/ecsa10/vigo_en.pdf, p. 3.

[41] E. Guild, 'Fundamental rights and EU citizenship', Contribution to Global Jean Monnet – ECSA-World Conference 2010, Brussels, 25–6 May 2010, http://ec.europa.eu/education/jean-monnet/doc/ecsa10/guild_en.pdf, p. 2.

[42] The Charter contains seven chapters: I. Dignity: right to life; II. Freedoms; III. Equality; IV. Solidarity; V. Citizens' Rights; VI. Justice; VII. General Provisions.

[43] The scope of the Charter extends Union citizens' rights (except for voting, free movement, and consular protection) to third-country nationals, thus diminishing the gulf between both; e.g. Charter Art. 41 lays down the right to good administration for every person, that is also for asylum seekers; see Guild (n. 41 above), pp. 2 and 9.

[44] Following the accession of the EU to the European Convention on Human Rights, every individual will be able to bring complaints against Member States, see: Report by French

The ToL (Article 6(1) TFEU, first subpara.) confers on the Charter of Fundamental Rights the same legal value as the Treaties, giving the same legal value to the provisions of the Charter in the social field. However, these provisions are essentially addressed to the EU institutions when they legislate, given that the 'provisions of the Charter shall not extend in any way the competences of the Union as defined in the Treaties' (Article 6(1), second subpara. TFEU).

Secondly, the ToL reinforces political aspects of European citizenship, by enhancing representative and participatory democratic rights. These reinforce the European Parliament as an access channel for citizens' representation in European political decision-making and European consultations for citizens' participation. Civil society will be more present in the democratic life of the EU. European citizenship will thus include the right of participation in the democratic life of the Union, namely in the EU's dialogue with civil society in all areas of EU activities (Article 11 TFEU).

Thirdly, provided that the regulation of the 'citizens' legislative initiative' will ensure a credible and viable mechanism, it will make Union citizenship also more meaningful for active political practice. If this instrument is strongly used, it can have an important impact on the EU's agenda-setting, thus complementing the rights of citizens by helping build a genuine European public space.

Following T. H. Marshall's conception of citizenship as a 'process of accumulation of bundles of rights by people', European citizenship has evolved in successive stages, but not exactly mirroring the historic development of its national correlate.[45] People in the EU do have progressively acquired 'bundles of rights', from economic and political to, most recently, social rights.[46] But the Charter promotes a qualitative

---

MEP Alain Lamassoure (EPP-ED, UMP) on 'European citizens and Community law implementation', presenting sixty-one proposals for rectifying four types of problems experienced by Europeans: 1. social security; 2. portability of social rights (pensions, unemployment, right to social assistance); 3. equivalence of diplomas; and 4. family issues (divorce, child custody, maintenance allowances, etc.); A. Lamassoure, 'Mission Report for President Sarkozy', 27 June 2008, www.alainlamassoure.eu/liens/975.pdf.

[45] T. H. Marshall, *Citizenship and Social Class* (Oxford: Oxford University Press, 1950).

[46] See U. Liebert, 'European social citizenship: Preconditions for promoting inclusion' in L. Magnusson and B. Strath (eds.), *A European Social Citizenship: Preconditions for future policies from a historical perspective* (Brussels: Peter Lang, 2004); compare critical perspectives: K. Hailbronner, 'Union citizenship and access to social benefits', *CMLR* 42 (2005), 1245, and A. J. Menendez, 'European citizenship after *Martínez Sala* and *Baumbast*: Has European law become more human but less social?', RECON Online Working Paper 5 (2009).

transformation of citizenship in two respects: first, an expansion of citizenship from rights that are limited to a territorially bounded nation state to multilayered citizenship in a Union of states; and, secondly, its development into a formidable instrument for socially re-embedding market citizenship. That is, cross-border mobility as an emanation of European individual economic freedoms – and, thus, a trigger of negative integration – turns into a mechanism that is constitutive for political and social rights, and, thus, becomes a precondition for social integration.

D   Summary

In this second part, a range of innovative or changed provisions introduced by the ToL have been identified that speak to attempts by the framers of the reform Treaty to bridge the disconnects between social and economic dimensions of European integration. Yet, whether this will remain largely constitutional rhetoric failing to address real-life problems, or whether the new Lisbon rules will become tools that effectively shape practices, is a wide-open question. Thus far, neither political scientists nor legal nor constitutional analysts have provided a systematic framework for analysis let alone a well-grounded scrutiny to respond to this issue.[47]

The next section will outline an institutionalist perspective for engaging with the political science literature, with the purpose of developing empirically founded propositions about the impacts of the Treaty reforms on the EU's practices.

III   Probing Lisbon Treaty rules in practice: contestations and propositions

In the evolving practices of EU politics and policy-making, can the Lisbon Treaty help develop a socially embedded European constitutionalism for guiding the European Union in its search for legitimate governance? This third part deals with this question in three steps: first, it

---

[47] Compare U. Pütter, *Die Wirtschafts- und Sozialpolitik der EU* (Wien: Facultas-Verl., 2009); F. Scharpf, 'The asymmetry of European integration or why the EU cannot be a "social market economy"', *Socio-Economic Review* 8 (2010), 211; M. S. Höpner *et al.*, 'Kampf um Souveränität? Eine Kontroverse zur europäischen Integration nach dem Lissabon-Urteil des Bundesverfassungsgerichts', *Politische Vierteljahresschrift* 51 (2010), 323.

surveys the controversial issues in the debate among political analysts on the one hand, and normative approaches by constitutionalists and social constructivists, on the other; secondly, I draw on an institutionalist political economic framework to develop empirically based propositions that qualify some of the (more sceptical) political science arguments and to further substantiate other (more constructivist) normative propositions; I conclude by taking a look at different policy fields where tensions between economic and social dimensions and problems of collective action are at stake.

A   Social and economic welfare issues in political science and normative debate

In post-industrial societies, the capacity of harmonising social welfare with economic efficiency – and thus the sustainability of the welfare state – seems to be under threat, challenged by globalisation, tertiarisation, new technologies, family instability and shrinking fertility rates.[48] In this changed context, the European Union has become a 'testing ground for the turf battle between national welfare states and EU market making'.[49] Thus, the political science and legal scholarly literatures are deeply controversial as regards the question of the viability of reconciling economic and social objectives of European integration. Premised on the assumption that the EU's 'social dimension' largely coincides with the achievements of the Continental and social democratic welfare state that European economic integration supposedly undermines, the following five contentions about the impacts of European integration on welfare societies are made:

(i)   The ToL presents another case of 'cheap talk' about 'Social Europe' that cannot cope with the 'hard' facts of liberal market expansion. In particular, when faced with problems of effective and legitimate social policy-making, soft norms will not help much: The European multi-tiered social policy will be 'left to the judges and the markets' jointly giving precedence to market freedoms over collective social

---

[48]   G. Esping-Andersen, *Social Foundations of Postindustrial Economies* (Oxford: Oxford University Press, 1999), p. 145.

[49]   S. Leibfried, 'Social policy? Left to the judges and the markets?' in H. Wallace, M. A. Pollack and A. R. Young (eds.), *Policy-Making in the European Union*, 6th edn (Oxford: Oxford University Press, 2010), pp. 253, 273.

rights.[50] Constrained by the 'double asymmetry of European integration'[51] EU governance allegedly privileges market-making policies over market regulation, and that is 'negative' integration over 'positive' integration.[52]

(ii) The EU's dominant mode of integration through law is also perceived to systematically bias the competition between the Anglo-Saxon 'liberal market' regime on the one hand and the Continental European and Scandinavian 'co-ordinated market' model of the social welfare state, on the other.[53] Where the labour market is subjected to non-discrimination or to environmental or other kinds of rules, the EU puts questionable burdens on 'third parties', and, moreover, it constrains Member State autonomy.[54] Ultimately, under the combined pressures of the EU's judicial and legislative action, the social welfare embedded market regime will lose out against its competitor, the liberal market embedded residual welfare state.

(iii) To make things worse, given the EU's heterogeneous interests and fragmented powers, its social policy can and will never be that of a supranational social welfare state.[55]

(iv) The politicisation of European integration contributes to making the dilemma between the thriving of the European internal market and the national social welfare state visible to the larger publics,[56] fuelling political contentions and opposition against the EU.

(v) Therefore, regarding the question of whether the European model of social capitalism can survive, European integration – especially through law – is perceived as a predicament rather than an asset.[57]

In sum, from this structural–institutionalist view, the EU is overdetermined to proceed down the road towards the 'tragedy of the

---

[50] *Ibid.*, p. 256. See also C. Joerges, 'The Lisbon judgment, Germany's "Sozialstaat", the ECJ's labour law jurisprudence and the reconceptualisation of European law as a new type of conflicts law' in A. Fischer-Lescano, C. Joerges and A. Wonka (eds.), 'The German Constitutional Court's Lisbon ruling: Legal and political science perspectives', ZERP Discussion Paper 1 (2010), p. 27.

[51] Scharpf (n. 47 above).   [52] *Ibid.*   [53] *Ibid.*, p. 243.   [54] *Ibid.*, p. 228.   [55] *Ibid.*

[56] Magnusson and Strath (n. 7 above), p. 11; D. Damjanovic and B. de Witte, 'Welfare integration through EU law: The overall picture in the light of the Lisbon Treaty' in U. Neergard, R. Nielsen and L. Roseberry (eds.), *Integrating Welfare Functions into EU Law: From Rome to Lisbon* (Copenhagen: DJØF, 2009), pp. 65–87.

[57] C. Offe, 'The European model of "social" capitalism: Can it survive European integration?', *The Journal of Political Philosophy* 11 (2003), 437.

commons'. That is, multilevel social deficits will accumulate so that EU Member States cannot fence off the evaporation of the social solidarity and welfare resources on which their very legitimacy – and indirectly that of the EU as well – relies.[58]

On the other hand, normative and social constructivist perspectives focus on socially embedded, post-, trans- or supranational varieties of 'constitutionalisation'. Following these approaches, the EU is believed to be capable of responding to economic challenges in more or less socially solidaristic ways. As its predecessors, too, the Lisbon Treaty is evaluated in terms of rules as tools for reconciling tensions between economic and social dimensions of European integration. Notwithstanding the critique of its shortcomings, the ToL is valued as an asset to help balance current EU asymmetries. To sum this controversy up, while European constitutionalisation is seen by sceptical political scientists as a key mechanism driving the asymmetries of European economic versus social and legal versus political integration, more optimistic normative and legal views suggest that it also is the tool for bridging the gap between Social and Economic Europe. Therefore, while the political view conceives of European constitutionalism as the problem, the normative approach cherishes it as the solution. In the following, an institutionalist approach is adopted for outlining the assumptions on which a realist assessment of the ToL can be grounded.

B   Coping with social and economic welfare dilemmas through multilayered polycentric self-governance: realist assumptions

In the second step, an institutionalist conceptual framework and assumptions are proposed to assess this debate, to qualify some of the (more sceptical if not pessimist) political science concerns, on the one hand, and to further substantiate some of the (more optimist) normative propositions, on the other hand, both of which have been outlined above.

1   Social and economic welfare dilemmas in the EU: a complex phenomenon

Comparative political economists have approached the dilemma of economic versus social integration in various ways, some pointing to structural impediments, others to interest-based political power

---

[58] Cf. Scharpf (n. 47 above), pp. 213–4, n. 1.

dynamics or to different ideational constructions.[59] Given the dynamics of the world polity, its impact on the fragmentation of European social and economic policies and, at the same time, growing cross-border interdependencies, the EU, and in particular the EMU Member States, cannot help trying to cope with the 'tragedy of the commons', on the one hand. On the other, in the context of the polycentric nature of the EU system of governance, the modes that are available to them decidedly transcend the capabilities of the national welfare state, while falling short of those of a supranational welfare state.

Tensions and contentions indicating frictions between 'Social Union' versus 'Market Europe' have been brought to light through contested ECJ decisions, but also at a range of other sites, including the Commission or the European Parliament, national constitutional courts or parliaments, the mass media, civil society and public opinion. Driven by the fragmented dynamics of social and economic rationalities that originate in the world polity[60] they are reflected in different for(u)ms, where the de- and re-coupling of economic practices and social norms are at stake:

- A first type of contention concerns the balance between recognising employers' economic freedoms versus workers' rights to self-organise for collective action is at stake.
- The second kind of interest conflict arises from the distribution of costs and benefits by EU regulatory decision-making and its differential impacts on various social groups; for instance, new rules may shift (at least short-term) burdens of non-discrimination on employers while granting benefits to disadvantaged groups who tend to be excluded from the labour market.
- A third kind of friction regards the definition of who is a member with what kinds of rights in the European polity and the Member States; this may infringe Member State autonomy in drawing the boundaries

---

[59] See P. Hall, 'The role of interests, institutions, and ideas in the comparative political economy of the industrialized nations' in M. I. Lichbach and A. S. Zuckerman (eds.), *Comparative Politics: Rationality, culture, and structure* (Cambridge: Cambridge University Press, 1997), pp. 174–5; Esping-Andersen (n. 48 above).

[60] John W. Meyer's 'reflections' on 'institutional theory and world society' and his analysis of the EU through the lenses of this 'world polity approach' convincingly makes the case for putting centre stage these larger systemic cultural dynamics in an analysis of social and economic European institutional development. See J. W. Meyer, 'Reflections: Institutional theory and world society' in G. Krücken and G. S. Drori (eds.), *World Society: The writings of John W. Meyer* (Oxford: Oxford University Press, 2009), pp. 36–66.

of membership and defining who has access to national welfare benefits; in these situations, struggles concern the enforcement of principles of monocentricity versus polycentrism.

- Socio-economic contestations also play out within the multilayered parliamentary field of the EU, namely through party ideological representation of liberal market values versus social and solidaristic ideas, and their justification and negotiations in legislative proceedings in national parliaments or the European Parliament. Also, the *contentious constitutional choice* in the Convention on the Future of Europe has faced EU Treaty reformers with such socio-economic tensions.[61]

- Public opinion is a further site where the global economic crisis 'has revealed the growing gap between official statistics and people's perceptions of their standards of living'.

- Finally, tensions can be found among the sector-specific rationalities within the European Commission and its different policy domains, with opposing principles, objectives, and addressees, such as 'Competition' versus 'Work and Social Affairs'. These different rationalities also affect the issue of appropriate *indicators for measurement* and, thus, the available stock of relevant empirical knowledge and information.[62] For instance, the countervailing logics of economic versus social policy are supposed to impose trade-offs between efficiency and equity.[63]

Adopting the world polity perspective, sociological institutionalists would generally expect norms and practices to decouple, with growing tensions between respective norms and objectives, and increasingly incoherent rationalities, posing challenges to states and governments.[64]

---

[61] Although designed to make the enlarged EU collectively more effective and legitimate, the 'Draft Treaty establishing a Constitution for Europe' and its successor, the ToL, caused tremendous internal conflict of interests that risked stalemate. See e.g. the book by Michael O'Neill, *The Struggle for the European Constitution* (London: Routledge, 2009).

[62] J. E. Stiglitz, A. Sen and J.-P. Fitoussi, *Mis-measuring Our Lives: Why GDP doesn't add up: The Report by the Commission on the Measurement of Economic Performance and Social Progress* (New York/London: The New Press, 2010). This assessment is premised on the assumption that the GDP growth as an indicator of overall economic health is too limited to assess how and whether the European economy is serving the needs of European society.

[63] J. Pisani-Ferry and A. Sapir, 'Last exit to Lisbon', Policy Contribution, Brussels/Bruegel, 13 March 2006, www.bruegel.org/uploads/tx_btbbreugel/pc_march2006_exitlisbon.pdf, p. 3.

[64] World polity approach by Meyer, see n. 60 above.

Multilayered polycentric self-governance provides an institutionalist
framework for coping with such challenges.

2   Multilayered polycentric self-governance: an institutionalist framework

An institutionalist perspective informed by concepts and insights from
constitutional political economy has emerged namely from the work by
political scientists James Buchanan, Peter Hall and Elinor Ostrom. These
authors suggest alternatives to dualist thinking in terms of the liberal
market versus the social state, revising ideas by Hayek and Habermas
alike. Contrary to economists advocating the free market and
'Rechtsstaat' as well as different from social democratic proponents of
regulation, political economists such as Peter Hall or Gosta Esping-
Andersen move beyond the traditional state–market dualism towards a
'third pole', aimed at capturing the complexity of interactions among
economic interests, social norms (or ideas) and institutional rules, and
ask how different configurations account for variations in public policies
and outcomes.[65]

The 'institutional analysis and development framework' and research
programme developed by Elinor Ostrom, Vincent Ostrom and their
research group provides a methodology for 'understanding structured
human interactions', 'linking action situations', assessing rule design and
'rules in use' as 'tools to cope with the commons', that is for solving the
problems of 'robust resource governance' and namely for coping with
threats to sustainability of self-governance through 'polycentric institutions'.[66] Rule design as well as 'rules in use' explain successful and failing
systems of self-governance, from the local to the global level.[67]

Complex polycentric systems may successfully cope with 'tragedies of
the commons', if self-governance (or governance by users) of common-
pool resources, of private and public goods is helped by explicit rules
which are used 'as tools to change outcomes'.[68] Theoretical and

---

[65]   See Hall (n. 59 above), pp. 174–207, Esping-Andersen (n. 48 above), pp. 178ff.

[66]   E. Ostrom, *Governing the Commons* (Cambridge: Cambridge University Press, 1990),
and *Understanding Institutional Diversity* (Princeton: Princeton University Press, 2005).

[67]   Robert Axelrod proposes 'that Ostrom's insights are valuable even for situations far
beyond the common-pool resources domain of her original project', and extends it to
both private goods and public goods; see R. Axelrod, 'Review Symposium: Beyond the
tragedy of the commons', *Perspectives on Politics* 8 (2010), 580; R. O. Keohane proposes
to extend her institutional framework to the international realm, see R. O. Keohane,
ibid., pp. 577–80.

[68]   Ostrom, *Understanding Institutional Diversity* (n. 66 above), pp. 215 *et seq.*

empirical research findings from this large-scale research programme suggests that there does not exist any blueprint, but that certain 'design principles' and 'coping methods for dealing with threats to sustainability' can be identified that distinguish successful from failing systems of governance. As one of the results, policy advice based on dichotomising the institutional world into 'the market' as contrasted to 'the state' has been proven 'grossly inadequate' and a misleading, if not dangerous 'oversimplification of our design options': Among other things, 'it reduces our awareness of the need to monitor outcomes and improve them over time through better processes of learning and adaptation'.[69]

Against rational choice accounts suggesting that social dilemmas are the result of individual actors' incapability of action co-ordination, we adopt the 'institutional analysis and development framework' proposed by Elinor Ostrom that places social norms and institutional rules, 'social capital' and 'networks' centre stage to explain how 'governing the commons' can become an alternative to the 'tragedy of the commons'.[70] Hence, for overcoming dilemmas of social and economic integration, we would ask whether social norms matter and how institutional rules work for putting them into practice. To facilitate and enable sustainable self-governance, by and large, successful cases of 'real-world experiments that have proved to be robust over time'[71] have been found to be characterised by seven types of underlying institutional rules.[72]

C   Reconciling Market with Social Europe: five sets of propositions

Here, we will revisit the sceptical contentions as to the collective-action problems involved in constructing the EU social and economic polity, in the light of constitutional approaches on the one hand, and institutional research, on the other. The key contention is that European multi-tiered social policy if 'left to the judges and the markets' will jointly give

---

[69] *Ibid.*, p. 256.

[70] For the 'tragedy of the commons', see G. Hardin, 'The tragedy of the commons', *Science* 162 (1968), 1243; for Ostrom's 'institutional analysis and development framework', see Ostrom, *Understanding Institutional Diversity* (n. 66 above), pp. 15 *et seq.* and 59 *et seq.*

[71] Ostrom, *Understanding Institutional Diversity* (n. 66 above), p. 257.

[72] For detailed definitions of these seven classes of rules – comprising position rules, boundary rules, choice rules, aggregation rules, information rules, payoff rules, scope rules – see E. Ostrom and S Crawford, 'Classifying rules' in Ostrom, *Understanding Institutional Diversity* (n. 66 above), pp. 186–209.

precedence to market freedoms over collective social rights.[73] If persistently constrained by the 'double asymmetry of European integration',[74] EU governance allegedly privileges market-making policies over market regulation, and that is 'negative' integration over 'positive' integration.[75] To qualify these contentions, institutional studies have come up with a number of lessons on design principles that have been found to be common to robust social-ecological systems that have successfully been proven to cope with 'commons dilemmas', while they were largely missing in those systems that failed to do so.[76] Five sets of propositions can be formulated to that respect.

First, for coping with the 'double asymmetries' among 'Social Europe' that rests on soft law and the 'hard' facts of Liberal Market Europe, the EU under the ToL disposes of innovative constitutional provisions. To attenuate tensions and balance both dimensions of integration, this new toolbox strengthens fundamental rights, namely in the social realm and collective action, as European constitutionalists have pointed out. By stepping up the EU's rights foundation, it will embed the European economic order – 'Market Europe' – in 'social constitutionalism', strengthening individual and collective social and political rights.[77] Accordingly, as the institutional analysis and development research has demonstrated, systems of self-governance will perform better if they provide for 'collective-choice arrangements' that 'authorise most of the individuals who are affected by a regime to participate in making and modifying its rules'.

Secondly, critics have pointed out that EU law related to economic freedoms progressively undermines the autonomy of Continental and social democratic welfare states.[78] Constitutional advocates have responded to this issue by highlighting the ToL's novel provisions on 'services of general interest'. In combination with the centrality of welfare values in the Treaty introduction, these provide a legal basis for 'welfare integration through EU law', thus acknowledging and better protecting Member welfare state autonomy.[79] In terms of practices, too,

---

[73] See Leibfried, n. 49 above, and Joerges in n. 50 above.

[74] See Scharpf in n. 47 above.

[75] See *ibid.* and *Governing in Europe: Effective and democratic?* (Oxford: Oxford University Press, 1999), pp. 43–83.

[76] For these 'design principles' see Ostrom 1990 (n. 66 above), p. 90 and Ostrom, *Understanding Institutional Diversity* (n. 66 above), pp. 259 *et seq.*

[77] B. Bercusson, 'The Lisbon Treaty and Social Europe', *ERA Forum* 10 (2009), 87; see also Schiek, ch. 1 in this volume.

[78] See Scharpf (n. 47 above).

[79] Damjanovic and de Witte (n. 56 above), pp. 65–87.

institutional designs have been found to perform better if rules provide 'minimal recognition of rights to organise' to 'users who can devise their own institutions that are not challenged by external governmental authorities' and have 'long-term tenure rights to the resource', such as the Member State welfare societies.

Thirdly, as regards the alleged EU's deficit in terms of a supranational social welfare state, the ToL offers at least a number of new clues for protecting the current '*acquis communautaire social*', by 'rethinking Treaty provisions on economic freedoms' or 'a different interpretive framework' aimed at countering threats from the Commission or from ECJ judgments threatening to dismantle collective social rights' achievements, at the EU level as well as in the Member States.[80] In the new and more complex institutional configuration of the EU, it empowers the European Parliament to grow beyond an occasional veto-player into a collective actor that makes a difference for EU social policy development.

Fourthly, while politicisation of European integration has undoubtedly fuelled Euro-scepticism that is harmful to the EU's popular support, constitutionalist readings of the ToL suggest that the introduction of the citizens' legislative initiative and civil society participation may help develop an inclusive, open and democratic form of European constitutionalism. To the degree to which these dynamics will be reflected by civil society organisations and mass public-opinion formation, politicisation of social policy issues will not necessarily undermine but may foster public support for the EU.

Finally, regarding the issue whether the European model of social capitalism – and which variety of capitalisms – will survive, European integration through law does provoke contentions, but also offers a key to rationalisation and legitimisation. Given the complex interdependencies of the social economies of Member States, a socially embedded European economic constitutionalism, arguably, can help rationalise the EU's diverse national welfare state systems in three ways: (1) by redefining who has a voice, with which costs and benefits; (2) by balancing scope of participation with intensity of impact of decisions on different individuals and groups; (3) by instituting 'reason' in a policy through creating conditions for free informed discourse.[81] The lessons from empirical institutionalist research suggest institutional design principles

---

[80] Bercusson (n. 77 above), p. 102.
[81] Oral communication by M Poiares Maduro, Global Jean Monnet – ECSA-World Conference 2010 'The European Union After The Treaty Of Lisbon' (Brussels, 25–26 May 2010).

that support this line: the centrality of 'well-defined boundaries' by membership rules that clearly define the boundaries of the system and individual or collective rights; specification of a 'proportional equivalence between benefits and costs' for users, related to local conditions and to rules requiring inputs; 'monitoring' of rules by 'monitors' who are the users themselves or, if not, are 'at least partially accountable to the users'; rules for 'graduated sanctions', so that 'users who violate rules-in-use are likely to receive graduated sanctions from other users, from officials accountable to these users, or from both.[82] European integration through law and politics disposes of 'conflict-resolution mechanisms' that hardly provide users with the necessary rapid access to low-cost arenas to resolve conflict among users or between users and officials. Yet, arguably, European political actors under the ToL will benefit from the use, implementation and development of the new formal rules for performing more effectively and legitimately the key functions of successful self-governance – that is, reconciling Market and Social Europe across the multiple layers and decentralised centres of the EU's nested enterprises.[83]

IV   Conclusions

For establishing whether the ToL will further empower 'Market Europe' or enhance a 'Social Europe' capable of coping with failures of markets and states, this chapter has examined two questions. First, regarding formal norms, what is in the Treaty for reconciling Social and Market Europe? Moreover, regarding rules in use, how will the EU under the ToL cope with the challenges of failing markets or states, i.e. with tensions between economic freedoms and social values, or the dilemmas of providing social welfare efficiently and equitably? The remaining most important issue is whether the EU under the ToL will further dismantle and disrupt or rescue and eventually transform the model of social capitalism, for which Europe has become known worldwide.

In the light of the ToL, both views – the sceptical and the constructivist ones – are in need of certain revisions. Neither approach sufficiently takes into consideration important social practices that the building of a socially and economically balanced European constitutional order

---

[82] For the specification and classification of seven broad types of rule 'as tools to change outcomes', see Ostrom and Crawford, 'Classifying rules' (n. 72 above), pp. 190–215.
[83] See n. 59 above.

involves. The structural–institutionalist approach, on the one hand, places politics centre stage but misses the discursive or interpretative dynamics of turning formal legal norms into institutions; by reifying these as structural constraints under which politics operates, it ends up with an overly deterministic and altogether pessimistic picture. By contrast, the normative approach puts the meaning of norms at the heart of the matter, thus conceiving of constitutionalisation as an open-ended, contingent process. Yet, for understanding the whole story of European constitutionalism, the design and interpretation of legal norms as formal rules is necessary but not sufficient. In addition, we need to look at 'rules in use' in relation to social constituencies' practices. That is, we ought to examine the historical and social contexts on which the construction of a legitimate economic and social polity relies. Therefore, European constitutionalisation is shaped by law but what its shape looks like is not the exclusive domain of courts and judges but depends on institutional development in historical and social contexts, namely through social constituents' practices. In this sense, as long as changes go on, the ToL will be in flux.

3

Constitutionalism between normative frameworks and the socio-legal frameworks of societies

NICOLE LINDSTROM

I Introduction

Writing in 2002, Fritz Scharpf warned: 'the only thing that stands between the Scandinavian welfare state and the market is not a vote in the Council of Ministers or in the European Parliament, but merely the initiation of . . . legal action by potential private competitors before a national court that is then referred to the European Court of Justice for a preliminary opinion. In other words, it may happen one day'.[1] The day appeared to come with the referral of two cases to the Court of Justice of the European Union (ECJ) in 2005: *Laval*[2] and *Viking*.[3] At issue in each case was whether industrial actions by unions to force firms to abide by nationally negotiated collective agreements constituted an infringement of free movement of services. Coming in the wake of contentious battles over the Services Directive[4] and in ongoing political negotiations leading up to Lisbon, the cases attracted a great deal of attention as to how the Court would reconcile these competing economic and social demands.[5] Moreover, given that the cases involved employers based in old Member States (Sweden and Finland) seeking to employ workers from new Member States (Latvia and Estonia), the cases also exacerbated ongoing concerns that eastward enlargement would spur a race-to-the-bottom in

---

[1] F. Scharpf, 'The European Social Model: Coping with the challenges of diversity', *JCMS* 40 (2002), 657.

[2] C-341/05 *Laval un Partneri Ltd* v. *Svenska Byggnadsarbetareförbundet and ors.* (*Laval*) [2007] ECR I-11767.

[3] C-438/05 *International Transport Workers' Federation and Finnish Seamen's Union* v. *Viking Line ABP and OU Viking Line Eesti* (*Viking*) [2007] ECR I-10779.

[4] Directive 2006/123/EC of 12 December 2006 on services in the internal market.

[5] B. Bercusson, 'The trade union movement and the European Union: Judgment day', *ELJ* 13 (2007), 279.

wages and social protections. With the ECJ ultimately ruling in favour of the employers the cases appeared to vindicate concerns raised by Scharpf and others that direct interventions by the courts pose the most significant threat to existing national socio-legal frameworks.

This chapter considers the tensions between market liberalisation and social protection within the enlarged EU through an in-depth analysis of the *Laval* and *Viking* cases. It suggests that political conflicts surrounding these two principles are not limited to strategic interactions between Member States seeking to preserve autonomy over social policy against intrusions by the Court, as some decoupling accounts might suggest. Instead it pursues a more disaggregated approach that considers how the cases provided windows of opportunity for a variety of societal actors – including supranational institutions, governments, and social partners – to advance two larger agendas: furthering economic liberalisation and protecting the principles underlying social Europe. With the ECJ ultimately ruling with the employers' positions, and against the expressed preferences of most old Member States, the rulings appeared to have strengthened the position of advocates of further liberalisation in the enlarged EU. Yet the rulings have also spurred a 'protective reaction' among societal actors seeking to retain and strengthen social protections against unfettered market forces.[6] While some of these reactions have been framed in national terms of strengthening Member State autonomy over social policy, the cases have also bolstered demands to develop a more cohesive social policy at the European level.

II   Between the Single Market and Social Europe

The revitalisation of the European project in the 1980s involved an explicit compromise: that the process of abolishing barriers to the free movement of goods, capital, services and labour (the single market) would proceed in tandem with maintaining social cohesion within and across its Member States (Social Europe). The so-called 'European Social Model' (ESM) has been heralded by its proponents as a unique, i.e. *European*, response to the competitive pressures of globalisation.[7] While the concept of the ESM in the 1980s focused on developing a common social policy at the European level, in practice the results have

---

[6] K. Polany, *The Great Transformation*, 2nd edn (Boston: Beacon Press, 2001).
[7] A. Giddens, P. Diamond and R. Liddle, *Global Europe, Social Europe* (Cambridge: Polity, 2006).

been more modest. Subsequent constitutional arrangements have tended to grant EU institutions authority over economic integration while leaving most matters of social policy to Member States. The separation of regulatory policies at the European level from redistributive policies at the domestic level is argued to be both more efficient and legitimate.[8] Fundamental decisions concerning taxing and spending are left to democratically accountable governments, while technocratic experts at the EU level focus on creating and overseeing the most effective market-making policies.

Numerous scholars argue that this tidy decoupling of economic integration and social integration is unsustainable.[9] For one, some claim that market integration places numerous *indirect* pressures on social integration as governments seek to respond to increased economic competition by weakening national regulations, reducing corporate taxation rates, and constraining social expenditures.[10] Secondly, others argue that national social policies and practices have been *directly* challenged by European institutions on the grounds that they are incompatible with single-market rules.[11] Neither outcome is unexpected to scholars like Gill who argue that the 'new constitutionalism' of the EU is indeed *designed* to 'separate economic policies from broad accountability in order to make governments more responsive to the discipline of market forces and correspondingly less responsive to popular-democratic forces'.[12] European integration, according to this view, is a political project that seeks to subsume all states and societies into a single logic of market competitiveness.[13]

[8] G. Majone, 'The common sense of European integration', *JEPP* 13 (2006) 607; A. Moravcsik, 'Reassessing legitimacy in the European Union', *JCMS* 40 (2002), 603.

[9] Scharpf (n. 1 above), p. 657; F. Scharpf, *Governing in Europe: Effective and democratic?* (Oxford: Oxford University Press, 1999); C. Offe, 'The European model of "social" capitalism: Can it survive European integration?', *The Journal of Political Philosophy* 11 (2003), 437; A. Follesdal and S. Hix, 'Why there is a democratic deficit in the EU: A response to Majone and Moravcsik', *JCMS* 44 (2006), 533.

[10] A. Hemerijck, 'The self-transformation of the European Social Model(s)' in G. Esping-Andersen (ed.), *Why We Need a New Welfare State* (Oxford: Oxford University Press, 2002).

[11] S. Leibfried and P. Pierson, 'Social policy: Left to courts and markets?' in H. Wallace and W. Wallace (eds.), *Policy-Making in the European Union* (Oxford: Oxford University Press, 2000); M. Höpner and A. Schäfer, 'A new phase of European integration: Organized capitalisms in post-Ricardian Europe', *West European Politics* 33 (2010), 344.

[12] S. Gill, 'European governance and new constitutionalism: Economic and monetary union and alternatives to disciplinary neoliberalism in Europe', *New Political Economy* 3 (1998), 5.

[13] B. van Apeldoorn, *Transnational Capitalism and the Struggle over European Integration* (London: Routledge, 2002).

Yet the question arises: does the process of European economic integration *inevitably* undermine social integration at the national and regional levels? The work of Karl Polanyi provides a useful framework to analyse the dynamic relationship between economic liberalisation and social protections. In *The Great Transformation*, Polanyi argued that every move towards market liberalisation is invariably accompanied by a countermove to embed markets within societies. Describing the rise of liberal market ideas in the nineteenth century, Polanyi argued that the attempt by early industrialists to portray the 'unshackling of the market' as an 'ineluctable necessity' was a move designed to naturalise what was an inherently political project.[14] In other words, liberal proponents sought to transform the *idea* of the 'self-regulating market' into a kind of 'inexorable law of Nature' in order to justify abolishing barriers to unfettered market competition.[15] But Polanyi famously decried this liberal creed as a 'stark utopia'.[16] Market economies are always and necessarily embedded in societies. Those sections of society most threatened by the expansion of the market look to the state to provide protection. Failure to protect societies against market forces, according to Polanyi, would lead to a 'plunge into utter destruction', the kind of breakdown of social order that he witnessed from interwar Vienna.[17] Writing in 1944, Polanyi thus sought to provide a warning of the dangers of unfettered liberalism and a prescription for more social and sustainable ways of organising economic life.

Post-war leaders heeded such lessons. John Ruggie, drawing on Polanyi, coined the term 'embedded liberalism' to describe this post-WWII order: a compromise that sought to promote liberal international trade and monetary regimes, but one predicated on embedding them within national societies.[18] This explicit compromise was institutionalised to varying degrees and different forms in European social welfare states. European governments pursued liberalising agendas at the international and European levels. But they did so largely on their own terms.[19] That is,

---

[14] Quoted in J. Caporaso and S. Tarrow, 'Polanyi in Brussels: Supranational institutions and the transnational embedding of markets', *International Organization* 63 (2009), 596.

[15] F. Block, 'Karl Polanyi and the writing of *The Great Transformation*', *Theory and Society* 32 (2003), 275.

[16] Polanyi (n. 6 above), p. 139.   [17] *Ibid.*, p. 163.

[18] J. Ruggie, 'International regimes, transactions, and change: Embedded liberalism in the postwar economic order', *International Organization* 36 (1982), 379.

[19] J. Best, 'From the top-down: The new financial architecture and the re-embedding of global finance', *New Political Economy* 8 (2003), 360.

states sheltered domestic industries from unfettered competition through trade protections, economic subsidies and regulations and protected societies by providing generous social welfare and regulating labour markets.[20] The objective of market liberalisation was thus subordinated to the goal of preserving domestic social security and economic stability. This embedded liberal compromise came under pressure first with the breakdown of Bretton Woods in 1971 and later with the passage of the Single European Act. Since then governments have gradually ceded autonomy over a wider range of economic policies to European and global authorities. Many observers argue that this shift marks a 'progressive disembedding of liberalism'.[21] In other words, the objective of domestic social cohesion now appears subordinated to the principle of European or global economic integration.

Yet Polanyi argued that efforts to disembed markets from societies were ultimately unsustainable. Moves towards market liberalisation are always met by countermoves to protect society from its negative repercussions. A crucial question, however, is how we demarcate the boundaries of societies to be protected. Polanyi never provided an explicit definition of society. Whether describing it as a 'relationship of persons' or 'social tissue' Polanyi's notion of society was designed to offer a holistic account of economic life that challenged the *homo economicus* assumptions of classical economists.[22] His empirical analysis of the double movement in *The Great Transformation* was clearly national in scope: how forces within British society reacted against the liberalising agenda of British industrialists and their allies in the British state. In his analysis of embedded liberalism, Ruggie also refers explicitly to the reassertion of '*national* political authority over transnational economic forces' (my emphasis) as the foundation of the post-war embedded liberal compromise.[23] Yet if one conceives of society in broader terms as ties that bind individuals together in economic and social life, then nothing precludes considering how transnational markets might be embedded in *transnational* societies.

---

[20] D. Bohle and B. Greskovits, 'Neoliberalism, embedded neoliberalism and neocorporatism: Towards transnational capitalism in Central-Eastern Europe', *West European Politics* 30 (2007), 443, 445.

[21] Best (n. 19 above), p. 363.

[22] K. Gemici, 'Karl Polanyi and the antinomies of embeddedness', *Socio-Economic Review* 6 (2008), 22.

[23] Ruggie (n. 18 above), p. 381.

III   Polanyi in Brussels? Transnational embedding of markets

Caporaso and Tarrow suggest that such a process of transnational embedding is underway in the European Union. In an article entitled 'Polanyi in Brussels' they argue that rather than disembedding markets, EU supranational institutions have sought to forge new social compromises at the European level. The authors examine the ECJ as one important agent in this process. Examining ECJ decisions on the free movement of labour the authors suggest that the 'ECJ is interpreting existing Treaty provisions and secondary legislation in an increasingly social way'.[24] In cases such as *S. E. Klaus*,[25] *Bronzino*[26] and *Mary Carpenter*[27] the Court considered whether Member States have the same obligations to workers and their families who cross nation-state boundaries as they do to workers within their national borders. In each case the Court ruled in favour of the worker. Caporaso and Tarrow summarise the Court's *S. E. Klaus* judgment as stating that 'the working life of the person concerned should be seen *as a whole*, and not just from the limited standpoint of a particular job in one country, at one period of time'.[28] They conclude that the ECJ and other EU institutions are emancipating labour-market exchanges from old (national) structures and re-embedding them in new (European) ones.

Caporaso and Tarrow thus seek to challenge the pessimistic accounts put forth by Scharpf, Gill and others that further European integration will necessarily threaten the historic social agreements that protected national societies from destructive market forces.[29] New compromises can be forged at the European level. These arrangements do not necessarily have to recreate a national welfare state model on a supranational scale. Nor do they necessarily have to be channelled through popular politics. Caporaso and Tarrow argue that the institutionalisation of social rights and protections at the EU level will be achieved through the transnational mobilisation of a diverse set of societal actors whose socio-economic demands cannot be met at the national level

---

[24] Caporaso and Tarrow (n. 14 above), p. 611.
[25] C-482/93 *S. E. Klaus* v. *Bestuur van de Nieuwe Algemene Bedrijfsvereniging* [1995] ECR I-03551.
[26] C-228/98 *Giovanni Bronzino* v. *Kindergeldkasse* [2000] ECR I-00531.
[27] C-60/00 *Mary Carpenter* v. *Secretary of State for the Home Department* [2002] ECR I-06279.
[28] Caporaso and Tarrow (n. 14 above), p. 607.
[29] Scharpf (n. 1 above); Gill (n. 12 above).

alone.[30] This can include individuals pursuing their rights through the courts.[31] It can also entail non-governmental organisations, interest groups, or social movements mobilising for expanded rights and protections at the European level working within and/or in co-ordination with supranational institutions.[32]

Two problems arise. The first is whether this loose coalition of individual litigants and interest groups seeking stronger social protections at the EU level constitutes a '*European* society'? In the thinnest Polanyian terms of different cross sections of society mobilising to seek protection from the market, perhaps so. Yet it is questionable whether such movements can be conceived, or whether they conceive of themselves, in more organic or solidaristic terms of 'society as a whole'.[33] Polanyi may be in Brussels (or Luxembourg or Strasbourg). But he's also in Stockholm, Paris and Riga. That is to say that the ties that bind individuals within national societies remain strong, far stronger to date than the ties that bind a European society comprised of twenty-seven diverse Member States. Moreover, the more citizens perceive EU institutions to be the primary agents pushing forward the painful process of market liberalisation (a popular perception that many national politicians are all too willing to nurture), the more we can expect that countermovements will be organised *against* the EU rather than within it. It is important to note here that Polanyi's conception of the countermovement was largely a defensive movement: arising spontaneously rather than following a coherent set of societal or political alternatives.[34] This insight helps to account for the seemingly spontaneous eruption of anti-EU sentiments across Europe that appear to have little in common except a desire to halt the advance of European integration.

This leads to a second concern. One might argue that a significant barrier to the development of a coherent social policy at the EU level – and indeed the creation of a European society more generally – is the diversity of national welfare state models amongst its members. These differences are significant not only in institutional or policy terms.

---

[30] Caporaso and Tarrow (n. 14 above), p. 613.
[31] L. Conant, 'Individuals, courts and the development of European social rights', *Comparative Political Studies* 39 (2006), 76.
[32] R. Cichowski, 'Courts, rights and democratic participation', *Comparative Political Studies* 39 (2006), 50; D. Mabbett, 'The development of rights-based social policy in the European Union: The example of disability rights', *JCMS* 43 (2005), 97.
[33] B. Silver and G. Arrighi, '"Double movement": The *belle époques* of British and U.S. hegemony compared', *Politics & Society* 31 (2003), 327.
[34] R. Munck, 'Globalization and contestation: A Polanyian problematic', *Globalizations* (2006), 180.

Of equal importance, according to Scharpf are 'differences in taken-for-granted normative assumptions regarding the demarcation line separating the functions the welfare state is supposed to perform from those that ought to be left to . . . the market'.[35] That is, citizens are attached to, or are 'embedded' in, very different societal conceptions of the ideal relationship between the state, market and society. These different normative assumptions underlying national welfare states also carry a high degree of political salience.[36] Scandinavian leaders agreeing to modify the core structures and functions of deeply embedded welfare states often do so at their electoral peril. Caporaso and Tarrow conclude that 'whether national welfare states will be cut back, modified, strengthened, or simply supplemented by social programs on a regional scale has yet to be decided'.[37] But this begs the question: decided by whom? The future of the ESMs is not simply a matter of economic imperatives but of ongoing political struggles. The pertinent question then becomes how different actors – namely European institutions, Member States and social partners – are engaged in struggles at the national and European levels over the future of Social Europe.

The next section considers this question through an in-depth comparative analysis of *Laval* and *Viking*. The Court's rulings in these two cases challenge Caporaso and Tarrow's claim that the ECJ interprets existing Treaty provisions and secondary legislation in an 'increasingly social way'. By ruling in favour of private firms seeking legal redress against industrial action, the cases suggest that the ECJ may instead be interpreting existing Treaty provisions and secondary legislation in an increasingly *liberal* way. Yet a reading of ECJ opinions in dichotomous terms of a liberal versus social leaning Court is bound to be analytically limited as well as inconclusive. Indeed, for every case in which the ECJ appears to favour a market-making interpretation of Treaties and secondary legislation, we can identify a case where it interprets them in a market-shaping direction. However, rather than viewing the Court as an independent actor in its own right or, alternatively, as upholding the preferences of Member States, we can pursue a more disaggregated approach to examine how the legal process enables and constrains different sets of actors.[38]

---

[35] Scharpf (n. 1 above), p. 650.   [36] *Ibid.*, p. 651.
[37] Caporaso and Tarrow (n. 14 above), p. 612.
[38] A. M. Burley, 'Europe before the Court: A political theory of legal integration', *International Organization* 47 (1993), 41; K. Alter, 'Who are the "masters of the Treaty?": European governments and the European Court of Justice', *International*

IV   Transnational disembedding of markets? *Laval* and *Viking*

The overarching legal question at stake in the *Laval* and *Viking* cases was how to adjudicate between two fundamental principles: the freedom of establishment and the free movement of services and the right of collective bargaining and action. The first is inscribed in EU Treaties (Articles 49 *et seq.* TFEU (ex Articles 43 *et seq.* EC) and Article 56 TFEU (ex Article 49 EC) and the latter within the 2000 Charter of Fundamental Rights of the European Union (Article 28). At issue in each dispute was whether industrial action by unions to force firms to abide by nationally negotiated collective agreements violates EU laws overseeing the free movement of services and the right of establishment. Given that both cases involved firms based in old Member States (Sweden and Finland) seeking to employ workers from new Member States (Latvia and Estonia) at lower wage levels, the cases also involved political issues related to enlargement, namely the legality of actions taken to prevent social dumping. The following case studies trace the process through which different domestic and European actors sought to influence and frame the political and legal issues at stake in the two cases.

A   The Laval *case*

In 2003 a Riga-based firm Laval un Partneri Ltd won a contract through its Swedish subsidiary (L&P Baltic Bygg AB) worth nearly €2.8 million to refurbish and extend a school in the Stockholm suburb of Vaxholm. Between May and December 2004 Laval posted thirty-five Latvian workers to carry out the contract. In June 2004 the Swedish construction union (Svenska Byggnadsarbetareförbundet, hereafter 'Byggnads') contacted Laval to argue that the Latvian posted workers should fall under existing Swedish national collective agreements for the building sector. By September 2004, Laval had not agreed to Byggnads' demands. Meanwhile Laval announced that it had signed a collective agreement with the Latvian Building Workers' Union that represented approximately 65 per cent of the Latvian workers posted to Sweden. Under this

Organization 52 (1998), 121; G. Garrett, D. R. Kelemen and H. Schultz, 'The European Court of Justice, national governments, and legal integration in the European Union', *International Organization* 52 (1998), 263; C. Carrubba, M. Gable and C. Hankla, 'Judicial behavior under political constraints: Evidence from the European Court of Justice', *American Political Science Review* 102 (2008), 435.

agreement Laval agreed to pay the Latvian workers approximately €9 per hour, in addition to covering accommodation, meal and transport costs. This wage was nearly double the average pay for construction workers in Latvia. Yet it was nearly half the rate of pay for Swedish construction workers in the Stockholm region. Under the Swedish national collective agreement, Swedish workers at the same site would make approximately €16 per hour, in addition to 12.8 per cent holiday pay.

In October 2004, five months after its first meeting with Laval, Byggnads announced it would initiate a blockade of the Vaxholm site. Laval organised a demonstration at the Swedish parliament on 3 December to protest at the impending action. But to no avail. A day later the blockade commenced, with Byggnads members preventing workers and deliveries from entering the site and picketing the premises with signs reading 'Swedish laws in Sweden'. In December the Swedish electricians union (Svenska Elektrikerförbundet) launched a solidarity strike and unionised cement suppliers ceased deliveries to the site. A month into the blockade, Laval went to the Swedish Labour Court (or *Arbetsdomstolen*) to argue that the Byggnads blockade and the electricians' solidarity strike were illegal and should cease immediately and requested compensation for damages. Two weeks later the court ruled that the blockade was legal under Swedish labour law. In January 2005, other unions launched sympathy actions. By February 2005, the Vaxholm municipality requested to terminate its contract. A month later L&P Baltic Bygg AB declared bankruptcy. In April 2005, the Swedish Labour Court referred the case to the ECJ for a preliminary ruling.

The Latvian firm did not pursue its case in isolation. Swedish employer associations were actively involved in supporting the Latvian firm's position in the case, not only politically but financially. Svenskt Näringsliv, the Confederation of Swedish Enterprise that represents 54,000 Swedish companies, contributed thousands of euros towards Laval's legal fees in bringing the case to a Swedish court.[39] The Latvian Minister of Foreign Affairs remarked at the time, 'Swedish lawyers are queuing to help us.'[40] Why Swedish employer associations and some Swedish opposition parties aligned themselves with the Laval position can be explained by internal political factors. Swedish employers have

---

[39] C. Jacobsoon, 'Baxläxa för Sverige i EU domston', *Dagens Nyheter* (19 December 2007).

[40] *Diena*, 'Zviedriem būs jātaisnojas par pāridarījumu Latvijas celtniekiem' ['The Swedes will have to defend themselves regarding the harm to Latvian builders'], 19 November 2004.

long sought to secure more firm-level autonomy in wage bargaining and increase the flexibility of the Swedish labour market more generally.[41] Thus the *Laval* case presented an opportunity for Swedish employers to challenge existing Swedish labour and social policies at the EU level.

With respect to the union, to counter claims made by both Swedish and Latvian critics that the Swedish unions' actions were discriminatory towards Latvian workers in Sweden (and foreign workers more generally) Byggnads stressed that the action was designed to protect the rights of all workers to fair wages and working conditions. To appeal directly to Latvian audiences Byggnads took out a full-page advertisement in a Latvian newspaper displaying the hands of Swedish and Latvian workers clasped in solidarity.[42] The advertisement was met with contempt or indifference by Latvian unions. The chair of the Free Trade Union Confederation of Latvia argued that the advertisement was about the continuation of the boycott, rather than a genuine appeal for solidarity.[43] Representatives of the Latvian Union of Construction Workers, which represented the Latvian workers in Vaxholm, expressed concerns that Byggnads had neglected to consult with them on the industrial action.[44] The head of Byggnads retorted that Swedish unions were reluctant to discuss the case with Latvian unions since Latvian union officials were 'clearly under pressure by the Latvian government to support Laval against Swedish union action'.[45]

In terms of the Swedish government, it waged a political battle on domestic and foreign fronts. The government knew that Laval presented a host of legal and political problems. Indeed, a 1994 report released before Sweden's accession to the EU had warned that many aspects of its Swedish social model did not conform to EU law. Yet such concerns were assuaged by an implicit understanding that the Commission would not actively pursue infringement proceedings against Swedish labour and social policies that may be in violation of EU directives. According to

[41] J. Pontusson and P. Swenson, 'Labour markets, production strategies and wage bargaining institutions', *Comparative Political Studies* 29 (1996), 223.

[42] C. Woolfson and J. Sommers, 'Labour mobility in construction: European implications of the Laval un Partneri Dispute with Swedish Labour', *European Journal of Industrial Relations* 12 (2006), 49–68.

[43] *Diena* (n. 40 above).

[44] *Diena*, 'Būvuzņēmums sniedz prasību Zviedrijas tiesā, valdība vērsīsies EK' ['Construction business makes a claim in Swedish court, government will turn to European Commission'], 7 December 2004.

[45] *Diena* (n. 40 above).

Anders Kruse, the head of the Swedish legal secretariat who prepared the Swedish position in *Laval*, it was only a matter of time before a legal case would be raised.[46] *Laval* presented such a case. Kruse argued that the government had only one choice to make: 'to defend the Swedish social model'.[47] Domestically the government faced pressure by Swedish employers and Swedish unions. On the one hand, the Swedish employers association accused the government of trying to pressure the labour court to rule against Laval. On the other hand, when the government publicly condemned picketers' slogans targeted against foreign workers, some union officials publicly condemned the government for abandoning Swedish workers. With the Social Democrats losing to a centre-right coalition in 2005, some trade unionists feared that the government would change its position in the case. Such fears proved to be unwarranted as the incoming government held steadfast to its position that collective action should prevail over economic freedoms. On the external front, Prime Minister Göran Persson argued during the blockade that Swedish unions had the 'right to take retaliatory measures' in order to 'ensure the survival of collective agreements'.[48] Later, leading up to the *Laval* hearings, in 2006 the Swedish government invited the agents of all the Member States to a special information meeting in the lead up to the *Laval* hearings aimed at presenting the Swedish position on the issues raised in the case. 'We were concerned that other member states didn't understand the Swedish social model', Kruse explains, 'so we invited them to come to Stockholm and ask questions.'[49]

While the ECJ considered the case, political debates continued outside the courts. In December 2005 then EU Commissioner for the Internal Market and Services, Charles McCreevy, announced during a visit to Stockholm that he would oppose the Swedish government and Byggnads position in the ECJ case, arguing that the Swedish unions' action against Laval violated free movement of services.[50] McCreevy's comments provoked outrage among trade unions across Europe, as well as among Swedish and Danish social democrats. Given that Denmark's industrial relations model is quite similar to Sweden's – based on voluntary collective bargaining rather than mandatory minimum wages – Danish actors weighed in on the impending decision. Former Danish Prime

---

[46] Personal interview, Gothenburg, Sweden, 19 March 2009.   [47] Personal interview.
[48] Quoted Woolfson and Sommers (n. 42 above), p. 55.   [49] Personal interview.
[50] Carsten Jørgensen, 'Swedish case referred to ECJ has major importance for the Danish model', EIROnline (2004), www.eurofond.europa.eu/eiro/2005/11/feature/dk0511102f.htm.

Minister Poul Nyrup Rasmussen suggested that McCreevy's comment had seriously undermined Swedish and Danish support for the EU.[51] This view that the dispute might have wider implications for Swedish support of the EU more generally was reinforced by the Swedish employment minister's comment that the question of Sweden's withdrawal from the EU would be raised. 'There are a lot of people out there', he said, 'who voted for EU entry in the belief that the Swedish model would stay intact.'[52] When the European Trade Union Congress (ETUC) asked European Commission President Jose Manuel Barroso to clarify whether McCreevy's comments reflected the view of the European Commission as whole, Barroso responded that 'In no way are we going against or criticizing the Swedish social model.'[53] When asked in a European Parliament hearing on the dispute to expand on his position, McCreevy remarked: 'Latvian trade union members are entitled to have their interests defended as much as Swedish trade union members . . . The real issue to me is what we mean by an internal market.'[54]

In its December 2007 decision, the ECJ recognised that the right of trade unions to take collective action is a fundamental right under Community law – and that the right to take collective action for the protection of workers against social dumping might constitute an overriding reason of public interest. However, the ECJ deemed that in the *Laval* case the Swedish unions' boycott violated the principle of freedom to provide services since the unions' demands exceeded minimal protections under national labour law. The ECJ decision thus reaffirmed the right to take industrial action under EU law, but was a blow to Sweden's voluntary collective bargaining system. The Swedish government expressed disappointment in the ruling. Swedish employment minister Sven Otto Littorin told the *Financial Times* that the centre-right government, which had supported the unions in the dispute, would now have to amend the law. 'I'm a bit surprised and a bit disappointed by the verdict', he said. 'I think things are working well as they are.'[55] Anders Kruse remarked: 'The free movement of services cannot take precedence over such fundamental rights as negotiating a collective agreement or staging an industrial action.'[56]

[51] S. James, 'Sweden: Lessons of the Vaxholm builders' dispute', World Socialist Web (2006), www.wsws.org/articles/2006/jun2006/swed-j27_prn.shtml.
[52] James (n. 51 above).   [53] *Ibid.*
[54] EurActiv, 'McCreevy defends stance in social model row', 26 October 2005, www.euractiv.com/en/socialeurope/mccreevy-defends-stance-social-model-row/article-146475.
[55] *Financial Times*, 'Europe loses when it legitimates low wages', 7 March 2008.
[56] BBC News, 'Latvian firm test EU labour laws', 9 January 2007.

Supporters of Laval's position voiced satisfaction with the ruling. The key counsel for Laval, Anders Elmér, remarked in the Swedish daily *Dagens Nyheter* that the ruling vindicated Laval's opposition to the blockade.[57] Svenskt Näringsliv also welcomed the decision. Its vice-president, Jan-Peter Duker, said: 'This is good for free movement of services. You can't raise obstacles for foreign companies to come to Sweden.'[58] Latvian public officials also weighed in on the debate. Latvian European Parliament Member Valdis Dombrovskis of the centre-right EPP-ED group suggested that the EU should consider putting protective mechanisms in place to safeguard companies that post workers from the 'arbitrary and unjustified demands of trade unions' and argued that 'the Laval ruling will shape the direction of the single market in the future'.[59] Jorgen Ronnest of the employers association Business Europe struck a more cautious note. While the ECJ ruling will contribute to 'improving the development of an internal market' by forcing legal clarity, Ronnest argued, policy-makers should first 'wait for member states to draw their own conclusions on what [the *Laval* and *Viking* judgments] mean for their national systems' – and 'only then we can see whether something has to be done at EU level'.[60]

Swedish labour unions, Swedish opposition parties and the ETUC condemned the ruling. While many commentators made a point of emphasising that the ECJ had upheld the fundamental right to strike – as well as to take actions to preserve national protections against social dumping – they concurred that the ECJ ruling presented a setback to the Swedish collective bargaining system and the ESM more generally. Speaking in front of a packed audience at a 26 February 2008 hearing before the European Parliament's Employee and Social Affairs Committee on the *Laval* and *Viking* cases, ETUC General Secretary John Monks argued that the rulings challenge 'by accident or by design' the European Parliament's position that the Services Directive places fundamental social rights and free movement of services on an equal footing. He remarks:

> The idea of social Europe has taken a blow. Put simply, the action of employers using free movement as a pretext for social dumping practices is resulting in unions having to justify, ultimately to the courts, the

[57] O. Carp, 'Motgång för Byggnads i EU-dom', *Dagens Nyheter*, 18 December 2007.
[58] Jacobsoon (n. 39 above).
[59] EurActive, 'European Social Model challenged by court rulings', 27 February 2008, www.euroactive.com/en/socialeurope/european-social-model-challenged-court-rulings/article-170567.
[60] *Ibid.*

actions they take against those employers' tactics. That is both wrong and dangerous. Wrong because workers' rights to equal treatment in the host country should be the guiding principle. Wrong because unions must be autonomous. And dangerous because it reinforces those critics of Europe who have long said that liberal Europe would always threaten the generally excellent social, collective bargaining and welfare systems built up since the Second World War.[61]

The Latvian unions had been relatively silent during the course of the dispute. Yet after the ruling, the president of the Latvian Free Trade Union Confederation, Peteris Krigers, remarked that the ECJ ruling would require unions to improve their cross-border communication channels.[62]

B   The Viking case

In October 2003, Viking Line, a Finnish ferry company, gave the Finnish Seamen's Union (or Suomen Merimies-Unioni, FSU) notice of its intention to reflag its passenger vessel *Rosella*. One of seven Viking vessels, *Rosella* runs routes from Sweden and Finland through the Baltic Sea archipelago to the Estonian capital Tallinn. Viking argued that in order to compete with other ferries operating on the same route, it intended to register the vessel in Estonia, where it had a subsidiary, and employ an Estonian crew. Replacing the Finnish crew with an Estonian one promised to reduce Viking's labour costs significantly due to the far lower levels of pay in Estonia than in Finland. Once the existing collective agreement between Viking and the FSU expired on 17 November 2003, the FSU was no longer under the Finnish legal obligation to maintain industrial peace and soon after gave notice of its intention to strike in order to prevent the reflagging. The union put forth two conditions to renew the collective agreement: (1) that regardless of a possible change of flags on *Rosella* Viking would continue to follow Finnish laws and Finnish collective bargaining agreements and (2) that any change of flag would not lead to any redundancy and lay-offs of current employees or change in terms and conditions of employment without union consent. The FSU justified its position in press statements by arguing that they were seeking to protect Finnish jobs.

---

[61] European Parliament, Hearing of Committee of Employment and Social Affairs, 26 February 2008.

[62] Michael Whittal, 'Unions fear ECJ ruling in *Laval* case could lead to social dumping' (2008), www.eurofond.europa.eu/eiro/2008/01/articles/eu0801019i.htm.

The dispute soon took on a transnational dimension. Responding to a request for support from FSU, in November 2003 the London-based International Transport Worker's Federation (ITF) distributed a circular to all of its affiliates requesting that they refrain from negotiating with Viking Line and threatening a boycott of all Viking Line vessels if they failed to comply. ITF, which represents 600 affiliated unions in 140 countries, had long campaigned against the use of 'flags of convenience' (or FOC). This policy seeks to establish genuine links between the nationality of ship owners and the vessel flag – in other words, combating the prevalent use of flags from tax and regulatory havens – and to enhance the conditions of seafarers on FOC ships. When Viking learned of the ITF circular it immediately sought an injunction to restrain ITF and FSU from the strike action. In the course of conciliation meetings Viking agreed that any reflagging would not lead to lay-offs. Yet the ITF and FSU refused to withdraw its circular.

A year later, in November 2005, Viking Line brought a case against the ITF in the UK courts. Viking could bring the case before the UK courts since its main objection was against the boycott threatened by ITF, which is headquartered in London. Viking claimed that the ITF, by threatening a boycott, infringed Viking's right of establishment with regard to the reflagging of the *Rosella*. The UK commercial court ruled in Viking's favour, granting an injunction against the unions. The ITF and FSU appealed the decision in the UK Court of Appeal, which subsequently lifted the injunction and referred a series of questions to the ECJ to resolve. The questions were twofold: (1) whether collective action falls outside the scope of Article 49 TFEU (ex Article 43 EC) – that is, whether the free movement of maritime services supersedes or is constrained by the right to take collective action – and (2) whether Article 49 TFEU (ex Article 43 EC) has a 'horizontal direct effect' in that private companies can appeal to Article 49 TFEU (ex Article 43 EC) in disputes with trade unions. In essence, the UK Court of Appeal asked the ECJ to decide, like in the *Laval* case, how to strike an appropriate balance between the right to take collective action and the fundamental freedom to provide services. ITF summarised the stakes of the case as involving 'an essential issue: whether, and to what extent, industrial action by unions in order to prevent the imposition of lower wage rates and terms and conditions of employment is permissible when ships transfer flags within Europe'.[63]

---

[63] International Transport Workers' Federation, 'European Court to rule on landmark labour case', 10 December 2007, www.itfglobal.org/transport-international/ti27-viking.cfm.

The ECJ held a hearing on 10 January 2007. Fifteen states and the European Commission submitted observations in the case. ITF General Secretary David Cockroft commented: 'The number of submissions shows how many states have recognized just how deep the impact of this case could be, and we applaud the court's determination to settle it.'[64] He continued:

> What's at issue here could hardly be more fundamental. The right to defend your job against the right of a business to do what it takes to up its profits; a Europe for the powerful or a Europe for its citizens. This is not about new entrants, or labor costs. It is about the rights and basic beliefs that most of us have always believed underpinned the European Union.[65]

On 23 May 2007 Advocate General Miguel Poiares Maduro delivered a preliminary judgment. Concerning the fundamental point of whether collective industrial action falls outside the scope of Article 49 TFEU (ex Article 43 EC), Maduro took a compromise position, arguing that EU provisions on establishment and freedom to provide services are 'by no means irreconcilable with the protection of fundamental rights or with the attainment of the Community's social policies'.[66] Maduro expressed the view that trade unions could take collective action to dissuade a company from relocating within the EU, so long as it did not partition the labour market along national lines or prevent a relocated company from providing services in another Member State. Departing from the Commission's submitted opinion in the case, Maduro argued that Article 49 TFEU (ex Article 43 EC) does have a horizontal effect, giving an employer the right to pursue a claim against a trade union for violating free movement of services and the right of establishment. However, Maduro argued that Article 49 TFEU (ex Article 43 EC) does not necessarily preclude a trade union from taking collective action to protect the interests of its workers, even if the result of the action might restrict free movement of services. The question of the legality of particular actions should be left to national courts to decide, according to Maduro, provided that there is no difference in the treatment of national and foreign companies. In a press release following Maduro's opinion, the ITF welcomed affirmation of the right of trade unions to take industrial action, but also expressed concerns that the ruling 'might

---

[64] ITF (n. 63 above).   [65] ITF (n. 63 above).
[66] Case C-438/05 Opinion of Advocate General Maduro, delivered on 23 May 2007, 2.

encourage businesses to believe that they can override those rights through a kind of cross-border hopscotch'.[67]

On 11 December 2007 the ECJ handed down its eagerly awaited judgment. The ECJ stated, consistent with Maduro's opinion, that collective action may be legitimate if its aim is to protect jobs or working conditions and if all other ways of resolving the conflict were exhausted. Concerning horizontal direct effect, the ECJ argued that private companies can appeal to Article 49 TFEU (ex Article 43 EC) in seeking relief from industrial actions. With respect to the *Viking* case, however, the Court ruled that the strike action threatened by the two unions to force the employer to conclude a collective agreement amounted to a restriction of Viking's freedom of establishment as set out in Article 49 TFEU (ex Article 43 EC). According to the Court, FSU's demands to force Viking to abide by Finnish collective agreements made reflagging pointless, given that the aim of reflagging was to reduce *Rosella*'s labour costs. Put another way, if Viking was prevented from reflagging its vessel to Estonia, then Viking, through its Estonian subsidiary, was denied the freedom to compete with other Estonian-based companies doing business under Estonia's lower minimum wage rates and laxer regulations. Yet the Court ruled that ITF's policy of combating the use of flags of convenience could, in general, be interpreted as a legitimate restriction of the right of freedom of establishment. The Court left it to the national courts to determine whether the objectives of collective action can be deemed proportionate to protecting workers' jobs and employment conditions and/or whether the action is in the public interest. If so, then collective action can infringe on the right of establishment and freedom to provide services. The ITF and FSU and Viking settled out of court in March 2008, the terms of which were not disclosed.

V   Concluding remarks

We can draw three sets of conclusions from this analysis. The first concerns the ECJ as an embedding or disembedding agent or, in other words, the extent to which we can argue that Polanyi is in Luxembourg. The analysis of the cases points to a basic but important fact that the Court cannot initiate policy on its own; it must react to cases brought

[67] S. McKay, 'European Court gives preliminary ruling on union cases over conflicting rights', EIROnline (2007), www.eurofond.europa.eu/eiro/2007/06/articles/eu0706029i.htm.

before it.[68] In the *Laval* and *Viking* cases, private firms appealed to the ECJ to intervene in industrial relations disputes. This suggests that while the ECJ may indeed provide new opportunities for individuals and interest groups to seek social protections at the European level, this opportunity also extends to private firms. Indeed, historically commercial interests have exploited these legal channels far more frequently and successfully to advance their interests at the domestic and European levels. This appears to leave trade unions in the defensive position of protecting national socio-legal frameworks against intrusions by the courts. Yet in both cases unions pursued more proactive and transnational strategies, with Swedish unions framing their actions as representing the interests of all European workers and the Finnish seamen's union joining forces with the international transport union. This suggests that trade unions' strategies are not only focused on preserving social bargains made in Stockholm or Helsinki. Unions increasingly recognise the need to invest in strengthening co-operation across national borders and forging new compromises in Brussels.[69]

A second conclusion concerns the relationship between the Commission and the Court in advancing European policy agendas. Caporaso and Tarrow suggest that the Commission and the ECJ work together to promote a social agenda at the European level, with the Commission supplying the Court with a 'concrete set of social regulations'.[70] Yet they can also join forces in promoting liberalising agendas. The Services Directive passed by the Council and Parliament in 2006 had watered down many of the most ambitious proposals put forth by former Internal Market Commissioner, Frits Bolkestein. But it also left wide scope for advocates of service liberalisation to pursue this agenda through legal means. If the Court looks to the Commission as a 'political bellwether' then *Laval* and *Viking* could be viewed as quite consistent with the Commission's long-standing commitment to liberalising the European service sector.[71] It is also notable that the Court went on to rule

[68] D. Wincott, 'A Community of law? "European" law and judicial politics: The Court of Justice and beyond', *Government and Opposition* 35 (2000), 3, 21.

[69] R. Hyman, 'Trade unions and the politics of the European Social Model', *Economic and Industrial Democracy* 26 (2005), 9; A. Bieler, *The Struggle for a Social Europe: Trade unions and EMU in times of global restructuring* (Manchester: Manchester University Press, 2006); K. Gajewska, 'The emergence of a European labour protest movement?', *European Journal of Industrial Relations* 14 (2008), 104.

[70] Caporaso and Tarrow (n. 14 above), p. 614.

[71] W. Mattli, 'Revisiting the European Court of Justice', *International Organization* 52 (1998), 185.

in *Rüffert* (C-346/06) that a *Land Niederachsen* provision that all public contracts must conform to collective wage agreements constituted an undue restriction on a Polish subcontractor's right to provide services.[72] This lends support to Scharpf's claim that the most significant challenges to national labour and social policies do not stem from decisions made by the Council of Ministers or the European Parliament but the initiation of legal actions through the courts.[73] But this leads to a final conclusion concerning the practical and political consequences of the verdicts.

One outcome might be a process of 'contained compliance' whereby affected states make revisions to existing laws to conform to the rulings.[74] Some have argued that introducing minimum-wage laws, or making collective agreements legally binding, poses a threat to the socio-legal principles underlying the Swedish (and Danish) social model based on voluntary agreements.[75] Others have called for pursuing secondary legislation that would raise the level of social and labour protections now allowed under the Posting of Workers Directive (PWD)[76] or introducing a 'social progress' clause in the treaties.[77] In October 2008 the European Parliament passed a resolution calling for a 're-assertion in primary law of the law of the balance between fundamental rights and economic freedoms in order to avoid a race to lower social standards'.[78] In December 2008 employment ministers in the European Council refused to consider proposals to strengthen the PWD. Yet just months after UK ministers had rejected consideration of the proposal in Brussels, the government was faced with a wave of

[72] Case C-346/06, *Rüffert v. Land Niederachsen* [2008] ECR I-1989.
[73] Scharpf (n. 1 above), p. 657.
[74] L. Conant, *Justice Contained: Law and politics in the European Union* (Ithaca: Cornell University Press, 2002).
[75] I thank Marie Pierre Granger for bringing this point to my attention. See also 'Förslag till åtgärder med anledning av Lavaldomen, Betänkande av Lavalutredningen' ['Report of the Committee Consequences and action in response to the *Laval* judgment'], Statens Offentliga Utredninglar (12 December 2008), 123, www.regeringen.se/content/1/c6/11/74/43/5d1a903d.pdf.
[76] Directive 96/71/EC of the European Parliament and of the Council of 16 December 1996 concerning the posting of workers in the framework of the provision of services.
[77] Bercusson (n. 5 above); J. Monks, 'European Court of Justice and Social Europe: A divorce based on irreconcilable differences?', *Social Europe Journal* 22 (2008), 26; C. Joerges and F. Rödl, 'Informal politics, formalized law and the "social deficit" of European integration: Reflections after the judgments of the ECJ in *Viking* and *Laval*', *ELJ* 15 (2009), 1.
[78] European Parliament A6-0370/2008.

strikes at home protesting the hiring of foreign workers at lower wages. Former UK Health Secretary Alan Johnson referred to the recent ECJ cases in his public response to the strikers' demands stating, 'As a result of those rulings we need to look again to make sure our intention of this free movement is actually being supported by workers themselves . . . and it is not based on [workers] being undercut on terms and conditions.'[79] Societal countermovements seeking to defend national socio-legal frameworks against moves towards further liberalisation are not confined to Member States with the strongest social protections to defend but are increasingly evident among the EU's most liberal members. The question remains whether this movement can be waged at the transnational level, spanning east and west.

[79] *Times Online*, 1 February 2009.

4

Observations on economic governance and the search for a European economic constitution

WOUTER DEVROE AND PIETER VAN CLEYNENBREUGEL

I Introduction

The project of 'European economic integration' has never been an end in itself.[1] Economic integration has, on the contrary, always been considered an instrument to attain non-economic goals.[2] Economic rule-making should in that respect facilitate and promote the realisation of non-economic objectives, including the protection of weaker (contract) parties, protection of the environment or prevention of climate change and protection of fundamental social rights.

Finding the right balance between non-economic goals and purely economic objectives in principle remains a matter for political decision-making. Political balancing is nevertheless said to take place within the confines of a European economic constitution framework. This chapter discusses and assesses that framework in the current stage of European integration.

At the time of the adoption of the founding EU Treaties, the economic constitution was well-known among German scholars as a concept to

---

[1] See the Memoirs of Jean Monnet, explaining the underlying philosophy of a peaceful, prosperous Europe: J. Monnet, *Mémoires* (Paris: Fayard, 1976), 323.

[2] Compare the Spaak Report (Report to the Heads of Delegation to the Ministers of Foreign Affairs, Brussels, 21 April 1956, consulted at www.ena.lu on 11 August 2010), p. 13: 'L'objet d'un marché commun européen doit être de créer une vaste zone de politique économique, constituant une puissante unité de production, et permettant une expansion continue, une stabilité accrue, un relèvement accéléré du niveau de vie, et le développement de relations harmonieuses entre les Etats qu'il réunit.' ['The purpose of a common market must be the creation of a large area with a common economic policy, so that a powerful unit of production is formed and continuous expansion is made possible, as well as an increased stability, an accelerated increase of the standard of living, and the development of harmonious relations between the Member States.' (English translation from www.ena.lu).]

justify the organisation of the national economic order.[3] Their so-called 'ordoliberal' model in particular is said to have influenced EU legal thinking and/or EU Treaties.[4] However, and without being able to confirm the accuracy of this claim, it appears that even the proponents of the ordoliberal model have had to adapt, if not abandon, their position in view of more recent judicial and political developments. Section II of this chapter briefly analyses those developments.

Building on that analysis, the chapter subsequently revisits the concept of economic constitution. Section III identifies a number of essential components in an economic constitution. Section IV assesses whether these components are present in the current Treaties. It will be argued that the Treaties at best constitute an 'open economic constitution', and perhaps no economic constitution at all.

The limited guidance offered by the Treaties affects the outlook of economic governance debates in the European Union. Section V explores the limited scope of the current European economic governance debate. It subsequently argues in favour of a broader and less nebulous governance debate in a fully developed European economic constitution framework.

II   From ordoliberalism to economic constitutional law to economic constitution

The concept of economic constitution is traditionally associated with the German school of ordoliberalism.[5] Ordoliberals considered individual freedom essential for organising a market economy. According to ordoliberal thought, unrestrained competition provided the fullest expression

---

[3] W. Möschel, 'Competition as a basic element of the social market economy', *European Business Organisation Law Review* 2 (2001), 716.

[4] C. Joerges, 'What is left of the European economic constitution? A melancholic eulogy', *ELRev* 30 (2005), 470.

[5] For background information on the origins of the concept, D. Gerber, 'Constitutionalising the economy: German neo-liberalism, competition law and the "new" Europe', *Am. J. Comp. L.* 42 (1994), 25. See also R. Ptak, 'Neoliberalism in Germany: Revisiting the ordoliberal foundations of the social market economy' in P. Mirowski and D. Plehwe, *The Road from Mont Pélerin: The making of neoliberal thought* (Cambridge, MA: Harvard University Press, 2009), pp. 103 *et seq.* W. Eucken is considered the founder of ordoliberalism. F. A. Hayek is frequently classified as an ordoliberal, in particular in relation to his *The Road to Serfdom* (Chicago: University of Chicago Press, 1944). Gerber argues that Hayek, just like Eucken considered free competition important, but did not, at least in later stages of his career, believe in strong state enforcement mechanisms (p. 32).

of individual freedom. Free competition therefore needed to be an end in itself.[6]

In order to achieve free competition, ordoliberals proposed the establishment of a pre-determined economic order by means of a fundamental legal framework or 'economic constitution'.[7] That constitutional framework had to guarantee free competition.[8] It would only tolerate government intervention in the market in order to preserve competition.[9] Discretionary public interventions in the marketplace were to be ruled out by the constitutional framework itself.[10] Only so could the 'perils' of both discretionary government interference and private anticompetitive action be avoided.[11]

The old liberal organisational framework conflicted with the classical post-World War II perception of governments actively intervening to design social policies.[12] Interventionist social protective measures would remain impossible if original ordoliberal ideas were strictly adhered to. Some scholars therefore argued in favour of a separation between social politics and the economic constitution.[13] Gradually, however, it was considered overly simple to separate an economic constitution from social and political constitutions, as the economy is intricately interwoven with social protection. Moreover, it was generally felt that at least some discretionary state intervention was needed in order for states to actively correct market injustices. To make markets function effectively, the once excluded 'social politics' were felt as a necessity in modern post-World War II states. The impossibility of a pure economic constitution based order has since become apparent at the level of Member States.

---

[6] This is at least the thesis of Möschel (n. 3 above), p. 713.

[7] W. Sauter, 'The economic constitution of the European Union', *Columbia JEL* 4 (1998), 28. The importance of the rule of law has been emphasised by Möschel (n. 6 above), p. 716; This has also been referred to as a moment of constitutional choice, see V. J. Vanberg, 'The Freiburg School: Walter Eucken and ordoliberalism', Freiburg Discussion Papers on Constitutional Economics 11 (2004), www.econstor.eu/handle/10419/4343, pp. 5, 7.

[8] Gerber (n. 5 above), p. 37; I. Maher, 'Re-imagining the story of European competition law', *Oxford Journal of Legal Studies* 20(1) (2000), 163.

[9] C. Joerges and F. Rödl, 'Social market economy as Europe's "social model"', EUI Working Paper 8 (2004), p. 13.

[10] *Ibid.*

[11] C. Mantzavinos, *Individuals, Institutions and Markets* (Cambridge: Cambridge University Press, 2001), p. 163.

[12] Mentioned by Joerges and Rödl (n. 9 above), p. 11.

[13] E. Laurent and J. Le Cacheux, 'What (economic) constitution does the EU need?', Document de Travail OFCE, Sciences-Po 4 (2007), p. 18.

A similar evolution can be observed at the European Union level. It is stated that the European Coal and Steel Community (ECSC) and European Economic Community (EEC) Treaties and policies at large have been influenced by ordoliberalism in some way, although the extent of that influence remains unclear.[14]

Orthodox ordoliberal theorists did consider a supranational free trade association to be an ideal organisational structure. Neither the ECSC nor the EEC reflected that ideal. The ECSC provided a regulated market mechanism that cannot however be said to have focused entirely on individual freedom. The EEC treaty incorporated free competition rules and provided for non-discretionary enforcement by the European Commission.[15] At the same time, the EEC Treaty also entrusted the European institutions with more discretionary powers.[16] The scope of those powers has been subject to severe criticism.[17] In order to address the challenges of social policy within the confines of a theoretical model, orthodox ordoliberal ideas have been mitigated following World War II by the rise of an enticing social market economy (*Soziale Marktwirtschaft*) concept. A social market economy still envisaged open and competitive (national) markets, but also aimed at enforcing social justice[18] and social protection of individuals without blindly relying on regular market mechanisms. This in turn required not only market supervision and enforcement[19] but also a more active role for government when markets would fail to offer 'social' protection. Discretionary state powers were considered important and necessary. The scope of the economic constitution framework therefore needed to be re-evaluated.

The *Soziale Marktwirtschaft* concept shifted the focus from competition as an expression of freedom, to competition as an instrument for attaining other objectives, possibly also social protection.[20] Building on the

---

[14] Gerber (n. 5 above), p. 74.   [15] *Ibid.*

[16] M. E. Streit and W. Mussler, 'The economic constitution of the European Community: From "Rome" to "Maastricht"', *ELJ* 1 (1995), 10.

[17] W. Röpke, 'Zwischenbilanz der Europäischen Wirtschaftsintegration. Kritische Nachlese' in *ORDO Jahrbuch*, 1959, 87; Streit and Mussler (n. 16 above), pp. 5–30. Röpke has often been said to be part of the ordoliberal school and is equally often credited as one of the fathers of the social market economy. Gerber did however indicate that Röpke's thinking differed in a number of ways from mainstream ordoliberalism because of an increased attention to values: Gerber (n. 5 above), p. 32. On Röpke's value orientations and his thinking, see J. Zmirak, *Wilhelm Röpke: Swiss localist, global economist* (Wilmington: ISI Books, 2001).

[18] W. Sauter, *Competition Law and Industrial Policy in the EU* (Oxford: Oxford University Press, 1997), p. 47.

[19] T. Drinoczi, 'Some elements of the economic constitution of the EU: Social market economy and relevant fundamental rights', *Free Law Journal* 1(1) (2005), 68.

[20] Joerges and Rödl (n. 9 above), p. 6.

ordoliberal premises, social market theorists argued that a balance should be developed between the rule of law, undistorted competition, individual freedom and social protection.[21] State powers should be clearly embedded and delineated in an economic constitutional framework and should allow government actors to restore the social balance in an economic order. Some scholars have labelled this 'liberal interventionism'.[22] Most recently, the importance of the role of social policy in an economic framework has been demonstrated by the Lisbon Treaty's explicit referral to a 'social market economy' as a policy goal.[23] Not unlike the original ordoliberal model, the framework itself limits the scope of public policy and action.[24]

Despite the shift from orthodox ordoliberal thought to an integration of social and market policies, the 'economic constitution' remained in place as an analytical tool in legal scholarship. However, its role has changed. From being a normative blueprint for a legal order in which economic rules constituted ends in themselves, economic constitution research grew more analytical.[25] Economic constitutionalism evolved into a description of a limited number of provisions in the Treaties and of their interpretation by the Court of Justice of the European Union. Those provisions and interpretations were named European 'economic constitutional law'. Analysis has so far focused on specific economic provisions in the EC Treaty (now Treaty on the Functioning of the European Union or TFEU), such as the free movement rules,[26] competition and industrial policy rules[27] or the relationship between competition and free movement rules.[28] More recently, services of general economic interest,[29]

---

[21] Joerges (n. 4 above), p. 468.

[22] W. Röpke therefore criticised continuing discretionary European Integration, see Röpke (n. 17 above).

[23] Art. 3.3 TEU.   [24] Joerges and Rödl (n. 9 above), pp. 17–19.

[25] G. Farjat, 'La Constitution économique de l'Europe et le couplage droit – économie' in Le Giepi (ed.), *La Constitution économique de l'Union Européenne* (Brussels: Bruylant, 2008), p. 89.

[26] M. P. Maduro, *We the Court: The European Court of Justice and the European economic constitution – a critical reading of Article 30 of the EC Treaty* (Oxford: Hart, 2000).

[27] Sauter (n. 18 above).

[28] J. Baquero Cruz, *Between Competition and Free Movement: The economic constitutional law of the European Community* (Oxford: Hart, 2002).

[29] See P. Behrens, 'Public services and the internal market: An analysis of the Commission's Communication on services of general interest in Europe', *European Business Organisation Law Review* 2 (2001), 469–92, analysing services of general interest within the framework of the economic constitution (the latter framework does however remain implicit); see as well O. Duperon, 'Service public ou service d'intérêt économique général?' in Le Giepi (ed.), *La Constitution économique de l'Union Européenne* (Brussels: Bruylant, 2008), pp. 223–38. For more detail see Neergaard, ch. 7 in this volume.

budgetary principles[30] and environmental protection[31] have equally been scrutinised.

It is clear that economic constitutional law analyses serve other goals than those addressed by the original economic constitution. From a model to aspire to, the 'economic constitution' has evolved into a tool for analysis of the general EU Treaty framework.[32]

Adopting a somewhat different approach, we develop in the following sections a normative account of possible components of an economic constitution and assess whether these components are present in the current EU Treaties. It will be argued that this is not or not entirely the case, so that the current EU Treaties at best constitute an 'open economic constitution', and perhaps no economic constitution at all.

III   Components of an economic constitution

In order to enrich economic constitution research, its conceptual boundaries have to be reconsidered. This section provides an overview of essential components of an economic constitution. The presence of these components reflects the nature and outlook of a given economic order.

It is accepted that an economic constitution should at least contain provisions determining the choice for an economic system, provisions providing for fundamental rights and provisions concerning competences of (governmental or non-governmental) economic actors.[33] We would like to add a number of additional components suitable to shape and structure economic policy-making, which would lead to the following list:

- choices among economic and non-economic values (hierarchisation)
- translation of the values and choices in legal principles, principles of good governance and/or rights

---

[30] C. Flaesch-Mougin, 'Les aspects constitutionnels du budget de l'Union européenne' in Le Giepi (ed.), *La Constitution économique de l'Union Européenne* (Brussels: Bruylant, 2008), pp. 181–94.

[31] I. Büschel, 'La constitution économique de l'Union européenne et l'environnement' in Le Giepi (ed.), *La Constitution économique de l'Union Européenne* (Brussels: Bruylant, 2008), pp. 279–94.

[32] Compare L. J. Constantinesco, 'La Constitution économique de la CEE', 13 *RTDE* (1977), 249. Constantinesco argues that an economic constitution reflects the structures of a given economic setting. The choice for a specific setting is not considered to be part of the constitution itself.

[33] T. Drinoczi, 'An introduction to the economic constitution(s) in Europe', www.eu-consent.net/library/deliverables/D11b_Team_5.pdf, pp. 11, 15, 22.

- guidelines and procedures for balancing the translated values where necessary
- a division of competences between different competent authorities
- instruments of decision-making
- enforcement mechanisms and supervisory tools
- foreign (economic) relations principles
- constitutional modification rules.

A   Values

The first component is the choice for a type of economic order. Choices can vary between very simple market, centrally planned or mixed economy models that involve conflicting economic and non-economic values. Choices made will determine the systemic relationship between the legal and economic systems and the ways in which the economy will be structured and upheld.[34] Political choices made at the time of the adoption of a constitutional framework will eventually provide an initial roadmap for economic policy.[35]

A choice will almost never appear directly from a constitutional text. The choice for a particular economic order can rather be extracted from the values reflected in that constitution. Values translated into legal principles (or principles of good economic governance) constitute the essential basis upon which the economic constitution is built. In van Gerven's view, economic values are reflected in legal principles underlying economic law provisions imposing rights and obligations to authorities and private persons alike.[36] They thus determine the nature and limits of economic policy-making.

Written constitutions often seem to contain only a limited number of legal principles, from which underlying economic values can be extracted. Scholars mainly identified as such principles the French

---

[34] A. Hatje, 'The economic constitution' in A. Von Bogdandy and J. Bast (eds.), *Principles of European Constitutional Law* (Oxford: Hart, 2006), p. 590.

[35] P. Verloren van Themaat, 'Recht en Economische Orde. Een oud probleem in een nieuw gewaad', *SEW* (1977), 262. They also guide the division of competences between the legislative and the judiciary. See P. Verloren van Themaat, 'Die Aufgabenverteilung zwischen dem Gesetzgeber und dem Europäischen Gerichtshof bei der Gestaltung der Wirtschaftsverfassung und der Europäischen Gemeinschaften' in E. J. Estmäcker, H. Möller and H.-P. Schwarz (eds.), *Eine Ordnungspolitik für Europa. Festschrift für Hans von der Groeben zu seinem 80. Geburtstag* (Baden Baden: Nomos, 1987), p. 425.

[36] W. van Gerven, 'Schets Van een Belgisch economisch grondslagenrecht', *SEW* (1971), 418.

revolutionary ideals of freedom, equality and solidarity,[37] said to be inherent in most modern Western European constitutions. However, it has also been acknowledged that these three values merely serve as classifying devices and would not suffice as foundations of an entire economic constitutional framework.[38] Furthermore, simply listing these three values next to each other would underestimate the complex yet necessary effort to balance values in a specific economic constitution.

The question arises as to whether any hierarchy between concrete values exists and whether, and if so how, different values have to be weighed against each other in concrete situations. The economic constitution should make clear how that weighing effort should take place. To give an example, does equality (including equal protection of everyone through legislation, as indirectly reflected in consumer protective provisions) have unconditional primacy over free market provisions or mechanisms? How can the concept of solidarity be aligned with the idea of individual freedom? What about the relationship between environmental protection and freedom of enterprise? The economic constitution should develop, or create the possibility of developing, a framework within which these questions can be answered and relationships and priorities between those values can be established. Balancing those principles constitutes an essential adjudicatory task in concretely defined cases. The institutional division of competences will determine whether the economic constitution itself or an institutional actor operating within the economic constitution engages in that adjudicatory task.

The choice of values and of their internal hierarchy results from a choice made by the competent actors in the economic order. Often, a close connection with political actors will exist so that the values provide guidelines for the economic policy of a certain economic area at a certain time.[39]

B Fundamental rights and balancing procedures

Fundamental rights could accompany legal principles in an economic constitution. Rights then mainly appear as a translation of values into

---

[37] P. Verloren van Themaat, 'Het Economisch grondslagenrecht Van de Europese Gemeenschappen' in *Liber Amicorum J. Mertens de Wilmars* (Antwerpen: Kluwer, 1982), pp. 379–81.

[38] *Ibid.*

[39] See also C. Joerges, 'States without a market? Comments on the German Constitutional Court's Maastricht judgment and a plea for interdisciplinary discourses', *EIOP* 1(20) (1997), http://papers.ssrn.com/sol3/papers.cfm?abstract_id=302713.

subjective entitlements. From an economic constitutional point of view, market operators are granted rights that facilitate their operations within the economic system. However, in order for fundamental rights to be part of an economic constitution, the legal system concerned has to recognise the concept of subjective rights, to be invoked by a person (natural or legal) against another person.

If that choice is made and fundamental rights are recognised as part of the economic constitution, some of those fundamental rights will appear to be more closely connected to economic life than others. Drinoczi engaged in an analysis of diverse European Union Member States' constitutional provisions and considered the right to property to be an economic fundamental right par excellence.[40] Freedom of enterprise is also mentioned as a typical fundamental right within an economic constitution.[41] That does not however imply that only those rights can play a role in an economic constitution. Rather, the extent to which fundamental rights are part of an economic constitution will be determined by the more general question how those constitutional values should be balanced. Just like procedures for balancing values (see above section III.A), procedures for balancing rights should therefore also be part of an economic constitution.

C Division of competences

An economic constitution usually also contains a division of competences between different authorities and market operators.[42] Competences could be granted to governmental agencies on central, regional, local political or economic levels. Purely private organisations such as professional associations or market operators might be granted competences as well.

It has been argued that an economic constitution should provide limits to the economic power of government and of private actors.[43] A division of competences is generally considered as the most efficient way to impose such limits (in contrast to the ordoliberal position which held that power should not be divided but contained). Based on a division of competences, Maduro subdivided three models of economic

---

[40] Drinoczi (n. 33 above), p. 16. Compare Art. 345 TFEU ('This Treaty shall in no way prejudice the rules in Member States governing the system of property ownership') and the protection of property rights through Art. 17 of the Charter of Fundamental Rights.
[41] Drinoczi (n. 33 above), p. 19.   [42] Hatje (n. 34 above), p. 590.   [43] *Ibid.*

constitution. The centralised model emphasises competences for economic regulation and ordering (and thus weighing different values and competences) within a supranational central organ, stating the vision and choice that the only way to regulate the market is through centralism.[44] A second model concerns decentralisation and makes Member States competent to determine their own economic policies, recognising each other's choices as being equal and supporting the ideal of a Common Market through non-discrimination.[45] The third, so-called competitive model is situated between the two others. It focuses on fundamental rights as being essential sources for legitimate supranational action.[46] This model emphasises individual freedom, an open market, free competition in general and freedom to contract and property-rights protection specifically.[47] Maduro himself recognised that the models are only abstract idealisations of reality.[48] Nevertheless, they can guide and structure choices made in a more orderly way.

D   Other components of an economic constitution

The following components support and enforce the choices, values and division of competences. They are crucial in any developed economic constitution, as they 'bring to life' the choices and values.

Instruments of decision-making are necessary to execute the values founding the economic constitution. Economic policy initiatives need to be implemented using instruments which the economic constitution provides for. As indicated, those instruments are embedded in a larger framework of values which need to be weighed. However, the instruments have to be neutral to some extent, able to support different (sets of) values.[49]

The use of legal instruments to safeguard economic policy choices and values requires at least some degree of surveillance or supervision. Surveillance can come in many variations, ranging from (close to) absence of any supervision to complete state supervision. In the European framework, the surveillance can be supranational, national or a combination of both. Surveillance or supervision necessarily requires enforcement in order to be effective. Enforcement may again vary, e.g. from purely private enforcement by market operators and self-regulation to public (governmental) enforcement, through public

---

[44] Maduro (n. 26 above), p. 110.   [45] Ibid.   [46] Ibid.   [47] Ibid.
[48] Drinoczi (n. 33 above), p. 30.   [49] Hatje (n. 34 above), p. 591.

authorities with competence to impose sanctions subject to judicial review.

Political constitutions at national level often cover foreign policy, reflecting the need for any political community to entertain relationships with other polities. In an economic constitution, the need for 'foreign policy' elements appears at least as strong: the economic constitution organises, defines and structures the basic framework of economic operations within a determined economic order. No economic order, not even a global one, does however operate in a vacuum. There will always be some interaction with other small-scale or larger economic orders. It is hereby submitted that the economic constitution should make clear how relationships are entertained with other economic orders (including access for foreign economic operators to the economic order), especially when the economic system pretends to constitute an 'open market'.[50]

Political constitutions equally contain provisions that recognise the principles of transition and modification, which allow the framework to adapt to specific needs. Just as contractual relationships can only be terminated in specific ways, a political constitution only can be modified using specific procedures, like general elections,[51] referenda[52] or specific voting requirements, offering guarantees for stability without endangering flexibility. Some national political constitutions even contain provisions that are supposed to remain unchanged (the German *Ewigkeitsgarantie*)[53] as long as the constitution remains in force. Incorporating similar provisions in an economic constitution appears to require a formal constitutional text.

IV   EU Treaties as economic constitution?

The following paragraphs assess whether and to what degree the components of an economic constitution mentioned above are present in the current EU Treaties.

---

[50] van Themaat (n. 37 above), p. 372, states that this external openness did e.g. not constitute a value within the former Comecon countries.
[51] See e.g. Art. 195 Belgian Constitution; Chapter 8 Dutch Constitution.
[52] See e.g. Art. 89 French Constitution.
[53] This untranslatable technical term of German constitutional law refers to Art. 79(3) of the German Constitution. That provision envelops a number of unchangeable fundamental constitutional principles.

A   Values

Article 4 of the pre-Lisbon EC Treaty mentioned an open market economy with free competition, as well as an economic and monetary union[54] as two guiding policy principles. Post-Lisbon, these principles are no longer present in Article 4 but have been moved further down (Article 119 TFEU), which might be seen by some as an indication that these principles no longer result from a fundamental choice. In addition, a number of crucial economic values and choices are now to be found in protocols annexed to the Treaties rather than in the Treaties' texts themselves. As was well-publicised, the role of the EU in ensuring undistorted competition in the internal market is now only explicitly mentioned in Protocol No. 27. Interestingly, a number of important values are written out in the Protocol on Services of General Interest.[55]

Despite their relocation, fundamental economic principles continue to provide the Treaties' texts. The principle of free movement is still omni-present.[56] Additional economic principles are stated in Article 119(1) and (2) TFEU, under the specific heading on economic and monetary policy. That Article explicitly refers to the internal market, co-ordination of economic policy, common goals and an open market economy.

The internal market concept by nature presupposes a market system. From that market-oriented perspective, concepts like openness, free competition and the economic and monetary union provide hard values that interact with other values such as the 'social market economy'.[57] A number of competing goals are defined in the Treaties. Article 3.3 of the Treaty on the European Union (TEU) assures equal treatment for women and men, in order to attain the goals set by the Treaties. Discrimination based on nationality is prohibited (Article 10 TEU) and solidarity between Member States constitutes an explicit goal (Article 3.3 TEU). Loyalty (Article 4.3 TEU), decision-making in conformity with the principles of proportionality and subsidiarity (Article 5 TEU), respect for human health (Article 11 TEU) and con-sumer protection (Article 12 TEU) are also mentioned. The protocols accompanying the Lisbon Treaty also explicitly incorporate values.

---

[54] Hatje (n. 34 above), p. 595.
[55] OJ C 306, 17 December 2007, 158. Art. 1 elaborates on shared values in services of general interest.
[56] Art. 26 TFEU. The Union's enforcement role is only to be found in Protocol No. 27 as mentioned above.
[57] Art. 3 TEU.

As already mentioned, the Protocol on Services of General Interest is an important example in that respect.

It is not entirely clear to what extent all these references reflect exclusively economic values underlying the Treaty framework. In our view, they should not be overestimated. The Articles also refer to the 'principle' of an open market economy. The open market economy thus constitutes a guiding principle that is to be taken seriously when developing a European economic policy. It cannot be held to reflect a definite all-determining choice. The Treaty framework does not explicitly and clearly opt for one specific market economy model. Rather, a large scope for flexible interpretation exists[58] and the determination of concrete economic policies is left open.[59]

As observed, values could be translated in vague principles of good economic governance or in legally enforceable rights. The values stated in the Treaties only provide clues as to what legal principles of good economic governance could be derived. The Treaties themselves do not however mention concrete procedures or guidelines for good governance.

B   Balancing mechanisms

Although liberty, equality and solidarity may not as such provide the foundations for an economic constitution (supra, III.A) many values identified in European economic law have been classified within one of those headings. Free movement of goods and free competition are said to stress the equality between undertakings within the economic framework of the Common Market. Even the value of a social market economy would express equality linked to solidarity and freedom. These core values can however be interpreted in various and often conflicting ways. They remain vague and hierarchisation is by and large absent.

The EU Treaties do not set out with sufficient clarity a procedure for the weighing of values. A considerable amount of discretionary power remains with political and judicial authorities.[60] The enhanced role of the Charter of Fundamental Rights in the post-Lisbon framework[61] provide a key example of judicial discretion. The broad economic policy guidelines reflect political discretion.

---

[58] Hatje (n. 34 above), p. 594. The author considers the open market to be a definite choice, which would seem to somewhat contradict the claim of elasticity.
[59] Sauter (n. 18 above), p. 50.   [60] Ibid.
[61] Charter of Fundamental Rights, published 17 December 2007, OJ C 303, 1.

Fundamental rights appear in many different places in EU law (e.g. in Treaty provisions and in ECtHR judgments, which the ECJ respects through the 'general principles of Union law'). Fundamental economic rights are expressed in Article 34 TFEU concerning measures having equivalent effect and in other anti-discrimination provisions in the Treaties. They appear to directly guarantee the protection of specific underlying values in the economic constitution.

The protection that fundamental economic rights can offer will never be complete and will only relate to individual problems. It has been argued that those rights may be set aside, albeit subtly, amounting to a de facto unenforceability of some of them.[62] The protection that fundamental economic rights can offer may be uncertain, as much will depend on the way in which courts, but especially the Court of Justice, apply and (re-)shape the economic constitutional principles. The ECJ appears not to defend the values of open markets and free competition to the full, but will weigh different interests[63] (an approach which some have characterised as 'conservative'[64]). The ECJ determines the relative weight of different values.[65] The judges consider whether or not other values or principles can justify measures that at first sight do not conform with the ideal of integrated markets.[66] It is important to stress that Treaty Articles themselves (e.g. free movement and competition law Articles) often demand such weighing of interests (by judges, by undertakings etc.).[67] Although judges play a role, this will always be limited. A judgment as such may provide insights into current economic constitutional relationships, but it will not be capable of establishing the infinite durability of those relationships. Judgments focus on a specific case, with specific facts and specific consequences.

The lack of choices in the Treaty framework is to a certain (but limited) extent compensated by the so-called 'broad economic policy guidelines', adopted in accordance with Articles 5 and 121 TFEU. Member States are required to co-ordinate their economic policies as a matter of European Union law. In order to attain that purpose, a specific procedure is followed, whereby the supranational level adopts

---

[62] See in that respect as well, Hatje (n. 34 above), p. 629.

[63] W. Wils, 'The search for the rule in Article 30 EEC: Much ado about nothing?', 17 *ELRev* (1993), 478.

[64] G. Wils, 'De bijdrage van het Hof van Justitie to de ontwikkeling van een Europese markteconomie' ['The contribution of the Court of Justice to the development of a European market economy'], unpubl. PhD thesis University of Leuven (1994), p. 754.

[65] Maduro (n. 26 above), p. 151.   [66] Wils (n. 63 above), p. 490.

[67] Wils (n. 64 above), p. 750.

'guidelines' to help Member States adapt their policies. These guidelines can be considered to constitute concrete applications of divergent values and principles underlying the European economic framework. It is interesting to see how solidarity or social policy values and principles play an important role in the development of those economic guidelines. The 'social' is present in the 'economic'. The 'economic policy' in the broad economic policy guidelines refers to the entirety of measures that should serve specific goals and be used to influence and steer the economic process.[68] 'Economic policy' in this regard concerns and promotes interventionist measures in the originally conceived free market.

Clearly, the European Union defines its economic policy in broader terms than the realisation of the internal market. This is mirrored in non-economic elements being contained in the broad economic policy guidelines, often by reference to the Lisbon Strategy goal which allures to sustainability and social cohesion.[69] As more specific examples, the 2001 guidelines refer to environmental protection and sustainable development,[70] and the 2005–8 guidelines stress gender mainstreaming.[71]

The guidelines remain essentially non-binding. Their enforcement may have been reinforced somewhat through Article 121(4) of the TFEU, according to which warnings and recommendations can be sent to Member States.[72] However, they do not impose concrete economic policy measures and are open-ended. They only provide basic guidance for choices to be made and are not reflected in the Treaty structure itself. That openness could create room for concrete measures that might be considered more or less interventionist. From this perspective, the European economic constitution rather consists of a European economic constitutional framework or model within the boundaries of which changing political or economic circumstances can influence constitutional aspects. The question remains of course whether such an openness to change is desirable for a constitution or, more fundamentally, whether one can speak of a constitution at all if such openness to change persists.[73]

---

[68] Hatje (n. 34 above), p. 606.
[69] 2003 Broad Economic Policy Guidelines, *European Economy* (2003), p. 59.
[70] 2001 Broad Economic Policy Guidelines, *European Economy* (2001), pp. 76–7: Enhance environmental sustainability.
[71] 2005–8 Broad Economic Policy Guidelines, *European Economy* (2005), p. 37.
[72] See Drinoczi (n. 33 above), p. 31 on this as well.
[73] From an ordoliberal point of view, such finding of an open constitution would constitute quite a problem, since discretionary competences would be institutionalised within the framework itself.

Currently and for lack of clear choices in the treaties, the hierarchisation between economic values or their translations into legal principles is
left to political and judicial practice. The case law of the ECJ (in all its
limits) determines the balance between economic and non-economic
values in EU law. The ECJ has often clarified, in individual cases, the
relationships between general values and concrete competences reflected
in the Treaties. In the *Leclerc* case[74] it recognised that the general
principles expressed in the Treaty should be applied in connection to
the Treaty Titles elaborating upon those specific competence fields.
Those titles do indeed apply the general principles in practice, as confirmed by the Court in *Bettati*.[75] National authorities, judges and private
actors cannot as such invoke the violation of those values or that one
value has not been granted proper attention.

On the other hand, and as already indicated, the role of ECJ judgments is
limited in that these judgments concern specific cases only, with specific
facts and specific consequences. Moreover, the Court of Justice reasons that
it would take the place of governmental institutions if it would directly value
the choice of principles having been weighed.[76] This being so, and given the
relative lack of clear and stable value hierarchisation in the constitutional
treaties (see above), policy-makers can relatively easily, and under only
marginal judicial control, change the constitutional framework's concrete
application, as long as they leave the broad, vaguely determined framework
of values and principles intact. Given that the broad economic policy
guidelines are not really enforceable, it would seem that the European
economic constitution, to the degree it exists, appears as a soft constitution,
with the exception of claims that can be brought within the confines of
vested case law relating to competition law or the internal market.

In the end, two positions can be defended with respect to the lack of
value-weighing criteria. Either this could be a choice of the framers of the
economic constitution, or it could be considered a denial to make any
choice regarding the development of an economic constitution. Under
either position, the Treaties do not offer clear guidance.

---

[74] Case 229/83, *Association des Centres distributeurs Édouard Leclerc and ors. v. SARL
'Au blé vert' and ors.* [1985] ECR 1, para. 8.
[75] C-341/95 *Gianni Bettati* v. *Safety Hi-Tech Srl* [1998] ECR I-4355, para. 75: 'Article 3 of
the Treaty determines the fields and objectives to which the activities of the Community
are to relate. It thus lays down the general principles of the common market, which are to
be applied in conjunction with the respective chapters of the Treaty devoted to their
implementation.'
[76] van Themaat (n. 37 above), p. 356.

C   Division of competences

The pattern of indeterminacy is also found in the division of competences among economic policy-makers. Even though the Treaties confer some competences exclusively to Union institutions,[77] they also contain and promote a vast number of shared competences. Even to the extent that values are made explicit,[78] clear operative criteria to guide value-weighing are absent; delineation of competences in that respect is variable and somehow dependent on the values at stake in a concrete legal situation.

The most that can therefore be said is that the European economic constitution is structured as an open economic constitution. The outlook of the European economic order is not planned or conceived, but rather left to political and judicial authorities to develop on a case-by-case basis. The constitutional framework as such does not provide clarity on how those authorities should act.

D   Other elements of a European economic constitution

Supervision and enforcement are crucial additional components. It would be difficult if not impossible to judicially enforce the principles and values underlying the economic constitution, and some will argue that this is not even desirable. However, the values may be turned into fundamental subjective rights granted to e.g. market operators (including consumers) and these may very well be enforceable. The increasing 'direct effect' of those fundamental rights may provide for an indirect but adequate enforcement tool when different values or principles conflict. As mentioned above, it is however highly unlikely that the current system of ECJ-based fundamental rights enforcement reflects an economic constitution.

In addition to fundamental rights, the European Union is only beginning to structure market supervision in different fields of law. Major supervisory projects have been developed in financial services, in competition law and in regulated industries. All in all, EU-supervisors supplement the national supervisory mechanisms and provide for additional room for deliberation and analysis. No general guidelines or values as to the organisation of market supervision can be found in the

---

[77] See Arts. 4 TEU and 3–4 TFEU.

[78] The abovementioned protocol on services of general interest provides a summary of concrete values, but does not establish a clear hierarchy between them.

Treaties. Different supervisory strategies seem to have been developed in different fields of law.

As observed, it can be expected that an economic constitution also needs to make clear how relationships with other economic orders are structured. In an EU context, the focus would lie on third-country economic orders or other supranational economic systems. Relationships between supranational constellations and the national sub-constellations of Member States are not included in those principles: they appear (implicitly) from the division of competences. In relation to third countries and entities, the Treaty framework does provide for a common commercial policy, focusing on harmonious development of world trade. Other elements are, however, not made explicit. For example, extraterritoriality clauses in competition and tax law are not developed in the constitutional treaties but in secondary legislation or court rulings.[79]

Finally, questions arise as to whether the economic constitutional framework can be altered according to specific provisions on transition and modification. Of course, the general provisions on treaty amendment apply.[80] Apart from these, as already indicated, flexibility prevails over stability. Whereas amendment of a true economic constitution should be accompanied by guarantees that underlying fundamental values and principles are respected,[81] the constitutional Treaties allow for shifts in values to occur at any time.

E   Absence of a European economic constitution?

It was already clear that the Treaties did not represent an ordoliberal blueprint for regulating the economy altogether. The question therefore arose, what values and choices the current treaties reflect and how they are translated in legal principles and fundamental rights; whether they contain a clear division of competences between different competent authorities, instruments of decision-making, enforcement mechanisms and supervisory tools, foreign (economic) relations principles and constitutional modification rules.

---

[79] See in that respect the Commission Guidelines on the effect on trade concept in Arts. 81–2 of the Treaty, http://eur-lex.europa.eu/LexUriServ/LexUriServ.do?uri=CELEX:52004XC0427(06):EN:NOT.

[80] Art. 48 TEU; see K. Lenaerts and P. van Nuffel, *Constitutional Law of the European Union* (London: Sweet & Maxwell, 2005), pp. 341–4.

[81] According to van Themaat (n. 37 above), p. 373.

The analysis in this part made clear that the Treaties do not reflect a fully fledged economic constitution. They incorporate a number of values and choices that appear open-ended and conflicting. In addition, they do not provide definitive guidance in creating one type of economic order. Neither do they exclusively demand 'ultraliberal'[82] policies. It is even incorrect to argue that the Treaties promote any concrete economic choice over another at all.

V   The economic constitution and economic governance

Despite the absence of a true European economic constitution, economic policy initiatives feature prominently in current EU discourse. However, absent a clear Framework of how economic governance should proceed, different policy proposals risk to remain stuck in mere rhetoric.

This part traces the roots of the current discourse on economic governance back to the older 'corporate governance' debate. It will briefly highlight differences and similarities between corporate and EU 'government governance'. It will be argued that the two pillars of corporate governance – informal guidelines and practical workability – have not entirely been replicated in EU government governance. In addition to being limited by the very nature of the governance concept, the current EU discourse on 'economic governance' is also limited in scope. The final sections of this part will highlight those limits and argue for a more inclusive, workable and practical discourse of EU economic governance by relying on the European economic constitution.

A   From corporate governance to government governance

The roots of European (economic) governance can be traced to the original corporate governance debate in the eighties and nineties.

The corporate governance debate focuses on the appropriate organisation of the administration and management of companies in general, and on the possible conflicting interests of shareholders and

---

[82] Compare A. T. J. M. Jacobs, 'The social Janus head of the European Union: The social market economy versus ultraliberal policies' in J. Wouters, L. Verhey and P. Kiiver (eds.), *European Constitutionalism beyond Lisbon* (Antwerp: Intersentia, 2009), pp. 111–30. To be clear, the author does not claim that European constitutional Treaties demand or promote 'ultraliberal policies'.

management in particular. Corporate governance was considered a means to instil trust, integrity and honesty in corporate relationships. Those relationships were thought to be best served by regulation through voluntary, non-binding codes of best practice. The codes demonstrated a more flexible and adaptable approach to changing circumstances. Binding legal provisions only played a minor role.[83]

The contribution of the corporate governance debate in responding to the abovementioned problems and interests is twofold. It raises awareness of governance problems but also provides a set of very concrete recommendations, flexible enough to be tailored to different circumstances. Concrete provisions emphasise the structure, competences and functions of audit committees[84] and remuneration committees.[85] In addition, specific provisions on the composition of the board of directors, management responsibilities, poison pills, golden parachutes, supermajorities, voting mechanisms and institutional shareholders have all been developed.[86] Over time, the abovementioned recommendations have grown into foundations and testing hypotheses of corporate governance research.[87] For example, Bebchuk *et al.* analysed the impact of twenty-four essential concrete provisions thought to be beneficial for management–shareholder relationships.[88]

Those concrete proposals were originally created exclusively to fit private corporations. Legal literature has subsequently transposed the debate to Continental European publicly held entities, which are (partly)

---

[83] In December 1992, the so-called 'Cadbury Committee' (named after its President Sir Adrian Cadbury) released its 'Report of the Committee on the Financial Aspects of Corporate Governance' and the associated 'Code of Best Practices' with nineteen concrete recommendations to promote accountability of directors to shareholders and to society at large. Although not binding, the recommendations had an enormous impact as companies listed on the London Stock Exchange were required to state in their accounts whether they had followed the recommendations and to motivate non-compliance. The 2008 Combined Code of Corporate Governance and the 2010 UK Corporate Governance Code heavily rely on those original proposals and can be found at www.frc.org.uk.

[84] On the audit committee, see section C.3 (including subsections C.3.1–C.3.7) of the 2008 Combined Code.

[85] See section B.2. of the 2008 Combined Code.

[86] An interesting overview is provided in an annex to L. Bebchuk, A. Cohen and A. Farrell, 'What matters in corporate governance?', 22 *Review of Financial Studies* (2009), 783. All of those elements are equally laid out in the 2008 Combined Code.

[87] American corporate governance scholarship often relies on the work of the Investor Responsibility Research Center Institute, www.irrcinstitute.org.

[88] Bebchuk, Cohen and Farrell (n. 86 above).

owned by the very same governments that regulate and supervise the commercial environment in which they operate. Concrete recommendations for corporate governance in such undertakings were developed as well.[89]

The evolution from corporate governance of publicly held undertakings to government governance is a logical next step. The very same issues which the corporate governance debate aims to solve – promoting integrity, solving conflicts of interest, choosing between concentration or division of power – also affect the political decision-making process. The very idea of governance codes as a more informal tool for regulating and solving conflicts of interest in political entities is obviously appealing but should be handled with care. Governments may resemble corporations in certain ways – with the legislator as a shareholders' assembly and the executive as a board of directors – but they serve different social and public goals. Different kinds of recommendations would seem more appropriate. Moreover, if they have to be applicable to a wide range of states and governmental or public-interest organisations, they risk not being very concrete and practicable. Accordingly, they risk lacking one of the major strengths of the recommendations made in the framework of the corporate governance debate, as the latter recommendations are concrete.

In our view as economic lawyers, it would appear that this risk has indeed materialised on the EU level. For instance, the EU responded to calls for good 'government governance' in its own institutional structure. Faced with complicated and long-winding legislative procedures, the European Commission developed a governance initiative to make EU policy initiatives more flexible, accessible and adaptable.[90] The Commission defined governance as 'the rules, processes, and behaviour by which interests are articulated, resources are managed, and power is exercised in society. The way public functions are carried out, public resources are managed and public regulatory powers are exercised is the major issue to be addressed in that context.'[91] It suggested a distaste to binding legal rules, similar to corporate governance.

However, it is submitted that when it comes to developing concrete maxims beyond vague principles, EU governance initiatives do

---

[89] See W. Devroe, 'Deugdelijk bestuur van overheidsondernemingen. (autonome overheidsbedrijven, publiekrechtelijke naamloze vennootschappen)' ['Corporate governance of publicly held undertakings'], *Tijdschrift voor Rechtspersoon en Vennootschap* (1998), 461.

[90] See the White Paper on European Governance, COM (2001) 428 Final, adopted on 25 July 2001.

[91] COM (2003) 615 Final, adopted on 20 October 2003, p. 3.

not appear as successful as earlier corporate governance initiatives. Momentous EU documents developing good governance or better regulation proposals mainly focus on the instruments of good governance, rather than on finding workable or practical governance recommendations or maxims.[92]

B   Broadening the limited scope of 'economic governance' within the EU governance discourse

The more general claim about lack of concrete proposals or rules flowing from the EU's governance discourse equally applies to economic governance. In addition, the term 'economic governance' itself appears to be too limited in scope. At present, it is only used in relation to monetary and budgetary policy co-ordination. It is therefore submitted that refocusing the EU economic governance debate requires both a broader and a more concrete governance discourse.

European economic governance was mentioned as early as in April 2003 when the Commission claimed to have adopted 'an instrument for European economic governance'.[93] In reality, the Commission only adopted a new set of broad economic policy guidelines (see above section IV.B). More importantly, the mandate of the 'Working Group on Economic Governance' that reported to the European Convention on this subject was limited to monetary policy, economic policy and institutional issues in these spheres. The working group provided recommendations on different subjects, but did not reach agreement on financial services regulation or tax matters, subjects outside the traditional scope of macro-economic co-ordination.

Debates on economic governance gained new attention in light of the 2010 budgetary crises in different Member States. In response, a 'task force for European economic governance' was created.[94] Even though the president proclaimed that 'We need to strengthen economic governance, in institutional terms, in order to be able to act quicker and in a more coordinated and more efficient manner', his remarks did not appear to

---

[92] See on better regulation in general, J. Wiener, 'Better regulation in Europe', 59 *Current Legal Problems* (2006), 447.

[93] Press release IP/03/508, 8 April 2003.

[94] The task force consists of the president of the European Council, the finance ministers, and representatives of the Commission, the ECB and the Eurogroup countries. See for activities and developments www.european-council.europa.eu/the-president/taskforce. aspx and http://ec.europa.eu/economy_finance/eu/index_en.htm.

presuppose a wider scope for 'economic governance' as such.[95] The Communication accompanying the task force meeting considers European economic governance and macro-economic policy co-ordination to be synonyms.[96] It proposes a revision of surveillance tools for macro-economic policy in order to support the newly created European stabilisation mechanism. Proposals in that regard are limited to adaptations for macro-economic surveillance, focusing on national fiscal frameworks, the excessive deficit procedure and compliance with the stability and growth pact.[97] Current discussions on European monetary policy are thus unlikely to provoke a shift to a broader interpretation of economic governance.

The strengthening of macro-economic policy co-ordination may distract attention from the need to develop a more inclusive economic governance concept. In order to take the Commission's words seriously and give credit to its 'desire to retain a broad perspective on European governance',[98] a fruitful debate on economic governance should supersede a purely macro-economic approach. Themes like regulation and implementation of rules, supervision, state and market, and ethics and integrity also deserve attention in a debate on EU economic governance, but are currently neglected. Only by including them within the confines of the debate, can a more enhanced European economic governance debate, focusing on practical recommendations, be developed.[99]

Supervision or surveillance of markets obviously reflects ex-ante good governance. To counter the current 'proliferation of supervisors' in the EU, a more integrated approach to supervision is needed, which no longer remains limited to a particular sector, level of authority or country but recognises supervision as a study object in its own right. The structure of national market supervisors is not harmonised at all in current EU practice. The drawbacks of this situation include, apart from the increased cost of supervision, the risks of legal uncertainty, of forum shopping and of inconsistencies and tensions between individual

---

[95] See remarks by Herman Van Rompuy following the first meeting, PCE 102/10, www. consilium.europa.eu/uedocs/cms_data/docs/pressdata/en/ec/114606.pdf, p. 1.

[96] *Reinforcing Economic Policy Coordination*, Communication COM (2010) 250, http://ec. europa.eu/economy_finance/articles/euro/documents/2010-05-12-com%282010%2925 0_final.pdf, pp. 2–3.

[97] *Ibid.* nn. 4–6.

[98] See e.g. the Commission's *Report on European Governance*, COM (2002) 705 of 11 December 2002, ec.europa.eu/governance/docs/comm_rapport_en.pdf.

[99] See on broadening economic governance W. Devroe, 'Challenges for economic governance and economic law in Europe', *Maastricht Journal of European and Comparative Law* 10 (2003), 335–44.

supervisors and regulators. More systematic thinking about supervision and prevention mechanisms in the light of more general economic choices to prevent market failure would provide a more in depth insight into the stakes in European economic governance.

The ethics debate too goes far beyond the scope of prevention in macro-economic policy co-ordination. Partly in response to a number of scandals in Europe, more stringent requirements of transparency and accountability have reached private market operators. New standards are developed[100] and applied more vigorously by ever more supervisors. The macro-economic reform proposals now intend to impose similar ethical standards on governments and aim at compliance through preventive mechanisms. Those standards nevertheless play a major role outside the scope of macro-economic co-ordination.

The contents of those debates are well-known. Missing from the picture, however, are concrete proposals, similar to those developed in order to improve corporate governance and reaching beyond macro-economic policy co-ordination.

C   Economic governance in terms of a European economic constitution

Thinking in terms of a European economic constitution may be of use when aiming to develop what is currently missing. We mentioned that a choice for a particular economic system was fundamental within an economic constitution (see section III.A above) but that EU Treaties mostly leave that choice open (see section IV.A above).

An economic constitution analysis may be of use here in four different ways. First, it would require choices to be made explicit and concrete recommendations to be made. Secondly, those choices and recommendations would be reflected within a framework and can be assessed and enforced in light of that framework. Thirdly, judicial actors within that framework would be capable of enforcing the limits of the economic constitution. Governance debates mainly focus on administrative action and the judicial role is mainly relegated to legal provisions outside the scope of governance debates. The economic constitution can provide a bridge between judicial and political discretion and their intertwinement. Fourthly, and finally, the economic constitution would guide

---

[100] One thinks of the new International Accounting Standards or the strengthened rules of conduct for financial intermediaries.

practitioners' and citizens' expectations. To the extent that the EU represents clear choices, controversial governance initiatives can be mitigated by the boundaries of the economic constitution. Citizens will equally be able better to assert rights and duties imposed or proposed in those governance initiatives. All in all, the balance between economic and non-economic rule-making would somehow be restored in a coherent theoretical framework.

Such ambitions may require a different approach to legal scholarship. A persuasive model of economic constitution may have to be developed, which does more than describe the indeterminate status quo of the Treaty framework (compare section II above on 'economic constitutional law') and yet provides concrete guidance to economic policy-makers. Thinking about a (new) European economic constitution at least challenges scholars to devise alternative models and persuade others. Debates on an EU economic constitution provide an immense opportunity to rediscover and uncover underlying values and possible choices made in economic governance, or in governance at large, within the EU on both the national and supranational level.

VI   Conclusions

This chapter discussed the role of the economic constitution as a structuring device for EU economic policy-making. It summarised the core components of the economic constitution and assessed whether or not the EU Treaties present an economic constitution. At the same time, it demonstrated the limited scope of current European economic governance debates and the need for a more enhanced economic constitutional structure to feed those debates.

It is clear that an economic constitution lays down fundamental economic rules and principles that formulate an economic order. Not every legal provision entailing economic consequences is incorporated into an economic constitution but only the foundations or essentials of an economic order, even if those foundations are not economic by nature.

What is currently labelled 'economic constitution' research often focuses on specific economic provisions in EU Treaties, such as the rules on free movement, competition and industrial policy, the relationship between free competition and free movement rules, services of general economic interest, budgetary principles and environmental protection. However, an economic-constitution approach is to be distinguished from an economic-constitutional law approach which is more positive-law-oriented and favours the study of constitutional law provisions regarding economic choices. Instead of starting out from the analysis of a particular set of rules we identified components of an economic constitution and checked whether they are present and how they are modelled in the European constitutional Treaties.

The following components of an economic constitution appear essential to us: economic and non-economic values, choices made between these values (hierarchisation of values) and translation of the values and choices into legal principles and/or rights; general economic objectives; guidelines and procedures for balancing the values where necessary; a division of competences between different authorities; instruments of decision-making; supervision and/or enforcement mechanisms; foreign (economic) relations principles; and constitutional modification rules.

Not all of these elements are present in the current European constitutional Treaties. The European constitutional framework does not represent an original ordoliberal blueprint for regulating the economy altogether. Rather on the contrary, its open-ended and seemingly conflicting provisions do leave much policy room for value-weighing between economic freedom and social policy-making. Most strikingly, no choice is made between different, sometimes potentially conflicting, values and objectives and no mechanisms are put in place to allow for a weighing of the different values and interests (other than ECJ case law, which by nature focuses on specific cases in a specific, also factual, context). It would appear that Europe 'wants it all'. All that can be confirmed is that a market system has been opted for. Within that market system, the constitutional Treaties allow for divergent policies to be developed.

Consequently, it could not be doubted whether the European constitutional Treaties constitute, contain or reflect any economic constitution at all. To the extent that they do, the European economic constitution seems at most structured as an 'open economic constitution', leaving room for ample inclusion of values by way of interpretation. As shown in this chapter, this will have several consequences, two of which deserve to be stressed. First, the content of European constitutional Treaties does not provide an excuse for not developing social integration nor for decoupling economic and social integration. Secondly, the search for a European economic constitution will necessarily have to be extended from the constitutional Treaties alone to other parts of economic policy and law, such as secondary legislation and case law. The inclusion of governance initiatives within that structure can enrich both economic constitution research and practical governance proposals.

PART II

Emanations of tensions between economic and social integration

5

Circular migration: A triple win situation? Wishful thinking or a serious option for a sustainable migration policy?

HILDEGARD SCHNEIDER AND ANJA WIESBROCK

I   Introduction

Ten years ago the Lisbon Strategy proclaimed that the EU was to become 'the most dynamic and competitive knowledge-based economy in the world'. In order to guarantee sustainable economic growth, full employment and an increase of highly skilled labour participants is considered to be essential. Beyond this, international migration must also be regarded in its global context, both socially and economically. From economists' perspectives, liberalisation of migration will achieve greater welfare benefits than liberalisation of trade in goods and services and of capital flows.[1]

In the light of Europe's declining fertility rates and an ageing population, the Member States and the EU, specifically in the 2009 Stockholm Programme, have argued in favour of a more demand-driven immigration policy even in a period of economic crisis. At the same time, the idea of temporary and specifically circular labour migration has regained increasing popularity.

Rather than seeing the process of return migration as a permanent phenomenon, scholars have identified more temporary patterns of return and re-migration that allegedly create a 'triple win situation' by benefiting countries of origin, host countries as well as individual migrants. This phenomenon has been called 'circular migration', indicating cyclical migratory movements and return as a stage in the process

---

[1] J. P. Trachtman, 'The role of international law in economic migration', Society of International Economic Law Working Paper 24 (2008); R. Freeman, 'People flows in globalization', National Bureau of Economic Research Working Paper 12315 (2006).

of moving between countries.[2] Circular migration is seen as a potentially effective tool for fostering economic development in the sending countries. At the international level, the concept of circular migration has been advocated by the United Nations, the World Bank,[3] and the International Organisation for Migration (IOM)[4] and the Global Commission on International Migration (GCIM).[5] In the EU, the concept of circular migration has been introduced more recently within the discourse on migration and development. The European Commission has stressed the development potential of circular migration within the context of labour migration to the EU. The so-called 'Blue Card Directive', adopted in May 2009, is intended to stimulate circular migration patterns.[6] In addition, national actors, such as the UK House of Commons[7] and the Dutch Social Economic Council (SER)[8] have issued reports investigating the possibilities of circular migration. In the broad policy discourses, circular migration is often presented as the 'triple win' situation being in the interest of the migrant, the home as well as the receiving state, a model of migrant management that would maximise gains and minimise costs of international human mobility.[9] Thus, migration policy becomes an integral part of economic development policies.

However, the question arises to what extent the cherished concept of circular migration differs from older forms of temporary labour migrations. The so-called 'guest-worker' policies of the post-war period had a similar objective of securing a temporary supply of labour whilst preventing the permanent settlement of labour migrants. It is open to doubt

---

[2] S. Ammassari and R. Black, *Harnessing the Potential of Migration and Return to Promote Development: Applying concepts to West Africa*, IOM Migration Research Series, 5 (2001), p. 26.

[3] World Bank, *International Labor Migration: Eastern Europe and the former Soviet Union*, World Bank, Europe and Central Asia Region (Washington DC, 2006).

[4] IOM, *World Migration 2005: Costs and benefits of international migration* (2005).

[5] Global Commission on International Migration, *Migration in an Interconnected World: New directions for actions* (2005).

[6] On the EU Blue Card see K. Eisele, *Making Europe More Competitive for Highly-skilled Immigration*, Maastricht Graduate School of Governance, Policy Brief No. 2 (2010).

[7] House of Commons International Development Committee, *Migration and Development: How to make migration work for poverty reduction* (London: The Stationery Office, 2004).

[8] Social and Economic Council, *Ontwerpadvies Arbeidsmigratiebeleid* (2007), p. 13.

[9] F. Pastore, 'Circular migration: Background note for the meeting of Experts on Legal Migration', Rabat, 3 and 4 March 2008, p. 3.

whether the concept of circular migration differs from those schemes, which are generally considered as a failure.[10]

Furthermore, immigration schemes and integration requirements as currently applied by various EU Member States may well counteract any form of circular migration potentially benefiting all parties involved.[11] Rather than seeing circular migration as a tool for fostering economic development in the countries of origin, national politicians seem to perceive it as a tool for control and limitation of any form of labour migration from third countries.

Hence, the legal framework in the Member States does little to stimulate circular migration. Notwithstanding existing differences in immigration, integration and labour migration policies among EU Member States, the main features of the national legal arrangements can be characterised as strict immigration requirements, limited duration of stay, uncertain prospects for return, tying of workers to specific employers and, in some Member States, compulsory and rigid integration measures for migrant workers and their families. Increasingly, EU Member States have introduced pre-entry integration/language requirements with an integration/language test to be passed at the national embassy before a visa is granted (e.g. the Netherlands, Germany and more recently France and the UK).[12] The national rules concerning highly skilled migrants are mostly not as severe as in the case of other economic migrants but do not guarantee e.g. an automatic right to return and free entry and residence in another Member State. It is questionable whether this legal framework coheres in any way with the concept of circular migration.

European migration policies are at a crossroad. Two quite different goals have dominated the migration policy discussion in the EU and the Member States during the past decade. On the one hand, many Member States have articulated the need for a vigorous integration policy.[13] On the other hand, due to demographic developments, the demand for highly skilled workers becomes more and more urgent in order to fulfil the targets now set by the Europe 2020 strategy in order to keep Europe's economic position on the global market. While some national polities

---

[10] S. Castles, 'The guest-worker in Western Europe: An obituary', *International Migration Review* 20 (1986), 761. See also Castles's reaction on the new temporary migration schemes: S. Castles, 'Back to the future? Can Europe meet its labour needs through temporary migration?', International Migration Institute (IMI) Working Paper 1 (2006).

[11] See ch. 8 by Carrera and Wiesbrock in this volume on the civic integration of immigrants.

[12] *Ibid.*, pp. 199ff.   [13] *Ibid.*, pp. 203ff.

are requesting increasingly stricter integration requirements (e.g. Denmark, France, Germany, the Netherlands and the UK), the same Member States try with various legislative initiatives to attract highly skilled migrants to enter their labour market.[14]

When the EU seeks to encourage circular and temporary migration schemes with the declared aim to stimulate economic migration of mainly highly skilled migrants to Europe while avoiding 'brain drain' in the countries of origin, this policy goal has to be brought in line with the national immigration and integration legislation of the Member States. The question arises, whether these very different policy goals can be achieved simultaneously or whether they contradict each other in such a way that certain clear policy choices will have to be made. In this chapter we will critically analyse the contradictory aims of national immigration and integration systems from a European and comparative perspective. After discussing the so-called 'guest-worker' policies of the 1960s as a historical predecessor of the concept of circular migration in three selected Member States (Germany, the Netherlands and Sweden), we will discuss the implications of the concept of circular migration in its current form at the international and European level. This will be followed by an assessment of present labour migration policies in the same three Member States. The chapter ends with some concluding observations on the potential of 'circular migration' as a serious option for a sustainable EU labour migration policy.

II   Circular migration: historical perspective

The relatively novel concept of circular migration bears striking similarities to the European guest-worker programmes of the post-war period that were inspired by the 'rotation principle'. Between the end of World War II and the 1970s–1980s most Western European countries tried to satisfy their rising demand for labour by relying on labour migrants from abroad. Their guest-worker programmes were largely based on the idea of a temporary inflow of labour migrants, who were expected to return to their country of origin after a number of years. The same ideology underlies the concept of circular migration. This section discusses the guest-worker programmes of three Member States (Germany, the Netherlands and Sweden) in order to evaluate in how far current labour migration policies differ from the previous approach.

---

[14] *Ibid.*, pp. 219ff.

A Germany

Germany is the country most commonly associated with the 'guest-worker model'. After World War II the German economy recovered rapidly, leading to a rising demand for labour that could not be fulfilled by relying exclusively on the domestic workforce. Consequently, from the late 1950s and 1960s onwards, Germany started to systematically recruit workers from abroad.[15]

The guest-worker model was essentially a form of temporary labour migration. Foreign workers were expected to return to their country of origin after a certain number of years. The then minister president of Baden-Württemberg, Hans Filbinger, introduced the 'principle of rotation' (*Rotationsprinzip*), implying that migrant workers were to return in order to be replaced by 'young and fresh' guest-workers on a regular basis.[16] Even though the idea of replacing older migrants with young guest-workers was unique to the guest-worker model, the similarities between the 'principle of rotation' and the currently advocated concept of circular migration are striking.

Yet, the return of labour migrants did not go as smoothly as expected. During the economic recession of 1967 the mechanism worked satisfactorily. A large number of guest-workers returned to their countries of origin, with the intention to come back as soon as the German economy had recovered.[17] This pattern changed with the economic recession and oil crisis in the 1970s. In that period the number of migrant workers continued to increase, in spite of the economic downturn. In 1973 the German government imposed a stop on the inflow of foreign labour, spurred by the oil crisis as well as concerns about the economic and social consequences of the rising immigration population. There is, however, no evidence that the inflow of foreign labour, and especially the large number of immigrants employed in specific industries, induced unemployment amongst the native German population in the 1970s and 1980s.[18]

---

[15] U. Herbert, *Geschichte der Ausländerpolitik in Deutschland: Saisonarbeiter, Zwangsarbeiter, Gastarbeiter, Flüchtlinge* (Munich: Beck, 2001), esp. pp. 200–10.

[16] D. Tränhardt, 'Inclusie of exclusie: discoursen over migratie in Duitsland', *Migrantenstudies* 18 (2002), 225–40.

[17] *Ibid.*

[18] M. Mühleisen, K. F. Zimmermann, 'A panel analysis of job changes and unemployment', *European Economic Review* 38 (1994), 793–801.

B   The Netherlands

The Netherlands equally experienced an inflow of labour migrants that were initially perceived to be temporary in the post-war period. However, as opposed to Germany, migration to the Netherlands was additionally characterised by movements from the former colonies of Suriname and Indonesia.

Between 1964 and 1975, immigration to the Netherlands was dominated by labour migrants from the Mediterranean countries, in particular Morocco and Turkey. The post-war boom of the Dutch economy in the 1960s resulted in a shortage of labour, especially in the low-skilled sector, that could not be filled with the native workforce.[19] Yet, as opposed to Germany, which started to sign labour recruitment agreements in the mid-1950s, the Dutch government only took action in the 1960s.

In any event, the Dutch immigrant population during the initial post-war years remained relatively small, at less than 5 per cent of the total population.[20] Italy and Spain, the countries with which the two first labour recruitment agreements were concluded, were the main source countries in the early 1960s. Around 11,000 Spaniards arrived in the Netherlands in 1965 alone. Yet, a large number of Spanish and Italian guest-workers returned to their country of origin after having worked in the Netherlands for a number of years. At the end of the 1960s, seven out of ten Spanish migrant workers had returned to their home country. A completely different pattern could be observed in respect of Turkish and Moroccan labour migrants. Rather than returning to their country of origin after having worked in the Netherlands for several years, most migrants from Turkey and Morocco decided to settle permanently and to bring their family members.[21]

Two years later than Germany, in 1975 the Dutch government imposed a stop on labour migration.[22] As a consequence, labour migrants were only allowed to enter the Netherlands if they were in possession of a work permit. In addition, high penalties for employing illegal workers were introduced. As in most other European countries,

---

[19] J. Heijke, *Migratie van Mediterranen: economie en arbeidsmarkt* (Leiden: Stenfert Kroese, 1986).

[20] P. Ireland, *Becoming Europe: Immigration, integration and the welfare state* (Pittsburgh: University of Pittsburgh Press, 2004), pp. 117–18.

[21] H. Nicolaas and A.H. Sprangers, 'De nieuwe gastarbeider: manager uit de VS of informaticus uit India', *Maandstatistiek van de bevolking* 9 (2000), 10.

[22] P. Lakeman, *Binnen zonder kloppen: Nederlandse immigratiepolitiek en de economische gevolgen* (Amsterdam: Meulenhoff, 1999).

the late 1970s and 1980s were dominated by an inflow of family migrants. As indicated above, a large number of guest-workers, especially from Turkey and Morocco came to settle permanently in the Netherlands, in spite of the fact that they were initially expected to return to their countries of origin in the wake of the economic crisis. For this reason, immigration from Turkey and Morocco rose rather than declined in the years after 1973. In the late 1980s, around 40,000 persons entered the Netherlands each year for the purpose of family reunification constituting 70 per cent of the total number of immigrants.[23] Yet, the Dutch government did not adopt any specific measures aimed at encouraging the return of guest-workers in that period.[24]

C   Sweden

Just as Germany and the Netherlands, Sweden saw an economic boom and an expansion of industry in the post-war period. Especially the early 1960s were characterised by a rising consumer demand, high economic growth rates and an increasing demand for labour. Consequently, the domestic workforce was complemented by workers from abroad. Labour migrants were recruited in their country of origin by individual companies or through the Swedish Labour Market Board in co-operation with the competent authorities in the sending countries. Other migrants arrived on a tourist visa in order to search for an employer upon arrival in Sweden.[25]

In the initial post-war years, labour migrants arrived mainly from the Nordic countries. Even though the first arrangements for an intra-Nordic movement of workers were already made in the 1940s,[26] the first formal agreement encompassing all Nordic countries was concluded in 1954.[27] The Passport Union established between Denmark, Sweden,

---

[23] E. M. Naborn, *Gezinshereniging. De overkomst van gezinsleden van migranten en Nederlanders* (Ministerie van Justitie, Wetenschappelijk onderzoek- en documentatie centrum, 1992), p. 2.

[24] J. Lucassen and R. Penninx, *Nieuwkomers, Nakomelingen, Nederlanders. Immigranten in Nederland 1950–1993* (Amsterdam: Het Spinhuis, 1994), p. 147.

[25] A. Århammar, 'Migration och integration – om framtidens arbetsmarknad. Bilaga 4 till Långtidsutredningen 2003/04', *SOU* 73 (2004), 30.

[26] On 1 October 1943, the requirement for Danish, Finnish, Icelandic and Norwegian citizens to hold a work permit when working in Sweden was abolished. Moreover, visa-free entry was granted to Norwegians, Danes and Icelanders in 1945 and to Finns in 1949.

[27] Agreement of 22 May 1954 between Denmark, Finland, Norway and Sweden on a Common Labour Market.

Finland, Iceland and Norway provided for the free movement of labour workers in the Nordic region, the abolition of work permit requirements for citizens of other Nordic countries and the abandonment of requirements to hold a passport and a residence permit when travelling to, and residing in, another Nordic country.[28] The 1954 Passport Union was supplemented in 1957 with the Nordic Passport Control Agreement,[29] which extended the right of travelling between the Nordic countries without passport controls to third-country nationals, and contained rules on the establishment of passport controls at the external borders. The largest group of Nordic workers arrived from Finland, due to the recession of the Finnish economy in the late 1960s and the active recruitment from Finland by many Swedish firms.[30]

Next to the free movement of labour from Nordic countries, the period after 1954 was characterised by a dismantling of restrictions with regard to the entry and settlement of foreign workers.[31] Even though the Swedish alien legislation of 1954 contained in principle a requirement that no domestic worker was available to fill the post, the 1950s and 1960s were dominated by a laissez-faire policy, allowing for the entry of labour migrants on the basis of a tourist visa. Upon arrival they were permitted to seek work and granted a work permit if they were successful in obtaining an employment contract. In addition, the Swedish government concluded labour recruitment agreements with several countries, including Italy, Hungary, Greece, Yugoslavia, Turkey and the British and American occupational forces in Austria.[32] As a result of such active recruitment policies, in the 1960s between 30,000 and 60,000 immigrants arrived in Sweden each year.[33] Yet, patterns of

---

[28] Protocol concerning the Exemption of Citizens of Denmark, Finland, Norway and Sweden from Requirements of Passport and Residence Permit during Residence in Other Nordic countries.

[29] Agreement of 12 July 1957 between Denmark, Finland, Norway and Sweden on the Abolition of Passport Control at the Intra-Nordic Borders, amended by an Agreement of 2 April 1973 including Iceland as a party and an amendment of 27 July 1979.

[30] For an analysis on gross and net migration flows between Finland and Sweden between 1962 and 1977 see P. Nyberg, *Emigration, ekonomisk tillväxt och stabilitet: en teoretisk undersökning kring emigrationens orsaker och effekter på medellång sikt* (Finlands Bank, Serie B:34, Helsingfors, 1980).

[31] C. Lundh, 'Invandrarna i den svenska modellen – hot eller reserv? Fackligt program på 1960-talet', *Arbetarhistoria* 2 (1994).

[32] J. Johansson, *'Så gör vi inte här i Sverige. Vi brukar göra så här.' Retorik och praktik i LO:s invandrarpolitik 1945–1981* (2008), p. 124.

[33] L. Jederlund, 'In transition: From immigration policy to integration policy in Sweden', *Scandinavian Review* 87 (1999), 1.

migration corresponded to the business cycles in Sweden, leading to an increase in the number of migrants in times of economic boom and a decrease in times of economic recession.[34]

The large inflow of foreign workers in the 1960s as well as rising unemployment rates led the Swedish government to gradually introduce immigration controls. The requirement for immigrants from non-Nordic countries to hold a work permit when arriving in Sweden was reintroduced in 1968.[35] As a consequence, foreign workers could no longer arrive in Sweden on the basis of a tourist visa and apply for a work permit after entry. Moreover, the labour market authorities and trade unions subjected labour migrants to an increasingly restrictive labour market test.[36] Just as in Germany and the Netherlands, the Swedish authorities put an end to labour recruitment policies in 1972. From then on, refugees and family migrants came to constitute the two main categories of immigrants to Sweden.

III   Circular migration: international perspective

The concept of circular migration in the EU emerged within the wake of it being the 'rage in international policy circles'.[37] International bodies such as the UN, the World Bank, the IOM and the Global Commission on International Migration (GCIM) have promoted circular migration as a way of fostering mobility to the benefit of both sending and host societies.

The UN Secretary-General, in its 2006 Report on International Migration and Development, talks about a 'new era of mobility' which is characterised by more temporary movements.[38] The Report sees potential for such temporary migration programmes to result in 'beneficial synergies for migrants, countries of origin and countries of destination'.[39] Migrants are considered to benefit from having a legal status,

---

[34] R. Ohlsson, *Ekonomisk strukturförändring och invandring: en undersökning av invandrare i Malmö under perioden 1945–1967* (Lund: Skrifter utgivna av ekonomisk, vol. XXV, 1978).

[35] See K. Ekenger and F. Wallen, *Invandring för tillväxt och nya job* (2002), pp. 7–8.

[36] See Chapter 5, Section 4, UtlF.

[37] S. Vertovec, 'Circular migration: The way forward in global policy?', IMI Working Papers No. 4 (2007), p. 2.

[38] United Nations, *International Migration and Development*, Report of the Secretary General (New York, 2006).

[39] *Ibid.*, p. 18.

countries of origin from remittances and return migration and receiving countries from the resident workforce.

Also the World Bank, in a 2006 study on labour migration in Eastern Europe[40] advocated circular migration as a means of decreasing brain drain by encouraging the transfer of knowledge and skills. According to the World Bank, circular migration programmes can reduce the negative economic effects of brain drain and the negative social effects that result from the separation of families in case of long-term migration.[41] Even though circular migration is not presented as the only feasible policy solution, the report underlines the potential of circular migration to allow for an effective matching of supply and demand for international labour and to satisfy the preferences of many migrants to spend short periods abroad.[42]

The IOM has dealt with the issue of circular migration in its World Migration Report 2005.[43] Considering the potential developmental benefits of circular migration, the IOM encourages receiving countries to use incentives and sanctions in order to ensure that temporary migration programmes are in fact temporary. Such measures may include scholarships for students with conditions attached regarding return, reimbursements of migrants' unused social insurance contributions after return, opening up more avenues for repeated temporary migration and making residence or dual citizenship available.[44] The IOM has also investigated in more detail the implications of circular migration schemes in certain regions, including Europe.[45]

The Global Commission on International Migration was set up by the UN Secretary-General Kofi Annan in December 2003 with the task of providing a framework for the establishment of a coherent global response to the issue of international migration. The Global Commission presented its final report, including conclusions and recommendations, in October 2005.[46] In its report the Commission encourages states and international organisations to 'formulate policies and programmes that maximize the developmental impact of return and circular migration'.[47] According to the Commission, temporary and circular migration

---

[40] World Bank, *International Labor Migration* (n. 3 above).
[41] *Ibid.* p. 109.   [42] *Ibid.* p. 98.
[43] IOM (n. 4 above).   [44] *Ibid.* p. 296.
[45] IOM, *Permanent or Circular Migration? Policy choices to address demographic decline and labour shortages in Europe* (Geneva, 2008).
[46] Global Commission on International Migration (n. 5 above).   [47] *Ibid.* p. 31.

movements are progressively replacing the old paradigm of permanent migrant settlement. The developmental opportunities spurred by this shift in migration patterns should according to the Commission be grasped by new migration policies. Consequently, it encourages states to adopt measures facilitating the movement of migrants between their countries of origin and destination. This includes the portability of pension benefits, the enhancement of opportunities for migrants to return to their country of origin on a regular or occasional basis, without losing residence rights in their country of destination and the creation of a more favourable business climate and decent working conditions in countries of origin.

Thus, numerous international organisations promote the implementation of circular or return migration schemes in order to maximise benefits for sending and receiving countries. Yet, it becomes clear from the abovementioned reports that a number of policies have to be put in place for circular migration policies to be successful.

The argument most frequently cited in order to defend policies of circular migration is the brain drain suffered by developing countries if they are continuously deprived of their brightest talents. This is especially the case if there has been a significant investment in the education of the migrants on the part of the developing countries. Returnees can make a substantial contribution to economic development not only by investing the money they accumulated in their country of migration but also by stimulating the transfer of technological and managerial know-how. Thus, the new group of circular migrants that maintains multiple attachments with various countries and communities is seen to be able to make a significant contribution to development by transferring financial capital as well as specialised knowledge and skills. The financial means as well as the work experience provided by returning migrants has the potential of boosting the economic growth, employment figures and innovation in the home country. High economic growth rates in turn can stimulate return migration, leading to a virtuous cycle to the benefit of the sending country.

Consequently, circular migration is often cited as one of the primary means of 'making migration work for development'. Yet, in addition to the interests of the developing countries that are often put forward, the industrialised countries have their own interests in promoting the concept of circular migration. For the receiving countries temporary migration schemes including circular migration constitute a convenient way of filling shortages in their labour markets.

IV   Circular migration: European perspective

In a European context, the concept of circular migration was brought up by the European Commission in its Communication on Migration and Development of 2005.[48] In the Commission document, circular migration is defined as a form of migration that is managed in a way allowing some degree of legal mobility back and forth between two countries. According to that document, circular migration can provide a stimulus for emigrants from developing countries to return and invest in their home country and contribute to the reduction of unemployment rates. Therefore, the Commission sees circular migration primarily as a suitable mechanism to mitigate the negative effects of brain drain for developing countries. In May 2007, the Commission published a Communication that is entirely devoted to circular migration and mobility partnerships between the EU and third countries.[49] The Commission uses the same working definition of circular migration as in its earlier Communication of 2005. This broad definition encompasses the re-entry of previous migrants for the purpose of temporary employment as well as the temporary engagement of migrants based in the EU in business, professional and voluntary activities in their country of origin. This does not preclude the possibility of granting returned migrants privileged admission to their former host state.[50] At the same time it is made clear in the Communication that the type of circular migration that the EU wishes to facilitate is essentially temporary migration.[51] According to the Commission 'if not properly designed and managed, migration intended to be circular can easily become permanent and, thus, defeat its objective'.

In December 2006, the European Council identified circular migration as one of the guiding principles in the development of an EU policy on legal migration. Under the heading 'A comprehensive European migration policy', the European Council deliberated that 'while respecting the competences of the Member States in this area, considerations will be given to how legal migration opportunities can be incorporated into the Unions' external policies in order to develop a balanced partnership with third countries adapted to the specific EU Member States'

---

[48] European Commission Communication, *Migration and Development: Some concrete orientations*, COM (2005) 390 Final of 1 September 2005.
[49] COM (2007) 248 Final, of 16 May 2007.   [50] *Ibid.* pp. 8–9.
[51] *Ibid.*, p. 8.

labour market needs; ways and means to facilitate circular migration will be explored'.[52] It invited the Commission to present proposals on legal migration, with a particular emphasis on ways and means to facilitate circular and temporary migration in order to develop a balanced partnership with third countries.[53]

In response to this invitation, the European Commission issued a proposal for a directive on the conditions for entry and residence of third-country nationals for highly qualified employment.[54] The so-called 'Blue Card Directive' was adopted in 2009[55] and will have to be transposed into national law by all Member States except Denmark, the UK and Ireland by 19 June 2011.[56] The directive aims at establishing a common EU-wide entry regime for labour migrants from third countries, pursuing highly qualified employment, being work for which higher education qualifications or at least three years' – or (when provided for by national law) five years' – relevant professional experience is required.[57] Applicants must be in possession of an employment contract or a job offer for at least one year. Moreover, their salary must comply with a certain minimum threshold to be set by the Member States, but amounting to at least 1.5 times the average gross annual salary in the Member State concerned.[58]

Successful applicants receive a Blue Card, granting them the right to reside and work in the territory of a Member State and to move to another Member State for highly qualified employment if certain conditions are fulfilled.[59] The Blue Card is valid for a standard period of validity of between one and four years, provided that their employment contract has an equal duration.[60] The directive is silent as regards the possibility to renew a residence permit. This means that highly skilled migrants are dependent on national law concerning the possibility of renewal. Consequently, after one to four years of employment in a Member State, labour migrants may be required to leave the country. At that moment highly skilled workers fall short of meeting the five-year residence requirement for obtaining long-term residence status which was introduced by Directive 2003/109/EC.[61] Thus, the Blue Card scheme

---

[52] European Council, Brussels 14/15 December 2006, Presidency Conclusions.   [53] *Ibid.*
[54] COM (2007) 637 of 23 October 2007.
[55] Directive 2009/50/EC on the conditions of entry and residence of third-country nationals for the puprposes of highly qualified employment, OJ L 155/17, 18.6.2009.
[56] Art. 23 of Directive 2009/50/EC.   [57] Art. 2(1)(g) of the directive.
[58] Art. 5(3) of the directive.   [59] See Art. 18 of the directive.
[60] Art. 7(2) of the directive.   [61] Art. 4(1) of Directive 2003/109/EC.

is an essentially temporary system, driven by the labour market neces-
sities of an ageing and declining EU population. In fact, recital 20 of the
preamble of the directive in the context of internal mobility of third-
country nationals explicitly refers to EU migration rules as being 'controlled' and 'demand-driven', indicating the focus on the Union's own
interests rather than those of the sending countries.

Under recital 11 of the preamble, the directive refers to the aim of
encouraging circular migration of highly qualified third-country workers from developing countries. To that end, highly skilled third-country
nationals are allowed longer periods of absence from EU territory than
those provided for under Directive 2003/109/EC. In derogation from
those provisions, highly skilled migrants are allowed to be absent from
EU territory for up to twelve consecutive months and eighteen months in
total during the five years before long-term residence status is reached.
After that status has been obtained, an absence of twenty-four consecutive months will be permitted.[62]

Moreover, it is stressed that Member States should 'refrain from
pursuing active recruitment in developing countries in sectors suffering
from lack of personnel'.[63] Ethical recruitment policies are to be developed in key sectors, particularly in the health sector[64] and the education
sector. The preamble of the directive underlines the importance of
monitoring the possible brain-drain effects of highly qualified schemes
and points to the necessity of adopting measures to facilitate circular and
temporary migration and to 'minimise negative and maximise positive
impacts of highly skilled immigration on developing countries'.[65]

Also in the 2009 Stockholm programme,[66] the European Council
underlines the importance of circular migration within the context of
maximising the positive and minimising the negative effects of migration
on development. The Commission is invited to present further proposals
to 'explore the concept of circular migration and study ways to facilitate
orderly circulation of migrants'.[67] Such circular migration is envisaged
to take place either within or outside the framework of specific

[62] Art. 16(3)–(4) of the directive.   [63] Recital 22 of the preamble.
[64] See also the European Programme for Action to tackle the critical shortages of health
workers in developing countries (2007 to 2013), Council and Member States
Conclusions of 14 May 2007 (Doc. 7189/07).
[65] Recital 22 of the preamble.
[66] Stockholm Programme, Council Document 17024/09, adopted by the European Council
on 10–11 December 2009.
[67] Point 6.1.2. of the Stockholm Programme.

programmes, including a study on the potential effects of different policy areas on 'increased temporary and circular mobility'.

In its Communications on Migration and Development[68] and on Circular Migration and Mobility Partnerships,[69] the European Commission has identified several crucial aspects related to circular migration and has encouraged Member States to take measures to make return for migrants an attractive option.

A crucial aspect to encouraging return is the portability of pension benefits. This problem applies in particular to highly skilled workers who are being sent by their employer to one of the developed countries on a short-term contract. The social security systems of the EU receiving states generally require even temporary migrants to make a periodic tax-based social security contribution. Migrant workers often do not benefit from the social security contributions made abroad after finalising their temporary employment in the host country due to the prohibition on exporting social security benefits. Workers who are not able to transfer their pension benefits back to their country of origin will be left without any possibility to claim their contributions, making the option of returning much less attractive, especially if they have lived and worked abroad for a number of years.[70] The Commission in its Communication on Migration and Development has stressed that the portability of pension benefits for returnees should be ensured. It maintained that Member States should ensure that contributions made by migrants are paid out to him/her in the country of origin after return either in the form of a pension or as a lump sum payment.[71]

In order to deal with this problem, India has started to conclude bilateral social security agreements with a number of countries, which provide exemption from social security contributions for workers with a short-term contract and/or exportability of pensions at the event of relocation. The first bilateral social security agreement was concluded with Belgium in 2006, followed by agreements with the Netherlands and Germany and negotiations with Denmark and Sweden underway. The agreements provide for social security co-ordination and in the case of Germany an exemption from social security payments for foreign workers remaining for a period of up to sixty months.[72]

---

[68] European Commission Communication (n. 48 above), p. 28.
[69] COM (2007) 248 Final, of 16 May 2007.
[70] UK House of Commons (n. 7 above), p. 45.
[71] European Commission Communication (n. 48 above), p. 28.
[72] Ministry of Overseas Indian Affairs (MOIA), *Annual Report 2007–08* (2008), p. 9.

Another crucial element of making migrants return to their home country is the option to return again to their host country. Migrants tend to be reluctant to return unless they are given some guarantee that they will be able to re-enter their (former) country of destination. This is especially the case if the migrant continues to be involved in some kind of business in the former country of residence. It can, however, also merely be based on the desire to keep a link to two countries and to maintain the option to live in the former country of destination, especially if the home country is characterised by a high degree of economic and political instability. Thus, migratory regimes in the receiving countries which include an option of multiple re-entries, such as temporary labour market access on a renewable basis or some kind of preferential access to work permits can play an essential role in inciting migrants to return. The Commission has proposed that workers who have already worked under temporary employment schemes and have returned at the end of their contract should be given priority for further temporary employment.[73]

A further proposition made by the Commission is that Member States could facilitate the possibility for financial institutions to open up special savings accounts that migrants can access upon return. The profit from such accounts could be maximised by offering favourable tax treatment, interest rate subsidies and a bonus payment at the time of return.[74] However, this suggestion comes very close to the much-criticised proposals of financial penalties in the form of a security bond or mandatory saving schemes. The first mechanism refers to the introduction of a financial security bond, to be paid by the employer or the worker himself upon migration. The bond will be confiscated by the receiving country in case the worker overstays his visa.[75]

The Commission has also stressed the importance of ensuring that the migrant's education and qualifications obtained in the country of residence will be recognised in the country of origin. Moreover, in the case of researchers and other professionals it should be ensured that they will be able to keep in touch with their former colleagues, for instance by way of web portals and fellowships for returning researchers.[76]

Additionally, one has to consider whether dual citizenship and voting rights for expatriates have to be stimulated as they may facilitate

---

[73] European Commission Communication (n. 48 above), p. 7.   [74] *Ibid.* p. 128.
[75] G. Epstein, A. Hillman and A. Weiss, 'Creating illegal immigrants', *Journal of Population Economics* 12 (1999), 3.
[76] European Commission Communication (n. 48 above), p. 128.

long-term circulation by enabling permanent migrants to maintain substantial personal and political attachments to both the country of origin and of destination. In the EU, holding dual nationality of two or more EU Member States has in most Member States become an increasingly common and accepted practice. It is seen now by many as part of the developments towards an ever closer Union and in some instance is even stimulated as an important element leading towards a European identity (e.g. Germany and France). The situation, however, is different when the nationalities of non-EU countries – specifically migrant-sending states – are at stake. In such cases for many migrant-receiving states, dual citizenship remains a highly contentious proposition, suspected of weakening loyalty to the state. In an age of mobility and globalisation, the toleration (and in some cases even the stimulation) of dual citizenship should, however, be considered beyond the border of the EU or the Council of Europe. Hereby various models could be taken into consideration. The introduction of the status of 'Overseas Citizenship of India' (OCI) for Indians living permanently abroad in 2005 – although not a genuine Indian citizenship – is already a step in this direction. Interesting examples of successful migration movements with a circular pattern of mobility are Hong Kong residents holding Canadian passports and moving back and forth between the two areas.[77] Very interesting is also the Spanish position which recognises and allows dual citizenship in a rather selective way concerning mainly Latin American countries, the Philippines and Equatorial Guinea. Further research is needed in order to see whether these cases of double membership stimulate successful patterns of circular migration as in the case of Hong Kong/Canada.

V   Circular migration: national perspectives

In most Member States entry regimes for highly skilled nationals are essentially temporary. Even though migrants have the possibility of obtaining a permanent residence permit after a certain number of years, this possibility is conditioned by the passing of increasingly difficult language and integration tests and may, in the worst case (Denmark), take up to seven years. In countries such as Sweden and Germany where it is possible to obtain a permanent residence permit immediately upon arrival, conditions for falling under the category of

---

[77] K. Newland, 'Learning by Doing: Experiences of circular migration', MPI Insight (September 2008), p. 4.

highly skilled worker have been extremely demanding. Thus, the focus of most Member States is clearly on granting access to their territory only temporarily and making the accession of more secure residence rights increasingly difficult.[78] Those migrants who stay temporarily in the Union mostly do not enjoy any protection from expulsion and may be asked to leave if they cease to fulfil the conditions for entry.

The understanding of the concept of circular migration from the perspective of the Member States becomes apparent when considering the initiative launched by the German and French interior ministers, Wolfgang Schäuble and Nicolas Sarkozy, in 2006. In the strategy paper 'German–French Initiative for a New European Migration Policy' submitted at an informal meeting of interior ministers from the six largest Member States (UK, France, Germany, Spain, Italy and Poland) on 26 October 2006, they promoted a closer co-operation of EU Member States in combating illegal migration as well as managing legal migration in particular by encouraging circular migration.[79] Rather than following the Commission in seeing circular migration mainly as a tool for fostering economic development in the sending countries, the two interior ministers openly revealed the real purpose behind circular migration, namely the control and limitation of migration. Circular migration is perceived as a concept that allows receiving countries to manage labour migration by way of introducing national quotas for specific professions.[80] Quotas are to be set according to the labour market needs and economic situation of the Member States and should be flexible enough to be adapted to changes in the labour market situation of each individual country. Moreover, such quotas are to be used in negotiations on readmission agreements (of illegal migrants) with third countries.[81] This reveals the explicit link made between allowing controlled and temporary labour migration in order to reduce illegal migration. The objective of economic development in the policy document is clearly subordinate to the goal of effectively managing labour migration to the EU.

[78] See A. Wiesbrock, *Legal Migration to the European Union* (The Hague: Martinus Nijhoff Publishers, 2010), pp. 363–415.

[79] German–French Initiative for a New European Migration Policy, presented at the Meeting of the Interior Ministers of France, Germany, Italy, Poland, Spain and the United Kingdom, Stratford-upon-Avon, 25–6 October 2006.

[80] *Ibid.* See also S. Angenendt, 'Circular migration: A sustainable concept for migration policy?', *SWP Comments* C (2007).

[81] *Ibid.*

Besides virtually forcing highly skilled migrants to return by restricting their residence rights or making the acquisition of permanent residence rights or citizenship increasingly difficult, the EU Member States have taken little action in order to encourage the return of migrants by way of positive incitements.

A   National perspectives: the Netherlands

Even though the concept of circular migration is propagated at the international, the European and the national level, restrictive immigration legislation in force in the Member States effectively prevents the circularity of migrants. As pointed out by several scholars, restrictive immigration policies will tend to encourage migrants to settle in the host country[82] and discourage them from investing let alone returning to their country of origin, thus preventing patterns of circular migration.[83]

In the fields of migration and development, the Dutch government has chosen to adopt an integrated approach.[84] In that context, the Ministries of Justice (department of migration) and of Foreign Affairs (department of development) have co-ordinated their policies and undertaken several joint initiatives. For instance, in the framework of the IOM Migration and Development in Africa (MIDA) programme, a scheme has been launched, which allows Ghanaian health workers in the Netherlands to return temporarily to Ghana and Ghanaian nurses to follow training and internship in the Netherlands. Another example is the 'Return of Qualified Afghans' project,[85] under which skilled migrants are encouraged to return temporarily to Afghanistan to make a contribution in the reconstruction process of their country.[86]

However, as argued by de Haas,[87] in spite of a striving for coherence between migration and development policy goals, the co-operation

---

[82] See e.g. G. Hugo, *Circular Migration: Keeping development rolling? Migration Information Source* (Migration Policy Institute, 2003).

[83] H. de Haas, 'International migration, remittances and development: Myths and facts', *Third World Quarterly* 26 (2005), 1243.

[84] DGIS (Directoraat-Generaal Internationale Samenwerking), *Verband tussen migratie en ontwikkeling* (Ministerie van Buitenlandse Zaken, 2004).

[85] The programme is carried out by the IOM and partly financed by the European Commission.

[86] See Kabinetsreactie op advies ACVZ, *Regulering en facilitering van arbeidsmigratie* (2004), p. 43.

[87] Statement made by H. de Haas at a conference on migration and development on 19 June 2006, www.worldconnectors.nl/pdf/27.pdf.

between the two ministries is in fact dominated by the Ministry of Justice. As a consequence, Dutch policies tend to perceive migration as a problem and to focus on the return of migrants to their country of origin. This is apparent from the two projects above, which focus largely on the return of Ghanaians/Afghans to their countries of origin.

Thus, the Netherlands focuses only on one part of the circular migration process, namely the return of migrants to their country of origin. The focus on the return-side of circular migration is also clearly apparent from policy documents issued by the Dutch government. The Dutch parliament defines circular migration as migration which implies the return to the migrant's country of origin.[88] In that respect, circular migration is used as an interchangeable concept with temporary migration.

According to the Parliament, temporary labour migration constitutes an adequate strategy to ensure benefits of the migration process for the migrant and the sending and receiving state. Yet, in that context it is seen to be crucial that the migrant returns to his country of origin after his contract has expired.[89] It is argued that temporary migration will lead to the possibility of accepting more migrants from developing countries, under the precondition that they return after a number of years to their country of origin or *go elsewhere*.[90] This statement is an indication of the main motivation behind circular migration policies, namely the self-interest of the receiving states. The Dutch government attaches great importance to the temporariness of labour migration, but the positive effects for the country of origin do not seem to be a major priority.

This conclusion is substantiated by the government's policy approach in respect of highly skilled workers. On 1 October 2004, a special scheme for highly skilled immigrants, the so-called 'knowledge migrant scheme' (*kennismigranten*) entered into force. The Dutch scheme defines eligible workers from third countries exclusively on the basis of a certain annual minimum salary which has been set at €47,565 for employees aged thirty years or older and €34,881 for employees younger than thirty years. However, the salary criterion does not apply to immigrants who will be working in the Netherlands in the context of conducting academic research (including university lecturers and researchers) and physicians

---

[88] See Tweede Kamer, *Verbanden tussen ontwikkeling en migratie* Vergarderjaar 2003–2004, 29 693, nr. 1 (2004), p. 30: 'Met circulaire migratie wordt bedoeld migratie in de loop waarvan de migrant al dan niet tijdelijk terugkeert naar zijn land van herkomst.'

[89] *Ibid.*, p. 41.   [90] *Ibid.*, p. 30.

training to be specialists.[91] Knowledge migrants must have concluded a valid employment contract with an employer based in the Netherlands, who has enrolled in the IND Highly Skilled Migrant Programme. The length of the residence permit depends on the length of the employment contract. Highly skilled workers with a permanent employment contract are eligible for a residence permit of five years.[92] This allows them to acquire a permanent residence and EU long-term residence status after five years of residence in the Netherlands. Within that period of time (in fact within three and a half years after their arrival) they must however comply with the integration requirements laid down in the Dutch Integration Act of 2007.

B   National perspectives: Sweden

In Sweden new rules concerning labour migration entered into force in December 2008.[93] The reform is designed to create an effective and flexible system for labour migration, which will make it easier for people to come to Sweden to work, and for Swedish companies to recruit labour from outside Europe. The new legislation will make it possible to grant work permits to third-country nationals who are offered employment, provided labour needs cannot be met through recruitment within Sweden or the EU.[94] It is important that the employment and wage conditions have to meet Swedish standards as established in so-called collective agreements and in order to prevent social dumping. Different to prior Swedish legislation in force, it is not anymore the Swedish Public Employment Agency which has to decide whether there is indeed a need for recruitment beyond the EU borders but the Swedish employers themselves decide whether they need to fill a particular vacancy with someone from outside Sweden or the EU.[95] Furthermore, the system applies not only to highly skilled workers but is based on a non-sectoral approach. This means the system applies to the complete Swedish labour market without the distinction of high- or low-skilled labour. Thus, in comparison with other EU countries, Sweden has one of the least restrictive labour migration policies. It has been argued that the current

---

[91]   Ministerie van Justitie, *Verruiming kennismigrantenregeling*, 4 December 2006.
[92]   Art. 3.59a Vreemdelingenbesluit 2000.
[93]   Lag (2008:884) om ändring i utlänningslagen (2005:716).
[94]   See Chapter 6, Section 2 Utlänningslagen.
[95]   Socialforsakringsutskottests betakande 2008/09:SfU3, Nya regler for arbetskraftsin-vandring, p. 1.

European approach to labour migration implies less openness than the Swedish system.[96] It would be regrettable if Sweden were to introduce a stricter system of labour migration as a consequence of European integration.

The concept of circular migration is high on the Swedish political agenda. In the coming future the Swedish government wants to analyse circular migration to and from Sweden today and in a historic perspective. Furthermore, Sweden wants to identify various factors that affect migrants' prospects for mobility and look into its own legislative framework as well as that of other Member States. It will be important to consider the effects these measures have on the development in the countries of origin.

In a letter[97] as well as a bill both entitled 'Sweden's Policy for Global Development',[98] the Swedish government has stated that it aims to ensure that the movement of labour migrants is facilitated and that obstacles to voluntary repatriation or return migration are abolished. According to the letter, the Swedish government should develop a policy on migration and development that promotes synergies between migration and development and highlights the development potential of increasing mobility for migrants and their countries of origin.[99]

In July 2009, the Swedish government appointed a parliamentary committee, mandated to identify and describe the conditions for migration to and from Sweden and to analyse the link between migration and development.[100] The 'Committee on circular migration and development' (Kommittén för cirkulär migration och utveckling, CiMU) will examine the impact of increased mobility in Sweden and in countries of origin. Its work will lead to suggestions for potential measures that could help to facilitate circular migration to and from Sweden in order to enhance the positive development impact of labour migration. Circular migration is broadly defined as temporary or more permanent, often recurring, movement between two countries. This includes migrants moving from their country of origin to a country of destination and then re-migration as well as migrants returning for a short or longer period of time to their countries of origin. The Committee, consisting of

---

[96] P. Lundborg, 'Invandringspolitik för cirkulär migration', Sieps 9 (2009), 33.

[97] Regeringens skrivelse, Sveriges politik för global utveckling (skr. 2007/08:89).

[98] Proposition Gemensamt ansvar – Sveriges politik för global utveckling (prop. 2002/03:122, bet. 2003/04:UU3, rskr. 2003/04:112).

[99] Ibid.

[100] Kommittédirektiv, Cirkulär migration och utveckling, Dir. 2009:53, Beslut vid regeringssammanträde den 2 juli 2009.

parliamentarians from seven political parties, will consult groups in Sweden that have experience and are affected by the regulation of circular migration. This includes a consultation group formed by the social partners as well as immigrant associations and organisations involved in development cooperation. The Committee will present its final report in 2011.

VI   Conclusion

Arguably, if it is to differ from the forms of temporary labour migration applied by Western industrialised countries since the 1960s, circular migration must include some kind of circularity, in the sense of an option to return temporarily or permanently to the (former) country of destination. Moreover, in order to guarantee that circular migration is beneficial to all three parties involved, the development impacts of such movements must be closely examined and essential rights of the migrants have to be secured.

In spite of an elaborate rhetoric of 'making migration work for development' in the sending countries, policies in the EU countries are in principle still very much based on economic self-interest. The Blue Card Directive 2009/50/EC can be seen as a significant step forward in harmonising rules on economic migration to the EU. It provides for a set of transparent and uniform entry conditions for highly skilled migrants and has the potential to make the EU more attractive for such migrants. However, the directive still suggests an essentially temporary period of residence of migrant workers in the EU. The policy approach in the Netherlands is even stronger in stressing the temporariness of labour migration and encouraging return. Yet, from a development perspective, rather than focusing on temporariness, migrant workers should be encouraged to stay in the host country for a longer time in order to enable them to accumulate sufficient resources to make return worthwhile. Arguably, the movement to a developed country for a limited duration of time is not enough to make migration work for development and allow migrants to return with a sufficient amount of savings. Moreover, it has been argued that from a human rights perspective, all temporary labour schemes should always contain some possibility to extend the temporary status to permanent residence rights.[101] From that

---

[101]   D. Papademetriou, 'Reflections on restoring integrity to the United States immigration system: A personal vision', *Insight* 5 (2005), 16, www.migrationpolicy.org/pubs/Insight_Sept05_5.pdf.

perspective the directive might run counter to the protection of essential rights of (highly skilled) migrants.

In spite of the short-term duration of their stay in an EU country, migrants are often subjected to demanding integration requirements. There is a certain controversy between stressing the temporariness of migration and demanding migrants to comply with comprehensive integration requirements. Moreover, during the period of time that migrants are merely accepted to stay temporarily, they are generally denied access to political and sometimes even socio-economic rights.

Restrictive immigration policies will tend to encourage migrants to settle in the host countries, and discourage them from investing in – let alone returning to – their countries of origin, thus preventing patterns of circular migration. On the other hand, very restrictive admission policies of some Member States, including even integration test will discourage the desired highly skilled migrants from third countries to consider the EU as a hospitable place to move to. Furthermore, the emphasis on the temporariness of current labour migration rules in the Member States runs counter to the objective high on the political agenda of most Member States, namely integrating third-country nationals into the host societies.

It is submitted that demographic concerns clearly demand more flexibility and openness in admission and settlement policies for economic migrants in Europe. Research has shown that immigration and citizenship policies influence specifically highly skilled migrants' decision-making when choosing a destination. The prospect of becoming a permanent member or at least a member with a guaranteed long-term resident status of an affluent and stable society is deemed to be a valuable 'good'. Indeed, highly skilled migrants and their families often put more weight on obtaining a secure membership in a stable and prosperous country than on remuneration and working conditions. The prolongation of the European long-term resident status should be made possible for migrants returning to their countries of origin. The guarantee of keeping the acquired long-term or permanent resident status can stimulate return mobility and investments in the country of origin while the loss of acquired residence rights will prevent such movements. Registration procedures could be introduced in order to prolong such a status.

Additionally, one has to consider whether dual citizenship and voting rights for expatriates have to be stimulated as they may facilitate long-term circulation by enabling permanent migrants to maintain substantial personal and political attachments to both the country of origin and of destination. In the EU, holding dual nationality of two or more Member States has in most Member States become increasingly common and accepted practice. It is seen now as part of an ever closer Union and in some instances even encouraged as an important element leading towards a European identity (e.g. Germany and France). In an age of mobility and globalisation the toleration of dual citizenship should, however, be considered beyond the border of the EU or the Council of Europe. The introduction of the status of 'Overseas Citizenship of India' (OCI) for Indians living permanently abroad in 2005 – although not a genuine Indian citizenship – is already a step in this direction. An open discussion concerning the acceptance of dual citizenship in order to stimulate circular migration should take place, especially also as political rights are mostly only granted to migrants who have acquired citizenship.

Thus, as long as the concept of circular migration remains tied to the notion of temporariness, it does not differ greatly from the much criticised guest-worker model of the 1960s. In order to make circular migration work for sending and receiving states, it has to be decoupled from temporary labour migration schemes. Rather than deterred, migrants should be encouraged to stay in the host country for a longer period of time, inter alia by granting them extensive socio-economic and political rights including under certain conditions access to dual citizenship. Circular migration in its current form, however, is not apt to guarantee a 'triple-win' situation for migrants, sending and receiving states nor to make migration work for development.

It will be up to the European institutions to formulate a sustainable European model of circular migration. This European model should be based on further research. This research should also include a historic perspective by comparing bilateral arrangements concluded in the 1960s with new arrangements made at the moment. Which lessons can we learn from the past? How far can the failure of the so-called guest-worker model be avoided in the case of circular migration policy arrangements? We have to keep in mind that only a sustainable and socially responsible migration policy will make Europe an attractive place for highly skilled migrants to move to and guarantee Europe's global economic market position.

6

European company regulation between economic and social integration

THOMAS BIERMEYER

I Introduction

A European SME [Social Market Economy] cannot come about, and SMEs at the national level will be destroyed, unless the politically uncontrolled dynamics of (negative) 'integration through law' can be contained.[1]

As demonstrated in the last chapters, through its early rulings in *Van Gend en Loos*[2] and *Costa* v. *ENEL*[3] the Court of Justice (ECJ) had created a European economic constitution. It was revolutionary in the sense that, through this constitution, a unique legal system was created which proved to be a powerful means of pushing forward liberalisation and economic integration. The famous cases *Viking*,[4] *Laval*[5] and *Rüffert*,[6] however, demonstrated the inability of this constitution to defend social norms in the same manner and raised the question as to whether and how the EU's economic dimension can be realigned with a social one. This chapter explores this issue taking a different field as a starting point: European company law. It is an area in which harmonisation attempts are nearly as old as *Van Gend en Loos* and the academic discussions even older.[7] While the clear objective of company law is to support profit maximisation, another goal is to regulate the diverging interests between shareholders, managers, creditors and employees. In the EU, several national models exist which afford different degrees of influence and

---

[1] F. W. Scharpf, 'The asymmetry of European integration, or why the EU cannot be a "social market economy"', *Socio-Economic Review* 8 (2010), 211, 234–5.
[2] Case 26/62 *Van Gend & Loos* [1963] ECR 1.
[3] Case 6/64 *Flaminio Costa* v. *E.N.E.L.* [1964] ECR 585.
[4] C-438/05 *Viking* [2007] ECR I-10779.   [5] C-341/05 *Laval* [2007] ECR I-11767.
[6] C-346/06 *Rüffert* [2008] ECR I-01989.
[7] P. Sanders, *Naar een Europese N.V.?* (Zwolle: W. E. J. Tjeenk Willink, 1959).

levels of safeguards to those constituencies. Whilst the German approach of a social market economy provides more influence to employees, the Anglo-Saxon liberal model in the UK grants more power to shareholders. European company law is therefore required to incorporate these contrasting social and economic approaches.

This chapter analyses the approaches to this issue found in internal market law by examining the developments in company law under the fundamental freedoms and European legislative instruments, such as the Cross-Border Merger Directive[8] or the Societas Europaea (SE) Regulation.[9] It will be argued that internal market law, in theory as well as in practice, has the clear economic objective of erasing barriers to trade. Member States can protect their national social values by invoking justifications inherent in the structure of the fundamental freedoms. However, in this context, the ECJ applies a very strict standard which does not leave much room for employee protection, for example. Whilst this arguably leads to a partial convergence of the models and limits national social standards, there is no conclusive evidence that domestic norms are endangered by regulatory competition between Member States. Therefore, it does not seem likely that there will be a *European* social and economic model in company law in the near future. In response to this, the European legislators have opted for company models which leave discretion to Member States as to the level of employee or creditor protection even in such legislative instruments as regulations.

The first part looks at the different constituencies of a company prior to explaining, in the next section, the different company law models in Europe. The third section discusses the impact of the fundamental freedoms on national company law and the final section examines European company law legislation.

II The constituencies of a company

Jensen and Meckling define companies as organisations that are 'simply legal fictions which serve as a nexus for a set of contracting relationships among individuals'.[10] The individuals were identified as the owners of the company, namely the shareholders, the management, its creditors,

---

[8] Directive 2005/56/EC of the European Parliament and of the Council of 26 October 2005 on cross-border mergers of limited liability companies, OJ L 310/1.

[9] Council Regulation (EC) No. 2157/2001 of 8 October 2001 on the Statute for a European Company (SE), OJ L 294/1.

[10] M. Jensen and W. Meckling, 'Theory of the firm: Managerial behavior, agency costs and ownership structure', *Journal of Financial Economics* 3 (1976), 305, 310.

the employees or any other contractual partner(s).[11] The company thereby solves the problem of how to mobilise capital from the financiers and/or how to organise large-scale production by managers.[12] In contrast to other contractual connections, companies establish long-term relationships between the individuals involved.[13] As Coase wrote in 1937, a company 'is likely ... to emerge in those cases where a very short-term contract would be unsatisfactory'.[14]

Yet the relationship between these different constituencies is not without conflict and is mostly described in terms of the agency or 'principal–agency' problem. The underlying issue is that the agent, that is the management, tends to act in its own interest instead of the interest of the principal (the shareholders). The reason is that, generally, the agent has better information than the principal, and therefore has an incentive to act opportunistically.[15] Within the company, the conflict exists furthermore between controlling shareholders and minority shareholders and between the company and non-shareholder constituencies such as creditors and employees.[16]

Corporate governance deals with and attempts to solve these issues. By means of adequate corporate governance, companies seek to achieve an effective interaction between the different constituencies of a company and ensure that each one receives its fair share.[17] The manner in which the power is divided amongst the constituencies depends very much on a given society's political and social views on the function and position of a company.[18] The influence of labour in the corporate governance process is an example. In the US, where the overall goal is profit maximisation, employees have little power. In European social democracies, employee representatives sit on the boards or assert influence in other ways.[19]

[11] W. Schön, 'The mobility of companies in Europe and the organizational freedom of company founders', European Company and Financial Law Review 3 (2006), 122, 126.
[12] M.J. Roe, Political Determinants of Corporate Governance: Political context, corporate impact (Oxford: Oxford University Press, 2003), p. 13.
[13] Schön (n. 11 above), p. 127.
[14] R.H. Coase, 'The nature of the firm', Economica 3 (1937), 386.
[15] R. Kraakman, The Anatomy of Corporate Law (Oxford: Oxford University Press, 2006), p. 21.
[16] Ibid., p. 195.
[17] G.S. Dallas, Governance and Risk: An analytical handbook for investors, managers, directors, and stakeholders (New York: McGraw-Hill Companies, 2004), p. 171.
[18] I. Lynch-Fannon, Working within Two Kinds of Capitalism (Portland: Hart Publishing, 2003).
[19] Roe (n. 12 above), pp. 201–4.

One way in which corporate governance is implemented is by means of company law.[20] As Kraakman puts it, company law has two general functions: (1) 'it establishes the structure of the corporate form as well as ancillary housekeeping rules necessary to support this structure', and (2) it seeks to mitigate the conflicts among the company's constituencies.[21]

Accordingly, it is already possible to identify the stakeholders and, secondly, to see why conflicts arise between them. The next paragraphs concentrate on the most important groups – (1) the shareholders, (2) creditors and (3) employees – in order to show what would happen if they were not protected.

One problem faced by shareholders and creditors is to obtain sufficient and correct information from the agent. Shareholders need the information in order to determine the risks and benefits of investing in a company. However, it might not be in the interest of the companies to provide the optimal quantity or quality of information. In the extreme, managers might intentionally provide incorrect information.[22] The most common device to mitigate the problems of inadequate information is to rely on mandatory disclosure.

The creditors might also face opportunism by the debtor. Prior to borrowing, the debtor, or shareholder, might lie about assets in order to receive a loan. After borrowing, he might dilute company assets or pursue risky projects because he knows that the creditor will bear the costs of a failed project.[23]

The rationale behind the protection of these constituencies is that better legal protection ensures that more of the company's profits returns, in terms of interests or dividends, to the investors. This leads to higher prices for stocks or cheaper loans given by the creditors and therefore enables more entrepreneurs to finance projects. Consequently, financial markets expand and eventually trigger the economy to grow.[24]

[20] Corporate governance is also built upon securities law, which determines the issuance and exchange of securities by setting disclosure and filing standards. However, insolvency law and the general commercial law also play an important role in assuring the positions of the owners, creditors and other stakeholders. (See Dallas, n. 17 above, p. 170). Finally, also corporate governance codes and self-regulation play a role. See also, in this volume, ch. 4 by Devroe and van Cleynenbreugel and ch. 9 by Kröger.
[21] Kraakman (n. 15 above), p. 21.
[22] R. Yalden, *Business Organizations: Principles, policies and practices* (Toronto: Emond Montgomery Publication, 2008), p. 472.
[23] Kraakman (n. 15 above), p. 72; R. La Porta, F. Lopez-de-Silanes and A. Shleifer, *Investor Protection: Origins, consequences, reform* (Cambridge, MA: National Bureau of Economic Research, 1999), p. 5.
[24] *Ibid.*, p. 3.

The reason for the protection of employees is a different one, based on a specific vision of the balance between the company's constituencies. Some even argue that it goes against efficiency and welfare gains.[25] For example, the US and the UK place company control into the hands of shareholders, which might seem justified as they are the owners of the company. Their objective, of course, is profit maximisation.[26] In other models, however, the market is seen as a vehicle for the organisation of the economy, but not the priority. Profit-making is balanced against social values, such as labour influence, in order to shield employees from opportunistic behaviour of other constituencies, for example in wage negotiations or lay-offs.[27] Employee protection is thus a policy choice[28] which is seen as a middle road between raw capitalism and socialism.[29] Examples of countries in which employees are represented in company boards are Germany, Spain, the Netherlands and Sweden.[30]

III   Different company law models in Europe

This section focuses on the manner in which the tensions between different constituencies are solved within different EU Member States. It is argued that the socio-economic environment determines the respective company law models of the countries.

The starting point is the 'varieties of capitalism' discussion of political economy, which presumes that there exist different kinds of capitalisms, particularly liberal and co-ordinated market economies (LME and CME). Both differ in terms of non-market co-ordination between firms, public influence in the market and a political mandate to

---

[25] K. Pistor, 'Co-determination in Germany: A socio-political model with governance externalities' in M. Blair and M. Roe (eds.), *Employees and Corporate Governance* (Washington: Brookings Institution Press, 1999), pp. 163–93.

[26] I. Lynch-Fannon, *Working within Two Kinds of Capitalism* (Oxford, Portland: Hart Publications, 2003), p. 9.

[27] R. Hyman, 'Britain and the European Social Model: Capitalism against capitalism?', IES Working Paper WP19 (November 2008), p. 7.

[28] T. H. Tröger, *Choice of Jurisdiction in European Corporate Law: Perspectives of European corporate governance* (2004, last revised 2007), electronically available at http://ssrn.com/abstract=568782.

[29] Roe (n 12 above), p. 30.

[30] In fact, Portugal, Italy, Belgium and the UK are the only countries in Europe that do not have any kind of worker board representation (see Kraakman (n. 15 above), p. 62).

redistribute welfare gains.[31] The theory regards companies to be the primary actors and presumes that their behaviour relies on means of market co-ordination. Whilst LMEs rather rely upon competition and formal contracting, CMEs focus on relationships with different stakeholders, such as associations, trade unions and regulatory systems in order to build long-term relationships.[32] Yet, certainly, as Scharpf notes, these are ideal-types, reflecting the 'golden age' of each approach.[33] Nevertheless, as a consequence of these differences, the varieties theory presumes different domestic corporate responses. This line of thinking can also be found in company law, where most authors distinguish between the Anglo-Saxon and the Continental model.[34] The Anglo-Saxon model of corporate governance is based upon the shareholders' interest.[35] It is argued that focusing on maximising shareholder returns advances overall social welfare. Creditors, workers and customers will only deal with the company if they expect to be better off. Therefore, the company has a high interest in ensuring that its business is beneficial for all parties dealing with the firm.[36] Rooted in market capitalism, one idea behind the model is that self-interest and decentralised markets function in a self-regulatory, balancing manner with minimal state intervention.[37] The co-operation between social partners is low, labour organisations are fragmented and employee influence is minimal. Banks play a minimal role in corporate ownership, while the stock exchange plays a strong

[31] M. Höpner and A. Schäfer, 'A new phase of European integration: Organized capitalism in post-Ricardian Europe', *West European Politics* 33 (2010), 344; P. A. Hall and D. W. Soskice, 'An introduction to varieties of capitalism' in P. Hall and D. Soskice (eds.), *Varieties of Capitalism: The institutional foundations of comparative advantage* (Oxford: Oxford University Press, 2001), pp. 8–9.

[32] See also the chapter by Kröger in this collection.

[33] F. W. Scharpf (n 1 above), pp. 234–5. He distinguishes between liberal and social market economies. The latter essentially reflect the system of coordinated market economies.

[34] P. Mäntysaari, *Comparative Corporate Governance: Shareholders as a rule-maker* (Heidelberg: Springer, 2005); also R. H. Schmidt and S. Grohs, 'Angleichung der Unternehmensverfassung in Europa aus ökonom. Perspektive' in S. Grundmann (ed.), *Systembildung und Systemlücken in Kerngebieten des Europäischen Privatrechts* (Tübingen: Mohr Siebeck, 2000), pp. 145–88.

[35] F. Allen and D. Gale, 'A comparative theory of corporate governance', Wharten Working Paper Series 3–27 (2002), pp. 1, 17.

[36] Kraakman (n. 15 above), p. 18.

[37] L. Cernat, 'The emerging European corporate governance model: Anglo-Saxon, Continental, or still the century of diversity?', *Journal of European Public Policy* 11 (2004), 147, 149.

role in corporate finance. The management is characterised by a one-tier board system.[38]

At the opposite end of the spectrum is the Continental model where the company pursues a broad variety of interests, inter alia those of the employees.[39] Contrary to the Anglo-Saxon system, the Continental model regards the market as a vehicle for economic organisation, but not as a political priority.[40] The German concept of 'social market economy' clearly reflects this philosophy. The role of the state is regulatory and there is much co-operation between social partners. Labour organisations are strong and the employees' influence through works councils and board representation is extensive. For example, in a public firm with more than 2,000 employees, half of the supervisory board seats are assigned to employees.[41] Banks play an important role in corporate finance, whereas the role of the stock exchange is limited. Management is characterised by a two-tier board system in which supervisory and executive responsibilities are separate.[42]

Armour analysed the protection of the different stakeholders within the French, German, UK, Indian and US systems. Regarding shareholders, France, Germany and the UK all had a high level of shareholder protection. The UK protected best against boards, followed by France, India and Germany. Regarding the protection against other shareholders (majority vs. minority shareholders), Germany ranked first, followed by France. The UK ranked fourth.[43] Concerning creditor protection Germany ranked first, the UK second and France fifth.[44] Finally, with regard to employee representation, Germany ranked first, France second and India and the UK shared third place.[45]

Based on the analysis above, a link can be identified between the socio-economic environment and different company law models. Where the UK favours a model that pursues the interests of shareholders, strong minority shareholder protection is not needed as ownership is dispersed. This stands in contrast to Germany and France, where minority

---

[38] M. Rhodes and B. van Apeldoom, 'Capital unbound? The transformation of European corporate governance', *Journal of European Public Policy* 5 (1998), 406, 410.

[39] Allen and Gale (n. 35 above), p. 1.   [40] Hyman (n. 27 above), p. 7.

[41] M. Gelter, 'Tilting the balance between capital and labour? The effects of regulatory arbitrage in European corporate law on employees', *Fordham International Law Journal* 33 (2010), 792, 802.

[42] Rhodes and van Apeldoom (n. 38 above), p. 410.

[43] J. Armour *et al.*, 'How do legal rules evolve? Evidence from a cross-country comparison of shareholder, creditor and worker protection', ECGI Working Paper 129 (2009), pp. 25–6.

[44] *Ibid.*, p. 27.   [45] *Ibid.*, p. 32.

shareholder protection is required in order to protect against concentrated ownership. Yet, due to the same characteristic, protection against the board (vis-à-vis managers) is more crucial in the UK than in Germany. In addition, and as a result of the liberal market philosophy, employees have rather little influence and therefore no seats on the management board in the UK, whereas they are highly influential, even on boards, in the social market economy of Germany. Consequently, there are at least two different socio-economic environments and corresponding company law models in the EU which need to be taken into account when developing European company law. Both models were arguably presented in their ideal-type. As the research done by Armour also shows, differences cannot always be explained by relying on the same assumptions. For example in the US, shareholder ownership is dispersed, yet there is no strong protection against boards. Furthermore, the last ten to fifteen years have shown a convergence of law in general.[46] However, as the discussion of EU legislation will show, the major faultlines are still present. The objective of this example was to show that company law does not exist in a legal vacuum but is instead adapted to national social values and to the economic structure of the country. If harmonisation of company law is the objective, those values and prerequisites need to be incorporated or one model is to augment its social standards or the other to lower them. The next part discusses the manner in which European law can influence national company law.

IV The relationship between national company law and European law

National company law is enacted by Member States. However, the EU has two different tools at its disposal to exert influence. It can either harmonise national company laws or scrutinise whether national law complies with the fundamental freedoms. The fundamental freedoms aim to abolish legal barriers to trade regarding goods, free movement of workers, services, capital and establishment. They ensure access to the national markets and that the factors of production compete under the same conditions.[47] This is also called negative

---

[46] *Ibid.*, p. 44.
[47] C. Teichmann, *Binnenmarktkonformes Gesellschaftsrecht* (Berlin: De Gruyter, 2006), p. 131. It should be noted that in practice conditions can hardly ever be the same and only a convergence is possible.

integration.[48] The fundamental freedoms cannot harmonise the legal differences between the Member States. Yet once the legal barriers have been eliminated, the state in which an activity is conducted should not matter.[49] This, however, also means that the fundamental freedoms do not suffice to achieve a completed internal market. As Teichmann notes, they take away the effect of contested national regulation, but they do not replace it with an alternative.[50] Therefore, the Treaty provides tools to harmonise national laws, which is also called positive integration.[51] This is enshrined in Articles 114–15 TFEU (ex Articles 94–5 EC), and further specific provisions such as Article 50 TFEU (ex Article 44 EC) for company law, which gives the Union the possibility of creating the alternatives named above.[52]

Based on positive integration, the European Commission originally envisaged full harmonisation of company law. Yet the efforts were only semi-successful, leading to directives on exotic issues of company law, as Timmermans refers to them, such as internal mergers, divisions of companies, one-man companies etc. Harmonisation of classic issues such as institutional structures, minority protection and directors' liability failed.[53]

Regarding negative integration, it is primarily the freedom of establishment which individual litigants (companies) use in order to extend the mobility of companies throughout Europe.[54] There are two different seats, the central administration and the registered office which, together, are a nexus to a variety of applicable laws to a company, such as company law (including employee board representation), insolvency law, securities law and tax law. The registered office is the official address of a company to which notices, letters and reminders will be sent.[55] The central administration is the place where the main decisions are taken.[56] If a company transfers

---

[48] A. M. El-Agraa, *The European Union: Economics and policies* (Harlow: Prentice Hall, 2004), pp. 1–2.

[49] Teichmann (n. 47 above), p. 57.   [50] Teichmann (n. 47 above), p. 130.

[51] El-Agraa (n. 48 above), pp. 1–2.   [52] *Ibid.*, p. 58.

[53] C. W. A. Timmermans, *Company Law as Ius Commune? First Walter van Gerven Lecture* (Antwerpen: Intersentia, 2002), p. 3. For a discussion of these first legislative instruments see N. Lutter, 'Konzepte, Erfolge und Zukunftsaufgaben Europäischer Gesellschaftsrechtsharmonisierung' in S. Grundmann (ed.), *Systembildung und Systemlücken in Gerngebieten des Euroäischen Privatrechts* (Tübingen: Mohr Siebeck, 2000), pp. 121–43.

[54] Note that also the free movement of capital can have an impact on company law, such as in the *Golden Shares* cases. Due to space constraints, those cases will not be dealt with.

[55] www.businesslink.gov.uk/bdotg/action/detail?type=RESOURCES&itemId=1073791048.

[56] V. Kruse, *Sitzverlegung von Kapitalgesellschaften innerhalb der EG* (Köln: Carl Heymanns Verlag, 1996), pp. 23 *et seq.*, and Opinion of Advocate General Darmon in *Daily Mail* (n. 65 below), paras. 7–8.

one or both seats to another country, it will fall under a different legal regime. In order to protect different constituencies of a company, many countries had prohibited the transfer of the seat through company law.

Within the EU, there are two main conflict-of-law rules used by Member States to determine whether a company is recognised under domestic law:[57] the incorporation theory[58] and the real-seat theory.[59] According to the real-seat theory, the central administration is the connecting factor to the company law while the incorporation theory uses the registered office for this function.

Countries adhering to the incorporation theory, such as the UK or the Netherlands, oblige companies to have their registered office within the country in order to be recognised as a domestic company. However, companies are allowed to transfer their central administration to another country. In a real-seat country, such as Germany before its company law reform,[60] a company is required to have its central administration within the country to fall under domestic law. Material company law also requires that the registered office remains within the country. Under both systems, if companies want to transfer their connecting factor to another country, they would be liquidated, which basically amounts to prohibiting them from transferring their seat.

The reason for the different approaches can be found in their origins. The real-seat theory allows strong state control and seeks to protect shareholders, employees, and creditors by precluding nearly all forms of abuse of law.[61] These groups can be adversely affected by the immigration of foreign

---

[57] F. M. Mucciarelli, 'Company "emigration" and EC freedom of establishment: *Daily Mail* revisited', *European Business Organization Law Review* 9 (2008), 267; S. Rammeloo, *Corporations in Private International Law: A European perspective* (Oxford: Oxford University Press, 2001), p. 282; H. Eidenmüller, 'Theorien zur Bestimmung des Gesellschaftsstatus und Wettbewerb der Gesellscahftsrechte' in H. Eidenmüller (ed.), *Ausländische Kapitalgesellschaften im deutschen Recht* (Munich: Beck, 2004), pp. 2–9.

[58] In 2007, the following European states adhered to this theory: Denmark, Ireland, the Netherlands, UK, Malta, Sweden, Czech Republic, Slovakia, Finland, Hungary, and Cyprus. Commission Staff Working Document: Impact assessment on the Directive on the Cross-border Transfer of Registered Office (2007), SEC (2007) 1707, p. 9, n. 16.

[59] In 2007, the following European states adhered to this theory: Belgium, Germany, Spain, France, Luxembourg, Portugal, Estonia, Norway, Austria, and Latvia. Commission Staff Working Document, p. 9, n. 18.

[60] Since company law reform, Germany now adheres to the incorporation theory.

[61] Rammeloo (n. 57 above), p. 14, Kruse (n. 56 above), p. 6; P. Behrens, 'Centros and company law' in G. Ferrarini, K. J. Hopt and E. Wymeersch (eds.), *Capital Markets in the Age of the Euro: Cross-border transactions, listed companies and regulation* (The Hague: Kluwer Law International, 2002), p. 506.

companies or migration of domestic companies because it can be difficult or impossible to enforce their rights.[62] The incorporation theory, on the other hand, was developed in eighteenth-century UK in order to adapt to the economic needs of the then colonial power. The company was able to incorporate under UK law but still be under the protection of the law at the place of the actual business activities.[63]

V   The conflict between national rules restricting seat transfers and the freedom of establishment

As the prohibition against transferring the seat negates the mobility of companies within the EU, the first case was brought before the ECJ in 1988. Yet, to begin with, since the Treaties of Rome in 1957, the EU guarantees the freedom of establishment to legal persons through the current Article 49 TFEU in conjunction with Article 54 TFEU (ex Article 43 in conjunction with Article 48 EC). The seat transfer is considered as falling under this fundamental freedom and, consequently, there is a prima facie conflict between the substantive company laws of the Member States prohibiting those transfers, the effect of the conflict rules, and EU law, which is supreme to both.[64] Thus, in the last twenty years, several cases dealing with this matter have been brought before the ECJ. The next paragraphs concentrate on the cases *Daily Mail*,[65] *Centros*,[66] *Überseering*,[67] *Inspire Art*[68] and, the most recent one, *Cartesio*.[69]

First, in *Daily Mail*, the ECJ addressed the question of whether limiting the departure of an 'emigrating' domestic company infringed the freedom of establishment. In this case, an English company had decided to transfer its central management to the Netherlands in order to benefit from tax advantages. Yet English tax authorities would only allow it upon a tax payment, which the company was not willing to pay.[70] The Court stated that the conflict rules of the Member States varied too much

---

[62] W. F. Ebke, 'Centros: Some realities and some mysteries', *The American Journal of Comparative Law* 48 (2000), 623, 625–6.
[63] Kruse (n. 56 above), pp. 6–7.
[64] G. Mäsch, 'EGBGB Art. 12: Begriff, Aufgabe und Ziele des IPR' in H. G. Bamberger and H. Roth, *Beck'scher Online-Kommentar* (2009), pp. 1–6.
[65] 81/87, *R* v. *HM Treasury and Commissioners of Inland Revenue, ex p. Daily Mail and General Trust plc* [1988] ECR 5483.
[66] C-212/97 *Centros* [1999] ECR I-1459.   [67] C-208/00 *Überseering* [2002] ECR I-9919.
[68] C-167/01 *Inspire Art* [2003] ECR I-10155.   [69] C-210/06 *Cartesio* [2008] ECR I-09641.
[70] Mucciarelli (n. 57 above), p. 279.

for a full application of Article 49 in conjunction with Article 54 TFEU and excluded cross-border transfers from the application of this fundamental freedom.[71]

In subsequent judgments, the impact of *Daily Mail* was limited to moving-out cases. Thus the following three judgments differed in the sense that, whilst *Daily Mail* concerned a company moving its seat out of a country, the other three judgments concerned companies moving in.

In *Centros*, decided by the Court in 1999, a Danish couple set up a UK company with a branch in Denmark, which basically meant that they transferred their central administration from the UK to Denmark. Yet the Danish authorities refused to register the branch. In their view, the couple sought to evade the Danish minimum capital requirements as the company did not conduct any business in the UK, but exclusively in Denmark. The Court finally ruled that the refusal infringed the company's freedom of establishment.[72]

In *Überseering*, the shares of a company set up in the Netherlands were purchased by a German businessperson. When the company started proceedings against a local creditor in Germany, the court found that Überseering had moved its central administration to Germany by the share transfer. Thus, according to the real-seat theory, German company law was applicable because the central administration was regarded as the connecting factor to German company law. Yet, due to the fact that the company had not been formed in accordance with German law, it lacked legal personality and could not open proceedings.[73] The ECJ declared that this view infringed the freedom of establishment. A Member State has to accept the legal capacity of a company duly established under the law of another Member State.[74]

While *Überseering* concerned the legal capacity and *ius standi* of a foreign company, the recognition of a foreign *lex societatis* by the host Member State had not been addressed. In the case *Inspire Art*, a UK company operated exclusively in the Netherlands and also had its central administration there. Under Dutch law, the company had to indicate that it was a pseudo-foreign company as it had presumably been

---

[71] Case 81/87 (n. 65 above), para. 20.
[72] W. Ringe, 'No freedom of emigration for companies?' *European Business Law Review* 3 (2005), 1.
[73] S. Lombardo, 'Conflict of law rules in company law after Überseering: An economic and comparative analysis of the allocation of policy competence in the European Union', *European Business Organization Law Review* 4 (2003), 301, 305, n. 12.
[74] Ringe (n. 72 above), p. 10.

incorporated in the UK only to evade Dutch company law rules. The ECJ ruled that such rules infringed Article 49 TFEU and that a Member State has to recognise a company operating in its territory under a foreign *lex societatis*.[75]

Looking at these developments, especially after *Überseering* and *Inspire Art*, it was disputed whether the real-seat theory could still be upheld in its original form.[76] Yet the revolution had only occurred in cases involving a Member State's recognition of a foreign company. In December 2008 the ECJ attempted to clarify its view on moving out cases by delivering the judgment in *Cartesio*. The case concerned a Hungarian company seeking to transfer its central administration to Italy whilst remaining under Hungarian company law. The Hungarian authorities prohibited *Cartesio* from doing so. Even though the Court ultimately ruled that the company could not rely on Article 49 TFEU in order to achieve its goal, it extended the cross-border mobility of companies in an *obiter dictum*. The ECJ decided that seat transfers are possible as long as the country-specific rules which determine the existence of a company are complied with. That means that if the factor connecting a company to a specific national company law is its place of central administration, the company has to transfer the central administration and, if required, the registered office in order to change the applicable company law.[77]

From a constitutional point of view, the case law shows tension in the institutional balance between the EU and national levels. Even though the Court formally already had the power fully to extend cross-border mobility in 1988 in the *Daily Mail* case, it decided that seat transfers would fall outside of the freedom of establishment. Also in subsequent case law, the ECJ was reluctant to bring cross-border seat transfers within the scope of the fundamental freedoms and thus to change the

---

[75] *Ibid.*, pp. 11–12.
[76] See e.g. G. Gänßler, "'Inspire Art' – Briefkastengesellschaften "on the Move"', *DStR* 50 (2003), 2167; K. Baelz and T. Baldwin, 'The end of the real seat theory (Sitztheorie): the European Court of Justice decision in Ueberseering of 5 November 2002 and its impact on German and European company law', *German Law Journal* 3 (2002), www.germanlawjournal.com/article. php?id=214; A. Engert, 'Rechtslage nach dem Ende der Sitztheorie' in H. Eidenmüller (ed.), *Ausländische Kapitalgesellschaften* (Munich: C. H. Beck, 2004).
[77] *Cartesio*, paras. 108–12. The interpretation of this decision is still disputed, but the prevailing view is that cross border mobility was enhanced. See e.g. R. B. van Hees, 'Het Cartesio-arrest en re-incorporatie binnen de Europese Unie', *V&O* 1 (2009), 5; G. J. Vossestein, 'Grensoverschrijdende zetelverplaatsing en omzetting van vennotschappen', *NTER* 5 (2009), 184; D. Deak, '*Cartesio*: A step forward in interpreting the EC freedom to emigrate', *Tax Notes International* 54 (2009), 493; O. Valk, 'Increasing corporate mobility through outbound establishment', *Utrecht Law Review* 6 (2010), 151.

regulatory balance in favour of the EU. Most probably, the Court also felt that the two theories were too different. The real-seat theory was based on a high level of protection of the stakeholders and the incorporation theory on a high level of freedom and Member States were in any case opposed to any harmonisation in this area. Article 293 EC, now repealed under Lisbon, allowed Member States to reach agreement on the mutual recognition of companies and, in 1968, the Convention on the Mutual Recognition of Companies, Firms and Legal Persons was signed by the original six EC Member States. However, the Netherlands had never ratified the Convention.[78] The European Commission had also published a proposal for a fourteenth Company Law Directive on the transfer of the registered office. It never even made it to the European Parliament or the Council and was finally abandoned in 2007.

The case law from *Centros* to *Inspire Art* had a major impact on jurisdictional arbitrage. While in 2001 only 516 German companies were registered in the UK and operated in Germany, in 2005 19,686 foreign companies were registered in the UK, 12,019 of which were operating in Germany. Here one can clearly see the impact of the Court and the 'economic constitution' which allowed individual commercial litigants to enforce their right to the freedom of establishment to break up one of the fortresses protecting domestic norms: the real-seat theory.

Did this process lead to regulatory competition either with the consequence of forcing countries to lower their standards or in the sense that companies choose the most favourable regulatory framework? According to several authors,[79] company law reforms in Europe provide a mixed picture. The freedom to contract has been extended in Italy, but limited in Spain. The minimum capital requirements have been abolished in France, yet they have not been touched in Spain or in Italy.[80] In Germany, the country in which the highest number of companies registered in the UK operates, the legislator contemplated lowering these requirements but eventually maintained the minimum capital requirement.[81] As a consequence, there is no

---

[78] W. Wymeersch, 'Company law in Europe and European company law', Financial Law Institute Working Paper 6 (2001), pp. 3–4.

[79] W. Bratton, J. McCahery and E. Vermeulen, 'How does corporate mobility affect lawmaking? A comparative analysis', ECGI Law Working Paper 91 (2008), p. 3; E. Kieninger, 'Aktuelle Entwicklungen des Wettbewerbs der Gesellschaften', German Working Papers in Law and Economics 14 (2007), pp. 20–1.

[80] *Ibid.*

[81] www.bmj.bund.de/enid/86beedd318f30cd645a8364e7b4a6d93,cf1b3a706d635f6964092 d0935363133093a0979656172092d0932303038093a096d6f6e7468092d093132093a095f 7472636964092d0935363133/Press/Press_Releases_zg.html.

clear trend towards a 'race to the bottom' of national standards in company law. This might also be in line with the finding that, until now, cross-border seat transfers mainly concern start-up companies which use this option in order to circumvent minimum capital requirements and social standards.[82] However, one should stress that only since December 2008 has it been possible, based on the *Cartesio* case, to change easily the legal company form, which in many EU countries also regulates employee board representation. Yet, so far, research done by Pütz shows that the number of companies operating in Germany, which would be required to have a system of employee board representation under German company law but operate under foreign law and thus do not have a system of co-determination, amounts to only thirty-seven. Compared to the number of over 2,000 companies operating under a system of employee board representation, the author concludes that, currently, there are not many companies using this option, nor is there pressure on the national regulator to adapt its social norms.[83] In addition, amongst German companies, it is not clear that they are themselves opposed to co-determination. It is even said that the reason behind the catalogue business company Otto's decision to sell its 22 per cent stake in the fashion company Zara was because the latter planned to change from a German GmbH into a Dutch B.V. & Co. KG. The consequence of this was that Zara would no longer be required to have a co-determination system while Otto did not want to appear as cutting the competences of the employee representatives.

However, one should keep in mind that firms are not only regulated by company law and that also the two different seats are not only the connecting factor to company law, but also to domestic insolvency law,[84] securities law[85] and tax law.[86] Thus, the considerations to make use of corporate mobility are much more complex. As insolvency law cases demonstrate, these decisions do not always reflect opportunistic behaviour, but sound deliberation between debtor and creditor in order to guarantee the survival of the

---

[82] Bratton, McCahery and Vermeulen (n. 79 above), p. 26.

[83] S. Sick, *Mitbestimmungsrelevante Unternehmen mit ausländischen/kombiniert ausländischen Rechtsformen* (2010), www.boeckler.de/pdf/mbf_2010_01_20_sick.pdf.

[84] J. Israel, *European Cross-border Insolvency Regulation* (Antwerpen: Intersentia, 2005); H. Eidenmüller, 'Abuse of law in the context of European insolvency law', *European Company and Financial Law Review* (2009), http://ssrn.com/abstract=1353932.

[85] L. Enriques and T. Tröger, 'Issuer choice in Europe', ECGI Working Paper 90 (2008), pp. 1–73.

[86] G. Maisto, *Residence of Companies under Tax Treaties and EC Law* (Amsterdam: IBFD, 2009).

company.[87] Further research will be needed in the following years in order to be able to give a solid conclusion as to the impact of the *Cartesio* case law on national socio-economic environments.

VI   Fundamental freedoms as a balancing test

A further aspect that needs to be taken into account is that the fundamental freedoms are, in theory, a balancing test. As explained before, Article 49 TFEU prohibits any restrictions on the freedom of establishment. This not only includes direct or indirect discrimination but, since *Kraus*, it also extends to rules which constitute a mere hindrance to the freedom of establishment.[88] Yet this does not mean that every restriction is a violation of the Treaty. The aim of the fundamental freedoms is to create an internal market by abolishing legal barriers to trade. However, there might be cases in which the objective of the internal market violates the interests of certain groups. As it has been acknowledged that those interests cannot simply be overridden, justification grounds were incorporated into the internal market law. This allows striking a balance between the objective of the fundamental freedoms and objectives of the public interest. Justifications can be found in Article 52 TFEU or in the mandatory requirements which have been developed by the Court. The justifications found in Article 52 TFEU are limited to public policy, public security and public health and can be used to 'heal' a discriminatory measure. The list of justification grounds under the mandatory requirements is open but can only be used for non-discriminatory measures, not for economic reasons.[89]

Yet a rule that allegedly violates the Treaty cannot simply be justified because it serves a public interest that is worth protecting. It must also be suitable for securing the attainment of the objective which it pursues, and it must not go beyond what is necessary in order to attain the goal.[90]

As restrictions in the field of company law are generally non-discriminatory,[91] Member States can use the mandatory requirements to justify restrictive rules. This means that they can attempt to put

[87] W. Ringe, 'Forum shopping under the EU Insolvency Regulation', Oxford University Legal Research Paper 33 (2008), pp. 1–33.

[88] C-19/92 *Kraus* v. *Land Baden Württemberg* [1993] ECR I-1663.

[89] P. Craig and G. De Búrca, *EU Law: Text, cases and materials*, 4th edn (Oxford: Oxford University Press, 2008), p. 802.

[90] *Kraus*, para. 32; C-55/94 *Gebhard* [1995] ECR I-4165, para. 37; *Centros*, para. 34; *Inspire Art*, para 133.

[91] Cf. *Centros*, para. 34 and *Inspire Art*, para. 131.

basically any justification ground forward which they can prove to be an 'imperative requirement in the public interest'.[92] It should be noted that, in *Überseering*,[93] the Court stated that a full negation of the freedom of establishment cannot be justified. Yet it acknowledged that measures might be justifiable on grounds of protection of the interests of minority shareholders, creditors, employees, and even tax authorities.[94] In *Inspire Art* and *Centros*, the Court also accepted the grounds of abuse of law and fraudulent conduct and fraudulent insolvency.[95] As one can see, the first grounds correspond to the stakeholders protected under the real-seat theory.

Consequently one might argue that Member States can therefore protect their social and societal values under the internal market law. Yet the following qualifications should be made.

First, even though the protection of employees, minority shareholders and creditors are justifications acknowledged by the Court, it has not yet accepted them in any of the cases. It is the ECJ which will determine whether for example minimum capital requirements are suitable and do not go beyond what is necessary in order to protect creditors. According to Teichmann, until now the Court has adopted an information model in its case law. In *Centros* and *Inspire Art*, the Court was of the opinion that the protection of creditors was a legitimate objective. Yet it found that minimum capital requirements were not necessary as the creditors would already be sufficiently protected by having information about the company form. In this case, it was enough for the creditor to know that the company was from the UK.[96]

Yet it should also be noted that in *Centros*, *Überseering* and *Inspire Art*, a company had been set up, the seat was moved to another country and it started to become economically active there. In such a case, the creditors cannot expect such a transfer and the resulting changes in law. Therefore, it might be that in such cases the Court would decide differently.[97]

A second qualification is that the approach of the justifications is very casuistic and therefore does not provide a high level of legal certainty. Due to the fact that Article 49 TFEU is directly applicable, national courts can assess whether a national rule violates the Treaty and thus

---

[92] *Inspire Art*, para. 109.   [93] *Überseering*, para. 93.   [94] *Ibid.*, para. 92.
[95] *Inspire Art*, para. 109.
[96] Teichmann (n. 47 above), p. 147; S. Grundmann, 'Ausbau des Informationsmodells im Europäischen Gesellschaftsrecht', *DStR* 6 (2004), 232.
[97] K. J. Hopt, 'Internationales Gesellschaftsrecht und europäische Einflüsse' in A. Baumbach, K. J. Hopt and H. Merkt, *Handelsgesetzbuch* (Munich: C. H. Beck, 2010), pp. 29–33.

can also assess them in the context of the mandatory requirements. This not only means that national courts might apply different standards than those adopted by the ECJ, but also that the courts of the twenty-seven Member States might decide in different ways and therefore develop different social and economic standards.

VII   Abuse of law and 'Social Europe'

Nevertheless one specific justification ground can be explored in more depth because there is existing case law in this area. It is the ground of behaviour abusive of Union law in order to circumvent national legislation. The underlying question is at which point a certain behaviour falls under jurisdictional arbitrage or so-called 'forum-shopping' and when it falls under an abuse of rights. The issue concerns the 12,000 letter-box companies which operate in Germany while having their registered office in the UK in order to circumvent German company law legislation. Whether and in which instances this is permissible is a question which the ECJ has answered in a couple of cases.

In *Cadbury Schweppes*,[98] the Court (further) developed a two-pronged test consisting of an objective and a subjective part.[99] The objective part signifies that the ECJ assesses the abuse of rights against the objectives pursued by the Union provision. The subjective part refers to the intention of the natural or legal person. The objective part can be proven by the existence of a 'wholly artificial arrangement', which is not an actual establishment of a company pursuing a genuine economic activity.[100] According to the Court, 'that finding must be based on objective factors which are ascertainable by third parties with regard, in particular, to the extent to which the [office] physically exists in terms of premises, staff and equipment'.[101] It should be noted that any legislation still needs to be proportionate in relation to the objective.[102]

However, it is important to note that this only appears to concern the situation in which a company relies on the freedom of establishment without pursuing the objective of this provision. The Court stated in *Inspire Art* that:

> as the Court confirmed in paragraph 27 of *Centros*, the fact that a national of a Member State who wishes to set up a company can choose

---

[98]   C-196/04 *Cadbury Schweppes* [2006] ECR I-07995.
[99]   The Court had already developed a less sophisticated version of the test in *Centros*, para. 25.
[100]   *Cadbury Schweppes*, paras. 54–5.   [101]   *Ibid.*, para. 67.   [102]   *Ibid.*, para. 57.

to do so in the Member State the company-law rules of which seem to
him the least restrictive and then set up a branch in other Member States
is inherent in the exercise, in a single market, of the freedom of establishment guaranteed by the Treaty.[103]

At that point, one might wonder what precisely the objective of this
provision is. In *Factortame*, the Court stated that the freedom of establishment presupposes the actual pursuit of an economic activity through
a fixed establishment in that state for an indefinite period.[104]
Consequently, a UK company, transferring its central administration,
does pursue the objective of the Treaty as it integrates into the host
Member State economy by pursuing an economic activity there.
However, one might seriously question whether this is more than a
formal argument regarding nationals of another Member State. When
a German national orders an English limited company via the
Internet,[105] and registers its branch in Germany, and therefore does
not even have to leave Germany, he clearly does not economically
integrate into a 'host Member State'. Nevertheless, one might state
that, after *Cartesio*, the abuse doctrine still prevents companies from
only transferring their registered office. To recap, the registered office is
the official address of the company to which letters and notices are sent.
For example in the UK, it does not even need to correspond to the
address where the business is actually carried out.[106] Therefore, it does
not involve any economic integration into the host Member State.

Consequently, the abuse-of-law discussion clearly shows the problem
of the integration of countries with different socio-economic standards
into one internal market. Theoretically, one standard should be as good
as the other. The only point of reference is the creation of an internal
market. This also led the Court to develop the doctrine of mutual
recognition in the *Cassis de Dijon*[107] case in the context of the free
movement of goods. Yet while this case concerned product requirements, it could in the context of company law, for example, be about a
social standard such as employee participation. From the point of view of
citizens of a sovereign nation state, their standard in this context might

---

[103] *Inspire Art*, para. 138.
[104] C-221/89 *Factortame and ors.* [1991] ECR I-3905, para. 20; C-246/89 *Commission* v.
UK [1991] ECR I-4585, para. 21–3.
[105] See e.g. www.wbc-ltd.de/html/ltd_grunden_-_warum_bei_uns.html.
[106] www.businesslink.gov.uk/bdotg/action/detail?type=RESOURCES&itemId=1073791048.
[107] Case 120/78 *Cassis de Dijon* [1979] ECR 00649.

belong to what they perceive as their national values, such as in the German social market economy. Notwithstanding the discussion as to whether registering in the UK and conducting business there can be legally qualified as an abuse of law, it is highly questionable whether such rulings add to the legitimacy and acceptance of the EU by its citizens and their understanding of what the project of the EU actually concerns.

VIII European company legislation

The next section examines the Cross-Border Merger Directive and the SE Regulation in order to illustrate how EU company law attempts to balance the diverging national approaches. Both instruments represent a different approach to the previous harmonisation attempts, especially reflecting the highly difficult negotiations. For example, regarding the SE Regulation, the Commission had submitted its first proposal in 1970; the original ideas stemmed from 1959; yet, agreement could only be reached in 2001.[108] First, the two legal instruments will be analysed before looking at the implications of both for the incorporation of national social and economic values into European company law.

A   Cross-Border Merger Directive

The directive, which entered into force on 26 October 2005, facilitates cross-border mergers of limited liability companies. Member States have to allow the merger between a domestic and a foreign EU limited liability company if the national law of the relevant Member States permits mergers between such types of companies.

As can be seen from Article 4 of the directive, the legislative instrument relies heavily upon national law. Companies do not only have to comply with the provisions and formalities of national law, but national authorities can also oppose a merger on grounds of public interest. As paragraph 2 of Article 4 specifies, the provisions and formalities specifically refer to the protection of creditors, debenture and holders of securities and shares and minority shareholders as well as employees as regards rights other than those governed by Article 16. Put simply, Article 16 on worker participation provides that if one of the merging

---

[108] P. Behrens, 'Europäische Gesellschaft' in M. A. Dauses (ed.), *EU-Wirtschaftsrecht* (Munich: C. H. Beck, 2010), p. 155; S. Pluskat, 'Die Arbeitnehmerbeteiligung in der geplanten Europäischen AG', *DStR* 35 (2001), 1483.

companies employs more than 500 workers and uses a participation structure and if the national legislation after the merger does not provide for the same level of participation, the rules of Directive 2001/86/EC (European Company) apply. The directive is discussed below.

The directive was required to be implemented by Member States by 15 December 2007. Given its nature as a directive, Member States could apply slightly different safeguards. Germany will be taken as an example.

The Second Act on the Amendment of the German Transformation Act (*Zweites Gesetz zur Änderung des Umwandlungsgesetzes*) implemented the directive in Germany. Summarising, the major points concerning third-party protection are the following:

(1) The shareholders of both companies have to approve the merger in accordance with the relevant national law.
(2) The creditors of the transferring company have to be provided with security if they can show within two months of the announcement of the Common Terms that the fulfillment of their claims might be jeopardised and that they cannot yet claim a settlement and that their claims have arisen before or within fifteen days of the publication of the Common Terms.
(3) Employee participation is regulated in the Act on Employee Participation in the case of cross-border merger and is very similar to the structure under the SE.
(4) Concerning minority shareholders, German legislation provides that if the transferring company is German it must offer to acquire the shares of those minority shareholders that oppose the merger.[109]

B European Company Statute

The objective of the European Company Statute was to create a 'European company' with its own legal framework in order to avoid the constraints of twenty-seven different legal systems within the EU. Since the previous section on the fundamental freedoms focused on seat transfers, this issue will also be dealt with in this section.

The Commission submitted its first proposal in 1970. Five years later, it published its second proposal. Both envisaged the SE as an autonomous European company law entity with a two-tier board and a system

---

[109] For this part see Freshfields, *Implementation of the EU Cross-border Merger Directive in Germany* (2007), pp. 1–10, www.freshfields.com/publications/pdfs/2007/may21/18736.pdf.

of co-determination modelled on the German approach. However, after the accession of the UK and Ireland to the European Community, these ideas were not feasible and the plan was dropped during the 1980s. The Commission started to lobby again for the SE in 1988 in the context of the completion of the internal market. Contrary to the 1970s, sensitive areas were left to national law. Still, the positions of Germany and the UK on co-determination were not compatible and it took another ten years until 2001 before agreement could be reached.[110]

The transfer of the registered office of a SE is found in Article 8 of the SE Regulation. The interests of creditors and holders of other rights in respect of the SE are protected by Member State legislation. A competent authority at Member State level will issue a certificate stating that those interests are sufficiently protected.[111] Furthermore, within the two months, the competent authority can oppose the transfer on grounds of public interest.[112] Finally, the SE may not transfer its registered office if proceedings for winding up, liquidation, insolvency or suspension of payments or similar proceedings are pending.[113]

As a consequence, it can be stated that the main constituencies are protected.[114] The study on the operation and the impacts of the Statute for a European Company[115] shows that 64 per cent of Member States chose to adopt safeguards for minority shareholders,[116] 48 per cent of Member States have implemented special protection for creditors[117] and 52 per cent have provided the public authorities with the right to oppose the transfer.[118]

The field of conflict with regard to the SE Regulation was employee participation and it was highly difficult to get political agreement on that

---

[110] Pluskat (n. 108 above), pp. 1483–4.   [111] Art. 8, para. 7.   [112] Art. 8, para. 14.

[113] Art. 8, para. 15.

[114] For a detailed discussion on the implementation of the SE in the Member States see D. van Gerven and P. Storm, *The European Company* (Cambridge: Cambridge University Press, 2006); K. Oplustil and C. Teichmann, *The European Company: All over Europe* (Berlin: De Gruyter, 2004).

[115] *Study on the Operation and the Impacts of the Statute for a European Company (SE) –* 2008/S 144–192482 (2009), http://ec.europa.eu/internal_market/consultations/docs/2010/se/study_SE_9122009_en.pdf.

[116] Austria, Germany, Denmark, Finland, Greece, Hungary, Latvia, Portugal, Poland, Czech Republic, Romania, Slovenia, Spain, France, Estonia. In all countries the safeguard is basically to have the shares redeemed. See *ibid.*, p. 76.

[117] Austria, Germany, Denmark, Finland, Greece, Latvia, the United Kingdom, France, Spain, Cyprus, Sweden and the Netherlands.

[118] Belgium, Cyprus, Denmark, Spain, France, Latvia, the Netherlands, Poland, Portugal, Sweden, the United Kingdom, Bulgaria and Greece.

matter.[119] In principle, certain information and consultation procedures have to exist for every SE. Board representation depends on the negotiations by a special body, which represents the employees of the company in the different Member States proportionate to their number. If 25 per cent of the employees were covered by co-determination, and this system is to be reduced through the establishment of the SE by merger, a two-third majority representing two-thirds of the employees that are employed in at least two Member States is required. The same holds for 50 per cent if a holding SE is created.[120] The special negotiation body has to come to an agreement within six months, otherwise a standard model applies.

The objective of this system was to incorporate both a system without board-level employee participation, such as in the UK, and a co-determination system, like in Germany. Naturally, this system is not perfect. UK-based companies are complaining about the additional costs of the negotiations which have to take place before creating any SE.[121] In Germany, on the other hand, commentators explain the high numbers of SEs present by the circumstance that, through this company law model, it is possible to 'freeze' employee participation due to the fact that there is no adaption necessary to increasing numbers of employees.[122]

C   The new mode of regulation: a way forward for a Social Europe?

Both pieces of legislation can be viewed in a line of legislative instruments, which are based on 'flexibility', 'voluntarism' and 'subsidiary'.[123] The mode has changed from a primarily substantive to a procedural legislative instrument. Harmonisation is reached by

[119] P. Storm, 'The Societas Europaea: A new opportunity?' in D. van Gerven and P. Storm (eds.), *The European Company* (Cambridge: Cambridge University Press, 2006), pp. 16–17.
[120] S. Schwimbersky, 'Worker participation in Europe: Current developments and its impact on employees outside the EU', *AIRAANZ* (2005), 189, 192.
[121] See e.g. The Law Society of England and Wales, *Consultation on the Results of the Study on the Operation and the Impact of the Statute for a European Company (SE)*, http://circa.eu ropa.eu/Public/irc/markt/markt_consultations/library?l=/company_law/statute_european/ registered_organisations/40law_wales-enpdf/_EN_1.0_&a=d, p. 4.
[122] J. Reichert, 'Experience with the SE in Germany', *Utrecht Law Review* 4 (2008), 28.
[123] B. Keller, 'The European Company Statute: Employee involvement – and beyond', *Industrial Relations Journal* 33 (2002), 424.

creating a common procedure for cross-border mergers, or a European company form, However, large areas of the substantive provisions are left to the Member States and to negotiation between social partners at a lower level, such as with employee participation in the SE.[124] Critiques of such a process might argue that those legislative instruments do not lead to 'true' harmonisation and are a smallest-common-denominator approach because no consensus could be found between Member States. However, a counter argument can be put forward. As this chapter shows, company law reflects a certain socio-economic environment which fundamentally differs among Member States. Moreover, simple preferences might also differ. As Teichmann notes, for some it is enough if there is a warning sign before a rather dangerous bend, others prefer having a guard rail.[125] Consequently, it is logical that consensus is difficult to reach, and it would also not be desirable as different national solutions to the tension between the company's constituencies reflect different domestic environments which also require different solutions.

Furthermore, with regard to the observation that an economic constitution, based on the fundamental freedoms, which is enforced by the ECJ practically only leaves very limited room for social values, one might even argue that this legislative approach might be a way forward for 'Social Europe'. Clearly, in the short run, it will not lead to a unified system of European social values. However, it allows incorporating domestic social values into a European economic constitution. The main argument here is that, theoretically, Union institutions have to comply with the fundamental freedoms. Consequently, the ECJ could scrutinise safeguards of the company's constituencies based on a European legislative instrument and determine whether they pose a legal barrier to the internal market.[126] However, in practice and in opposition to the Member States, the institutions have a wider discretion. The ECJ will only find a violation of the fundamental freedoms if the weighing of interests by the institutions has been manifestly wrong.[127] Still, it needs to be kept in mind that the Court can still

---

[124] *Ibid.*, p. 439.   [125] Teichmann (n. 47 above), p. 149.

[126] Case 37/83 *Rewe-Zentral AG* v. *Direktor der Landwirtschaftskammer Rheinland* [1984] ECR 1229; C-284/95 *Safety Hi-Tech* v. *S & T* [1998] ECR I-04301.

[127] Case 233/94 *Germany* v. *Parliament and Council* [1997] ECR I-02405; 31/88 *FEDESA* [1990] ECR I-04023; Teichmann (n. 47 above), p. 154.

scrutinise the Member State legislation, to which the directive or regulation refers, in the normal way as to the compatibility with the fundamental freedoms.[128]

IX   Conclusion

Taking the quote of Scharpf at the outset of this chapter and comparing it with the foregoing sections of this chapter, one has to conclude that his statement is supported by the findings in company law. A European economic *and social* constitution does not seem to be emerging.

Certain qualifications have to be made, however. One should keep in mind that the internal market allows the balancing of the fundamental freedoms against justifications invoked by the Member States. Yet, when looking at past case law, one does not become too enthusiastic about this possibility. The Court applies a very strict standard which does not leave much room for employee protection measures, for example. However, in the same breath one also needs to stress that the ECJ has not yet had the opportunity to rule on, for example, measures protecting the German co-determination system.

Moreover, until now, there is little evidence that corporate mobility has led to regulatory competition that seriously endangers domestic social models. The number of companies which take advantage of this opportunity is too small and, as the case of the catalogue company Otto shows, certain social norms are still strong.

Finally, when regarding European company legislation, the focus in this chapter is on the Cross-Border Merger Directive and the SE Regulation. The approach of the European legislators to the tension between different social and economic values is to adopt procedural instruments and leave issues such as the safeguards made available to the company stakeholders to Member States and social partners to address. Such a method arguably acknowledges that Europe wants to exist as one entity; however, it also recognises that this entity still contains twenty-seven different sovereign countries. As is often stated: Europe – unity in diversity.

As argued in the last part, this method might actually be a way forward for a 'Social' Europe. European legislation that incorporates different national social values can be shielded more easily from the impact of the fundamental freedoms as enforced by the ECJ. This would restore the

---

[128]   C-205/07 *Gysbrechts* [2008] ECR I-09947.

institutional balance on two levels – between Member States and the EU, but also inter-institutionally between the Court and the legislative bodies. It also has the potential of bringing the European project closer to its citizens. If Europe wants to move forward, the European institutions should not feed the fear of their citizens that the EU can simply override their values and preferences, but show that they actually respect them.

The consequence of the foregoing is, however, not that a European economic and social constitution will never come into existence. If company law is responsive to its socio-economic environment, it will converge at the same speed as Europe is integrating or converging as a society, and not as a political construct.

7

Services of general economic interest under EU law constraints

ULLA NEERGAARD[*]

I Introduction

In his Opinion in the *Federutility* case, Advocate General Colomer observed that:

> In the early days of the welfare state, certain areas of the economy were set apart from the free market philosophy with the aim of reducing the distance between the 'dominated *lebensraum* (living space)' and the 'effective *lebensraum*'. Inspired by ideals which went beyond the strictly economic – enshrined in the time-honoured continental legal concept of *service public* – state intervention in some sectors was intensified, monopolies were created and regulation was increased. Since the Single European Act, when competition was installed as the new deity on 'the altar of political ideas', public service has become an obstacle to be overcome in the name of a liberalisation on which all hopes were pinned. The creation of an open market is the first step of this policy, but once barriers have been removed there remain certain requirements which the market alone is not able to meet. Hence the origins of public intervention, in the form of 'services of general interest' and 'public service obligations', imposed by the authorities on undertakings in liberalised sectors in order to safeguard public interests which, because they are inalienable,

---

[*] This is a revised version of a paper presented at the conference 'European Economic and Social Constitutionalism after the Treaty of Lisbon', 4 September 2009 (University of Leeds). Certain parts may be seen as a development of previous works such as U. Neergaard, 'Services of general (economic) interest: What aims and values count?' in U. Neergaard, R. Nielsen and L. M. Roseberry (eds.), *Integrating Welfare Functions into EU Law: From Rome to Lisbon* (Copenhagen: DJØF, 2009); and U. Neergaard, 'Services of general economic interest: The nature of the beast' in M. Krajewski, U. Neergaard and J. van den Gronden (eds.), *The Changing Legal Framework of Services of General Interest in Europe: Between competition and solidarity* (The Hague: T. M. C. Asser Press, 2009), pp. 17–50. In principle, only material which has come to my knowledge before 1 January 2010 has been included.

cannot be left to market forces to take care of. It is the great challenge of economic law today to define the limits of this state activity. So far, the question has only arisen in connection with the existence of exclusive rights or the financing of these services and rarely in relation to public service obligations. It is precisely this aspect with which the present reference for a preliminary ruling is concerned.[1]

One of the most fundamental problems at present is how to understand and solve the problems connected with economic and social dimensions of European integration, as well as deciding how far the initiation of this development should go. An area where these considerations are particularly present is the area concerning services of general economic interest (SGEIs) as very eloquently expressed recently by Advocate General Colomer in the above quotation.[2] SGEIs constitute an EU legal concept and may in simplified terms be viewed as related to the more national terms 'public services' or 'welfare services'. During the last one or two decades, SGEIs have moved from almost anonymity to the very centre stage of legal and political debate in the EU, situated as they are in the middle of apparently antagonistic interests of liberalisation and welfare.[3] The purpose of this chapter is to examine the development in this area, in light of the process of constitutionalism which the regulation of these services has undergone.

The development of the Treaty texts will be touched upon as these represent the 'hardest' law in the examined field, and also are likely to be 'constitutional' in nature (section II).[4] In addition, the case law of the Court of Justice will be included (section III).[5] Both sources of law will be

---

[1] Opinion of Advocate General D. Ruiz-Jarabo Colomer of 20 October 2009 in Case C-265/08, *Federutility and ors.* v. *Autorità per l'energia elettrica e il gas* (decided on 20 April 2010, n.y.r.), paras. 1–4. Footnotes included in the original version of the quotation have been omitted.

[2] Hereinafter to be referred to as SGEIs. Regarding the definition of these concepts see e.g. Neergaard (see * above), pp. 17–50. Also see D. Damjanovic and B. de Witte, 'Welfare integration through EU law: The overall picture in the light of the Lisbon Treaty' in U. Neergaard, R. Nielsen and L.M. Roseberry, *Integrating Welfare Functions into EU Law: From Rome to Lisbon* (Copenhagen: DJØF, 2009), which contains an insightful analysis with the point of departure taken in the concept 'welfare services'.

[3] See e.g. M. Krajewski, 'Providing legal clarity and securing policy space for public services through a legal framework for services of general economic interest: Squaring the circle', *EPL* (2008), 377.

[4] Concerning the soft law in this area, see U. Neergaard, 'SGEIs: The Commission soft law and legislative approach including the Treaty of Lisbon' in E. Szyszczak *et al.* (eds.), *Developments in Services of General Interest* (forthcoming).

[5] Pursuant to Art. 19 TEU, the terminology regarding the European courts now is: 'The Court of Justice of the European Union shall include the Court of Justice, the General

examined from an evolutionary point of view in order to trace more exactly the contours of the transformation which is likely to have taken place. On this basis, some final conclusions are stated (section IV).

II   The development in the Treaties

In what follows, a fairly quick glance is taken at the Treaty texts including the Treaty of Rome, the Treaty of Amsterdam and the Treaty of Lisbon (ToL). The Treaty of Maastricht and the Treaty of Nice are not of direct relevance here, and thus are not dealt with.

A   The Treaty of Rome

The birthmarks of the EU are to be found with the establishment of the original European Economic Community pursuant to the Treaty of Rome which entered into force on 1 January 1958. This was, as the name itself already indicates, largely a Community with only an economic character, the focus being primarily on economic integration. This original premise should not, however, be viewed as being identical to a premise of a market economic ideology always to rule. Especially Article 90 EEC (later Article 86 EC and now Article 106 TFEU) – which necessarily must be of particular interest here – should be seen as not completely allowing for solely a market economic ideology to prevail. This provision had the following wording which, with the exception of the numbering of the provisions which are referred to, in principle is unaltered until today:

> 1. In the case of public undertakings and undertakings to which Member States grant special or exclusive rights, Member States shall neither enact nor maintain in force any measure contrary to the rules contained in this Treaty, in particular to those rules provided for in Article 7 and Articles 85 to 94 [later Articles 12 and 81–9 EC and now Articles 18 and 101–9 TFEU].
> 2. Undertakings entrusted with the operation of services of general economic interest or having the character of a revenue-producing

Court and specialised courts . . .' This terminology is used throughout the present chapter, also in situations of reference to case law rendered before the entering into force of the Lisbon Treaty. Therefore, what often has been referred to as the European Court of Justice will here be referred to as the Court of Justice. Also, an analysis of judgments from other courts of relevance is not systematically included, as it is considered sufficient to limit the analysis to judgments from the highest court in the hierarchy.

monopoly shall be subject to the rules contained in this Treaty, in particular to the rules on competition, in so far as the application of such rules does not obstruct the performance, in law or in fact, of the particular tasks assigned to them. The development of trade must not be affected to such an extent as would be contrary to the interests of the Community.

   3. The Commission shall ensure the application of the provisions of this Article and shall, where necessary, address appropriate directives or decisions to Member States.

Regarding SGEIs, Article 90 EEC (ex Article 86(2) EC and now Article 106(2) TFEU) naturally is of central importance, as the concept is explicitly mentioned here.

B   The Treaty of Amsterdam

In the Treaty of Amsterdam, which entered into force 1 May 1999, Article 7D EC (ex Article 16 EC and now Article 14 TFEU) began with the following wording:

> Without prejudice to Articles 77, 90 and 92 [ex Articles 73 and 86–7 EC, and now Articles 93 and 106 and 107 TFEU], and given the place occupied by services of general economic interest in the shared values of the Union as well as their role in promoting social and territorial cohesion, the Community and the Member States, each within their respective powers and within the scope of application of this Treaty, shall take care that such services operate on the basis of principles and conditions which enable them to fulfil their missions.[6]

It is noteworthy that the provision was inserted in the beginning of the Treaty concerning principles, rather than close to what has now become Article 106 TFEU. It is generally viewed as a rather ambiguous provision.[7] In addition, mention should be made of Declaration 13 to Article 7D (ex Article 16 EC and now Article 14 TFEU) in which it is stated that:

---

[6] Concerning this provision, see among others the Commission, *Report to the Laeken European Council. Services of General Interest*, COM (2001) 598, pp. 17 *et seq.*; W. Frenz, 'Dienste von algemeinem wirtschaftlichen Interesse', *Europarecht* 36 (2000), 901; M. Ross, 'Article 16 E.C. and services of general interest: from derogation to obligation?', *ELRev* 30 (2000), 22; E. Szyszczak, 'Public service provision in competitive markets', *Yearbook of European Law* (2001), 62.

[7] See e.g. W. Sauter, 'Services of general economic interest and universal service in EU law', *ELRev* 38 (2008), 172.

> The provisions of Article 7D of the Treaty establishing the European
> Community on public services shall be implemented with full respect for
> the jurisprudence of the Court of Justice, inter alia as regards the prin-
> ciples of equality of treatment, quality and continuity of such services.

Some Member States had actually wanted a change of what was still
designated as Article 90 EC (ex Article 86 EC and now Article 106
TFEU), but the Commission – most likely supported by some other
Member States – was strongly against this. The result of the negotiations
only became the insertion of Article 7D EC (ex Article 16 EC and now
Article 14 TFEU).[8] As expressed by Duff, there is probably no more stark
exposure in the Treaty of the division between those who wish to regulate
in order to protect public utilities and the like, and those who wish to
make them competitive, than indicated in this provision.[9] In addition, it
may be mentioned that the Commission has unsuccessfully worked on
the insertion of a new paragraph in the 'old' Article 3 EC concerning
services of general interest (SGIs).[10]

C   The Treaty of Lisbon

The ToL contains several elements of interest to the present analysis
which will therefore be introduced in what follows.

First, it is noteworthy that Article 86 EC once again survives in an
unchanged version[11] – this time in what is now called the Treaty on the
Functioning of the European Union (TFEU). It is renumbered as Article
106 TFEU.

Secondly, Article 16 EC has been altered to the following – however
renumbered Article 14 TFEU:

> Without prejudice to Article 4 of the Treaty on European Union or to
> Articles 93, 106 and 107 of this Treaty, and given the place occupied by
> services of general economic interest in the shared values of the Union as

---

[8] See J. L. Buendia Sierra, *Exclusive Rights and State Monopolies under EC Law: Article 86
(formerly Article 90) of the EC Treaty* (Oxford: Oxford University Press, 1999), pp. 330 *et
seq*. Also see Commission, *Services of General Interest in Europe (96/C281/03)*, paras.
71–4; L. Flynn, 'Competition policy and public services in EC law after the Maastricht
and Amsterdam Treaties' in D. O'Keeffe and P. Tworney (eds.), *Legal Issues of the
Amsterdam Treaty* (Oxford: Hart Publishing, 1999), pp. 196–7.

[9] A. Duff, *The Treaty of Amsterdam: Text and commentary* (London: Federal Trust, 1997),
p. 84.

[10] Commission (n. 8 above), paras. 71–4.

[11] Except for the renumbering of the provisions, which it refers to.

well as their role in promoting social and territorial cohesion, the Union and the Member States, each within their respective powers and within the scope of application of the Treaties, shall take care that such services operate on the basis of principles and conditions, particularly economic and financial conditions, which enable them to fulfil their missions. The European Parliament and the Council, acting by means of regulations in accordance with the ordinary legislative procedure, shall establish these principles and set these conditions without prejudice to the competence of Member States, in compliance with the Treaties, to provide, to commission and to fund such services.

The last sentence constitutes a completely new addition. This sentence had previously in the legislative history of the provision been formulated in what then was Article III-6 as: 'European laws shall define these principles and conditions.'[12] The wording in the final version must be viewed as a much softer legal basis. Nevertheless, as it has been put forward by Sauter, the change implies that in future we will have two competing, or concurrent, legal bases for legislation on SGEIs, namely a new one in Article 14 TFEU based on co-decision between the European Parliament and the Council, and one for Commission directives in Article 86(3) EC as before (now Article 106(3) TFEU).[13]

Thirdly, reference should also be made to one of the protocols annexed to the Lisbon Treaty. Number 26 concerns explicitly SGEIs, and it is stated that the High Contracting Parties wish to emphasise the importance of these.[14] Article 1 stipulates that:

---

[12] Also see e.g. J. Baquero Cruz, 'Services of general interest and EC law' in G. de Búrca (ed.), *EU Law and the Welfare State: In search of solidarity* (Oxford: Oxford University Press, 2005), p. 178; C. H. Bovis, 'Financing services of general interest in the EU: How do public procurement and state aids interact to demarcate between market forces and protection?', *ELJ* 11 (2005), 81; Commission, *Communication from the Commission to the European Parliament, the Council, the European Economic and Social Committee and the Committee of the Regions. White Paper on services of general interest*, COM (2004) 374, p. 12; Damjanovic and de Witte (n. 2 above), pp. 86 *et seq.*; S. Rodrigues, 'Vers une loi europé-enne des services publics', *Revue du Marché commun et de l'Union européenne* (2003), 503; E. Szyszczak, 'Legal tools in the liberalisation of welfare markets' in Neergaard, Nielsen and Roseberry (see * above), pp. 294 *et seq.*; S. de Vries, *Tensions within the Internal Market: The functioning of the internal market and the development of horizontal and flanking policies* (Groningen: Europa Law Publishing, 2006), pp. 161 and 381.

[13] Sauter (n. 7 above), p. 172.

[14] Regarding the origin of this protocol, see among others Appendix 3 of Conseil Economique et Social, 'Analysis of the implications of the Lisbon Treaty on services of general interest and proposals for implementation', Discussion paper drawn up by European experts (2008); D. C. Le Bihan and A. Moriceau, 'Services d'intérêt économique general et valeurs communes', *Revue du Marché commun et de l'Union europénne* 519 (Juin 2008), 358.

> The shared values of the Union in respect of services of general economic interest within the meaning of Article 14 of the Treaty on the Functioning of the European Union include in particular: – the essential role and the wide discretion of national, regional and local authorities in providing, commissioning and organizing services of general economic interest as closely to the needs of the users; – the diversity between various services of general economic interest and the differences in the needs and preferences of users that may result from different geographical, social or cultural situations; – a high level of quality, safety and affordability, equal treatment and the promotion of universal access and of user rights.

Article 2 stipulates that:

> The provisions of the Treaties do not affect in any way the competence of Member States to provide, commission and organise non-economic services of general interest.

As it has been put forward by Sauter, although the fact that it was felt necessary to adopt this protocol highlights the deep concerns held by the Member States that something essential may slip from their control on this issue, in reality the protocol might appear not to add much of substance as regards SGEIs themselves.[15]

Finally, it should be mentioned that pursuant to Article 6 TEU, the Union recognises the rights, freedoms and principles set out in the Charter of Fundamental Rights of the European Union of 7 December 2000, as adapted at Strasbourg on 12 December 2007, which shall have the same legal value as the Treaties. Thus, with the Lisbon Treaty having entered into force, the legal effect of the Charter has changed significantly. Therefore, Article 36 thereof – placed in Title IV on 'Solidarity' – should be mentioned.[16] In this provision, it is stated that:

> The Union recognises and respects access to services of general economic interest as provided for in national laws and practices, in accordance with the Treaty establishing the European Community, in order to promote the social and territorial cohesion of the Union.[17]

---

[15] Sauter (n. 7 above), p. 173.

[16] Regarding the interpretation of this provision, see in particular Baquero Cruz (n. 12 above), p. 178. Also see in opposite direction Romano Prodi who, in a speech concerning *Services of general economic interest and the European model of development*, SPEECH/ 03/63, CEEP dinner, Brussels, 5 February 2003, p. 4, expresses that: 'The Charter of Fundamental Rights explicitly recognises the citizenship dimension of services of general interest. It makes access to such services a fundamental right.'

[17] For the sake of completeness, reference may also be made to two additional provisions in the Charter, namely Art. 34 which deals with social security and social assistance and Art. 35 which deals with healthcare.

D   Observations so far

Regarding the Treaty amendments over the years, several observations may be put forward. First, it may be noticed that over the years more and more provisions have been established regarding SGEIs, thereby strengthening the European consitutional dimension of SGEIs. Secondly, the provisions of interest are no longer only situated in the context of competition law, but by now are placed in quite different contexts, thereby indicating a different impact compared with the orig- inal point of departure. Thirdly, several new aspects are being taken into consideration, including for instance an emphasis on a high level of quality, safety and affordability, equal treatment and the promotion of universal access and of user rights. Also to be mentioned in this regard, ever since the Treaty of Amsterdam, it has been recognised that SGEIs in themselves take a place in the 'shared values of the Union' and they have a role to play in 'promoting social and territorial cohesion'. In addition, it was emphasised with the abovementioned Declaration 13 that the prin- ciples of equality of treatment and quality and continuity of public services are of central importance. These principles seem more or less upheld in the ToL, in particular in the abovementioned protocol. Fourthly, a trend absolutely worth mentioning as well is the 'rights dimension'; it is of central interest that SGEIs have a place in the Charter itself. In this way, it has become evident that constitutional rights of some kind have arisen in this area; rights which have tradition- ally been left to the Member States to decide whether they should be enforceable and if so, to take control of their actual enforcement. Fifthly, yet another trend to mention concerns the changed legal basis which has occurred with the Lisbon Treaty entering into force. Article 14 TFEU includes an improved legal basis which is of interest in this context as it emphasises the very changed place the regulation of SGEIs is given, and may give more room for both economic and social integration through harmonisation as such. The degree of social integration to occur will, among other factors, depend on the definition of the concept SGEIs, i.e. to what degree this concept will include social tasks. Altogether, SGEIs may be seen as gaining a larger and larger importance in constitutional terms, and there seems more scope for social integration through the constitutional changes which have taken place over the years.[18]

---

[18] In relationship to this, it should be noted that the former Art. 3(1)(g) EC states that the activities of the Community shall include: 'a system ensuring that competition in the

III   The case law of the Court of Justice

The focus in this section is to examine the interpretation of Article
106(2) TFEU (ex Article 86(2) EC) by the Court of Justice in order to
gain a better understanding of SGEIs in this context. As it is widely
known, the internal market law rules have for a long time been read as
involving a balance between free movement and alternative national
aims, e.g. as expressed in Article 36 TFEU (ex Article 30 EC) or the
Cassis de Dijon justification, which often may be viewed as allowing for
interests which, in a broad sense, are social in character. At this point, it
is of interest to analyse how SGEIs have been dealt with by the Court of
Justice in the context of competition law rules, especially Article 106
TFEU (ex Article 86 EC), in order to see if any indications are to be found
regarding the balancing between economic and other aims and values.
This again has an importance in the understanding of economic and
social integration. After all, the understanding of Article 106 TFEU (ex
Article 86 EC) by the Court of Justice could to a certain degree constitute
some guidance as to the future shaping of SGEIs at the political level.

In the case law, Article 106(2) TFEU (ex Article 86(2) EC) has
primarily had a role to play as a kind of exemption to the combined
reading of Articles 106(1) and 102 TFEU (ex Articles 86(1) and 82 EC),
and the following analysis is mainly limited to the interpretation of
Article 106(2) TFEU (ex Article 86(2) EC) in this context.[19] Here, the
Court of Justice has rather often viewed the granting of exclusive rights
and related issues as contrary to these provisions unless justified primarily under reference to Article 106(2) TFEU (ex Article 86(2) EC). The
guiding principle is the so-called *Höfner* criterion, which implies that
national measures which create a situation in which an undertaking
cannot avoid infringing Article 102 TFEU (ex Article 82 EC) are incompatible with the Treaty.[20] Buendia Sierra has stated that: 'Therefore, all
exclusive rights are in principle contrary to Article 86(1) and 82 [now

internal market is not distorted'. In the Lisbon Treaty this aim could be said to have been
'moved' to Protocol 27 with the following content: 'The High Contracting Parties,
considering that the internal market as set out in Article 3 of the Treaty on European
Union includes a system ensuring that competition is not distorted . . .'
[19] For the sake of completeness, it should be mentioned that Art. 106(2) TFEU
(ex Art. 86(2) EC) possibly also could have a role to play with regard to other Treaty
provisions, which may already follow from the term 'in particular' included in the
wording of the provision which indicates that the reference to the competition provisions is not exhaustive.
[20] C-41/90 *Klaus Höfner and Fritz Elser* v. *Macroton GmbH* [1991] ECR I-1979, para. 27.

Articles 106(1) and 102 TFEU] unless they can be justified for the general interest reasons and they respect the principle of proportionality.'[21] Others are more sceptical as to the scope of the combined reading. For instance, Maillo states that 'there is no automatic abuse, nor can the grant of an exclusive right be considered to be prima facie illegal'.[22] Under all circumstances, since the nineties, the EU has increasingly put pressure on national measures, especially exclusive and special rights. The underlying rationale behind this development seems to be driven by a market economic ideology.[23] Therefore, the possibility of justification pursuant to Article 106(2) TFEU (ex Article 86(2) EC) has grown in importance, and it is of interest to analyse how the balance between the more market–economic ideological approach pursuant to Article 106(1) TFEU (ex Article 86(1) EC) is contrasted with Article 106(2) TFEU (ex Article 86(2) EC) which apparently allows for other aims and values to be considered.

In more detail, there now follows, first, a few introductory remarks about the exemption.[24] Then, a synthesis of what may be deducted from an analysis of the judgments of relevance is put forward.

---

[21] Buendia Sierra (n. 8 above), p. 189.

[22] J. Maillo, 'Article 86 EC: Services of general interest and EC competition law' in G. Amato and D. Ehlermann (eds.), *EC Competition Law: A critical assessment* (Oxford: Hart Publishing, 2007), p. 624. See also for the same perception e.g. de Vries (n. 12 above), p. 158. Also see a possible support for this point of view, e.g. Case C-209/98 *Entreprenørforeningens Affalds/Miljøsektion (FFAD)* v. *Københavns Kommune* [2000] ECR I-3743, paras. 67–9.

[23] See further U. Neergaard, 'Public service concessions and related concepts: The increased pressure from Community law on Member States' use of concessions', *Public Procurement Law Review* (2007), 387; 'Modernising Article 82 EC: With particular focus on public and otherwise privileged undertakings', *Europarättslig Tidsskrift* (2007), 54. Regarding the related provisions, it is noteworthy that the Court of Justice has stated that: '... Article 86(1) EC precludes Member States, in the case of public undertakings and undertakings to which they grant special or exclusive rights, from maintaining in force national legislation contrary to Articles 43 EC and 49 EC', which pursuant to the judgment includes concessions granted without prior public procedure. See Case C-347/06 *ASM Brescia SpA* v. *Comune di Rodengo Saiano* [2008] ECR I-5641, para. 61.

[24] The provision contains several legal concepts of great importance, which however will not be defined here, as the available amount of space does not allow this. Concepts of relevance are especially 'undertakings', 'entrustment', 'revenue-producing monopoly', 'particular tasks', 'development of trade' and 'interests of the Community'. Ordinary textbooks on competition law will often contain an analysis of these. Regarding 'services of general economic interest', I have already, in n. 2 above, made reference to some of the literature of relevance. The concept 'obstruct' will be of central interest in the analysis of the case law below, i.e. in section III A.1.(a). Other details as to the application of the provision are left out here for the same reason.

A   The exemption under Article 106(2) TFEU (ex Article 86(2) EC)

This provision has given rise to great interpretational difficulties, or as it has been explained by Baquero Cruz:

> When judges were first confronted with Article 86(2) [now Article 106(2) TFEU], a provision unprecedented in other legal systems, it was certainly difficult to find operational and legal tests that reflected the economic ideas underlying that provision. And it remains difficult, at present, to devise a legal test that grants the necessary margin of action to political institutions without leaving the rules underenforced or unenforced.[25]

In principle, the importance of the provision lies in the possibility of an otherwise unlawful national measure being considered as legal. At the same time, an activity, which has been legitimised by such a measure, or the like, may also in this way find its 'immunity'.

Article 106(2) TFEU (ex Article 86(2) EC) has not until the nineties been given importance by the Court of Justice. In this context, Buendia Sierra explains that the originally very restrictive interpretation of the prohibitions of Articles 37 and 106(1) TFEU (ex Articles 31 and 86(1) EC) made the exemption contained in Article 106(2) TFEU (ex Article 86(2) EC) almost superfluous.[26] The reason was that if exclusive rights and related legal constructions were not, in general, prohibited there was no need for an exemption. Since the interpretation of Article 106(1) TFEU (ex Article 86(1) EC) has now severely changed, the importance of Article 106(2) TFEU (ex Article 86(2) EC) has become increasingly significant.

The underlying conflict relating to Article 106(2) TFEU (ex Article 86(2) EC) may be expressed by the following words of the Commission:

> The real challenge is to ensure smooth interplay between, on the one hand, the requirements of the single European market and free competition in terms of free movement, economic performance and dynamism and, on the other, the general interest objectives. This interplay must benefit individual citizens and society as a whole. This is a very tricky balancing act, since the goalposts are constantly moving: the single market is continuing to expand and public services, far from being fixed, are having to adapt to new requirements.[27]

---

[25] Baquero Cruz (n. 12 above), p. 171. Also see e.g. Ross (n. 6 above), p. 23, who has a similar message, as he states: 'As is well documented, [footnote omitted] the interpretation of this provision has produced a long line of complex and at times abstruse case law, with difficulties being encountered in relation to virtually all its aspects.'

[26] Buendia Sierra (n. 8 above), pp. 273 et seq.

[27] Commission, Services of General Interest in Europe (96/C281/03), para. 19.

The way in which the Court of Justice has so far met this challenge, is the focus of what follows.

B   Synthesis of what may be deduced from the case law

The following synthesis of what may be deduced from an analysis of the case law is divided into two parts, where the first explains the analytical framework applied by the Court of Justice, and the second contains an examination of the character of the exemption.

1   The analytical framework used by the Court of Justice

In a decision as to whether Article 106(2) TFEU (ex Article 86(2) EC) can imply 'immunity' to an otherwise unlawful anti-competitive state measure or activity legitimised by such a measure, the Court of Justice will often apply a two-step-test, possibly supplemented by a third and/or fourth step.[28] Thus, the Court of Justice might follow the following pattern of argumentation:

(1) whether a SGEI is entrusted
(2) whether the application of the rules on competition obstructs the performance, in law or in fact, of the particular tasks assigned to the undertaking(s)
(3) whether the principle of proportionality in the strict sense – pursuant to which it shall be examined whether a less anti-competitive measure could reach the same result – is fulfilled
(4) whether the development of trade is not affected to such an extent as would be contrary to the interests of the Community.

It should be emphasised that this is only meant to constitute a simplified picture of the scheme of thinking which the Court of Justice is likely to use. However, this is not always applied. In other words, derogations may occur, especially because this field of law is still under development and therefore characterised by a relatively high degree of uncertainty and unpredictability.

The steps are applied cumulatively, so that they all in principle should be answered in the positive as a condition for 'immunity'. The individual step should therefore only be applied if the examination of the previous step leads to a positive result. In many cases, the examination ends after

---

[28] As a condition for applying the test, it is inter alia assumed that an undertaking in the sense of Art. 106(2) TFEU (ex Art. 86(2) EC) is involved.

the first two steps. In case the answer to the examination under the second step is positive, the rules of competition will not be applicable in order to condemn the measure in question, etc., unless the Court of Justice finds it necessary to examine the third or the fourth step, which may lead to another result. However, neither the third nor the fourth step are applied that often, but if applied and the answers to the relevant questions are in the negative, the measure, etc., will be condemned. In what follows, the second and the third step will be given particular attention.[29]

(a) **The second step** The criterion of obstruction plays a central role in deciding whether there exists what may be called a legitimate interest in the shape of the performance of a particular task as a justification for a limitation of competition. If it may be found that the application of the competition rules *obstruct* the performance, in law or in fact, of such a particular task, these rules will after all not be applicable. Thereby, the involved distortion of competition may be upheld.

In the process of development regarding the criterion of obstruction, *Sacchi* (1974) may be viewed as constituting the first milestone, as it contains the first infant attempt to formulate the framework of application. In this case, the word 'incompatible', used in the English version, is central.[30] This strict formulation is followed up in *Höfner* and *ERT*, where the same term is applied.[31] In *Merci*, the term 'obstruct' is used.[32] The originally strict approach may possibly be viewed as inspired by the ideology of market-building, where the exemptions should be construed narrowly and the conditions to invoke the exemptions should be applied strictly.[33]

The second milestone may be viewed as being set approximately twenty years later with *Corbeau* (1993), as expressions such as 'necessary', 'economically acceptable conditions', and 'economic equilibrium',

---

[29] Regarding the first step, reference may be given to the work by Neergaard (see * above).
[30] Case 155/73 *Italian Republic* v. *Giuseppe Sacch*i [1974] ECR 409, para. 15.
[31] Case C-41/90 *Höfner*, para. 24; C-260/89 *Elliniki Radiophonia Tileorassi AE* v. *Dimotiki Etairia Pliroforissis and Sotirios Kouvelas* [1991] ECR I-2925, para. 33. However, see Baquero Cruz (n. 12 above), p. 187, who does not find that the term 'incompatible' necessarily constitutes a strict approach.
[32] C-179/90 *Merci convenzionali porto di genova SpA* v. *Siderurgica Gabrielli SpA* [1991] ECR I-5889, para. 26.
[33] de Vries (n. 12 above), p. 165.

are given decisive weight.[34] This apparent shift to a more gentle and nuanced approach seems confirmed in *Almelo*.[35]

The third and, for the time being, last milestone may be said to be established only a few years later with the *Gas and Electricity Monopoly* cases (1997). In these cases the strict interpretation which the Commission pleads for is rejected, the Court of Justice concluding that, for the Treaty rules not to be applicable to an undertaking entrusted with a SGEI under Article 86(2) EC (ex Article 90(2) EC), it is sufficient that the application of those rules obstruct the performance, in law or in fact, of the special obligations incumbent upon the undertaking, but it is not necessary that the survival of the undertaking itself be threatened.[36] It is somehow surprising that the Court of Justice in *Chemische Afvalstoffen* (1998) again establishes a strict version of the criterion of objection as it is here required that the undertaking in question without the contested measure 'would be unable to carry out the task assigned to it'.[37] However, this approach is not repeated in the subsequent cases and *TNT Traco* (2001) demonstrates how flexibly the Court of Justice by now seems to relate itself to the issue. In this case, it is stated that it may prove necessary not only to permit the undertaking entrusted with the task of operating the universal service, in the general interest, to offset profitable sectors against less profitable sectors, but also to require suppliers of services not forming part of the universal service to contribute, by paying dues of the kind at issue in the main proceedings, to the financing of the universal service and in that way to enable the undertaking entrusted with that task to perform it in conditions of economic stability.[38] When the criterion of obstruction becomes formulated as a test of whether the privileged undertaking can perform its task, in the general interest, on 'economically acceptable conditions', it is indicated that the services in

[34] C-320/91 *Criminal proceedings against Paul Corbeau* [1993] ECR I-2533, paras. 13–20.
[35] C-393/92 *Gemeente Almelo and ors. v. Energibedrijf Ijsselmij NV* [1994] ECR 1477, paras. 46–50. Several commentators have expressed the point of view that with the judgment a large step is taken towards a more gentle approach towards 'services of general economic interest'. See e.g. Baquero Cruz (n. 12 above), p. 190, who himself, however, is rather sceptical.
[36] e.g. C-157/94 *Commission* v. *Kingdom of the Netherlands (Dutch Electricity Monopoly)* [1997] ECR I-5699, para. 43. See e.g. Ross (n. 6 above), pp. 25–6, concerning the interpretation of this ground.
[37] C-203/96 *Chemische Afvalstoffen Dusseldorp BV and ors.* v. *Minister van Volkshuisvesting, Ruimtelijke Ordening en Milieubeheer* [1998] ECR I-4075, para. 67. See in this regard also e.g. Ross (n. 6 above).
[38] C-340/99 *TNT Traco SpA* v. *Poste Italiane SpA and ors.* [2001] ECR I-4109, para. 55.

question can be provided in an economic equilibrium. Therefore, it may be necessary for the privileged undertaking to offset profitable sectors against less profitable sectors.[39]

On the basis of an analysis of the development of the case law, the impression left is thus that the criterion has been applied differently in the individual cases.[40] The general impression is also that the Court of Justice since 1993 has demonstrated a certain degree of reluctance in applying the competition provisions, when the involved organs perform a task of a public character, or as it has been expressed by Flynn:

> while the Court's judgments discussed above curtailed the previous flexibility offered to Member States in the manner in which they offered public services through state-owned or state-favoured enterprises, since 1993 it has, nevertheless, displayed more reserve in its application of the competition rules to bodies with a public-service mission. This reticence has been displayed in two ways; the definition of 'undertaking' for the purposes of identifying the material scope of the competition rules, and the applicability of the limited exemption from the competition rules contained in Article 86(2) [now Article 106(2) TFEU].[41]

As a continuous feature the cases are in themselves giving the impression of a reasonable balancing of the often contradictory interests involved, and seem to demonstrate a certain tolerance towards those distortions of competition which almost always seem to follow in the wake of SGEIs. Article 106(2) TFEU (ex Article 86(2) EC) implies in the majority of cases that distortions of competition to a large degree may be upheld. In other words, it is in principle a rather strong rule of exemption. In more practical terms, this means that the Member States' freedom in this field may largely be considered to be upheld, provided that the conditions following from the provision are fulfilled. In legal literature, this impression that the possibility of exemption pursuant to Article 86(2) TFEU (ex Article 86(2) EC) has developed in the direction

---

[39] As an example of the application of the criterion, reference may also be made to Case C-209/98 *FFAD*, para. 78, where it is held that a grant of an exclusive right is necessary to ensure that a high-capacity centre was guaranteed a significant flow of waste. Furthermore, reference may be made to joined cases C-147/97 and C-148/97, *Deutsche Post AG v. Gesellschaft für Zahlungssysteme mbH (GZS) and Citicorp Kartenservice GmbH* [2000] ECR I-0825, para. 50.

[40] See e.g. Advocate General Jacobs' Opinion of 23 October 1997 in C-203/96 *Chemische Afvalstoffen*, para. 107.

[41] Flynn (n. 8 above), p. 193.

of being more and more gentle may find support. For instance, Hancher expresses that the scope of the exemption:

> might well be wider than any of the exemptions available either under Article 36, 56 and 66 [ex Articles 30, 46 and 55 EC and now Articles 36, 52 and 62 TFEU], or in terms of the 'mandatory requirements' and it may be seen as an additional safety net which will 'save' national measures which would otherwise have failed to meet the conditions for exemptions.[42]

In the same direction, it has for instance been stated by Malaret that:

> Although initially the attitude of the Commission and the Court of Justice appeared to be focused entirely on ensuring the prevalence of the rules on competition, [footnote omitted] more recent decisions show signs of a more moderate position.[43]

Nevertheless, it has to be stressed that the interest of the performance of particular tasks does not weigh absolutely over the interest of competition. The most correct description seems to be that the Court of Justice will perform a reasonable balancing act in a given situation. It is the core function of the exemption to give room for 'other interests' rather than purely competition interests. The idea of a balancing act may be said to have been expressed by the Court itself as, for instance, it decides in the *Dutch Electricity Monopoly* case that:

> in allowing derogations to be made from the general rules of the Treaty in certain circumstances, Article 90(2) [later Article 86(2) EC and now Article 106(2) TFEU] seeks to reconcile the Member States' interest in using certain undertakings, in particular in the public sector, as an instrument of economic or fiscal policy with the Community's interest in ensuring compliance with the rules on competition and the preservation of the unity of the common market.[44]

Attention should in particular be given to the expression 'reconcile', whereby it seems confirmed that the interest of competition should not

---

[42] L. Hancher, 'Case C-320/91 P, Procureur du Roi v. Paul Corbeau, Judgment of the full Court, 19 May 1993', *CML Rev* [1994], 121. However, one has to be aware that in actual fact, it may be very difficult to compare the strength of the exemptions in the two different legal regimes.

[43] E. Malaret, 'Public service, public services, public functions, and guarantees of the rights of citizens: Unchanging needs in a changed context' in M. Freedland and S. Sciarra (eds.), *Public Services and Citizenship in European Law: Public and labour law perspectives* (Gloucestershire: Clarendon Press, 1998), p. 78.

[44] C-157/94 *Dutch Electricity Monopoly*, para. 39.

necessarily weigh more than 'other interests' or the other way around. This is also stressed in the following paragraph 40 of the same judgment:

> The Member States' interest being so defined, they cannot be precluded, when defining the services of general economic interest which they entrust to certain undertakings, from taking account of objectives pertaining to their national policy or from endeavouring to attain them by means of obligations and constraints which they impose on such undertakings.

(b) The possible third step   The Court of Justice only includes the third step concerning the principle of proportionality in the strict sense in a very few cases. For instance, in *Chemische Afvalstoffen* it decided that even if the task conferred on the undertaking in question could constitute a task of general economic interest, it is for the Member State involved to show to the satisfaction of the national court that that objective cannot be achieved equally well by other means.[45] The reference to what may be classified as the principle of proportionality is said by the Court of Justice to have been pointed out by Advocate General Jacobs in his Opinion. Yet Advocate General Jacobs refers to the Commission as his source of inspiration.[46] The principle also seems to be mentioned in *Sydhavnens Sten & Grus* (2000).[47] Even though Advocate General La Pergola seems to suggest its application in *Deutsche Post* (2000), the Court of Justice itself does not explicitly include it in its decision here.[48] That the Court generally only seldom explicitly includes the principle of proportionality may not necessarily imply that it is without importance, but perhaps rather that its application could be controversial.[49]

As the analysed field of law still constitutes a rather immature area, it is fair to emphasise that the principle of proportionality is not yet too clearly defined, which may in itself be a kind of disturbance in any discussion of the issues. Thus, here its definition has been limited to only referring to an examination of whether a less anti-competitive measure could reach the

---

[45] C-203/96 *Chemische Afvalstoffen*, para. 67.
[46] Opinion of the Advocate General Jacobs delivered on 23 October 1997 in C-203/96 *Chemische Afvalstoffen*, para. 108. Also see e.g. C-157/94 *Dutch Electricity Monopoly*, paras. 56–65.
[47] C-209/98 *FFAD*, para. 80.
[48] Opinion of Advocate General La Pergola delivered on 1 June 1999 in Joined Cases C-147/97 and C-148/97 *Deutsche Post*, para. 30.
[49] See e.g. Buendia Sierra (n. 8 above), p. 304; Baquero Cruz (n. 12 above), pp. 187, 196 *et seq*. See esp. p. 197, where it is indicated that: 'Proportionality, especially a strict version thereof, would give excessive weight to competition.'

same result.[50] In other words, it is a requirement that a given instrument to reach a given aim must not be more restrictive than necessary.[51] Hereby, the expression is given a different meaning than that given to it by Buendia Sierra, as he seems to view the entire criterion of obstruction as a principle of proportionality.[52] However, distinguishing the criterion itself from an individual test of whether the principle of proportionality in the strict sense is fulfilled could seem analytically more correct as the Court of Justice itself could be claimed to have done so. Also, this is the scheme of thinking dominating the case law on the parallel free movement rules. For the sake of completeness, it should be mentioned that the many weaknesses of the present stage of development in this regard have given rise to discussion in legal literature.[53]

2 The character of the exemption

It may be considered what kind of legitimate interests may justify an exemption pursuant to Article 106(2) TFEU (ex Article 86(2) EC). As a point of departure, the legitimate interest which may be invoked is the assurance that those particular tasks which have been entrusted to one or several privileged undertakings are capable of being performed.

Besides this observation, it may be noted that the Court of Justice is rarely specific in its application of this element. Often the examination becomes mixed up with the examination of whether a SGEI is involved. This impression is gained from e.g. expressions such as 'the task of general interest'[54] or 'justified by a task of a public service of general economic interest'.[55] The same impression may be gained from a case like GT-Link, where the Court of Justice states that: 'It does not follow, however, that the operation of any commercial port constitutes the

---

[50] In general, the principle of proportionality is not an unambiguously applied principle in EU law, which in itself is a difficulty in the present context.

[51] Compare with U. Neergaard and R. Nielsen, EU Ret, 5th edn (Copenhagen: Thomson, 2009), pp. 59 et seq. and 258. Also see Communication from the Commission, Services of General Interest in Europe (2001/C17/04), para. 23, where the Commission states that it has to be ensured: 'that any restrictions of competition and limitations to the freedoms of the internal market do not exceed what is necessary to guarantee effective fulfilment of the mission'. Finally, see Sauter (n. 7 above), pp. 186–8.

[52] Buendia Sierra (n. 8 above), pp. 300 et seq. Also see in the same direction e.g. de Vries (n. 12 above), pp. 163 et seq.

[53] See esp. Baquero Cruz (n. 12 above), pp. 195–6.

[54] Case 66/86 Ahmed Saeed and Silver Line Reisebüro GmbH v. Zentrale zur Bekämpfung unlauteren Wettbewerb e.V. [1989] ECR 803, para. 57.

[55] C-18/88 Régie des télégraphes et des téléphones v. GB-Inno-BM SA [1991] ECR I-5491, para. 22.

operation of a service of general economic interest or, in particular that all the services provided in such a port amount to such a task.'[56] In a case like *Almelo*, the Court is more explicit than usual regarding the definition of the particular task. Thus, it is here specified that the involved undertaking must ensure that throughout the territory in respect of which the concession is granted, all consumers, whether local distributors or end-users, receive uninterrupted supplies of electricity in sufficient quantities to meet demand at any given time, at uniform tariff rates and on terms which may not vary save in accordance with objective criteria applicable to all customers.[57]

It might be that in certain more recent cases it is possible to detect a certain tendency towards a more independent examination of the concept of SGEIs and 'particular tasks' to include 'other interests'. In principle, it might be that interests such as public health, public security or the environment could be invoked in themselves. Some support for such a possibility could be said to be found, for instance, in the *Dutch Electricity Monopoly* case, where the interest in ensuring the supply of electricity on the basis of costs that are as low as possible and in a socially responsible manner is touched upon to some extent.[58] In the *French Gas and Electricity Monopoly* case, the interest in, among others, continuity of supply and equal treatment between customers or consumers also seems to be given weight.[59] Furthermore, it may be mentioned that in *Corsica Ferries France* the interest in the safety of port waters seems to be of importance.[60] In addition, it may be mentioned that in *Albany*, which is one of the judgments in the *September Trilogy*, the Court of Justice states that the supplementary pension scheme at issue fulfils an essential social function within the Dutch pensions system by reason of the limited amount of the statutory pension, which is calculated on the basis of the minimum statutory wage.[61] To this may also be added that in *Sydhavnens Sten & Grus* it seems to play a role in the outcome of the case that the interest of the environment is involved.[62]

---

[56] C-242/95 *GT-Link A/S* v. *De Danske Statsbaner (DSB)* [1997] ECR I-4449, para. 52.

[57] C-393/92 *Almelo*, para. 48.

[58] C-157/94 *Dutch Electricity Monopoly*, para. 63.

[59] C-159/94 *Commission* v. *French Republic* [1997] ECR I-5815, para. 89.

[60] C-266/96 *Corsica Ferries France SA* v. *Gruppo Antichi Ormeggiatori del porto di Genova Coop. Arl and ors.* [1998] ECR I-3949, para. 45.

[61] C-67/96 *Albany International BV* v. *Stichting Bedrijfspensioenfonds Textielindustrie* [1999] I-ECR 5751, para. 105.

[62] See for the same perception, de Vries (n. 12 above), p. 163. Also the Commission accepts that considerations such as environmental protection, could be admissible as legitimate grounds, see Commission, *Services of General Interest in Europe* (96/C281/03), para. 25.

Finally, it could be that the interest of public health could have had a role to play in *Ambulanz Glöckner*, as the obligation involved consisted of providing a permanent standby service of transporting sick or injured persons in emergencies.[63]

In this context, it is of interest to mention that the Court of Justice in *Chemische Afvalstoffen* actually concludes that rules such as the contested long-term plan is in conflict with Articles 106 and 102 TFEU (ex Articles 86 and 82 EC) when these provisions 'without any objective justification' and without being necessary for the performance of a task in the general interest, have the effect of favouring the national undertaking and increasing its dominant position.[64] The formulation may also – in light of what was stated above – be viewed as an expression by the Court of Justice that it finds that the interpretation of Article 106(2) TFEU (ex Article 86(2) EC) should be transformed into a test more like the one prevailing in the 'internal market law universe', so that a wide amount of considerations can be invoked by Member States. Buendia Sierra seems to be convinced that 'other interests' in the broad sense have an importance within the framework of Article 106(2) TFEU (ex Article 86(2) EC), as he has stated:

> Today it is obvious that many restrictions concerning public or privileged undertakings (and therefore falling within Article 86(1) [now Article 106(2) TFEU]) may be justified for non-economic reasons, such as the protection of public health (this may be the case of alcohol monopolies) or the promotion of culture (television monopolies). The Court of Justice has made clear that these restrictions can also in some cases benefit from the exception in Article 86(2) [now Article 106(2) TFEU].[65]

---

[63] C-475/99 *Firma Ambulanz Glöckner* v. *Landkreis Südwestpfalz* [1991] ECR I-8089, para. 55. See for the same perception, de Vries (n. 12 above), p. 168.

[64] C-203/96 *Chemische Afvalstoffen*, para. 68.

[65] J. L. Buendia Sierra: 'Article 86: Exclusive rights and other anti-competitive state measures' in J. Faull and A. Nikpay (eds.), *The EC Law of Competition* (Oxford: Oxford University Press, 2007), p. 321. Also see e.g. Ross (n. 6 above), pp. 25–6. Furthermore, it may be mentioned that E. Rousseva, 'The concept of "objective justification" of an abuse of a dominant position: Can it help to modernise the analysis under Article 82 EC?', *The Competition Law Review* 2 (2006), 35, finds that: 'public policy concerns in fact serve as a justification for abuses under Article 86(2) which provides a derogation from the provisions of the Treaty, including the competition rules. However, this exemption only applies to the extent necessary to enable an undertaking entrusted with the provision of services of general economic interest (SGEI) to provide the service. The justification is the need to perform SGEI in the interest of the public. Although the text of the provision refers to services of "economic interest", the objective contemplated in the provision is of a non-economic nature and is comparable to that of other interests enumerated in Article 30 or in the open list of mandatory requirements recognized by the Court.'

Furthermore, reference may be made to de Vries, who finds that the term SGEIs appears to include 'horizontal and flanking policy interests'.[66] The author stresses that Article 106(2) TFEU (ex Article 86(2) EC) seems to have a broader scope than the exemptions to the rules on free movement, which are basically of a purely non-economic nature.[67] Also, the author seems to find that considerations such as environmental protection, public health, and culture may be invoked within the context of Article 106(2) TFEU (ex Article 86(2) EC).[68]

Altogether, it seems appropriate to assume that there are certain indications of a tendency implying that justifications in the direction of those acknowledged pursuant to the *Cassis de Dijon* doctrine may grow in importance within the context of Article 106(2) TFEU (ex Article 86(2) EC). However, this is not the same as saying that an individual possibility of exemption as the *Cassis de Dijon* doctrine itself – which may be applied independently of the Treaty based rules of exemptions e.g. in Article 36 TFEU (ex Article 30 EC) – is in force, but rather that it might be possible to invoke such justifications due to a somewhat progressive interpretation of Article 106(2) TFEU (ex Article 86(2) EC). In this way, there appears to be a movement towards a certain degree of convergence in the pattern of argumentation by the Court of Justice regarding the possibility of exemption between, on the one hand, free movement rules and, on the other, the part of the competition rules considered earlier. But, if taking place at all, this is still only at a very introductory and uncertain stage.[69]

C   Observations so far

Regarding the development of the case law, it may be observed among other things that the 'market' element seems to weigh heavier than the 'social' element. In other words, there has to be a good reason for setting aside competition and what that exactly could be is still not clearly defined. In terms of economic integration and social integration, Article 106 TFEU (ex Article 86 EC) may possibly be understood in the light of having been formulated in that period of early days where the focus was primarily about economic integration and when the social dimension was by and large viewed as being left for Member States to organise.

---

[66]   de Vries (n. 12 above), pp. 160 and 379.   [67]   *Ibid.*, pp. 160 and 163.

[68]   *Ibid.*, esp. pp. 165–71.

[69]   Concerning the tendency towards an increased degree of convergence among the individual free movement rules, see Neergaard and Nielsen (n. 51 above), ch. 6.

IV Conclusion

The analysis of the development traced on the basis of the two examined sources of law demonstrates that the significance of SGEIs has changed remarkably – and that the legal complexity has increased significantly – over the years. A tendency towards multi-level socio-economic integration of European society seems to take place. Also, in the words of Prechal, SGEIs have constitutional status, and: 'The recognition of access to services of general economic interest in the Charter, the prominent place these services have in the EC Treaty, as a shared value and a task for institution and Member States, and their status as a component of – social – citizenship all point in the direction of a constitutional guarantee.'[70] Altogether, in general the impression gained is that in the area of SGEIs – which originally was primarily left to national policy-makers – the EU becomes more and more involved. Not only economic integration but also social integration becomes of greater and greater significance. When an increased interest regarding more social tasks is taken at the level of the EU, among other things the limits of the application of competition as the 'new deity on "the altar of political ideas"' – as it is framed in the quotation introducing this chapter – will need further development.

---

[70] S. Prechal, 'Fundamental rights and the liberalization of service markets' in J. van de Gronden (ed.), *EU and WTO Law on Services: Limits to the realization of general interest policies within the services markets?* (Alphen aan der Rijn: Wolters Kluwer, 2009), p. 71.

PART III

Studying cases of possible tensions

Civic integration of immigrants: A challenge to proportionality and non-discrimination in the common European immigration policy?

SERGIO CARRERA AND ANJA WIESBROCK

I Introduction

Within the last decade, European migration law has undergone significant changes, starting with the entry into force of the Treaty of Amsterdam in 1999 and cumulating in the 2009 Lisbon Treaty. Title IV of the Amsterdam Treaty for the first time established (shared) Community competence to legislate on migration law. Ten years later, several aspects surrounding the conditions of entry and residence of third-country nationals (TCNs) are regulated at the European Union (EU) level. Yet, for a long time, the extent to which the Union has competence to legislate in the domain of integration of TCNs was a matter of debate between the European Commission and the Member States. The Lisbon Treaty has put a (formal) end to this ongoing discussion by introducing an explicit legal basis for the adoption of legal measures supporting Member States' integration policies.[1]

Be that as it may, the struggle between nationalism and Europeanisation has been one of the major factors for the emergence of a dual framework for integration at EU level, composed of European immigration law and the Framework for the Integration of TCNs (hereinafter the EU Framework on Integration). The dynamics characterising the development of a European immigration policy have favoured the emergence of a new understanding of integration of TCNs which is fundamentally transforming traditional assumptions considering integration policies for TCNs as promoting social inclusion,

---

[1] Art. 79(4) TFEU. This article, however, excludes explicitly the harmonisation of national laws in this area.

non-discrimination and access to individual rights. Integration requirements for TCNs are increasingly used as a tool of migration control aiming at limiting the number of immigrants having access to security of entry and residence and family life, as well as European rights.

Civic integration has become increasingly part of national legislations implementing European immigration law. The civic dimension of integration consists of programmes, tests and/or courses demanding TCNs to know, understand and respect the receiving society's history, institutions and common shared values. The concept of civic integration in immigration law also presents both an internal and an external dimension. An internal dimension takes the shape of a programme, course, test or a contract applying once a TCN has 'newly' entered the state's territory and aims at residing there legally. An external dimension consists of an evaluation and/or a course imparted in the consular and diplomatic authorities of the EU Member States in third countries about the way of life and values of the nation state involved.

This chapter assesses the tensions inherent in the relationship between civic integration of TCNs and the set of general principles guaranteeing the rule of law and fundamental rights in the common EU immigration policy. A comparison of the internal and external dimensions of civic integration in three selected Member States (France, Germany and the Netherlands) will allow us to identify common dilemmas and deficits shared between their national laws and policies in light of the principles of proportionality and non-discrimination. We conclude that as a consequence of the progressive Europeanisation of immigration policy, Member States are no longer free at times to use civic integration as a derogative clause for TCNs to have access to European rights and freedoms as recognised in EU immigration law.

II   Civic integration: The European context

Policies for integration[2] of TCNs (integration policies) in a European context have been dominated by alternative governance strategies, materialising in a dual regulatory framework: European immigration law

---

[2] This chapter uses the term 'integration' for a process by which a foreigner to the EU, a TCN, is accepted as a legal resident in one of its Member States. This is in line with EU legislation and policy documents on TCNs. The other chapters in this volume use the term 'European integration' in the wider sense of general European integration theory. They refer to European integration as a process bringing different states and regions together into a larger unit.

and the EU Framework on Integration. Different from the former, the EU Framework on Integration does not fall into the category of European law, but it rather constitutes a soft policy mechanism lacking any legally binding force upon the Member States and falling outside the European method of co-operation. In both contexts integration methods have been subject to profound transformation during the last ten years of European integration. The European approaches on integration of TCNs have evolved from a classical understanding of integration as security of residence, family reunification, equal participation, fair treatment and non-discrimination (which predominated European immigration policy discourses from the 1970s until 1999), towards integration as an immigration rule, as a 'condition' or a 'measure' constituting a derogative clause (exception) in the hands of Member States conditioning access by TCNs to socio-economic inclusion and membership.[3]

This mutation is mainly the result of a strategy pursued by certain Member States to transfer to the European level some elements pertaining to their national immigration legislation and integration policies. They have used integration as a norm in immigration law in order to keep a higher degree of discretionary power when granting European rights and freedoms to TCNs. Integration 'measures' and 'conditions' represent key tools in this strategy which have been implemented during the negotiations of the legislative initiatives on legal immigration inside the Council, and which have been subsequently promoted through the exchange of practices on integration policies within the scope of the EU Framework on Integration. This style of regulation used in EU immigration law has encouraged some Member States to transpose its provisions in the form of 'civic integration programmes, tests and courses', and their promotion as 'good' or 'best' practices' in the EU Framework on Integration.

Two directives have been of especial importance in the regulation of the conditions for entry, residence and family reunion of TCNs: the directive concerning the status of TCNs who are long-term residents,[4]

---

[3] S. Carrera, *In Search of the Perfect Citizen? The intersection between integration, immigration and nationality in the EU* (Leiden: Martinus Nijhoff Publishers, 2009). Refer also to D. Kostakopoulou, S. Carrera and M. Jesse, 'Doing and deserving: Competing frames of integration in the EU' in E. Guild, K. Groenendijk and S. Carrera (eds.), *Illiberal Liberal States: Immigration, citizenship and integration in the EU* (Aldershot: Ashgate, 2009), p. 167.

[4] Directive 2003/109/EC concerning the status of third-country nationals who are long-term residents, OJ L 16/44, 23 January 2004.

and the one on the right to family reunification.[5] The directive on TCNs who are long-term residents recognises an EU status of long-term resident for those who have resided 'legally' for a period of five years in the territory of a Member State, and provides a set of social rights and freedoms and protection against expulsion.[6] Article 5 presents 'the conditionality of integration' by saying that 'Member States may require third-country nationals to comply with integration conditions, in accordance with national law'. The directive on the right to family reunification establishes common standards and criteria for TCNs residing lawfully in a Member State to be reunited with their family members.[7] It creates a subjective right to family reunification,[8] but Article 7 stipulates that '2. Member States may require third country nationals to comply with integration measures, in accordance with national law.' Article 7 has left the door open for some Member States to apply integration measures for all those TCNs not falling within this legal category even *before* they have been granted family reunification and when they are still abroad in their country of origin (i.e. integration abroad).

A similar move can also be seen within the EU Framework on Integration.[9] Integration functions as a programme, a course or a module (inside or abroad) that includes the knowledge and respect of national and European values and fundamental norms, principles and 'ways of life' of the Member States. This is illustrated by the Common Basic Principles of Immigrant Integration Policy (CBPs).[10] The civic dimension of integration can be seen particularly in CBPs 2 and 4. CBP2 states that integration implies respect for 'the basic values of the EU'. This principle involves the obligation by 'every resident in the EU'

---

[5] Directive 2003/86/EC on the right to family reunification, OJ L 251/12, 3 October 2003.

[6] K. Groenendijk, 'The Long-term Residents Directive, denizenship and integration' in A. Baldaccini, E. Guild and H. Toner (eds.), *Whose Freedom, Security and Justice? EU immigration and asylum law and policy* (Oxford: Hart Publishing, 2007), p. 429.

[7] H. Oosterom-Staples, 'The Family Reunification Directive: A tool preserving member state interest or conducive to family reunification unity?' in A. Baldaccini, E. Guild and H. Toner (eds.), *Whose Freedom, Security and Justice? EU immigration and asylum law and policy* (Oxford: Hart Publishing, 2007), p. 451.

[8] K. Groenendijk, 'Family reunification as a right under Community law', *European Journal of Migration and Law* 8 (2006), 215.

[9] H. Urth, 'Building a momentum for the integration of third-country nationals in the European Union' (2005), *European Journal of Migration and Law* 7 (2005), 163.

[10] Council of the European Union, Justice and Home Affairs Council Meeting 2618th, Brussels. 'Common Basic Principles on Immigrants Integration', 14615/04, 19 November 2004.

to adapt and adhere closely to the basic values of the Union and the laws of the Member States and demands the Member States to ensure that all residents 'understand, respect, benefit from, and are protected on an equal basis by the full scope of values, rights, responsibilities, and privileges established by the EU and Member State laws'.[11] CBP4.1 emphasises that 'basic knowledge of the host society's language, history and institutions is indispensable for integration'. Both CBPs therefore justify the introduction, or legitimise the existence, of civic orientation programmes at national level. They also are aimed at constituting the basis upon which European Modules for Migrants Integration (EMMI) are expected to be developed in the future.[12] The EU Framework on Integration has constituted a supranational policy venue for the legitimisation of 'the moving of ideas' on national civic integration programmes as 'good practices'.

III   Civic integration: The national context

This section presents a comparative account of civic integration policy programmes and legal measures in three EU Member States: France, Germany and the Netherlands, which constitute paradigmatic examples about the use of civic integration measures. Their key role in relation to the final output of the negotiations inside the Council around the most relevant EU legal and policy measures so far adopted on immigration and integration further justifies our geographical selection. In order to ascertain the compatibility of civic integration with these general principles, we will assess the objectives, material and personal scope of the external and internal dimensions of civic integration in these three selected Member States.

A   The external dimension of civic integration

1   The public intended purpose

The Netherlands was the first European country to introduce 'integration-abroad' requirements. On 22 December 2005, the Dutch parliament adopted an 'Integration Abroad Act' (*Wet inburgering in*

---

[11] *Ibid.*

[12] The Stockholm Programme of December 2009 also calls for strengthening Member States' efforts toward the identification of 'European modules to support the integration process'.

het buitenland, WIB), which entered into force on 15 March 2006. Since 2006, immigrants are required to demonstrate basic knowledge of the Dutch language and society when entering the Netherlands.[13] In order to justify the introduction of a new immigration requirement for family migrants, the explanatory memorandum to the Integration Abroad Act[14] refers to the marginalisation and lack of integration of a growing number of migrants in the Netherlands, one-third of whom come for the purpose of family reunification or family formation. The Cabinet intended to put an end to this 'process of marginalisation' by requiring immigrants who are likely to face difficulties in integrating after arrival to start with the integration process already prior to arrival.[15]

However, behind the official objective of fostering and facilitating the integration process of newcomers lies the more implicit aim of reducing the number of family migrants to the Netherlands. It follows from the explanatory memorandum to the Act that the requirement to pass an integration exam abroad is intended to stimulate potential immigrants to carefully consider whether applying for admission to the Netherlands is worthwhile.[16] The purpose of the Integration Abroad Act as a tool of immigration control also became clearly apparent from the government's decision to raise the level of the requirements on 15 March 2008.[17] On the basis of an assessment carried out in 2007,[18] which showed that candidates had a higher level of language proficiency than expected and that a majority of applicants passed the test, the number of questions that must be answered correctly in order to pass the test was increased.

The external dimension of civic integration was introduced in France by the *Loi relatif à la maîtrise de l'immigration, à l'intégration et à l'asile* n° 2007–1631 of 20 November 2007.[19] This law represented a major transformation of the classical French Republican integrationist philosophy.[20] One of the main official justifications offered by the French government for this legislative reform to take place was the need to

---

[13] Art. 16(1)(h) Vreemdelingenwet.

[14] Memorie van Toelichting, Kamerstukken II, 2003–2004, 29700 nr. 3.

[15] *Ibid.*   [16] *Ibid.*   [17] Kamerstukken II 2006–07, 29 700, nr. 40.

[18] TNO-rapport, *Onderzoek naar de kwaliteit van het inburgeringsexamen buitenland*, TNO-DV 2007 C053.

[19] Loi n° 2007–1631 de 20 novembre 2007 relative à la maîtrise de l'immigration, à l'intégration et à l'asile, Journal Officiel no. 270 of 21 November 2007.

[20] C. Laborde, 'The culture(s) of the Republic: Nationalism and multiculturalism in French Republican thought', *Political Theory* 29 (2001), 716.

transpose into French law the Council Directive 2003/86 on the right to family reunification.[21] Similarly to the Dutch case, the first paragraph of the Explanatory Memorandum of the original *Projet de Loi* also made reference to the high number of residence permits so far granted in France on the basis of family reunification in contrast with other channels of 'legal' immigration.[22]

In Germany, a language test as a precondition for spousal reunification was introduced in 2007.[23] According to Section 30(1) No. 2 of the Residence Act (as amended), incoming spouses must be able to demonstrate basic knowledge of the German language in order to be granted a residence permit for the purpose of family reunification. However, as the pre-entry language requirement does not contain any 'civic element', a discussion of its official and implicit objectives goes beyond the scope of this chapter.[24]

2   Material scope

In the Netherlands, according to Article 16(1)(h) *Vreemdelingenwet*, an application for a temporary residence permit may be denied if a foreigner, who is categorised as a 'newcomer' pursuant to the Integration Act (*Wet inburgering*) and does not fall within one of the exceptions, fails to demonstrate a basic knowledge of Dutch language and society. Passing the test is a precondition for the acquisition of a provisional residence permit (*Machtiging tot voorlopig verblijf*, MVV). The requested knowledge has to be proven by way of passing an integration test abroad, as specified in the Integration Abroad Act. The test is carried out in Dutch embassies and consists of a civic and a language part. As regards the civic component, applicants are asked a number of questions about topics such as the geography of the Netherlands, Dutch history, the Dutch constitution and government. The necessary preparation for the test lies entirely within the responsibility of the potential applicants, who may acquire a 'practice pack' for a price of approximately €70.

---

[21] Directive 2003/86/EC on the right to family reunification, OJ L 251/12, 3 October 2003.
[22] C. Borrel, 'Enquêtes Annuelles de Recensement 2004 et 2005: Près de 5 million d'immigrés à la mide de 2004', Insee Première N° 1098 (2006).
[23] Gesetz zur Umsetzung aufenthalts- und asylrechtlicher Richtlinien der Europäische Union, BGBl. I, p. 1970.
[24] See A. Wiesbrock, 'Discrimination instead of integration? Integration requirements in Denmark and Germany' in E. Guild, K. Groenendijk and S. Carrera (eds.), *Illiberal Liberal States: Immigration, citizenship and integration in the EU* (Aldershot: Ashgate, 2009).

The Decree 2008–1115 implementing the Law 2007–1631 includes the details for the practical application of civic integration abroad in France.[25] The competent public authority in charge of organising the courses and the evaluation is the Office français de l'immigration et de l'intégration (hereinafter the French Office of Immigration and Integration, FOII). Article R311–30–1 provides that the latter can delegate all or part of these functions to third parties (*organismes*), something which leaves the door open for the involvement of the private sector in the delivery and testing of 'civic integration'.[26]

Every TCN over sixteen and under sixty-five years old, after the expiry of sixty days from the presentation of application for family reunification, will be subject to an evaluation carried out by the FOII about their degree of knowledge of the French language and the values of the Republic. Article R311–30–2 of the *Code de l'entrée et du séjour des étrangers et du droit d'asile* (CESEDA) states that the test will take the form of a series of oral questions in a language that the applicant will understand. Reference is made to Article R311–22 of the CESEDA which stipulates that civic formation training consists of 'the presentation of French institutions and the values of the Republic', including equal treatment between men and women, secularism and the rule of law. If the results are considered to be 'insufficient', the foreigner will 'benefit' from civic formation training, lasting for a minimum of half a day in the field or fields in which the insufficiency has been found (Articles R311–30–4 and R311–30–5 of CESEDA).

The foreigner will then be subject to a second evaluation. The law does not expressly specify the extent to which non-justifiable non-attendance to the civic formation training might negatively affect the decision for delivering a visa by the consular authorities. However, Article 411–8 expressly provides that family reunification, and the delivery of the visa, will be 'subordinated' to the presentation of a certificate of attendance on the training or integration course. Therefore, it is in our view clear that the certificate of attendance will actually constitute another indirect 'condition' for the actual delivery of the visa.

[25] Décret no. 2008–1115 de 30 octobre 2008 relatif à la preparation de l'integration en France des étrangers souhaitant s'y installer durablement, Journal Officiel of 1 November 2008.
[26] I. Michalowski, 'Liberal states: Privatized integration policies?' in E. Guild, K. Groenendijk and S. Carrera (eds.), *Illiberal Liberal States: Immigration, citizenship and integration in the EU* (Aldershot: Ashgate, 2009).

As stated above, Germany does not require any civic knowledge from potential migrants, but the passing of a language test at level A1 of the CEFR constitutes a requirement for spousal reunification.[27]

3 Personal scope

The integration-abroad test in the Netherlands must be passed by foreign citizens between the age of sixteen and sixty-five who are planning to apply for permanent residence. Yet, citizens of several developed countries, from whom an authorisation for temporary stay is not required, are exempted from the integration test.[28] Apart from EU/EEA nationals, this includes migrants from Switzerland, the US, Canada, Japan, South Korea, Liechtenstein, Monaco, Australia and New Zealand. According to the explanatory memorandum to the Integration Abroad Act this distinction on grounds of nationality is justified on the basis of the fact that countries whose citizens are exempted have a comparable level of economic, social and political development to European countries.[29] Therefore, the argument goes, in respect of their admission there is no risk of an inflow of migrants that will result in problems in respect of integration and social cohesion. However, it has been argued that the tests discriminate indirectly on the basis of ethnic origin, as they apply only to migrants from certain non-Western countries.[30] Further exemptions apply to Surinamese nationals who have followed secondary education in the Dutch language, persons with a work permit, self-employed persons, knowledge migrants (*kennismigranten*) and family members of persons with an asylum residence permit.[31]

In accordance to the Law 2007–1631 and Decree 2008–1115, the following categories are exempted from civic integration abroad in France: first, those providing evidence of having followed a minimum of three years of secondary studies in one French school abroad or in a francophone educational establishment; secondly, those having followed a minimum of one year superior studies in France; thirdly, those for whom account is taken of public order, state of war, natural or technological disasters which imply serious difficulties for displacement or putting into danger the security of the foreigner, or those for whom the civic formation training implies constraints which are incompatible

---

[27] s. 30(1) No. 2 *Aufenthaltsgesetz*.
[28] Art. 16(1)(h) Vreemdelingenwet jo. Arts. 3 and 5 Wet inburgering.
[29] Kammerstukken II, 2003/04, 29 700, No. 3, p. 19.
[30] Human Rights Watch, *The Netherlands: Discrimination in the name of integration* (2008), www.hrw.org/backgrounder/2008/netherlands.
[31] Art. 17(1) Vreemdelingenwet.

with their physical or financial capacities, or their professional obligations (Article 311–30–10 of CESEDA). No further exemptions have been
included.

Even though the German pre-entry language test does not contain a
civic element, it is interesting to note that the exemptions and justifications for exemptions under German law are very similar to the exemptions applied in the Netherlands. Categories of persons that are
exempted from taking a pre-entry language test include highly qualified
workers[32] and persons who are not required to obtain a visa in order to
enter Germany on grounds of their nationality,[33] that is citizens of the
EU/EEA, Switzerland, Australia, Israel, Japan, Canada, South Korea,
New Zealand, the United States, Andorra, Honduras, Monaco and San
Marino.[34] According to the German government, the difference in treatment on grounds of nationality is justified as it is in the particular
interest of Germany to encourage the immigration of nationals from
these countries.[35] This argument has been supported by the
Administrative Court of Berlin in a case of December 2007, where it
was concluded that the principle of equal treatment enshrined in Article
3(1) of the German Basic Law is not infringed if citizens of certain
countries enjoy an exemption from the language requirement.[36]

B   The internal dimension of civic integration

1   Purpose

France has framed civic integration in the shape of a contractual obligation on the side of TCNs. The so-called welcome and integration
contract (*contrat d'accueil et d'intégration*, CAI) seeks to institutionalise
and formalise into a contractual logic the integration of TCNs into the
French nation for having access to security of residence in France.[37] The
contract used to be of a voluntary nature,[38] but with the entry into force

---

[32] s. 30(1), second sentence, No. 1 jo. 19 AufenthG.
[33] s. 30(1), third sentence, No. 4 AufenthG.
[34] s. 41(1) and (2) AufenthV.
[35] Bundestags-Drucksache 16/520, Bundestags-Drucksache 16/5498, p. 6.
[36] Verwaltungsgericht Berlin, 19 December 2007, VG 5 V, 22.07. (InfAuslR 2008, 165 = DVBl. 2008, 396).
[37] S. Carrera, *A Comparison of Integration Programmes in the EU: Trends and weaknesses* (Brussels: CEPS, 2006).
[38] Loi relative à la maîtrise de l'immigration, au séjour des étrangers en France et à la nationalité of November 2003.

of the Sarkozy Law II – *Loi relative à l'immigration et à l'intégration* No. 2006-911 of 24 July 2006[39] – it became mandatory. According to the Explanatory Memorandum of the *project de loi* (N° 2986), one of the main purposes behind the introduction of the conditionality of Republican integration was to reinforce the '*parcours d'intégration républicaine*'. It was considered that durable settlement by TCNs in the country should be reserved to those who have chosen to respect 'French Republican values'.[40] The conditional (obligatory) nature of the CAI was introduced at times of transposing Directive 2003/109 into the French legal system.

The purported official objectives for the application of an integration test in the Netherlands has been the acquisition by foreigners residing permanently in the Netherlands of sufficient knowledge of the Dutch language and society in order to participate in society.[41] The new Integration Act (*Wet Inburgering*) that entered into force on 1 January 2007[42] has the additional purpose of increasing the speed and effectiveness of the integration process. The Dutch legislator referred inter alia to the EU Common Basic Principles on Integration and the explicit possibility granted to Member States in Directives 2003/86 and 2003/109 to impose integration conditions upon TCNs to justify the application of an integration test.[43]

As regards the official purpose of the German orientation course, *Aufenthaltsgesetz* refers to the acquisition of knowledge of the legal order, the culture and the history of Germany. The Ordinance on Integration Courses (*Integrationskursverordnung*) contains a more precise definition of these areas of knowledge, referring in particular to the principals of the rule of law, equal treatment, tolerance and religious freedom. The overall objectives of the orientation course are the acquisition of an understanding for the German state system, the development of a positive attitude towards and identification with the German state, knowledge of the rights and duties as residents and citizens, the

---

[39] JORF, No. 170, 25 July 2006, p. 11047. See Conseil Constitutionnel, 20 juillet 2006, n° 2006-539 DC, JO 25 juillet 2006, p. 11066; N. Guimezanes, 'Loi de 24 juillet 2006 relative à l'immigration et à l'intégration', *La Semaine Juridique – Édition Générale* 36 (2006), 1623, 1624.

[40] This was stated in the Rapport n° 3058 of M. Thierry Mariani, député, 26 avril 2006, www.senat.fr/dossierleg/pjl05-362.html.

[41] Kammerstukken II 2005–06, 30 308.

[42] Wet van 30 november 2006, houdende regels inzaken inburgering in de Nederlandse samenleving (*Wet Inburgering*).

[43] Kammerstukken II 2005–06, 30 308.

development of competences to the self-acquisition of knowledge, participation in German society and the acquisition of intercultural competences.[44]

2 Material scope

In France, no formal civic integration test is being applied. However, Articles L. 311.9 and 314-2 of the CESEDA prescribe the subordination of the granting of the first *carte de résident* to the fulfilment of the condition of Republican integration to French society by the TCN. The degree of integration will be evaluated taking into account the commitment of the person involved to respecting the principles governing the French Republic and knowledge of French language.

In addition to language instruction,[45] the CAI foresees a civic formation training course and an informative session about 'life in France'. The civic formation training, provided in Article L. 311-9 of the code, according to Article R. 311-22 of the Decree N° 2006-1791, will specifically comprise a presentation of French institutions and of 'the values of the Republic'. Further, the contract also foresees a session offering information concerning 'lifestyle in Republican France' as stipulated in Article R. 311-25 of the decree. The failure to integrate into French society will justify the application of sanctions by the state. The sanction will consist of not being granted the permanent residence permit, or a negative decision regarding the renewal of the temporary administrative status of stay.

The Law 2007–1631 also invented another version of the welcome and integration contract, this time related to the official conception of Republican integration of the family in French society (*'Contrat d'accueil et d'intégration pour la famille'*, CAIF). The new Article 311-9-1 of CESEDA imposes on those TCNs holding a permanent residence permit and her/his family having benefited from family reunification, to both conclude with the French state a contract which will oblige them to follow a course on 'the rights and duties of parents in France', and to ensure a proper schooling of their children. In those cases where the contractual conditions are not respected either by the TCN or her/his spouse, they may be penalised with a financial sanction consisting of the cessation of family social benefits granted by the French state, and eventually administrative sanctions consisting of a refusal to renew the

---

[44] Bundesamt für Migration und Flüchtlinge, *Konzept für einen bundesweiten Integrationskurs. Überarbeitete Neuauflage* (2009), pp. 24–5.
[45] For an in-depth analysis see Carrera (n. 3 above).

'*carte de séjour temporaire*' or grant the '*carte de resident*', and hence to eventual expulsion from the country.

In Germany, the integration programme consists of a basic and follow-up language course and a civic orientation course, with the exception of newcomers who already possess sufficient language skills. The curriculum for a uniform federal orientation course introduced in January 2009 includes subjects dealing with German politics, history and society.[46] The acquisition of a permanent right of residence depends on the fulfilment of the integration requirement. It is a precondition for the acquisition of a settlement permit under Section 9(2) *Aufenthaltsgesetz* that the applicant has a basic knowledge of 'the legal and social order and living conditions' in the Federal Republic. This requirement can only be fulfilled by success-fully completing an integration course, unless one of the exemptions applies. In addition, the ordinary participation in integration courses is one of the considerations to be taken into account when prolonging a temporary residence permit. According to Section 8(3) *Aufenthaltsgesetz* the repetitive violation of the obligation to participate in integration courses can lead to a refusal to prolong the temporary residence permit of a foreigner who does not have a right to acquire a residence permit. In case a right to prolong the residence permit does exist, denial is still possible unless the TCN can submit proof that his/her integration into society and social life has occurred by other means.

Pursuant to Article 21(1)(k) *Vreemdelingenwet*, TCNs wishing to acquire a permanent residence permit in the Netherlands must have passed an integration exam (*inburgeringsexamen*). In January 2007, the obligation for TCNs to participate in a language course and an orienta-tion course (*maatschapij orientatie*) was abandoned, giving way to a requirement to acquire Dutch language skills and knowledge of Dutch society by self-study.[47] A failure to pass the test will lead to the denial of a residence permit. This means that a TCN's unwillingness or inability to comply with the integration requirement will inevitably lead to his/her expulsion from the Netherlands. The civic element of this obligation to integrate requires immigrants to acquire knowledge on 'Dutch society', in particular on the following topics: work and income, behaviour, values and norms, living, health and healthcare, history and geography, admin-istration, the state and the rule of law and education.[48] According to Article 7(1) *Wet Inburgering*, an integration test has to be passed within

[46] s. 17 *Integrationskursverordnung*.   [47] Art. 7 jo. 13(2) *Wet Inburgering*.
[48] Art. 2.10(1) *Besluit Inburgering*.

three and a half years by persons who have passed the integration exam abroad on the basis of Article 16 *Vreemdelingenwet* and within five years in all other cases where a duty to integrate exists. The test consists of a central and a decentralised component.[49]

The central component contains three elements, namely a digital practical test, a Dutch oral language test and a knowledge test on Dutch society.[50] In the decentralised component immigrants are examined on a number of practical situations which they might encounter in the Netherlands.[51] The overall costs for the test amount to €230, consisting of €126 for the central part plus €104 for the decentralised component.[52] It is notable that the civic knowledge test and the language test are conducted at the same level as the previous citizenship test and that the diploma obtained serves as a valid proof of being integrated for naturalisation. This means that the level of integration that is required by immigrants after three and a half years of residence in the Netherlands is the same as that demanded from potential citizens.

3   Personal scope

In France, the following categories are exempted from signing the CAI according to Article L 311–9 of the CESEDA: first, those foreigners providing evidence of having followed a minimum of three years of secondary studies in one French school abroad or in a francophone educational establishment; secondly, those having followed a minimum of one year superior studies in France (Article R 311–19); thirdly, those TCNs holding residence permits (as well as their family members and children older than sixteen years old) falling within the category of intra-corporate transferees (Article L 313–10 of CESEDA); fourthly, those holding a residence permit mentioning 'competences and skills' ('*La carte de séjour portant la mention compétences et talents*') stipulated by Article L 315–1; fifthly, foreigners between sixteen and eighteen years

---

[49]   Art. 13(3) *Wet Inburgering*. (The legislation uses the term '*praktijk deel*' (practical part) for the decentralised component, although both the decentralised and the centralised component provide for a '*praktijkexamen*' (practical test). To avoid confusion, the notions used by the Dutch government in their English language explanation are used here, see www.ind.nl/en/inbedrijf/overdeind/veelgesteldevragen/ Wet_inburgering_nat uralisatie.asp.

[50]   Art. 3.9(1) *Besluit Inburgering*.   [51]   Art. 3.7 *Besluit Inburgering*.

[52]   See the IND website at www.ind.nl.

old meeting the conditions for the acquisition of French nationality foreseen in Article 21–7 of the Civil Code (Article L 314–12 of CESEDA).

Participation in integration courses in Germany is mandatory for all newly arriving immigrants who are permanently residing in Germany on the basis of a residence permit or a settlement permit and who are not able to communicate in the German language at a basic level.[53] In addition, resident TCNs who receive unemployment benefit II or have 'special integration needs' are obliged to follow an integration course.[54] Participation is open on a voluntary basis and provided that enough places are available to other resident TCNs, EU citizens and German nationals who are in special need of integration.[55] The following categories of TCNs are exempted from the 'obligation' (*Teilnahmeverpflichtung*) of attending an integration course: first, persons who are undergoing any form of education, training or vocational training in Germany; secondly, persons who have attended comparable education measures in Germany; thirdly, persons for whom continuous participation is considered to be unfeasible or unreasonable; fourthly, long-term residents who have already attended integration courses in other Member States.[56]

In the Netherlands, the obligation to integrate (*inburgeringsplichting*) applies to legal TCNs in the sense of Article 8(a–e) or 8(l) *Vreemdelingenwet* who are residing in the Netherlands for non-temporary purposes or are religious preachers.[57] Thus, all non-EU/EEA immigrants between the age of eighteen and sixty-five, whose purpose of stay is of a non-temporary nature, must pass an integration exam.[58] The requirement applies to both newcomers as well as *oudkomers*, who were already living in the Netherlands at the moment of entry into force of the Integration Act. Exemptions apply to several categories of foreigners. First, immigrants who have followed at least eight years of compulsory education in the Netherlands are presumed to possess sufficient Dutch language skills.[59] Secondly, foreigners who are able to present special diplomas or certificates, proving that their knowledge of the Dutch language and society is already adequate are exempted.[60] Acceptable means of proof are secondary or higher educational diplomas obtained in the Netherlands, Belgium or Suriname and Level

---

[53] s. 44(1) jo. 44a(1) *Aufenthaltsgesetz.*   [54] s. 44a(2) *Aufenthaltsgesetz.*
[55] s. 44(4) *Aufenthaltsgesetz.*   [56] s. 44a(1)–(2a) *Aufenthaltsgesetz.*
[57] Art. 3(1) *Wet Inburgering.*
[58] ss. 3 and 5(1) *Wet Inburgering.* Religious leaders and spiritual counsellors have to pass an integration exam even if their stay is merely temporary.
[59] s. 5(1)(b) *Wet Inburgering.*   [60] s. 5(3) *Wet Inburgering.*

A2 certificates from integration courses followed in accordance with the 1998 *Wet Inburgering Nieuwkomers*. Foreigners with pre-knowledge of the Dutch language also have the possibility of taking a 'short exemption test', consisting of the electronic practice test and the societal knowledge test conducted at a higher language proficiency level (B1) than the regular test. Thirdly, certain vulnerable groups are exempted from the integration requirement, including illiterates and persons suffering from a physical or mental illness who can demonstrate that they have made an effort to learn Dutch and can prove on the basis of an independent assessment that they will not be able to learn Dutch within the next five years.[61] The Integration Act also includes a broader exemption for persons who cannot be expected to pass the integration test due to the Netherlands' international human rights obligations.[62]

IV   Common deficits of national civic integration measures

There are two major deficits affecting the internal and external dimensions of civic integration relating to the principles of proportionality and non-discrimination.

A   *Proportionality*[63]

Proportionality has become one of the most important components of the general principles of EU law.[64] The Court of Justice has considered this principle to be particularly appropriate when reviewing the legality of administrative actions adopted by EU Member States in the scope of EU law. Settled case law has considered it necessary to ensure proper protection of the individual whose European rights might be endangered in the phase of national transposition. Even if the nature of Directives 2003/109 and 2003/86 have been considered as cases of 'minimal harmonisation' allowing a large margin of discretion to the Member States, they do constitute EU law and recognise a number of substantive rights and procedural guarantees below which threshold national authorities cannot cross. This has been confirmed by the Court of Justice in *European Parliament* v. *Council*,[65] where it was held that Directive

---

[61] s. 6 *Wet Inburgering*.   [62] s. 5(2)(d) *Wet Inburgering*.
[63] P. Craig, *EU Administrative Law* (Oxford: Oxford University Press, 2006).
[64] T. Trimidas, *The General Principles of EU Law* (Oxford: Oxford University Press, 2006).
[65] C-540/03, *European Parliament* v. *Council*, 27 June 2006 [2006] ECR I-5769.

2003/86 imposes precise positive obligations, with corresponding clearly defined rights on the Member States, where the latter are not left with any margin of discretion.[66] The Court also ruled that the fact that the concept of integration was not defined in the directive could not be interpreted as authorising the Member States to employ that concept in a manner contrary to general principles of EU law, in particular to fundamental rights. It therefore concluded that Member States cannot employ an unspecified concept of integration.[67]

The subjectivity, mandatory nature and intended public goal of civic integration measures in our three EU Member States can be identified as the most crucial factors at times of evaluating their compatibility with the general principle of proportionality. Our review will consider the three-pronged phases of evaluation which have traditionally characterised the Court of Justice's operability of this EU principle: suitability, necessity and proportionality *stricto sensu*.[68]

1 Subjectivity

A certain tension arises when considering the inherently subjective nature of civic integration in relation to the principle of proportionality. Civic integration functions as an exception or a derogative clause for TCNs to have access to security of residence and rights as provided by national immigration legislations and at times EU immigration law. This concept leaves too much discretion to the imagination of the national public authority or private actor conducting the evaluation when determining whether the applicant is integrated into 'the national set of values and symbols' or 'at the margins' of the canon national model. The indeterminate character of the civic dimension leaves therefore a wide margin of appreciation to the imagination of the evaluation agent. In the context of immigration legislation, and particularly those administrative aspects that have been subject to Europeanisation, the non-proportionate character of civic integration conditions constitutes a domestic mechanism endangering the legal certainty and foundations of the common European immigration policy.

After looking at the ways in which civic integration is tested and practised across the three EU Member States under study, it remains difficult to ascertain the existence of any objective criteria and procedure

---

[66] Para. 60.   [67] Para. 70.

[68] N. Emiliou, *The Principle of Proportionality in European Law: A comparative study* (The Hague: Kluwer Law International, 1996).

meeting the paradigm of legal certainty. National immigration law does not seem to provide a 'sufficiently clear and precise' definition of 'civic integration' which is accessible to all persons concerned and which prevents illiberal interferences by state authorities or private actors at times of granting (temporary or permanent) residence permits or visas to TCNs. The principle of legal certainty demands that individuals need to know the legal consequences of their actions and that the quality of the law is as high and objective as possible in order to prevent 'exceptionalism' by public authorities beyond any remits of legality.[69] The principle of legality has been considered to be of particular relevance by the European Court of Human Rights (ECtHR) in Strasbourg when deciding about the compatibility of an impugned national measure derogating a human right with the principle of proportionality. By way of illustration, in the case *Liu and Liu* v. *Russia*[70] the ECtHR held that the expression 'in accordance to the law', which is a constitutive element of the proportionality test, does not only require that the measure should be based on national law but also refers to the quality of the law in question. The ECtHR concluded that this would demand that the law would not only be accessible to the individual concerned but also formulated in a manner offering sufficient precision to enable her/him to foresee the consequences, delimit the scope of discretion by national authorities and be drafted in a sufficient clarity to provide the individual a proper level of protection against any arbitrary interference. Moreover, the principle of legal certainty is now also part of Article 49 of the EU Charter of Fundamental Rights, which applies to anyone, including TCNs.[71]

The category of 'values' is by definition vague, indeterminate and subject to divergent interpretations and ideologies. There is a presumption by the nation state and certain officials and professionals of politics, however, about the existence of a crystal-clear meaning of 'national identity' and a commonly shared understanding of what national values and symbols actually are and mean. Any attempt to provide a definition in law of the notion of 'national' (customs, ways of life, symbols, values etc.) would lead to huge conflicts which would go beyond any 'migration-related debate' and which would propagate across the entire

---

[69] For a brief analysis of relevant ECJ case law on the principle of legal certainty see P. Craig and G. de Búrca, *EU Law* (Oxford: Oxford University Press, 2007), pp. 551–8.

[70] *Liu and Liu* v. *Russia*, Application No. 42086/05, 6 December 2007.

[71] Charter of Fundamental Rights of the European Union, 2007, C 303/01, 14 December 2007.

citizenry, conflicting directly with the principles of pluralism, non-discrimination and respect for diversity upon which the EU liberal democracies are supposed to be founded. Such a definition would face the challenge to meet ever evolving social practices and plurality of identities across the constructed nation, as well as different interpretations and visions about the liberal boundaries of nationalism.

Further, what are the legal mechanisms and judicial guarantees provided in national immigration law for TCNs to mount a legal challenge against a decision rejecting family reunification on the basis that they are not 'civically' integrated? The answer to this question is particularly unclear in the context of integration-abroad requirements, but the internal dimension of civic integration also raises similar critical concerns. This answer, however, has also profound implications in respect of the fundamental right to an effective remedy as enshrined in Article 47 of the EU Charter.[72]

2 Mandatory nature

Another point of contention in light of the principle of proportionality relates to the mandatory nature of civic integration and the effects of non-compliance by the applicant. National civic integration measures fail to pass 'the less restrictive and onerous test' and therefore can be considered not to be necessary. In all countries under consideration pre-entry integration tests and compliance with integration conditions and/or participation in a state-organised integration course are obligatory. This, we have argued, is also the case in France even though at first instance one could be inclined to think that integration abroad is 'facultative' for the actual delivery of a visa. The degree of civic knowledge is also an issue of concern in this respect. TCNs are required to acquire knowledge of the receiving state's institutions, history, language and values in order to enter the country, have access to security of residence and, in the case of France, enjoy the fundamental right of respect for family life. The proportionality of the civic integration test is highly questionable in the Netherlands, where the requirements in order to acquire a secure residence status are as high as those applied to future citizens in the scope of naturalisation tests.

If the applicant fails to be civically integrated, national immigration laws foresee a set of sanctions. The failure to comply with the integration

---

[72] E. Brouwer, *Digital Borders and Real Rights: Effective remedies for third-country nationals in the Schengen information system* (Leiden: Martinus Nijhoff Publishers, 2007).

requirement can lead to the denial of a permanent residence status. In all three countries, TCNs who do not comply with national integration conditions will not be able to acquire an EU long-term residence permit in light of Directive 2003/109. In addition, even though it is not always explicitly stated in national immigration law, the non-compliance with integration conditions will in all three countries result in the expulsion of TCNs, as the holding of a temporary residence permit is generally limited to a certain period of time prior to the acquisition of a permanent residence permit. In Germany, an unsatisfactory integration process can in extreme cases even lead to a refusal to prolong a temporary residence permit. A similar situation occurs in the Netherlands where a failure to pass the test will lead to the denial of the residence permit and expulsion from the country. In addition to residence-related sanctions, legislation in all three countries envisages the application of fines in the event of non-compliance with the obligation to integrate. In the context of family reunion, the CAIF in France foresees that if the contractual obligations are not met, including those of 'civic nature', the family will be penalised with a financial sanction freezing access to family social benefits, the eventual refusal of renewing the temporary residence permits and expulsion.

3   The intended public goal

Is civic integration necessary to achieve 'the intended public goal' pursued by national immigration legislations? When looking at the political justifications put forward by most of the governments across the EU Member States analysed in this chapter, it is clear that one of the main intended public goals behind its use is a better management of migration and diversity. Civic integration functions as an instrument for migration control, as a selection mechanism of the kind of immigrants who will be allowed to enter and reside in the state. As we have shown above, the general purpose of civic integration abroad has been the reduction of the number of entries for the purposes of family reunification. The introduction of a requirement of passing a civic integration exam has primarily aimed at reducing the number of residence permits granted for these very purposes. Integration abroad in France has already proved to be quite effective towards that goal and it appears that the application rates will decrease even further. This is also evident when looking at the case of the Netherlands, where the integration test introduced by the Integration Abroad Act was later on considered to be 'too easy' because of the high success rates of candidates passing the exam and this led to increasing the degree of difficulty of the questions. Therefore, making family reunion more difficult, and making family migrants delay and even cancel their intended settlement, appears to be the predominant intended public goal driving civic integration abroad.

It is interesting to note that the arguments substantiating the legis-lative measures making use of civic integration have often alluded to practices already existing in other EU Member States as well as the obligation to transpose EU immigration law. For instance, the French government mentioned the Dutch integration policy before making mandatory the CAI and introducing integration abroad. Germany's language requirement abroad also found a source of inspiration in the Netherlands. Here we refer back to the effects of 'the exchange of ideas' between EU Member States' representatives taking place within the scope of the NCPs in the EU Framework on Integration. The 'Dutch approach on integration' has indeed constituted a model for other countries in the EU in the development of civic integration measures and programmes for TCNs. In addition, the transposition of EU immi-gration law has been often instrumentalised by certain governments to pass new amendments in their national legislation making use of civic integration measures as a tool for a restrictive immigration policy. In France, for instance, the introduction of civic integration abroad, the obligatory nature of the CAI and the CAIF were partly justified in light of the transposition of Directives 2003/109 and 2003/86.

B   Non-discrimination

The examination of the personal scope purported by the internal and external dimensions of civic integration shows a widely diversified pic-ture regarding the persons who are covered or exempted from taking the programmes, tests or contracts. There appears to be however a common presumption that certain categories of TCNs are already very well integrated or do not need to be integrated into 'the nation' and its perceived values, symbols and 'way of life'. This is most prominently the case for nationals of EU Member States who cannot be subject to any civic integration tests or measures as a condition for exercising their freedom to move and reside in another Member State of the Union. There are additionally certain migrants who are not obliged to pass a civic integration evaluation on a completely different basis. For example, among the group of TCNs who are exempted from taking the CAI and the CAIF in France are those benefiting from the residence permit mentioning 'competences and skills' ('*La carte de séjour portant la mention compétences et talents*'), and therefore considered as 'highly skilled' following the logic of *immigration choisie* (selective immigration policy) which has driven French immigration policy in recent years. In respect of pre-entry integration requirements, the same holds true for 'knowledge migrants' in the Netherlands and 'highly qualified migrants' in Germany. Moreover, both countries provide an exemption from the integration-abroad requirement for nationals from certain countries, who do need a visa/provisional residence permit to enter the country, such as nationals from the US, Canada, Japan, South Korea, New Zealand, Monaco and Liechtenstein. The question arises whether this difference in treatment can be considered to constitute an infringement of EU and/or international law.

When considering the arguments invoked by the German and Dutch authorities in order to justify the difference in treatment, it is notable that in both cases reference is made to the level of economic and social development of the countries whose citizens are exempted from integration-abroad requirements. However, distinguishing migrants exclusively on the basis of the level of development of their country of origin can be seen as discrimination on grounds of ethnic origin. This argument was made by Human Rights Watch in a 2008 report entitled 'The Netherlands: Discrimination in the name of integration'. The report argued that by providing a 'blanket exemption' for some 'Western' nationalities the test was disproportionate in aims and nature and constituted a violation of Article 14 and Protocol 12 of the European Convention on Human Rights.[73]

The main difficulty in challenging the exemption of some nationals from the integration-abroad requirements relates to the distinction between discrimination on grounds of ethnic origin and nationality discrimination.[74] Differences of treatment based on nationality are explicitly exempted from the scope of the EU non-discrimination directives.[75] It is also not clear whether a right to non-discrimination based on nationality in respect of TCNs can be derived from Article 21 of the

---

[73] Human Rights Watch (n. 30 above).

[74] A. Wiesbrock, *Legal Migration to the European Union* (The Hague: Martinus Nijhoff, 2010), p. 535.

[75] Directive 2000/43/EC implementing the principle of equal treatment between persons irrespective of racial or ethnic origin, OJ L 180/22, 19 July 2000, Directive 2000/78/EC establishing a general framework for equal treatment in employment and occupation, OJ L 303/16, 2 December 2000.

Charter of Fundamental Rights. Moreover, the ECtHR has stressed that states must be able to give preference to citizens of countries with which they hold a strong connection. Thus, it is likely to accept the existence of strong economic ties between two countries as a legitimate objective for the exemption from integration-abroad requirements.[76] Yet, at the same time the Court has underlined that a difference in treatment based exclusively on the ground of nationality must be based on very weighty reasons in order to be justified.[77] Accordingly, when considering the preferential treatment of citizens of countries with a similar socio-economic background and strong economic ties with the host country, the main question will be the proportionality of the means employed.

V Europeanisation and civic integration of TCNs

One of the immediate consequences of the progressive Europeanisation processes over immigration law is that Member States' discretional powers in the allocation of rights and security of residence to TCNs are diminished and subjected to EU rule of law. Member States' actions within the scope of EU law are subject to the supervision of the Commission and the judicial control and interpretation provided by the Court of Justice. The foundations and institutional arrangements characterising the EU legal system increasingly demarcate the boundaries for the legality of Member States' discretion also in the scope of EU immigration law.

By inserting integration measures and conditions inside some of the Articles of Directives 2003/109 and 2003/86, Member States' actions not only have to comply with the objectives and provisions thereby stipulated, but also with the EU-law general principles developed by the Court of Justice's jurisprudence, such as proportionality. Both the directive on long-term resident status and that of family reunification offer a European framework of rights, freedoms and guarantees to TCNs which all participating Member States need to ensure in practice. Any exceptions applicable to those rights will be closely monitored by the

---

[76] In *Andrejeva* v. *Latvia* the Court accepted the 'protection of the country's economic system' as a legitimate aim for a difference in treatment on grounds of nationality, see *Andrejeva* v. *Latvia*, Application No. 55707/00, 18 February 2009, para. 68.

[77] *Ibid.*, para. 87; *Gaygusuz* v. *Austria*, Application No. 17371/90, 16 September 1996, para. 42; *Koua Poirrez* v. *France*, Application No. 40892/89, 30 September 2003, para. 46.

Commission and the Court of Justice. Here the abovementioned Court of Justice's case *European Parliament* v. *Council*[78] has been central. The Court offered a fundamental contribution to the interpretation of the limits of Member States' actions in respect of fundamental rights while implementing European immigration law, and the discretion that Directive 2003/86 leaves them in relation to derogations from these rights. This ruling also reduced the margin of appreciation that the directive on the right to family reunification might have offered to Member States in the phase of national implementation, including the use of 'civic integration' measures and conditions. The Court ruled that any integration should have, according to Recital 12 of the preamble of this directive, the general objective of 'facilitating the integration of third country nationals in Member States by making family life possible through reunification'.

The limited degree of discretion held by Member States at times of transposing EU immigration law in their domestic legal systems has been also confirmed by the Commission Report on the application of Directive 2003/86 on the right to family reunification,[79] where it confirmed that:

> The admissibility of integration measures under the Directive depends on whether they respect the principle of proportionality. Their admissibility can be questioned on the basis of the accessibility of such courses or tests, how they are designed and/or organised (test materials, fees, venue, etc.), whether such measures or their impact serve purposes other than integration (e.g. high fees excluding low-income families).

In light of the comparative analysis provided in Section III above, the conditions highlighted by the Court of Justice and the Commission for the admissibility of integration measures (including those of a civic nature) remain questionable and pose a series of deficits in relation to the general principles of proportionality and non-discrimination. This undermines the goals of Directives 2003/109 (ensuring security of residence and that the main criterion for acquiring the status of long-term resident is the length of residence) and 2003/86 (making family life possible) and the substance of EU rights that they provide for TCNs.

---

[78] C-540/03 *European Parliament* v. *Council* [2006] ECR I-5769.
[79] European Commission, *Report on the Application of the Directive 2003/86 on the Right to Family Reunification*, COM(2008) 610, Brussels, 8 October 2008.

VI   Conclusions

Civic integration measures and conditions for TCNs constitute an illustrative case study of the ongoing struggles between nationalism and Europeanisation surrounding immigration and integration policies in Europe. Certain EU Member States have managed to fundamentally transform some of the traditional conceptual understandings of integration in EU law from one focusing on social inclusion, security of residence and access to rights to another one where integration becomes an instrument of a restrictive immigration policy in the form of a condition in immigration law for having access to a visa and/or residence permit. This has been particularly the case when looking at the introduction of integration 'conditions' and 'measures' within the body of Directives 2003/109 and 2003/86, which mainly represent derogative clauses in the hands of national administrations when determining the allocation of EU rights and procedural guarantees to TCNs. It has been particularly during the phase of national transposition of these directives where the civic dimensions of integration have been reinforced and further proliferated across several national arenas in Europe. The promotion of civic integration policies by certain EU Member States has also taken place through the exchange of 'good' practices and 'lessons learned' between Member States in the scope of the EU Framework on Integration.

It has been shown that the internal and external dimensions of civic integration programmes pose major deficits in respect of the principles of proportionality and non-discrimination. The relationship between civic integration and proportionality remains an issue of concern. This is evidenced when assessing the inherently subjective nature of civic integration examinations, their mandatory nature and set of sanctions applied in case of non-compliance by the applicant. The disproportionate nature of a majority of these measures is further supported by the intended public goal which is pursued, i.e. limiting the entries of TCNs for family reunion and reducing the number of long-term resident permits. Further, the differential treatment applying to the personal scope and the exemption of certain categories of ('Western', highly skilled and rich) foreigners from the obligation to pass the civic test leads to the incompatibility of integration measures with the principle of non-discrimination.

We have then moved into an examination of the implications of using civic integration as a condition for TCNs to have access to rights provided in EU immigration law and the multifaceted effects emerging from an increasing Europeanisation of migration law at EU level. It has been argued that by subjecting the access to EU rights and guarantees granted by European immigration law to civic integration programmes and tests, the Member States' strategies have been to win back their national sovereignty when determining who is entitled to rights and liberty, and who is included and can claim membership in the European polity. The deficits identified in the three EU Member States under analysis are therefore transferred to the common European immigration policy, something which endangers its compatibility with the general principles of the rule of law and fundamental rights. However, the results of Europeanisation processes on immigration law also make them subject to the supervision by the Commission and the judicial control by the Court of Justice, which are there to ensure that the substance and goals of European rights and freedoms of individuals are respected and not subject to exceptional public measures going beyond the remits of the rule of law.

The nexus between a secure immigration status and adherence to national/European identity leads to the stigmatisation of the vulnerable foreigner who is in search of security of residence and social solidarity. Integration paradoxically contributes to social exclusion and insecurity of the vulnerable migrant who is demanded 'to know and understand' national values and identity in order to access the legality of entry and residence in Europe. Europeanisation processes have therefore until now brought legitimacy to certain nationalistic approaches on integration rooted in conservative perceptions and stereotypes considering diversity as a threat to 'social cohesion'. The European immigration policy should not continue legitimising the continuance of these critical national practices and restrictive immigration policies by adding a 'European identity' dimension to civic programmes/tests. Instead a 'post-national' approach should be favoured. This approach should continue fostering the more traditional approaches of integration in EU law and policy that considered integration of TCNs as a social process leading to equality and membership of all individuals in Europe.

9

Corporate social responsibility: Assessing the scope for an EU policy

SANDRA KRÖGER

I Introduction

> When I give food to the poor, they call me a saint. When I ask why the
> poor have no food, they call me a communist.[1]

While the asymmetry of the economic and social dimension of the
European integration project has been thoroughly analysed and documented,[2] it remains open as to what could and should be done to achieve
a more balanced integration process. In particular, it is disputed whether
related efforts should focus on the national or supranational level and
whether these efforts should be of a regulatory or soft-law nature. With
regulation having become more difficult after the Eastern enlargement
rounds, considerable attention has been directed towards so-called new
modes of governance, in particular the open method of co-ordination
(OMC). Another instrument that emerged on the EU agenda in the
context of the Lisbon Strategy in 2000 is 'corporate social responsibility'
(CSR). The aim of CSR is to call upon firms' sense of responsibility to
contribute to certain social standards, to social cohesion, to environmental awareness or sustainable development.[3] CSR could thus be seen
as an attempt to balance the economic and social dimensions of the
European integration project. This chapter asks, in an explorative way, in
how far a European CSR policy that would work in favour of the social
dimension is possible in light of the institutional differences between
Member States.

---

[1] H. Camara, *Spiral of Violence* (London: Sheed and Ward, 1971).
[2] See for more detail and references chs. 1 and 2 of this volume.
[3] European Council, Lisbon European Council, 23 and 24 March 2000, Presidency Conclusions, 2000.

In practice, CSR refers to a range of different business activities, such as symbolic PR-concepts, the integration of CSR into the risk management of the firm or strategic renewal of production modes and products. It can include advanced employees' protection against risks, training measures, social and eco labels, higher levels of environmental performance via recycling or pollution abatement or stakeholder dialogue, to name only a few. It relates to a discussion about the responsibilities of firms towards society and reacts both to the retrenchment of public welfare government and to the increased influence of non-governmental organisations (NGOs) in policy-making and the claims they represent.[4]

CSR can be linked to two major strands of political science theory. It has been addressed, on the one hand, by the governance literature which prominently discusses public–private partnerships and the involvement of private actors in (public) policy development and implementation.[5] From such a functional perspective, it may be asked which governance tasks are performed better by firms than by public authorities and how both sets of actors co-operate with another in networks of exchange. Public actors have incentives to include private actors as the former increasingly lack resources, given that the latter bring relevant expertise to a policy process, and since involving them early on is likely to improve the effective implementation of policies. Private actors have incentives to co-operate with public actors as it provides them with the opportunity to influence or even forgo legislation and, thus, possibly prevent high compliance and implementation costs.

Another perspective is adopted by political economy approaches to which the present study belongs. Here, scholars are interested in evolving power relations, interest politics and their linkage to processes of global and regional economic integration. From such a perspective, CSR policies have been described in three ways. They can be implemented as reflections of legal obligations, they can mirror a shift from hard to soft law or they can be conceived as a substitution of regulation altogether as

[4] J.P. Doh and T.R. Guay, 'Corporate social responsibility, public policy, and NGO activism in Europe and the United States: An institutional-stakeholder perspective', *Journal of Management Studies* (2005), 47.

[5] C. Gribben, K. Pinnington and A. Wilson, *Governments as Partners: The role of the central government in developing new social partnerships* (Copenhagen: The Copenhagen Centre, 2001); J. Nelson and S. Zadek, *Partnership Alchemy: New social partnerships in Europe* (Copenhagen: The Copenhagen Centre, 2000).

firms seek to avoid institutionalised regulatory frameworks while states are under the pressure of downward regulatory competition.[6]

The remainder of this contribution is organised as follows. In the next section, CSR definitions and the main theoretical debates surrounding them will be presented. In the third section, the analytical grip of this contribution will be developed. Doing so, I will draw on the differentiation between social and liberal market economies and on the differentiation between soft and hard law. The fourth section investigates, in an explorative way, the United Kingdom and Germany as representative cases of the two types of economies. In the fifth section, against this background, the development of the CSR agenda at the EU-level is evaluated before the final section concludes and discusses the findings.

II   CSR between the business case and societal ownership

Before exploring CSR in two selected Member States, it is important to gain a better understanding of what CSR is actually about and what its normative and ethical foundations are. In this section, an overview of the relevant literature is provided permitting us to evaluate subsequently to which model the EU adheres.

One of the most prominent positions in the CSR debate has been formulated by Milton Friedman.[7] According to him, firms are only responsible to the shareholder value, and their primary role is to increase the value of the firm by any legal means available. Managers must only respect the basic rules of society (such as excluding fraud) and their legal obligations (paying taxes) while activities which do not increase profitability should be avoided. Social engagement of firms and the connected tendency to collectivism in his view constitutes a threat to the freedom of society and a step towards socialism, while in the ideal free market no one can coerce others and co-operation is voluntary. For Friedman, to identify and to fight social shortcomings and inequalities is the role of

---

[6] O. de Schutter, 'Corporate social responsibility European style', *European Law Journal* 14 (2008), 203; A. Apostolakou and G. Jackson, 'Corporate social responsibility in Western Europe: An institutional mirror or substitute?', University of Bath, School of Management, Working Paper Series 1 (2009); D. Kinderman, 'Why do some countries get CSR sooner, and in greater quantity, than others? The political economy of corporate responsibility and the rise of market liberalism across the OECD 1977–2007', WZB Discussion Paper SP III (2009), p. 301.

[7] M. Friedman, 'The social responsibility of business is to increase its profits', *New York Times*, 13 September 1970.

the state and of individuals. Managers who spend money for social aims take on tasks of the state and thereby contribute to the strengthening of the state's role within the firm.

By contrast, William J. Bowen, in 1954, had defined CSR as 'the obligation of businessmen to pursue those politics, to make those decisions, or follow those lines of action which are desirable in terms of the objectives and values of our society'.[8] In a similar vein, it is argued that the 'social responsibility of business encompasses the economic, legal, ethical and discretionary expectations that society has of organizations at a given point of time',[9] and that 'businessmen apply social responsibility when they consider the needs and interests of others who may be affected by business actions. In doing so, they look beyond their firms' narrow economic and technical interests.'[10] From this perspective, firms are an integral part of society. They depend on society in their development and therefore need to be legitimated by society. Since society provides business with a friendly and stable environment and with a well-trained workforce, business has to take into consideration societal demands and expectations and needs to 'pursue those policies, to make those decisions, or to follow those lines of action which are desirable in terms of the objectives and values of our society'.[11] In this view, CSR may be realised as a response to legal obligations, such as environmental or employment legislation, as well as an activity going over and above legal obligation.

More recently, the term 'society' has been replaced by 'stakeholders'.[12] According to stakeholder theory, *strategic* considerations lead firms to include the external environment into entrepreneurial strategies and activities as a factor for success. Freeman argues that this new strategy has become necessary due to the more complex and changed production conditions as well as the rise and recognition of new actors, the stakeholders. Stakeholders are all those actors who can influence the

---

[8] Cited in A. B. Carroll, 'Corporate social responsibility: Evolution of a definitional construct', *Business & Society* 38 (1999), 268, 269.

[9] A. B. Carroll, 'A three-dimensional conceptual model of corporate social performance', *Academy of Management Review* 4 (1979), 497, 500.

[10] *Ibid.*, p. 272.

[11] H. Bowen, *Social Responsibilities of the Businessman* (New York: Harper & Row, 1953), p. 6.

[12] R. E. Freeman, *Strategic Management: A stakeholder approach* (Boston: Pitman, 1984); F. G. A. Bakker, P. Groenewegen and F. Hond, 'A bibliometric analysis of 30 years of research and theory on corporate social responsibility and corporate social performance', *Business & Society* 44 (2005), 283.

economic performance of a firm or are affected by it.[13] Their inclusion in corporate activities is deemed critical for success:

> Shifts in traditional relationships with external groups such as suppliers, customers, owners and employees, as well as the emergence and renewed importance of government, foreign competition, environmentalists, consumer advocates, special interest groups, media and others, mean that a new conceptual approach is needed.[14]

Stakeholder theory is therefore interested in systematically addressing the question of which stakeholders are legitimate stakeholders, and which ones do not require management attention. As Mitchell, Agle and Wood argue, firms will respond to those stakeholders who possess at least one of the following attributes: power, legitimacy and urgency; the more attributes they possess, the more likely are they to be influential on the firm.[15]

Stakeholder theory has paved the way for what is commonly referred to as the 'business case'. CSR as a business case is a strategy for competitive advantage in which firms engage based on the anticipated benefits from these activities.[16] The business case perceives of increased profits as the only legitimate goal of corporate governance, but recognises that due to a changing social and political environment, particularly changed consumer demands and increased influence of NGOs on policy-making, what is required in order to achieve profitability has changed.[17] In such an environment, firms can no longer afford to ignore the issues that are brought forward by these actors since doing so may be costly, from decreasing profits to corporate ruin. Empirical research supports this interpretation of CSR, showing that dialogues with stakeholders are mainly organised around risky issues and in sectors that are particularly exposed to the public, i.e. to NGOs.[18]

Overall, these diverse approaches to CSR perfectly mirror the ambiguities and the political and theoretical contestations surrounding the

---

[13] Freeman (n. 12 above), p. 46.   [14] *Ibid.* p. 27.

[15] R. K. Mitchell, B. R. Agle and D. J. Wood, 'Toward a theory of stakeholder identification and salience: Defining the principle of who and what really counts', *Academy of Management Review* 22 (1997), 853.

[16] A. McWilliams and D. Siegel, 'Corporate social responsibility: A theory of the firm perspective', *Academy of Management Review* 26 (2001), 117.

[17] K. Trebek, 'Exploring the responsiveness of companies: corporate social responsibility to stakeholders', *Social Responsibility Journal* 4 (2008), 349.

[18] M. V. Huijstee and P. Glasbergen, 'The practice of stakeholder dialogue between multinationals and NGOs', *Corporate Social Responsibility and Environmental Management* (2007), 10.1002/CSR; Apostolakou and Jackson (n. 6 above).

concept. Each expresses a different understanding of the role of, and relationships between, firms, public authorities, stakeholders and the larger society. The ambiguities of the concept, it has been argued, may be one of the very reasons for its success.[19] The next section develops a framework for conceptualising a European CSR policy.

III   Conceptualising a European CSR policy

If assuming that enhancing social justice is considered a normatively valid goal of the EU, a European public good, the market in which firms operate will need public regulation and should not be left to self-appointed regulators.[20] Such reasoning might support a European CSR policy. The question is in how far a European CSR policy, which would work in favour of the social dimension of European integration, is possible in light of the institutional differences between Member States and the dominating soft-law character of CSR. In order to answer this question, this section will review two different strands of theory-building.

There are two literature streams which are interested in comparative socio-economic research.[21] One is the socio-political classification of Gøsta Esping-Andersen into 'three worlds of welfare capitalism'.[22] The other, the 'varieties of capitalism' of Hall and Soskice,[23] is a political–economical classification which builds on the former but shifts the emphasis to the firm. Esping-Andersen classifies welfare states as 'regimes' and argues that each is the outcome of specific political coalitions that had formed in the post-war period. He differentiates between liberal (Anglo-Saxon), Christian-democratic (Continental) and social-democratic (Scandinavian) welfare states in ideal-typical manner. The

---

[19]   de Schutter (n. 6 above), p. 203.
[20]   A. C. Neal, 'Corporate social responsibility: Governance gain or laissez-faire figleaf?', *Comparative Labor Law and Policy Journal* 29 (2008), 1.
[21]   While both theories have attracted criticism, their value still consists in 'their theoretical contributions and heuristic classification of ideal types': J. A. Ahlquist and C. Breunig, 'Country clustering in comparative political economy', Max Planck Institut für Gesellschaftsforschung Köln, MPIfG Discussion Paper 5 (2009), p. 3.
[22]   G. Esping-Andersen, *Social Foundations of Post-Industrial Economies* (Oxford: Oxford University Press, 1999); G. Esping-Andersen, *The Three Worlds Of Welfare Capitalism* (Cambridge: Polity Press, 1990).
[23]   P. A. Hall and D. W. Soskice, 'An introduction to varieties of capitalism' in P. A. Hall and D. W. Soskice (eds.), *Varieties of Capitalism: The institutional foundations of comparative advantage* (Oxford: Oxford University Press, 2001), p. 1.

three regimes differ to the extent to which they provide for tax-financed social services. While all three offer a minimum protection against poverty and sickness, the liberal regime leaves further protection to the market and individual prevention, while the two other regimes offer more ambitious protection schemes, in particular with regard to unemployment and pensions. Only the social-democratic regime, however, offers encompassing social services for children, the disabled and sick which are being taken care of either by the market (liberal) or the family (Christian-democratic) in the other two regimes. The consequence is that levels of taxes as well as of social equality are highest in states that belong to the social-democratic regime type.

The varieties of capitalism (VoC) perspective emphasises the notion of 'institutional complementarities' according to which 'the presence (or efficiency) of one [institution] increases the returns from (or efficiency of) the other'.[24] Five such complementarities are identified:[25] the financial system, corporate governance, the organisation of industrial relations, the education and training system and the mode for the transfer of innovations within the economy.[26] Hall and Soskice divide the European economies into ideal-typical liberal and co-ordinated market economies (LMEs and CMEs); LMEs are characterised by arm's length, competitive relations, competition and formal contracting, and the operation of supply and demand in line with price signalling. CMEs are dependent on non-market relations, collaboration, credible commitments and deliberative calculation on the part of firms. LMEs focus on radical innovation while CMEs are centred on incremental innovation.[27] According to the authors, the institutional complementarities of the two types of market economies are able to explain these specific innovation patterns. If the institutional complementarities are correctly calibrated, the performance increases and so does the comparative institutional advantage of the firm. The main argument of VoC is thus that both types of economies need not converge towards one model of capitalism, but may co-exist by making use of their respective comparative advantages in specific sectors and by making specific adjustments to external pressures as they see fit.

Apostolakou and Jackson[28] propose using VoC in order to account for institutional differences within Europe with regard to CSR. Their

---

[24] *Ibid.*, p. 16.   [25] n. 23 above, pp. 17–33.
[26] For a critical discussion of the theory of complementarities, see M. Höpner, 'Corporate governance reform and the German party paradox', *Comparative Politics* 39 (2007), 401.
[27] Hall and Soskice (n. 23 above), pp. 38–44.
[28] Apostolakou and Jackson (n. 6 above).

evidence shows that in CMEs, CSR is a largely implicit practice while it constitutes an explicit attempt to substitute for weak welfare institutions in LMEs.[29] They found a strong inverse correlation between CSR practices and the strength of institutional co-ordination, regulatory standards and social and ecological performances, in the sense that LMEs engage more in CSR than CMEs.

Most recently, Fritz Scharpf has suggested integrating both typologies into a single one in order to differentiate between 'social market economies' and 'liberal market economies' in the EU.[30] The latter would consist of the Anglo-Saxon and East European market economies while the group of social market economies would consist of the Continental and Scandinavian Member States. In the present study, the UK and Germany are chosen as ideal-types of liberal and social market economies in order to evaluate how CSR is approached in these two Member States. It is crucial to take into account the institutional differences of the respective types of capitalism as these institutional structures presumably influence the ways actors in these Member States approach CSR and thus their position towards CSR at EU-level.

Besides the institutional differences that we need to bear in mind, we also must take into consideration the fragile character of CSR. For most authors as well as for most business and political actors, CSR is an instrument belonging to the array of 'soft law'.[31] The latter consists of objectives, guidelines, targets, codes, etc. none of which is legally binding but which 'nevertheless may have practical effects',[32] for instance through learning effects or pressures that arise from public exposure. Defenders of soft law argue that due to its flexibility and experimental character, it would be better suited than hard law to deal with the increasing complexity and uncertainty while at the same time lowering transaction costs; that institutional diversity would not allow for harmonisation; that it allows for the inclusion of a broad range of actors in

---

[29] Implicit here means that CSR activities are part of daily practices without being labelled as CSR activities while explicit refers to CSR activities which are labelled as such. See also D. A. Matten and J. Moon, 'Implicit and explicit CSR, a conceptual framework for the understanding of corporate social responsibility', *Academy of Management Review* 33 (2008), 404.

[30] F. Scharpf, 'Weshalb die EU nicht zur sozialen Marktwirtschaft werden kann', *Zeitschrift für Staats- und Europawissenschaaften* 7 (2009), 419.

[31] Kinderman (n. 6 above).

[32] F. Snyder, 'Soft law and institutional practice in the European Community' in S. Martin (ed.), *The Construction of Europe: Essays in honour of Emile Noel* (Dordrecht: Kluwer Academic Publishers, 1993), p. 198.

policy-making, that thereby it would increase the legitimacy of policies and governance more broadly; that it might even induce more lasting change than hard law by changing people's minds through learning processes.[33] Opponents of soft law by contrast argue that a single and ultimate (hierarchical) source of authority is needed; that law should be uniform and bind all parties of the same political community; that soft law does not allow for a clear separation of powers; that courts should be in the centre of accountability and that law that is not enforceable is no law; that non-compliance cannot be sanctioned; and that legitimacy requires the consent of elected representatives.

Some authors consider CSR is not the same as a mere soft-law instrument because it may take effect in a legal context, with legal consequences, in particular through litigation. It may even be binding, as in certain forms of mandatory social and environmental reporting, codes of conduct or social labelling.[34] However, the same authors also show that these more binding forms of CSR can primarily be found outside of the EU. Other authors, such as de Schutter, have suggested that an EU CSR strategy can be most successful if hybrid forms of regulation are used, e.g. through legally binding measures that establish minimum standards with which CSR measures must comply if used in external communications, public procurement legislation or statutory accounting standards integrating CSR.[35] For the present purpose, we define CSR as self-regulation by business that may take the form of either soft or hard law.

In the context of the EU, soft law has been used increasingly since the early 1990s, in particular in policy areas with political deadlocks such as social policy. Accordingly, there has been a vivid scholarly debate about the merits and pitfalls of soft law ever since the OMC was introduced in 2000.[36] On one side are those who argue that such instruments suit the demands of subsidiarity of the EU and allow for meaningful learning processes. On the other side are those who perceive them as a back door

---

[33] J. Cohen and C. Sabel, 'Directly-deliberative polyarchy', *ELJ* 3 (1997), 313; D. Trubek and L. Trubek, 'Hard and soft law in the construction of Social Europe: The open method of coordination', *ELJ* 11 (2005), 343.

[34] L. Compa, 'Corporate social responsibility and workers' rights', *Comparative Labour Law and Policy Journal* 30 (2008), 1; H. Ward, 'Legal issues in corporate citizenship', Report of the International Institute for Environment and Development (2003), www.iied.org/pubs/pdfs/16000IIED.pdf.

[35] de Schutter (n. 6 above), pp. 222–3, 228–35.

[36] S. Kröger, 'The open method of coordination: Underconceptualisation, overdetermination, depoliticisation and beyond' in S. Kröger (ed.), 'What we have learnt: Advances, pitfalls and remaining questions in OMC research', *EIOP* special issue 13 (2009), 1.

through which neoliberal policies are introduced, as forums in which unaccountable actors implement normatively laden policies or as an instrument that in any event is not capable of preventing welfare-state retrenchment.[37]

When exploring the potential of a European CSR policy as a means of fostering the social dimension of European integration, it is thus necessary to reflect both the institutional diversity of Member States and the fragile character of CSR. While the former is a central reason why new modes of governance have been introduced to begin with, the latter is characterised by high volatility and dependence on the goodwill and the preferences of the relevant actors.[38]

The next section addresses the question of whether we find the expected institutional diversity with regard to CSR practices in the cases of the UK, a liberal market economy, and Germany, a social market economy.

IV   Varieties of CSR: The United Kingdom and Germany

A   United Kingdom[39]

The UK comes close to the ideal-type of a liberal market economy. This type of economy is characterised by individualism in which the market and policies invite individual actors rather than consensus-based collective agency.[40] Such economies typically have an outsider system of corporate control. Equity markets are characterised by relatively dispersed ownership by financial institutions. The market for corporate control, in turn, is supposed to provide the external control mechanism to align manager and shareholder interests. UK takeover regulation takes place under the self-regulatory framework of the City Code on Takeovers and Mergers, which is highly restrictive of the use of defensive tactics against takeover bids. Organised labour is not involved in corporate

---

[37] C. Offe, 'The European model of "social" capitalism: Can it survive European integration?', *Journal of Political Philosophy* 11 (2003), 437.

[38] S. Kröger, *Soft Governance in Hard Politics: European coordination of anti-poverty policies in France and Germany* (Wiesbaden: Verlag für Sozialwissenschaften, 2008).

[39] Policies of the coalition between the Conservative Party and the Liberal Democrats under Prime Minister David Cameron and Deputy Prime Minister Nick Clegg, which took office in 2010, are still under development and are thus not evaluated in this chapter.

[40] C. Crouch, 'The state: Economic management and incomes policy' in P. Edwards (ed.), *Industrial Relations: Theory and evidence in Britain*, 2nd edn (Oxford: Blackwell Publishers, 2003), p. 105.

decision-making, and works councils remain rather weak. The Cadbury Code (1992) constituted the first model of a self-regulatory corporate governance code in the European Union, and served as point of reference for many other national corporate governance codes. It was also the first in a series of self-regulatory corporate governance reports in the UK. When the New Labour government came into office in 1997, it emulated the self-regulatory, voluntaristic and shareholder-oriented model favoured by the finance industry, rather than enacting fundamental changes in corporate governance. In this type of economy, voluntaristic policies such as CSR enjoy more resonance than in corporatist societies such as Germany. It is therefore not surprising that the New Labour government strongly supported CSR. The UK has even been identified as the 'only European country that has a noteworthy history in CSR'.[41]

The British CSR policy can be explained by the British welfare philosophy in general and by developments in the 1980s in particular. Since urban decay and serious social exclusion problems became apparent, in juncture with massive urban riots, rising unemployment, inflation and public debt in the early 1980s, the state was facing an increasing legitimacy crisis, associated with a decreasing steering capacity. The crisis was responded to by a retreat of the state as a regulator and a provider of social services and goods, by an austerity policy, welfare cuts and an appeal to the social responsibility of non-state actors.[42] It became accepted that traditional welfare-state instruments should be renewed, and that the business community had a role to play in this renewal, in fighting poverty and in protecting the environment, leading to the concept of 'business in the community' which has since become commonplace in the UK. Inner-city tours for business leaders were organised by the government in order to encourage engagement of business in recognising and resolving social problems. CSR was not perceived as altruism, but as good for long-term business success and for wider society as a protection of its social licence to trade. Business certainly also had the motivation to engage in CSR in order to prevent further government regulation. In addition to governmental pressure, campaigns from large watchdog NGOs such as Amnesty International and

[41] R. Steurer, 'The role of governments in corporate social responsibility: characterising public policies on CSR in Europe', *Policy Sci* (2009), published online 9 May 2009, 7.

[42] J. Moon, 'Government as a driver of corporate social responsibility', University of Nottingham, ICCSR Research Paper Series 20 (2004); L. Albareda, J. M. Lozana and T. Ysa, 'Public policies on corporate social responsibility: The role of governments in Europe', *Journal of Business Ethics* 74 (2007), 391.

the World Wildlife Fund certainly also contributed to the development of a CSR policy. The rise of CSR was thus 'part of a wider re-orientation of governance whereby business was increasingly not only operating in its market mode but also in a network mode with government and non-government organisations'.[43]

The New Labour government between 1997 to 2010 drove CSR policy, introducing a minister for CSR, a ministerial steering group and a co-ordinating team. The government was responsible for enlisting the help of companies; it created a CSR umbrella group, the Business in the Community (BITC) and a Community Action Programme, an annual CSR report, and operated numerous partnerships with business organisations so as to encourage CSR.[44] The government stated that CSR was:

> the business contribution to our sustainable development goals. . . . The base level of responsible behaviour for any organisation is legal compliance and the Government has a role to play in setting standards in areas such as environmental protection, health & safety and employment rights. . . . Our approach is to encourage and incentivize the adoption of Corporate Social Responsibility, through best practice guidance, and, where appropriate, intelligent [i.e. soft-law] regulation and fiscal incentives.[45]

The emphasis upon CSR as a 'voluntary' instrument is also illustrated by the former Energy Minister, Malcolm Wicks, who stated:

> We want to provide the right policy framework to support it while letting business decide how to apply it. The position of Government is that CSR is something over and above the legal requirements and we feel it's best as a voluntary activity. Where the society judges that something is so crucial there should be at least a minimum standard, then we should legislate for it. But I would see CSR as the social policies of companies and essentially something that is added to that.[46]

The voluntaristic approach of the UK to CSR was also expressed in its 2001 response to the European Commission's Green Paper on CSR (see below) in which the British government argued that the best CSR approach would be the use of best practice. The government rejected

---

[43] Moon (n. 42 above), p. 1.

[44] J. Moon and D. Vogel, 'Corporate social responsibility, government, and civil society' in A. Crane (ed.), *The Oxford Handbook of Corporate Social Responsibility* (Oxford: Oxford University Press, 2004), p. 303; S. Scott, 'Corporate social responsibility and the fetter of profitability', *Social Responsibility Journal* 3 (2007), 31.

[45] Former UK government website, quoted in Steurer (n. 41 above), p. 11.

[46] M. Wicks, who held responsibilities for CSR issues, 14 March 2006, cited in Neal (n. 20 above), p. 472.

EU regulation on CSR because it held that standardisation was a risk to innovation.[47] While the governmental approach to CSR is thus based on voluntarism, it nevertheless adopts measures of intervention in order to promote corporate CSR action.[48]

Whereas government activity is thus alive and kicking, in-depth research about CSR activities of firms is rather scarce. Comparative studies show that British businesses have higher rates of stakeholder engagement and social reporting than they do in any other European state except Norway.[49] BITC is the single largest business association for CSR and now has over 800 members, 'including most of the major British-based multi-nationals and accounting for 20% of private sector employment'.[50] Changes have also been observed in the firms, such as an increase in CSR posts, greater attention paid to CSR issues by the board, the use of CSR-related codes in specific firm policies, employee volunteering schemes or even an inclusion of CSR in corporate branding.[51] CSR also plays an increasing role in annual reports and general corporate communications. Accordingly, it was noted that 'reporting on CSR among the Top 250 FTSE [Financial Times Stock Exchange] companies increased by nearly 150%, from 54 to 132 companies between 2001 and 2003'.[52] Some of the CSR activities are clearly related to governmental initiatives, such as those related to occupational pension funds. Since 2000, occupational pension funds should disclose how they take account of social, environmental and ethical factors in their investment decisions.[53] Another example is a 'Code of Conduct on Principles on Security and Human Rights' that the British government introduced. The code provides guidance to companies that operate in areas of conflict and that seek to ensure security for their personnel. A third example is the Extractive Industries Transparency Initiative (EITI) which seeks to increase transparency in payments made by firms and revenues to government in the extractive industries.[54] Further financial instruments that were intro-duced, with the help of a massive publicity campaign, were tax breaks for donations to civil society organisations (CSOs) that the government

---

[47] Steurer (n. 41 above), p. 17.
[48] Albareda, Lozana and Ysa (n. 42 above), p. 402; Moon (n. 42 above).
[49] Apostolakou and Jackson (n. 6 above).   [50] Moon (n. 42 above), p. 15.
[51] Ibid., p. 16.   [52] Ibid.
[53] C. A. Williams and R. V. Aguilera, 'Corporate social responsibility in a comparative perspective' in A. Crane et al. (eds.), The Oxford Handbook of Corporate Social Responsibility (Oxford: Oxford University Press, 2008), pp. 452, 456.
[54] M. Cuesta Gonzalez and C. V. Martinez, 'Fostering corporate social responsibility through public initiative: From the EU to the Spanish case', Journal of Business Ethics 55 (2004), 273, 283.

adopted in 2000. This measure grants tax exemptions for employees who donate money to CSOs via an approved payroll giving agency. The government committed itself to add 'a 10% supplement on all Payroll Giving donations from 2000 to 2004. As a result, Payroll Giving donations increased from £29 million in 1999 to £89 million coming from more than 5 million employees in recent years.'[55] The consequence of these measures was that public awareness of CSR issues was greatly enhanced.

However, there are also reservations against government-led CSR initiatives. Some argue that 'British companies react badly to multiple initiatives from the government that encourage business participation in social issues' and would, if so, only use it in order to have access to additional funding.[56] Others have highlighted implementation gaps, such as low reporting of gender impacts and performance and 'significant instances of non-disclosure of gender information' and 'a great disparity between information collected, used internally and communicated to specific stakeholders on the one hand, and that which gets reported on the other'.[57] Mixed results are also reported by a research team that brought together British CSR experts in a workshop series. Participants found that there was much noise about CSR, but few outputs and that with regard to corporate accountability the 'debate has gone backwards',[58] that employment relationships were not incorporated into CSR and that firms were picky on the issues they focus on with regard to CSR.

Overall, the case of the UK confirms that the institutional specificities of the liberal market economy have significantly shaped national CSR policies. The government of the UK has, in the past, actively supported the development of a CSR policy based on voluntary participation, quite different from the German case, where governments, firms and unions have been more hesitant or even resistant.

B   Germany

Germany represents the standard model of a social market economy which combines economic and personal freedom with social justice, the

---

[55] Steurer (n. 41 above), p. 11.   [56] Albareda, Lozana and Ysa (n. 42 above), p. 398.

[57] K. Grosser and J. Moon, 'Best practice reporting on gender equality in the UK: Data, drivers and reporting choices', University of Nottingham, ICCSR Research Paper Series 35 (2006), p. 40.

[58] H. Ward and C. Smith, *Corporate Social Responsibility at a Crossroads: Futures to CSR in the UK to 2015* (London: International Institute for Environment and Development, 2006), p. 15.

result being a consensus-oriented culture between the economy and the state.[59] Companies are considered 'good citizens', with a duty of socially responsible behaviour which includes transparency, corporate citizenship and local and/or regional engagement through partnerships and pacts.[60] The incorporation of employers' organisations and their members through codified rights and duties (towards their employees, unions and society at large) was an integral part of Rhenish capitalism.[61] Two governance arrangements have proved central for the social market economy in Germany. On the one hand, corporatism acted as a political mode of steering, supported by the social partners and connected both in a highly solidaristic system. State support of entrepreneurial freedom went hand in hand with the state-led assignment of an entrepreneurial role that transcended profit maximisation. Enterprises were expected to live up to certain social and environmental standards, such as to negotiate collective wage agreements with the union(s), to train young school leavers in the context of the dual training system, to contribute to a considerable extent to social insurance, and, last but not least, to pay taxes. On the other hand, the joint network of banks, insurances and enterprises acted as an economic steering instrument which, by way of bank-mediated insider corporate finance, through shares and credits, secured the existence and survival of German enterprises in a comparatively protected sphere. In this way, it can be said that in the traditional corporatist German social economy, certain forms of social responsibility of enterprises were institutionalised.[62] However, due to diverse pressures, this ideal-typical model has undergone a process of transformation in the direction of a liberal market economy.[63]

---

[59] J. Beckert, 'Wer zähmt den Kapitalismus' in J. Beckert et al. (eds.), *Transformation des Kapitalismus* (Frankfurt am Main: Campus, 2006), p. 425.

[60] Albareda, Lozano and Ysa (n. 42 above).

[61] F.-X. Kaufmann, *Herausforderungen des Sozialstaates* (Frankfurt am Main: Suhrkamp, 1997); W. Streeck, *Korporatismus in Deutschland. Zwischen Nationalstaat und Europäischer Union* (Frankfurt am Main: Campus, 1999).

[62] In Germany, the idea of CSR is embodied in constitutional law (Art. 14 GG: 'Eigentum verpflichtet. Sein Gebrauch soll zugleich dem Wohl der Allgemeinheit dienen' ['Property entails obligations. Its use shall also serve the public good']), official translation available from www.btg-bestellservice.de/pdf/80201000.pdf.

[63] Kinderman (n. 6 above); T. Niechoj, 'Does supranational coordination erode its national basis? The case of European labour market policy and German industrial relations' in S. Kröger (ed.), 'What we have learnt: Advances, pitfalls and remaining questions of OMC research', *EIOP* special issue 1(13) (2009).

Because the firm is traditionally committed to social goals and because of the strong corporatism in Germany, governments have traditionally given limited attention to an explicit CSR policy. It is only since the first decade of this century that the first timid steps towards a CSR policy have been undertaken.[64] Therefore, research on CSR in Germany has so far focused on how firms have taken up related practices. Unfortunately, existing research is not comparable due to different definitions of CSR and different units of analysis. For instance, the Bertelsmann foundation investigated both the external and the internal dimensions of societal responsibility of firms.[65] A study conducted by FORSA,[66] commissioned by the initiative *Neue soziale Marktwirtschaft* focuses on the voluntary societal engagement of company owners. The Hans-Böckler foundation, in turn, conducted a study with standardised questionnaires and a limited number of qualitative interviews in 2004, investigating CSR practices of large (German) enterprises.[67] Braun and colleagues conducted a representative study in 2006 about CSR practices of small, medium and large companies.[68] Finally, Kinderman investigated German CSR networks and associations.[69]

According to Braun, 96% of the firms under investigation have been voluntarily engaged in other forms than sponsoring.[70] Other studies find a minimum of over 80% of engagement[71] and a maximum of more than 90%.[72] Firm engagement occurs throughout sectors and regardless of size.[73] In two out of three cases, it happened as a reaction to societal demand. Which forms do CSR activities take in Germany?[74] Donations

---

[64] Cuesta-Gonzalez and Valor Martinez (n. 54 above), p. 282; D. Kinderman, 'The political economy of corporate responsibility in Germany 1995–2008', Mario Einaudi Center for International Studies: Working Paper Series No. 5 (October 2008).
[65] Bertelsmann Stiftung (ed.), *Die gesellschaftliche Verantwortung von Unternehmen* (Gütersloh, 2005).
[66] FORSA/Gesellschaft für Sozialforschung und statistische Analysen, *Corporate Social Responsibility in Deutschland* (Berlin, 2005).
[67] The sample number is thirty-two (works councils), Hans-Böckler-Stiftung 2004.
[68] S. Braun, 'Gesellschaftliches Engagement von Unternehmen', *Aus Politik und Zeitgeschichte* 31 (2008), 6; S. Braun (ed.), *Gesellschaftliches Engagement von Unternehmen. Der deutsche Weg im internationalen Kontext* (Wiesbaden: VS Verlag für Sozialwissenschaften, 2010).
[69] Kinderman (n. 6 above).   [70] Braun (n. 68 above).
[71] F. Maaß and R. Clemens, 'Corporate Citizenship. Das Unternehmen als guter Bürger' in Institut für Mittelstandsforschung Bonn (ed.), *Jahrbuch zur Mittelstandsforschung* 2 (2002).
[72] FORSA (n. 66 above).   [73] The minimum size of firms considered was ten employees.
[74] In what follows, I will draw on Braun if not indicated otherwise.

in money (83.4%) or in kind (59.7%) are the most common forms. Other forms such as the establishment of foundations (3.8%) or local or national campaigns are scarcer. However, over 60% support their employees in their engagement in some way or another (use of firm resources, personal and, to a lesser degree, work time). Most of this engagement happens locally (almost 75%) whereas 14.5% of the firms are engaged nationally and 13.6% internationally. One consequence of these local and/or regional roots is that most firms, in particular the larger ones, are co-operating with local associations (often business) when getting engaged (70%). Other co-operations are realised with educational institutions (43.7%), welfare associations (37.8%) or with local administrations (35.6%). Turning to the topics of engagement, the most important external activities are sports and leisure whereas education and training, the local community and social affairs play a secondary role. Internally, the safeguard of employment, of production sites and of training places for the young are by far the most important issues. They are considered more important than the external activities with regard to the reputation of the firm. Other topics that matter in the CSR debates, such as equal opportunities or the pursuit of International Labour Organisation (ILO) work norms in the production chain matter less in the perception of German enterprises. In their study, Hauser-Ditz and Wilke find that only twelve out of thirty-six firms which are listed on the German stock exchange are committed to the social and environmental ILO standards, eighteen undertook particular measures to train their employees, twenty-four were engaged socially in their region, and fifteen pursued a dialogue with critical stakeholders.[75]

What can we say about the reasons for entrepreneurial engagement? Approximately 33% of the engaged firms see their engagement explicitly as a part of the firms' strategy to maximise profits; for 36%, it is a means of improving the balance sheet or the competitive position; 12.9% pursue their engagement with an action plan; and 12.3% use instruments in order to evaluate their engagement. This situation is mirrored by the fact that most enterprises pursue CSR activities in a personalised manner, i.e. without a coherent firm concept. It is worth mentioning that the strategic use of CSR activities increases with firm size, and so do the respective planning and evaluation activities. Accordingly, firms noted

---

[75] A. Hauser-Ditz and P. Wilke, *Corporate Social Responsibility – Soziale und ökologische Verantwortung von Unternehmen. Eine Betriebsrätebefragung zu den Handlungsfeldern für Arbeitnehmervertretungen*, Diskussionspapier (Hamburg, January 2005).

in the stock market are committed to CSR in their mission statement, and the majority of them document respective activities on a regular basis.[76]

Work councils have a rather reserved evaluation and tend to perceive of CSR activities as prestigious advertising through which firms seek to present themselves as good (corporate) citizens. However, they also perceive the opportunities that CSR can offer in terms of more transparency between different production sites and in terms of positive effects created through increased reputation and increased motivation of employees. The rather sceptical view that unions and works councils have towards CSR is linked to their traditional prerogative to deal with and co-regulate such internal issues as the level of income and income protection, work conditions, work time, health, safety etc. With regard to CSR activities, however, not only do they tend to be soft in nature and therefore against unions' preferences, but also transnational NGOs have been the main pusher of CSR activities thus far, thereby depriving the unions somewhat of their privileged position as a negotiation partner in this field.[77] Along these lines, a study conducted in 2004 finds that in two-thirds of all cases, work councils were not involved in the CSR activities, such as the development and adoption of codes of conduct in their firms. The last third mainly concerns large firms in which the participation of work councils in CSR activities seems to rank a little better. In general, they do participate when a traditional topic of co-determination is at stake (work–life balance). However, an uneasiness remains as many perceive CSR as a threat to their credibility and as a means by which a firm might buy co-operation – and avoid loss of profits – by introducing artificial CSR activities.[78]

The sceptical attitude towards CSR by German firms is reflected in the reactions to the Commission's related initiatives. The employers' associations made clear in their reaction to the Green Book of the European Commission that they did not see any margin towards higher standards in Germany. An informal consensus existed with the second Red-Green government (2002–5) that no CSR initiatives should be made which could end in hard legislation. Changes in social reporting were also not adopted. The German government considers voluntariness as the main principle of CSR. Binding regulations by the EU or other Member States

[76] *Ibid.* [77] *Ibid.*
[78] G. Mutz and J. Egbringhoff, *Gesellschaftliche Verantwortung von Unternehmen. Die Rolle der Arbeitnehmervertretung* (Berlin/Munich: Hand-Böckler-Stiftung, 2006).

are rejected. Still, the EU may set incentives in the form of technical help, money or expertise. Measures for monitoring are perceived critically as they would not be in line with the principle of voluntariness. By contrast, seals of quality and the exchange of information are welcome.[79]

The critical position of the Schröder government towards the European CSR policy was backed both by employers' organisations and trade unions. The former had already resigned in 1999 from the European Business Network for Social Cohesion (known as CSR Europe since 2000), judging that its activities were a 'show with little substance'[80] that had little to do with the European welfare state in which binding regulation prevailed. The German unions remained reserved towards the CSR initiative of the Commission, too, but for different reasons. Whereas the DGB (*Deutscher Gewerkschaftsbund*) did welcome in principle the main goals of CSR, it also expressed doubts as to the effectiveness of the envisioned instruments and the voluntary character of CSR. The main way for a firm to meet its social responsibilities, so the argument went, was to obey the law and collective bargaining agreements.[81] Certain instruments such as social reporting or codes of conduct were welcomed, while related own measures or initiatives did not follow. A likely explanation of the reservation on the part of the German trade unions was their fear that employers might use CSR to substitute legally binding standards and participation rights transforming them into voluntary agreements.

Comparing the UK and Germany confirms that the institutional specificities of a liberal – in contrast to a social – market economy also shape different forms of CSR policies. While the government of the UK has actively in the past supported the development of a CSR policy based on voluntary participation, German governments and firms have been much more hesitant or even resistant. While the impact of CSR policies in terms of social integration in the UK often remains unclear, equivalent activities or policies often constitute an integrated part of German firms without being branded as CSR.

---

[79] C. Bussler, 'Ergebnisse des EU-Konsultationsprozesses zu Rahmenbedingungen für die soziale Verantwortung von Unternehmen' in A. Fonari and C. Bussler (eds.), *Sozial- und Umweltstandards bei Unternehmen: Chancen und Grenzen* (Munich: Digitaldruck leibi. de, 2005), p. 43.

[80] Representative of Bayer, quoted in Kinderman (n. 6 above), p. 28.

[81] DGB, 2001, 'Stellungnahme zum Grünbuch der Europäischen Kommission Europäische Rahmenbedingungen für die soziale Verantwortung der Unternehmen'.

V   A European CSR strategy?

CSR has been promoted in the EU as a new discourse and modern form of governance, in particular by the European Commission. This section traces this evolution and locates it in its broader environment.

A   The development of CSR discourse by the Commission

CSR emerged on the EU agenda as part of the Lisbon Strategy. At the summit in March 2000, the European Council called upon companies' sense of social responsibility to promote lifelong learning, work organisation, equal opportunities, social inclusion and sustainable development.[82] As has been noted, it was no coincidence that this call emerged precisely in the context of the Lisbon Strategy.[83] The primary goal of this strategy was to increase European competitiveness in relation to other world regions, and a classical regulatory framework for goals related to the social dimension of European integration was not perceived as a political option. Instead, heads of state and government decided to rely on more discursive tools such the OMC or CSR. With the mid-term review of the Lisbon Strategy in 2004 and a large conservative majority in the European Council, the orientation towards competitiveness and growth became even clearer and these soft tools weaker still.[84]

In July 2001, the promotion of CSR became more outspoken when the Commission published its Green Paper 'Promoting a European framework for corporate social responsibility'.[85] The goal of the initiative was to develop a European framework for CSR activities so as to render them more coherent, convergent and transparent – with the help of a public

---

[82]   European Council 2000 (n. 3 above).

[83]   de Schutter (n. 6 above).

[84]   U. Liebert, 'The politics for a Social Europe and the Lisbon process' in Lars Magnussion and Bo Strath (eds.), *European Solidarities: Tensions and Contentions of a Concept* (Frankfurt aM: Peter Lang, 2007), p. 267.

[85]   Commission of the European Communities, *Green Paper Promoting a European Framework for Corporate Social Responsibility*, 2001. The general context of the CSR initiative had been set by previous documents, namely N. Lebessis and J. Paterson, 'Evolution in governance: What lessons for the Commission? A first assessment', European Commission Forward Studies Unit Working Paper (Brussels, 1997); Commission of the European Communities, Communication from the Commission to the Council, the European Parliament, the Committee of the Regions and the Economic and Social Committee, *The Competitiveness of European Enterprises in the Face of Globalisation – How it can be Encouraged*, COM (98) 718 Final, Brussels, 20 January 1999.

authority, the European Commission. Once more, CSR was perceived as a contribution to the goal of the EU to become the most competitive regional economy of the world.[86] It was assumed that social responsibility of firms could contribute to a competitive advantage. Related costs should therefore be seen as investment rather than loss. In order to convince firms of such investments, the Green Paper seeks to sensibilise relevant actors about CSR, in particular about the training of managers and employees, reporting and audit, the advantages of labels, and the sensibilisation of financial markets.

The Commission defines CSR as a 'concept whereby companies integrate social and environmental concerns in their business operations and in their interaction with their stakeholders on a voluntary basis', thus adopting a definition that is centred on voluntarism. According to the Green Paper, CSR includes both the internal (inside the company) and the external dimension. The internal dimension relates to human resource management and means that employees should, in the best interest of the firm, be supported, trained and protected against risks and dangers. The external dimension relates to the contact and dialogue with local communities and other stakeholders and their demands.

After the presentation of the Green Paper, as is common practice, a phase of public consultation followed which attracted approximately 300 answers,[87] with a heavy bias towards firm contributions coming from the UK (twenty-eight) while only two German firms replied. Basically, the European Round Table of Industrialists (ERT) voiced its marked opposition to standardised CSR practices and reporting, while more far-reaching approaches envisioning a common, more binding framework for CSR and related social and environmental reporting, as demanded by unions[88] and NGOs, were stopped by the resistance of employers.[89]

In July 2002, the Commission presented its Communication 'Corporate social responsibility: A business contribution to sustainable

---

[86] *Ibid.*, para. 20.

[87] These include answers from governments (22), international organisations (42), firms and sectoral organisations (104), social partners (61) amongst which 12 national level trade unions, NGOs (37), science and individuals (37), and political parties (1); see Bussler (n. 79 above).

[88] Trade unions generally reject CSR as it transfers more power to managers. They also criticise the voluntary character of the concept that potentially replaces legal obligations and future regulation. Insofar as they accept it, they ask for an independent monitoring agency (ICTU (Untitled response to the Commission Green Paper) 2001, http://europa.eu.int/comm/employment_social/soc-dial/csr/pdf2/082-SFnjNAT_ICTU_Ireland_011221_cn.pdf).

[89] Hauser-Ditz and Wilke (n. 75 above), p. 4.

development'.[90] The Commission argued that a common framework for
CSR – and therewith Community action – was necessary as current
practices were not transparent and could not be compared. They therefore could be a source of market distortion and of confusion for consumers and investors alike. Companies should adopt management
schemes and codes of conduct built on ILO fundamental conventions
and OECD guidelines for multinational enterprises. Reporting obligations should be established and eco and social labels developed. Further
suggested activities included increasing knowledge about CSR and its
impacts, exchange of good practices at EU level, supporting the convergence and transparency of CSR practices in order to develop a
common framework, identifying areas where additional action is needed
at EU level and establishing a European CRS forum.[91]

Originally, the aim of the CSR forum was to promote transparency
and convergence of CSR practices and instruments. According to the
Communication, the forum should promote exchange and evaluate
existing CSR practices, establish a common approach and common
guidelines and identify areas where further EU action was needed.
These goals should be advanced and realised with the involvement of
all affected stakeholders in order to assure acceptance and credibility.
The responsibility for organising these tasks was shifted to the forum
while a monitoring function by the Commission was not foreseen. This
was the result of three roundtables between April and June 2002 in which
business voiced opposition to any sort of constraining CSR activities.
The idea to identify further areas where EU action was needed was also
dropped. Instead, the mandate was now to improve knowledge about the
relationship between CSR and sustainable development, to facilitate the
exchange of good practices and to explore the possibility of common
guiding principles for CSR policies.[92] While the forum should thus
suggest solutions to increase transparency and convergence, it was not
allowed to point to further necessary EU action. After twenty months of
work, a final report was published in June 2004. The report remained

---

[90] Commission of the European Communities, *Communication Concerning Corporate
Social Responsibility: A business contribution to sustainable development*, COM/2002/
347 Final, Brussels, 2 July 2002. The Communication was given additional weight by the
ensuing document of the Council of the European Union, *Resolution of the Employment
and Social Policy Council on CSR*, Brussels, 2–3 December 2002.

[91] Initially, the European Parliament proposed to establish such a forum, de Schutter (n. 6
above), p. 212.

[92] Commission of the European Communities (n. 90 above).

unspecific and did not recognise the necessity of a public CSR policy. It reflected the lowest common denominator of those involved and what they were able to achieve without a co-ordinating and monitoring agent.

B   The second Communication on CSR

After the final report of the CSR EMS forum, almost two years passed by before new CSR activity emerged on the EU horizon. In March 2006, the Commission presented its second Communication on CSR 'Implementing the partnership for growth and jobs: Making Europe a pole of excellence on CSR'.[93] In the context of the revised Lisbon Strategy, it was not surprising that it was even more business-friendly than the first Communication, resulting in the abandonment of the idea of a common regulatory framework. Instead, the Communication stated that because CSR was fundamentally about voluntary business action, an approach involving additional obligations and administrative requirements for business risked being counterproductive regarding the principles of better regulation. The second CSR Communication was in line with the revised Lisbon Strategy which focused on competitiveness, growth, and the need to create a business-friendly environment, while neglecting social objectives.

Acknowledging that enterprises are the primary actors of CSR, the Commission decided that it could best achieve its objectives by working more closely with European business. It therefore announced its backing for the launch of a European alliance on CSR, a concept drawn up on the basis of contributions from business active in the promotion of CSR.[94] The second striking change was that the Commission gave up the principle of equality of social partners (and other stakeholders) as it exclusively invited business to the CSR dialogue. It thereby confirmed its alignment with the business case for CSR activities while abandoning the idea of a public policy. At EU level, CSR was to be pursued in the context of a European alliance on CSR. This alliance was designed to provide a space for mutual learning that was open to business representatives only: 'It is not a legal instrument and is not to be signed by enterprises, the

---

[93] Commission of the European Communities, *Implementing the Partnership for Growth and Jobs: Making Europe a pole of excellence on CSR*, COM/2006/136 Final, Brussels, 22 March 2006.
[94] *Ibid.*, p. 3.

Commission or any public authority. It is a political process to increase the uptake of CSR amongst European enterprises.'[95]

In the period 2000–6, we have thus observed three major shifts. The first concerns a shift from substance to process due to the abandonment of CSR as a public policy. Originally introduced in order to arrive at a common policy, the ambition now is to provide a platform for exchange. The second change relates to the abandonment of formal equality of social partners in favour of business. The third concerns changing the meaning of CSR. While CSR was conceived as a politically and socially necessary responsibility of business at the turn of the century, it is now depicted as detrimental to competitiveness and should only occur as long as it increases profits and is something in which politics has no role to play.[96] The EU thereby clearly endorsed the 'business case' for CSR which only promotes it as far as it raises profitability.

These changes of CSR of the EU are obviously embedded in a larger political context. The unprecedented large majority of social-democratic governments in the Council had given way to a conservative majority, as reflected by the choice of Manuel Barroso as Commission president in 2004. Thus, the social dialogue had accordingly and markedly passed its heyday.[97] In the new political context, the power of trade unions had become weaker, workers' rights had been restricted to the area of labour law 'while company law, and even more so corporate governance regulation, have become increasingly focused on the rights of shareholders, and have been integrated into capital market law'.[98] It is thus no surprise that the original stakeholder model made way for a model of 'shareholder democracy'.[99]

VI Conclusion and discussion

As set out in the introduction, this chapter is interested in how far a common CSR policy that would work in favour of the social dimension is possible, in light of the institutional differences between Member States

---

[95] n. 93 above, p. 3.   [96] *Ibid.*
[97] A. Schäfer and S. Leiber, 'The double voluntarism in EU social dialogue and employment policy' in S. Kröger (ed.), 'What we have learnt: Advances, pitfalls and remaining questions of OMC research', *EIOP* special issue 1(13) (2009).
[98] L. Horn, 'The transformation of corporate governance regulation in the European Union: Towards a marketisation of corporate control', PhD Thesis, Political Science department, University of Amsterdam, 2008, p. 79.
[99] Moon and Vogel (n. 44 above), p. 316.

and the dominating soft-law character of CSR. In order to answer this question, I have first introduced CSR concepts and theories. Secondly, the institutional diversity that a common CSR policy would need to take into account has been established as well as the fragile nature of CSR between soft and hard law. Subsequently, the approach to CSR in the UK and in Germany – as representatives of the liberal and the social market economies, respectively – has been scrutinised. In the UK, CSR was found to have emerged in the context of Thatcherism and its efforts at deregulation. Here, the terminology of CSR as voluntary activity has been strongly embraced and related activities have been encouraged by governments since the late 1990s. The empirical implementation by firms ranges from ignorance to engagement. In Germany, the concept has been welcomed more hesitantly by the relevant actors while activities that figure as CSR activities in the UK are in many cases part of established firm action. Finally, the development of CSR by the EU has been sketched. It was shown that the EU has opted for CSR as soft law. The Commission's efforts were not very ambitious to start with, and they became even less so after the coming into force of the first Barroso Commission in 2004.

Now, can we still picture a European CSR policy developing that could set meaningful incentives for the social dimension of European integration? Caution is in order. Besides a vague terminology, responsibility is mainly defined by companies themselves, rather than being socially defined. As a consequence, firms are likely to embrace those activities – if any – that enhance their reputation and that are likely to increase their profits. While these activities must not be counterproductive to the dimension of European integration, they set different priorities and may be withdrawn in times of crisis. At EU level, CSR emerged under the strong influence of the UK and in the context of the search for competitiveness to which the Lisbon Strategy tried to give an answer. In its framework, market competition is heavily regulated while social cohesion goals are dealt with by non-binding instruments such as voluntary business activity or the OMC. It thus becomes apparent that content and mode of governance are linked to one another.[100] While issues of market integration are dealt with by hard law and the European

---

[100] A. Nölke, 'Private governance in international affairs and the erosion of coordinated market economies in the European Union', Cornell University, Mario Einaudi Center for International Studies Working Paper Series 3 (2008), p. 27.

Court of Justice, the topic of social responsibility of firms is left to the uncertain world of soft law.

What about the claim that CSR can take legal forms or provoke legal consequences through peer pressure and thereby be a useful instrument for enhancing the social dimension of European integration? There may be future developments in this direction, depending both on firms' willingness to get engaged and on continued civil society pressure and informed consumers,[101] neither of which are structurally available in all sectors and all parts of the production chain. Even so, CSR in its light European version cannot provide the same sort of institutionalisation of social solidarity as hard law can.[102] After all, CSR emerged both in the UK and the EU in the context of deregulation as a means to foster competitiveness. CSR therefore deserves attention in that it contributes to the framing of social relationships. It is more debatable whether it also deserves attention as a means of fostering the social dimension of European integration. Instead, it may be seen as an expression of the decline of institutionalised social solidarity[103] and as such might receive more attention on the EU agenda in the years to come.

[101] Compa (n. 34 above).
[102] S. M. Hart, 'Self-regulation, corporate social responsibility, and the business case: Do they work in achieving workplace equality and safety?', *Journal of Business Ethics* 92 (2009), 585.
[103] Kinderman (n. 6 above).

10

Services of general interest provision through the third sector under EU competition law constraints: The example of organising healthcare in England, Wales and the Netherlands

IDA WENDT AND ANDREA GIDEON

I Introduction

It is commonplace that directly applicable EU Treaty law exerts influence on various social fields at national level, including healthcare. There has been ample debate about the impact of free movement rights and public healthcare systems, recently complemented by an analysis of the relationship between public healthcare and EU competition law. This case study aims to highlight a different aspect of the tensions between social and economic dimensions of European integration.[1] By providing healthcare as a service of general interest, some Member States have taken recourse to the 'third sector', consisting of not-for-profit organisations offering social services based on a specific ethos. At the same time, a need to respond to ever diversifying social demands has developed. Co-operating with not-for-profit organisations as service providers as well as including them in the process of conceptualising services may be one way to respond to this. Such inclusion can be perceived as enhancing social integration through active civil society participation – a strategy which may also be suitable to enhance social dimensions of European integration.

This case study will therefore investigate whether the application of the – fundamentally economic – EU competition law provisions predominantly constitutes an opportunity or a threat to not-for-profit organisations providing healthcare services as an alternative to public provision and commodification. In order to provide a background for

[1] On these see Schiek in ch. 1 of this volume.

this analysis, section II places the welfare state, the market and the third sector into a historical and theoretical perspective. This will be followed in section III by an overview of the public healthcare structures in the three countries selected for analysis (England, Wales and the Netherlands) and their recent tendencies to enhance or reduce market mechanisms. Section IV sketches more particularly the position of third-sector providers as a special group of non-public providers in those healthcare systems. Ultimately, section V presents the analysis of European competition law effects. The results of this study then will be integrated in a conclusion.

II   Contextualising the welfare state, the market and the third sector in Europe

The background of this study is related to four fields of discussion. First, there has been a process of reforming European welfare states, by which they have transitioned from a purely public sector endeavour towards another, market-governed, sphere, allowing increasing space for third-sector actors.[2] Secondly, the relationship between the market and the public sector is a theme in itself, which goes beyond the welfare state.[3] Thirdly, finding 'third ways' between the market and the state has also been a general policy trend in Europe and at EU level.[4] Finally, the

---

[2] See further C. Pierson, *Beyond the Welfare State*, 2nd edn (Cambridge: Polity, 1998) in particular chs. 5 and 6; J. Lewis, 'The state and the third sector in modern welfare states: Independence, instrumentality, partnership' in A. Evers and J.-L. Laville (eds.), *The Third Sector in Europe* (Cheltenham/Northampton, MA: Edward Elgar, 2004); specifically on healthcare H. Rothgang *et al.*, 'The changing role of the state in healthcare systems', *European Review* 13 (2005), 187; J. Holmwood, 'Three pillars of welfare state theory: T. H. Marshall, Karl Polanyi and Alva Myrdal in defence of the national welfare state', *European Journal of Social Theory* 3 (2000), 23.

[3] See further A. Haagsma, 'The EU citizen between the market and the state', *Web JCLI* 5 (2005); A. M. Sbragia, 'Governance, the state, and the market: What is going on?', *Governance* 13 (2000), 243; A. A. Goldsmith, 'The state, the market and economic development: A second look at Adam Smith in theory and practice', *Development and Change* 26 (1995), 633; R. Voigt (ed.), *Abschied vom Staat – Rückkehr zum Staat?*, IfS-Werkstatt (Munich: Universitätsdruckerei der Universität der Bundeswehr München, 2000).

[4] See further A. Evers, 'Mixed welfare systems and hybrid organizations: Changes in the governance and provision of social services', *Intl Journal of Public Administration* 28 (2005), 737; H. K. Anheier, 'The third sector in Europe: Five theses', Civil Society Working Paper (2002); J. Kendall, 'Terra incognita: Third sectors and European policy processes' in J. Kendall (ed.), *Handbook on Third Sector Policy in Europe: Multi-level processes and organized civil society* (Cheltenham/Northampton, MA: Edward Elgar, 2009); A. Evers and J.-L. Laville, 'Social services by social enterprises: On the possible

influence of EU law on national welfare systems has been widely dis-cussed.[5] While these trends are too wide to be described fully here, the following offers a short overview of the core developments relevant for this case study.

Protecting citizens against typical risks through welfare-state institu-tions is widely seen as one of the pillars of the European Social Model.[6] To illuminate the background of this, it is necessary to have a closer look at the origins of the welfare system, its basic models and its crisis.

With industrialisation in Europe a growing number of people moved from rural communities to the cities in order to find work, leaving behind their ground, the extended family or the guild as social back-ups. With increasing competition for jobs, unemployment and low wages became a problem. In this climate not-for-profit organisations (often unions and friendly societies) started to provide old age, accident and other social insurances. These, however, did not cover every worker let alone every citizen. Action from the government seemed required. The beginning of the welfare state was then made in Germany with the first social insurances being introduced by statute (1883 health insur-ance, 1884 accident insurance, 1889 old age and disability insurance). They focused on workers, required a contribution and provided for benefits in accordance with the contributions paid. They were adminis-trated by independent bodies under public supervision. As the laws establishing them were introduced by Chancellor Otto von Bismarck, welfare systems based on a social insurance style are hence called Bismarck systems.[7]

For most European countries, the time of the Great Depression and the post-war periods provided the background for increasing

contributions of hybrid organisations and a civil society' in A. Evers and J.-L. Laville (eds.), *The Third Sector in Europe* (Cheltenham/Northampton, MA: Edward Elgar, 2004).

[5] See further M. Dougan, 'The spatial restructuring of national welfare states within the European Union: The contribution of Union citizenship and the relevance of the Treaty of Lisbon'; U. Neergaard, 'Services of general economic interest: What aims and values count?'; specifically on healthcare, V. Hatzopoulos, 'Services of general interest in health-care: An exercise in deconstruction?' all in U. Neergaard, R. Nielsen and L. Roseberry (eds.), *Integrating Welfare Functions into EU Law: From Rome to Lisbon* (Copenhagen: DJØF, 2009); G. de Búrca, 'Towards European welfare?' in G. de Búrca (ed.), *EU Law and the Welfare State* (Oxford: Oxford University Press, 2005).

[6] See further Schiek in ch. 1 of this volume.

[7] See A. Rohwer, 'Bismarck versus Beveridge: Ein Vergleich von Sozialversicherungssystemen in Europa', *Ifo Schnelldienst* 61 (2008), 26; E. Eichenhofer, *Sozialrecht*, 4th edn (Tübingen: Mohr-Siebeck, 2003), pp. 15 *et seq*.; R. Waltermann, *Sozialrecht*, 4th edn (Heidelberg: Müller, 2004), pp. 22 *et seq*.

development of European welfare systems. Of particular influence here was a report by William Henry Beveridge to the British House of Commons in 1942. It suggested a system providing the entire population with standard benefits financed from general taxation. The UK and the Scandinavian countries followed this approach and these systems are therefore called Beveridge systems. Due to later modernisations, the Bismarck and the Beveridge systems no longer exist in any purity, as most national welfare systems combine elements of both.[8]

Welfare systems experienced a period of functioning well and welfare rights made it into national constitutions and into international instruments. After the oil crisis in the beginning of the 1970s, however, economic depression, higher unemployment rates and an ageing society put increasing pressure on welfare states. In addition, uniform and centralised provision of social services, in line with Taylorism,[9] increasingly fractionised with the diversification of life cycles in European societies. These trends necessitated individualisation and rationalisation of social services. European states started to curb their welfare systems for budgetary reasons and experimented with commodification, leaving former public services to market forces.[10]

According to Esping-Andersen, however, commodification seems to contrast with the whole idea of welfare systems.[11] The theory explains the aim of welfare systems as establishing de-commodification, thus providing individuals with means to support themselves independently from the market. It might therefore be argued that leaving their welfare systems to market forces threatens these de-commodification aims. In addition, healthcare provision by the market does not necessarily lead to the desired individualisation of services. In this respect third-sector participation in welfare arrangements can offer an opportunity to

---

[8] See M. Bruce, *The Rise of the Welfare State* (London: Weidenfeld and Nicolson, 1973), pp. 136 *et seq.*, 238 *et seq.*; Rohwer (n. 7 above), pp. 1 *et seq.*; F. Noordam, *Hoofdzaken socialezekerheidrechts*, 3rd edn (Deventer: Kluwer, 2004), p. 5; C. J. J. H. van Voss, *Inleiding sociaal recht*, 4th edn (Den Haag: Boom Juridische uitgevers, 2005), pp. 256 *et seq.*

[9] Taylorism refers to a management theory that rigorously separates the planning from the execution of the task. Tasks are divided in small segments and have to be performed exactly as planned. See further D. M. Berwick, 'Improvement, trust, and the healthcare workforce', *Qual Saf Health Care* 12 (2003), 448.

[10] See A. Evers and J.-L. Laville (n. 4 above), pp. 241 *et seq.*; G. Bonoli, 'Classifying welfare states: A two-dimension approach', *JnlSoc.Pol.* 26 (1997), 351, 356 *et seq.*; Noordam (n. 8 above), pp. 3, 6; van Voss (n. 8 above), pp. 257 *et seq.*

[11] See e.g. G. Esping-Andersen, *Social Foundations of Postindustrial Economies* (Oxford: Oxford University Press, 1999), pp. 43 *et seq.*

provide differentialisation corresponding to societal differentiation without commodification, as third-sector organisations are often closer to the individual and work on a not-for-profit basis.[12] Third-sector organisations therefore have increasingly been enabled and encouraged in recent years to participate in social service provision.[13]

The third sector[14] is generally defined as a common sector of organisations which operate according to a certain ethos supporting a specific unselfish aim. As these aims can vary significantly, the third sector mostly is defined negatively as non-governmental and non-profit in distinction to the state and the market. Sometimes it is defined as part of civil society, but sometimes it is also differentiated from it by the criterion of formality. This means that, despite not operating in the same professional way as state administration or commercial firms, third-sector organisations are organised in a less informal way as e.g. private households.[15] This general international definition is, however, not taking account of specific features of the European third sector, which differs in some respects from the US one. Basically the European tradition uses a more historical and thus broader approach including also not-for-profit organisations that are not strictly speaking non-profit and 'hybrid' organisations overlapping with the other two sectors. In Europe, the third sector is more involved in policy-making and service delivery at national levels and attempts are made to include it in European policies as well, inter alia in the open method of co-ordination (OMC) as part of the Lisbon Strategy. This gives the European third sector a unique opportunity to provide healthcare (and other welfare) services as an alternative to commodification and state provision.[16]

On the other hand, however, despite health (Article 168 TFEU (ex Article 152 EC)) and social security (Articles 151 *et seq.* TFEU (ex Articles 136 *et seq.* EC)) being primary responsibilities of the

---

[12] See further on this E. Ostrom, 'Gemeingütermanagement – eine Perspektive für bürgerschaftliches Engagement' in S. Helfrich and Heinrich Böll-Stiftung (eds.), *Wem gehört die Welt? Zur Wiederentdeckung der Gemeingüter* (Munich: Oekom, 2009).

[13] See Bonoli (n. 10 above), pp. 353 *et seq.*; Evers and Laville (n. 4 above), pp. 237 *et seq.*

[14] Other terms used are, e.g. voluntary sector, voluntary and community sector, non-profit sector and social economy. See P. Alcock, 'A strategic unity: Defining the third sector in the UK', *Voluntary Sector Review* 1 (2010), 5 *et seq.*

[15] See *ibid.*, pp. 7 *et seq.* with further references.

[16] See further A. Evers *et al.*, 'Defining the third sector in Europe' in A. Evers and J.-L. Laville (eds.), *The Third Sector in Europe* (Cheltenham: Edward Elgar, 2004), pp. 11 *et seq.*; J. Kendall, 'The third sector and the development of European public policy: Framework for analysis?', Civil Society Working Paper 19 (2001), pp. 2 *et seq.*

Member States, national welfare systems are influenced by hard EU law. The fundamental freedoms and the citizenship provisions open up welfare systems to all EU citizens. Furthermore, the introduction of market principles in welfare areas such as health can also bring these services into the ambit of EU competition law. This might have consequences for third-sector involvement. Therefore this case study will undertake to investigate the effects of competition law on the third sector providing healthcare as an alternative to public provision and commodification in England, Wales and the Netherlands.[17]

III   Healthcare systems in England, Wales and the Netherlands between public service and commodification

The examples of two UK countries and the Netherlands have been chosen, because they represent two different types of public healthcare systems. While the UK National Health Service (NHS) follows the Beveridge model, the Netherlands – as many other Continental states[18] – have a health insurance system according to the Bismarck model. In addition, both the UK and the Netherlands have experimented with the introduction of market mechanisms. After devolution in 2000,[19] however, the two UK countries have taken rather different directions. While England progressed in the direction of marketisation, Wales chose a route towards re-de-commodification.

A   The NHS system

In 1948, a revolutionary overhaul of the UK health system took place whereby it moved from a privately funded arrangement to a new system in which services free of charge for everyone at the point of delivery funded through taxation were provided. Its management was to be achieved through a centralised system: the NHS. Successive modernisations have been undertaken since the 1970s; most significant among these are the 1990s reforms which were aiming at creating a more competitive system of

---

[17] See further on the influence of EU law on healthcare e.g. Hatzopoulos (n. 5 above); A. P. Van der Mei, 'Cross-border access to health care within the European Union: Recent developments in law and policy', *European Journal of Health Law* 10 (2003), 369. On EU law influence on national welfare in general see e.g. Eichenhofer (n. 7 above), pp. 42 *et seq.*; Noordam (n. 8 above), p. 113.

[18] e.g. Austria, France and Germany.

[19] Scotland has long had a separate system, even before the political devolution in 2000.

health service provision. After the political devolution in 2000 England and Wales developed their own very diverging systems. Their basic features are laid down in the National Health Service (England) Act 2006 and the National Health Service (Wales) Act 2006, which specify the individual systems in accordance with the National Health Service (Consequential Provisions) Act 2006. After the general election in 2010 the coalition government is discussing further changes.[20]

1   The English system

The new English[21] system continued in this line towards bureaucratic reform and the opening of competitive markets as the old top-down integrated NHS system was regarded as increasingly untenable. In the new system, the NHS buys health services for the patients from different providers, the quality of which is assessed by semi-independent agencies according to a governmental framework. These features increased competition and made the system similar to the one in the utility sector.[22]

While the Secretary of State, the Department of Health and, at the next level, the Strategic Health Authority are still responsible for the allocation of funds and the running of the NHS in general, most of the actual managing is undertaken by Primary Care Trusts (PCTs). The PCTs control 80 per cent of the NHS budget and have a threefold role. First, they have a complex relationship with general practitioners (GPs); the GPs provide primary care[23] as independent practitioners but also

---

[20] See S. Abbott, S. Procter and N. Iacovou, 'NHS purchaser–provider relationships in England and Wales: The view from primary care', *Social Policy & Administration* 43 (2009), 1; D. Hughes and P. Vincent-Jones, 'Schism in the church: National Health Service systems and institutional divergence in England and Wales', *Journal of Health and Social Behaviour* 49 (2008), 400, 403, 407; D. Ngo *et al.*, *Supervising the Quality of Care in Changing Healthcare Systems: An international comparison* (University of Rotterdam, 2008), p. 37; P. Vincent-Jones and C. Mullen, 'From collaborative to genetic governance: The example of healthcare services in England' in O. de Schutter and J. Lenoble (eds.), *Reflexive Governance* (Oxford: Hart Publishing, 2010), pp. 150 *et seq*. On the changes discussed by the coalition government see n. 29 below.

[21] While Scotland, Northern Ireland and Wales have their own governments and follow their own policies in certain fields after devolution, the UK government is still responsible for England. See further www.direct.gov.uk/en/Governmentcitizensandrights/UKgovernment/Devolvedgovernment/DG_073306.

[22] See Hughes and Vincent-Jones (n. 20 above), p. 404; Vincent-Jones and Mullen (n. 20 above), pp. 147 *et seq*.

[23] Primary care is the first instance general healthcare provided by e.g. GPs and dentists. See further The King's Fund, 'Primary and community care' (2009), www.kingsfund.org.uk/topics/primary_and_community_care/; Care Quality Commission, 'How the NHS is

contribute to the commissioning and procurement activity of the PCTs and provide clinical expertise and input into them. Secondly, the PCTs provide community healthcare[24] themselves. Finally, they act as commissioners for secondary[25] and tertiary[26] care.[27]

For the latter two forms of care, PCTs enter into contracts with health service providers to purchase health services for the consumers (patients). The providers can either be public (traditional NHS trusts and new semi-independent NHS Foundation Trusts, which operate as corporate entities), private commercial (Independent Sector Treatment Centres (ISTCs) which conduct NHS work while being owned by private enterprises as well as regular private providers)[28] or the third sector.[29] They are all paid standard tariffs for each individual service (payment by result (PbR)). The aim of this mechanism is to increase competition and deliver better services rather than lower prices. Special quality payments (called CQUINS) are possible if certain standards and performance targets are met. Patients are given increasing choice between providers,

---

structured' (2010), www.cqc.org.uk/usingcareservices/healthcare/makingdecisionsa-boutnhshealthcare/howthenhsisstructured.cfm.

[24] Community care services cater to special needs and comprise e.g. meal delivery for the elderly and home visits to families with new babies (Patient Plus 'Community Care' (2008), <http://www.patient.co.uk/doctor/Community-Care.htm>, The King's Fund (n. 23 above)). From April 2011, commissioning and provision of services will have to be separated. Accordingly, most PCTs will have to commission community care to other providers (Department of Health, 'Revision to the Operating Framework for the NHS in England 2010/2011' (2011) <http://www.dh.gov.uk/publications>, p. 9 and 'Transforming Community Services: overview' (2010), <http://www.dh.gov.uk/en/Healthcare/TCS/Abouttheprogramme/DH_121964>).

[25] Secondary care is specialist health care provided mostly in hospitals and emergency care. The former is known as elective care (Care Quality Commission (n. 23 above), NHS, 'NHS structure' (2010), <http://www.nhs.uk/NHSEngland/thenhs/about/Pages/nhsstructure.aspx>).

[26] Tertiary or specialised care for rare illnesses is not provided by each hospital but only in specialised centres which also conduct research. Special rules apply to the commissioning. Very specialised care is organised nationally (S. Kerr and I. Anderson, 'Service innovations: Developing a specialised (tertiary) service for the treatment of affective disorders', Psychiatric Bulletin, 30 (2006), 103 et seq. with further references).

[27] See Abbott, Procter and Iacovou (n. 20 above), pp. 2 et seq., Hughes and Vincent-Jones (n. 20 above), pp. 404 et seq.; Ngo et al. (n. 20 above), pp. 36 et seq.; Vincent-Jones and Mullen (n. 20 above), Annexes A and B.

[28] The ISTCs are long term commissioned while the regular private providers often work on an ad hoc basis. See Hughes and Vincent-Jones (n. 20 above), p. 405; Vincent-Jones and Mullen (n. 20 above), Annexes A and B.

[29] Plans are being discussed in the coalition government to abolish PCTs having GPs organise the commissioning and to turn all NHS hospitals into foundation trusts. See further N. Triggle, 'NHS "to undergo radical overhaul"', BBC News, 12 July 2010, www.bbc.co.uk/news/10557996.

who are encouraged to promote their services. Under the 'Any Willing Provider' scheme, which applies to elective care, patients even have completely free choice between all providers meeting the national standards. The system is overseen by semi-independent bodies; the providers have to comply with the requirements set by the Care Quality Commission (CQC), which stands outside the Department of Health. NHS Foundation Trusts are also monitored by the regulatory agency MONITOR.[30]

2   The Welsh system

The Welsh system, on the other hand, reversed the market system and returned to a more integrated state service system. The aim thereof is to ensure governmental responsibility for the improvement of healthcare and to achieve this improvement within a community rather than leaving the system open to market forces. The relatively small size of Wales provided an advantage in the attempt to achieve a well-functioning integrated system.[31]

The system is based on planning and co-ordination between the Welsh governmental bodies. At the top level the Committee of Assembly for Health and Social Services, the Welsh Minister for Health and Social Services, and the director of the NHS in Wales are in charge of health services. Twenty-two local health boards (LHBs), which are placed under three regional NHS offices and, unlike the English equivalent, cover the same area as the local authorities, undertake the organisation of primary, community and secondary care. Tertiary care is commissioned for the whole of Wales by Health Commission Wales, an executive agency of the Welsh Assembly Government (WAG). As regards secondary and community care the LHBs purchase the services

[30] See Abbott, Procter and Iacovou (n. 20 above), p. 3; Hughes and Vincent-Jones (n. 20 above), pp. 404 *et seq.*; C. Newdick, 'Charities in the health care market: Can trust survive NHS competition?', *The King's College Law Journal* 18 (2007), 415 *et seq.*; Ngo *et al.* (n. 20 above), pp. 36 *et seq.*; Vincent-Jones and Mullen (n. 20 above), Annexes A and B; Department of Health, 'Primary care trust procurement guide for health services', 25 March 2010, www.dh.gov.uk/en/MediaCentre/DH_4015576, pp. 6 *et seq.*

[31] See S. L. Greer, *Four Way Bet: How devolution has led to four different models for the NHS* (London, 2004), p. 4; Hughes and Vincent-Jones (n. 20 above), pp. 401, 406; Labour/Plaid Cymru, 'One Wales: A progressive agenda for the government of Wales' (2007), http://wales.gov.uk/about/programmeforgovernment/strategy/publications/onewales/?lang=en, p. 8; T. Jewell and J. Wilkinson, 'Health and social care regulation in Wales: An integrated system of political, corporate and professional governance for improving public health', *JRSH* 128 (2008), 306.

from integrated NHS trusts, English NHS hospitals and independent hospitals (private or third sector). The latter play a much smaller role, however. There are no semi-independent Foundation Trusts or ISTCs in the Welsh system. Furthermore, prices for treatments are individually negotiated between commissioners and providers. The purchases have to be in line with the LHBs' Annual Service and Commissioning Plans, which are based on strategies negotiated with the local authorities, and have to be agreed upon in regional commissioning groups consisting of LHBs, local authorities and NHS Trusts. Ultimately, annual operating frameworks (AOFs) are concluded between every organisation and the WAG represented by the director of the respective regional NHS offices. On this basis long-term agreements are set up. Only in exceptional cases such as extremely long waiting lists for surgeries, do patients have a limited choice between providers (second-offer scheme). Plans[32] to completely end the use of private providers by 2011 are being discussed in the Welsh government.[33]

Also the supervision looks different from the English system. While in England the overseeing bodies are semi-independent, the Welsh Healthcare Inspectorate is fully integrated in the governmental structure.[34]

B   The Dutch system

Successive efficiency-driven modernisations of the Bismarck-type healthcare system resulted in long waiting times and decreased the number of care providers. Also, from the late 1980s the government was advised to develop a more competitive healthcare system. As a reaction to these trends, a radically modified system was introduced in 2006 on the basis of the new *Zorgverzekeringswet* (Healthcare Insurance Act). The new system privatised all sickness funds and henceforth private insurers purchase primary and secondary care (*eerstelijns-* and

---

[32] Labour/Plaid Cymru (n. 31 above), p. 9.
[33] See Abbott, Procter and Iacovou (n. 20 above), p. 3; Greer (n. 31 above), pp. 13 *et seq.*; Hughes and Vincent-Jones (n. 20 above), pp. 406 *et seq.*; Labour/Plaid Cymru (n. 31 above), pp. 9 *et seq.*; M. Longley, 'Health care systems in transition: The Welsh report' (WHO Regional Office for Europe on behalf of the European Observatory on Health Systems and Policies, 2004), pp. 3 *et seq.*; M. Aylward, 'Health Commission Wales: A review' (Wales Centre for Health, 2008), www.wales.nhs.uk/sites3/docopen.cfm?org id=222&id=99810&uuid=BDD78622-1143-E756–5C584B471069B525, pp. 9, 12 *et seq.*
[34] See Hughes and Vincent-Jones (n. 20 above), p. 406.

tweedelijnsgezondheidszorg) for patients ('consumers') from different providers.[35] The funds negotiate prices, volumes and quality of care and service levels directly with the providers. Statutory obligations protect the public interest in respect of quality, accessibility and financial sustainability of healthcare and make the system a public one, despite its private definition ('managed competition').[36]

While the new system increases patients' choice and responsibility, it also allows insurers to sign contracts with 'preferred providers'. The negotiation power of these providers is amplified and groups of patients are channelled towards them. Primary care (or 'first access' care) is provided by GPs, dentists, physiotherapists, etc. as independent practitioners. Secondary care is provided by specialists inside and outside hospitals and is often not directly accessible for patients without referral from a GP. Traditionally, hospitals in the Netherlands are third-sector providers. Recently ownership by shareholders has started, subject to restrictions on the distribution of profits.[37] Only university hospitals are public and there are also only a few private commercial clinics.[38] Some

---

[35] The largest health insurer in a particular region is also responsible for a third type of care under the Exceptional Medical Expense Act 2003 (*Algemene Wet Bijzondere Ziektekosten*, AWBZ), which is a public service task. It is organised as a national social insurance, i.e. a collective and compulsory fund for costs that are not insurable on an individual basis. In particular it covers hospital care provided for longer than 365 days, but also nursing and medical care of elderly people and people with disabilities in care institutions and home care (*thuiszorg*).

[36] Y. Bartholomée and H. Maarse, 'Empowering the chronically ill? Patient collectives in the new Dutch health insurance system', *Health Policy* 84 (2007), 163. In particular private insurers have to guarantee a statutory package of basic healthcare defined by the Ministry of Health (*zorgplicht*). Basic health insurance coverage is compulsory and acceptance of any Dutch resident is mandatory (*acceptatieplicht*). The objective of the statute is that patients ('consumers'), by exercising their right to choose their insurer and health plan, can positively influence accessibility and improve the quality of care. This system of creating one single market for private health insurance has been endorsed by the European Commission in its decision of 3 May 2005 (N 541/2004 and N 542/2004), http://ec.europa.eu/competition/ state_aid/register/ii/by_case_nr_n2004_0540.html.

[37] 'Ruimte en rekenschap voor zorg en ondersteuning', letter of 9 July 2009 to the lower house by the Ministry of Health, pp. 30 *et seq.*, http://parlis.nl/pdf/kamerstukken/KST133509.pdf. In 2006 the Slotervaart hospital in Amsterdam was taken over by an investor in order to avoid its dissolution. See www.nvma.nl/index.php?option=com_content&view=article&cat_id=1: nieuwsitem&id=1186.

[38] Consequently, the Dutch third sector in health is one of the largest in the world. See E. M. van den Berg and T. Brandsen, 'The Dutch Third Sector and the European Union: Connecting citizens to the EU?' (Scientific Council for Government Policy, 2007), www. wrr.nl/content.jsp?objectid=4039.

community and specialised healthcare services[39] are still provided by public bodies rather than being financed by insurance contributions. Supervision of the system is organised centrally by the Dutch Healthcare Authority (*Nederlandse Zorgautoriteit*, NZa) established in 2006.

IV   The position of third-sector providers in the three healthcare systems

Within the group of non-public providers, third-sector organisations have a special status as they do not work in order to maximise profit. This allows them to generate trust amongst the public. Already before the turn to a more market-based system, voluntary organisations took part in health and social care provision in the countries under scrutiny here. In the UK, however, their role was only additional to the NHS, in which case they were supported by grants rather than the commissioning of services. These grants were significantly cut in the 1980s and charities were encouraged to compete. In England they now form an integral part of healthcare provision, while they play a mere additional role in Wales. In the Netherlands, the third sector is the traditional provider of secondary healthcare. Therefore no particular system of support for third-sector healthcare providers exists apart from the compulsory insurance system through which secondary care is financed. Under the statutory provisions of the Dutch Healthcare Market Organisation Act, any care provider is required to negotiate prices and quality with health insurers in order to have their services remunerated. All these developments required changes in the organisations' administration forcing them to operate more commercially.[40] Accordingly, in order to retain public trust the third sector had to become careful regarding the kind of contracts it would take over.[41]

---

[39] e.g. medical examination of the population by the *Gemeentelijke gezondheidsdienst* (GGD) on the basis of the *Wet Publieke Gezondheid 2008* (Public Health Act) and basic medical care for children under four by the community healthcentre.

[40] Further, on the difficulties for the third sector and organisational changes within them see Vincent-Jones and Mullen (n. 20 above), p. 166. On the particularities of the Dutch third sector, see van den Berg and Brandsen (n. 38 above); T. Brandsen and W. van de Donk, 'The third sector and the policy process in the Netherlands: A study in invisible ink' in J. Kendall (ed.), *Handbook on Third Sector Policy in Europe: Multi level processes and organised civil society* (Cheltenham/Northampton, MA: Edward Elgar, 2009), p. 140.

[41] See C. Hogg, *Citizens, Consumers & the NHS: Capturing voices* (Basingstoke/New York: Palgrave Macmillan, 2009), p. 170; Newdick (n. 30 above), p. 415.

A   England

The idea behind the competitive system in England is to improve health-care provision by giving the government the possibility to issue rules by which all the providers have to comply and create competition within the boundaries of these rules. Furthermore, PbR increases competition for better services, e.g. shorter waiting times, cleaner hospitals, etc., rather than for lower prices. This has been reported to have led to improvements in some of these fields, especially in reducing the length of waiting times.[42]

However, difficulties do occur on the side of the commissioners[43] as well as on the side of the providers, especially the third sector. Traditionally, third-sector providers tried to offer independently a service to the public regardless of economic constraints and governmental priorities. Now they have to win contracts from the government often through tightly specified procurement arrangements. The NHS contracts require high performance indicators no matter which kind of provider gets the contract (often referred to as 'level playing field') to achieve fair competition. Therefore even though the aim of third-sector providers is not to gain profit and the profit they do gain is used to support their primary charitable goal and not to satisfy shareholders, it is nevertheless necessary that they organise themselves in a 'profitable' way to be able to compete (e.g. they have to make sure the standard tariffs also cover overhead costs and adjust their services accordingly or make a conscious decision to subsidise them, otherwise they risk running at a loss). Furthermore, PbR means that care providers will only be paid for the procedures they perform. If therefore an organisation does not attract enough patients it might not survive. More than for public[44] or commercial providers, such requirements to be competitive are difficult for the third sector without changing their public mission and risking loss of trust.[45] However, other than in competitive markets where suspiciousness and prospective lawsuits lead to compliance with rules, trust plays an important role in healthcare where the patient is vulnerable and

---

[42] *Ibid.*, pp. 415 *et seq.*

[43] See further on the problems on the side of the PCTs, Vincent-Jones and Mullen (n. 20 above), pp. 154 *et seq.*; Abbott, Procter and Iacovou (n. 20 above), pp. 5 *et seq.*, 10 *et seq.*

[44] Further on the power of big NHS providers see Abbott, Procter and Iacovou (n. 20 above), pp. 5 *et seq.*

[45] Further on the difficulties for the third sector and organisational changes within them see Vincent-Jones and Mullen (n. 20 above), p. 166.

relies on the doctor. As a consequence third-sector providers might turn away from bidding for such contracts.[46]

Despite these difficulties the new system also offers opportunities to voluntary organisations as they enjoy societal trust. Furthermore, they can be more transparent about possibly diverging interests than commercial providers (who might have to fear losing customers if they declare that they did not recommend a certain treatment in order to increase profit for their shareholders) as those are still charitable interests (and if they only perform services that coincide with their primary goal there might not even be diverging interests). In addition, they can also try to influence policy-making via public patient-involvement processes. The possibilities that third-sector involvement can offer are recognised by the government which tries to encourage[47] the third sector to compete in the health market.[48]

B   Wales

In Wales third-sector healthcare organisations receive support from the state through grants and participate in public procurement, whilst the latter has gained in importance in comparison with the former. The procurement is subject to European procurement directives and UK procurement policy and allows private commercial and third-sector providers to compete in a level playing field.[49] Despite the integrated approach focusing mainly on the NHS, the Welsh government recognises advantages of voluntary organisations such as closeness to the patient and trust the public has in them and therefore tries to encourage their participation in the areas chosen for public procurement.[50]

However, third-sector organisations face many difficulties when attempting to bid for a public tender. Most of the issues are based on the fact that third-sector organisations are often smaller and inexperienced with public tendering. They might frequently have no access to 'start-up capital', be less

---

[46] See Newdick (n. 30 above), pp. 415 *et seq.*; Vincent-Jones and Mullen (n. 20 above), pp. 164 *et seq.*

[47] See e.g. Department of Health, 'No excuses. Embrace partnership now: Step towards change!' (2006).

[48] See Newdick (n. 30 above), pp. 418 *et seq.*; Vincent-Jones and Mullen (n. 20 above), p. 165.

[49] On the question of dominance of NHS providers and the problems that this causes for the commissioning bodies see Abott, Procter and Iacovou (n. 20 above), pp. 5 *et seq.*, 10 *et seq.*

[50] See Welsh Assembly Government (WAG), 'Procurement and the third sector: Guidance for the public sector in Wales' (2008), https://www.buy4wales.co.uk/PRP/10693.file.dld, pp. 4 *et seq.*

involved and informed at the early stages of planning tenders and might not be able to cope with the high level of bureaucratic duties imposed, especially if the contract concerned is only short term. Moreover, as there are no standard tariffs in Wales, they need to make a bid on the basis of full economic costs and compete with professional undertakings. However, third-sector organisations are often unaware of this and might bid on unrealistic prices. This means they later have to support the contract with their own means. Sometimes public authorities therefore take their bids less seriously than those from commercial undertakings and NHS providers, especially as the latter ones often are in a particularly strong position after having had a near monopoly before the turn to the market system in the 1990s. Moreover, procurement contracts might involve additional goals besides the actual service such as environmental and social aims which again might be more difficult to be met by voluntary organisations. In addition, the risks in public procurement are often on the side of the providers as they do not have any control over demand risk. This is especially difficult for the third sector. A specific problem for voluntary organisations in comparison to commercial ones is also that they lobby for their clientele which is sometimes against a certain government policy. Public authorities might then be uncomfortable with that situation and prefer a different provider.[51]

While several of these problems concern all non-public providers, some of them exist especially in the third sector. Therefore, the Welsh government has issued guidelines for public authorities when undertaking public procurement to enable the third sector to participate. This includes, inter alia, early consultations, training for tendering, considering longer-term contracts, reducing administrative burdens and the possibility of advance payments.[52]

C   The Netherlands

The role of the third sector in the Netherlands traditionally is a strong one in secondary care as hospitals used to be, and still are, almost exclusively organised as not-for-profit foundations.[53] However, since the objectives of

---

[51] See WAG (n. 50 above), pp. 7 *et seq.*; Abbott, Procter and Iacovou (n. 20 above), pp. 5 *et seq.*, 10 *et seq.* (especially on problems on the side of the commissioning bodies with strong NHS providers).

[52] See WAG (n. 50 above), pp. 12 *et seq.*

[53] Under the legal form of *stichting* traditional hospitals may make a profit, but the latter has to be reinvested in view of a social or ideal aim. See also n. 38 above.

the 2006 system in the Netherlands are comparable to those described above for England, third-sector providers in this country also need to organise themselves in a 'profitable' way to be able to meet the competitive conditions that healthcare purchasers require from them. The adaptation to the new system requires hospitals to negotiate separately with all insurers rather than with one representative of all insurers as previously, which increases transaction costs for hospitals[54] and the bargaining power of insurers. Furthermore, the system of managed competition induces negotiability of prices, quality and care volumes. Hospitals are faced with hard negotiations as insurers realise considerable savings through price cuts.[55] Negotiating quality confronts hospitals with requirements and indicators of multiple insurers,[56] if they cannot obtain the status of a preferred provider to a limited number of insurers.[57] Some hospitals have chosen to combine quality and price so as to correct errors at their own expense in return for higher initial payments.[58]

The new system also places hospitals in competition with their peers. Often they differentiate their services from each other by specialisation and investment in different technologies in order to attract (new) patients. Some hospitals, however, lack sufficient resources to do so. The reformed hospitals also redirect patients with complex clinical pictures to the public university hospitals for financial reasons: the refunding of their treatment is no different from that for patients with a less complex clinical picture.[59] The treatment of the latter is thus more lucrative.

V   The effects of EU competition law on third-sector providers in the three healthcare systems

The foregoing shows that the introduction of market mechanisms has affected the position of third-sector providers in healthcare. To assess these effects from a legal perspective this section investigates the effects of

[54] S. Meijer, R. Douven and B. van den Berg, 'Recent developments in Dutch hospitals' (2010), CPB Memorandum No. 239, www.cpb.nl/nl/pub/cpbreeksen/memorandum/239/memo239.pdf, p. 22.
[55] Ibid., pp. 5, 16.
[56] The requirements formulated by insurers fulfil a similar function as indicators used in public procurement.
[57] At the same time, a 'preferred-provider' policy might bear the risk of preventing patients to go to their local hospital if the latter is not included; consequently hospitals might lose market shares. Arguably, the latter is a consequence of the rationale of the Healthcare Insurance Act. Meijer, Douven and van den Berg (n. 54 above), p. 17.
[58] Ibid., p. 16.   [59] Ibid., p. 22.

EU competition law on the third sector providing healthcare as an alternative to public provision and commodification. First, there follows an assessment of whether competition law at all applies to healthcare provision and in particular to third-sector providers. Three separate subsections then consider consequences of the Treaty prohibitions on cartel agreements, abuse of a dominant position and state aid for third-sector providers in the respective national systems. The last subsection turns to the possible justification of restrictions of competition for healthcare providers as providers of services of general economic interest.

A   EU competition rules and healthcare by the third sector

Healthcare provision in England, Wales and the Netherlands will be subject to EU competition rules only if the providers of healthcare qualify as undertakings under the relevant Treaty provisions. That is the case where they exercise an economic activity,[60] regardless of whether they are organised as public, private or third sector.[61] Healthcare qualifies as an economic activity if, *in principle*, it can be carried out under market conditions, i.e. by a private actor with a view to profit.[62] As such this is conceivable for many healthcare services in the three countries under scrutiny, in particular in England and the Netherlands where all care providers have to compete with each other. However, activities not provided under market conditions do not fall under the definition of 'undertaking'.[63] In Wales, those areas of

---

[60] C-41/90 *Höfner and Elser (Höfner)* [1991] ECR I-1979, para 21: 'The concept of an undertaking encompasses every entity engaged in an economic activity, regardless of the legal status of the entity and the way in which it is financed'. This definition is by now established case law, see e.g. C-309/99 *Wouters and ors.* [2002] ECR I-1577, para. 46.

[61] This wide interpretation derives from the aims and objectives of the EU to establish an internal market. An entity might be treated as an undertaking with regard to some of its activities, while others fall outside the sphere of competition law. See C-6/72 *Continental Can* [1973] ECR 215, para. 25; 118/85, *Commission* v. *Italy (AAMS)* [1987] ECR 2599, para. 7; Opinion by AG Poiares Maduro in C-205/03 *FENIN II* [2006] ECR I-6295, para. 10; T-155/04 *SELEX* [2006] ECR II-4797, paras. 54 *et seq.*; C-49/07 *MOTOE* [2008] ECR I-4863, para. 25.

[62] C-475/99 *Ambulanz Glöckner* [2001] ECR I-8089, para. 20. It is not relevant whether an entity is profit-seeking.

[63] 118/85, *AAMS*, para. 7; AG Poiares Maduro in C-205/03 *FENIN II*, para. 13 (for a critique see AG Jacobs in C-222/04 *Cassa di Risparmio di Firenze* [2006] ECR I-295, para. 78). The Court has, inter alia, acknowledged that entities do not fall within the ambit of EU competition law, if they conduct activities with social objectives, e.g. organising and managing social security and certain insurance schemes in accordance with the principle of solidarity, and act under state supervision (ECJ C-180–184/98 *Pavlov* [2000] ECR I-6451, para. 118; Case C-218/00 *INAIL* [2002] ECR I-691, paras. 37 *et seq.*).

integrated healthcare provision that are provided exclusively by the NHS and for which the NHS hospitals are generally not in competition with each other, might not be offered under market conditions, in particular as they are financed through a tax-based system (Beveridge model). It is conceivable for a Member State to withdraw parts of its healthcare system on the basis of the case law that recognises certain activities to be outside of competition law if they are of a purely social nature.[64] More generally, it is perceivable that also third-sector organisations may be excluded from competition law if they resign themselves to purely social activities.[65]

Generally speaking, however, third-sector providers in the three healthcare systems have to be regarded as undertakings under EU competition law. Their exercise of an economic activity therefore not only subjects them to the prohibition clauses of EU competition law but also allows them to challenge developments in the market by other parties, i.e. public and commercial providers and public authorities.[66]

B Third-sector providers under Article 101 TFEU (ex Article 81 EC)

The restriction of competition is at the heart of Article 101(1) TFEU (ex Article 81(1) EC) and defines its scope.[67] In brief the concept refers to methods by which undertakings can reduce uncertainty about the future conduct of other market participants, be it through agreements, concerted practices or decisions, and which serve the purpose of orchestrating their economic activities.[68] Article 101(1) TFEU prohibits such methods as they are in conflict with the aim of competition law, which

---

[64] See esp. Case C-218/00 *INAIL*, para. 31: 'According to settled case-law, Community law does not affect the power of the Member States to organise their social security systems', inter alia quoting Cases C-158/96 *Kohll* [1998] ECR I-1931, para. 17 and C-157/99 *Geraets-Smits and Peerbooms* [2001] ECR I-5473, para. 44. The aspect of solidarity was decisive for Member States being allowed to withdraw activities from competitive markets in Cases C-159,160/91 *Poucet et Pistre* v. *Assurance Générales de France* [1993] ECR I-637, paras. 18 *et seq.*; T-319/99 *FENIN* [2003] ECR II-357, para. 37 and C-264 *et al./01 AOK Bundesverband* [2004] ECR I-2493, paras. 45 *et seq.*

[65] Again this could be based on the case law excluding purely social entities from the undertaking status. *Ibid.*

[66] Acts of public authorities can be challenged where they enable undertakings to escape from the constraints of EU competition law, 13/77 *INNO* v. *ATAB* [1977] ECR 2115, paras. 30–3.

[67] See A. Jones and B. E. Sufrin, *EC Competition Law*, 2nd edn (Oxford: Oxford University Press, 2004), p. 158.

[68] See 8/72, *Cementhandelaren* [1972] ECR 977; T-41/96 *Bayer AG* v. *Commission* [2000] ECR II-3383, para. 64.

is to foster competitive markets. Such markets require competitors to compete for better prices, better quality and better choices in terms of variety. A certain level of uncertainty on future conduct, market power and developments is inherent to competitive markets. Not every agreement necessarily is prohibited under competition law, however, and the decision has to be taken on a case-by-case basis in order to assess the anti- and pro-competitive aspects thereof.

This requirement can have positive and negative consequences for third-sector providers. Since competition law applies to all market players, third-sector providers of healthcare can invoke Article 101(1) TFEU in cases where their access to a particular healthcare market is inhibited by other parties. This could be promising where, despite the introduction of certain competitive elements in the market, other providers should become the preferred providers at the exclusion of voluntary organisations in particular tender procedures as this could be regarded as a vertical cartel. While the former English government had suggested the NHS providers to become preferred providers,[69] such a policy seems unlikely under the new coalition government, which is favouring the 'any willing-provider policy'.[70] In areas open for competition in Wales, EU public-procurement rules are followed and no preferred-provider policy is in place there. Therefore, the occurrence of a vertical cartel seems to be unlikely in these two countries. The situation is different for the Netherlands where private health insurers are authorised by law to pursue a policy of preferred providers. Where a network of preferred providers with a number of health insurers would, however, result in excluding particular hospitals from participating in the market, this could constitute an infringement of Article 101 TFEU.

Another situation in which third-sector providers could invoke Article 101(1) TFEU is that of horizontal cartels where non-competitive prices or conditions are imposed as the consequence of an agreement between a string of healthcare providers (e.g. specialised in the provision of particular care for a particular group of patients).[71] Competition law

---

[69] See e.g. A. Stratton, 'Burnham faces private healthcare sector challenge over NHS "bias"', *guardian.co.uk*, 6 January 2010, www.guardian.co.uk/society/2010/jan/06/nhs-challenge-private-healthcare-sector-competition.

[70] See e.g. D. Campbell, 'What's in store for public services under the coalition – on health', *guardian.co.uk*, 19 May 2010, www.guardian.co.uk/society/2010/may/19/public-services-policy-coalition-government.

[71] See NMa, *Richtsnoeren voor de zorgsector* (March 2010), www.nmanet.nl/nederlands/home/Actueel/Markten/Zorg/Index.asp.

may then provide an opportunity for third-sector providers as an outsider to gain (more competitive) access to the service provision.

The same argument can, however, also have chilling effects for third-sector providers who co-operate extensively, e.g. by exchanging best practises or establishing non-interference agreements. As seen in section II of this case study, the European tradition in its definition of the third sector also covers not-for-profit organisations that are not strictly non-profit and e.g. operate in co-operatives. The spirit of co-operation is an integral part of such organisations' identity and a way of establishing themselves against commercial providers. Such co-operation practises might, however, be regarded as collusion and could be challenged under Article 101(1) TFEU by competitors.[72]

C   Third-sector providers under Article 102 TFEU (ex Article 82 EC)

A particularly powerful instrument to be invoked is Article 102 TFEU (ex Article 82 EC), the subject of which mainly is the control of unilateral behaviour of a dominant firm. Dominance is a position of economic strength (market power) that enables one or more undertakings to prevent effective competition being maintained on the relevant market.[73] The question of what behaviour constitutes an abuse of economic power depends on the assessment of the facts of the individual case and is closely linked with the diagnosis of dominance on a market. This means that some behaviour may be deemed competitive, or at least neutral, when engaged in by non-dominant undertakings, while being classified as abusive when engaged in by dominant undertakings. Dominant and non-dominant firms are thus in crucially different positions.[74]

---

[72] The ECJ has in the past qualified cooperation within cooperatives as illegitimate cartels, e.g. T-61/89 *Dansk Pelsdyravlerforening* v. *Commission* [1992] ECR II-1931, paras. 52–4 with reference to joined Cases 209–213/84, *Ministère public* v. *Asjes and ors.* [1986] ECR 1425; 45/85, *Verband der Sachversicherer* v. *Commission* [1987] ECR 405. There was some deliberation whether co-operation could be justified due to the special character of a cooperative, but this was rejected in the end.

[73] 27/76, *United Brands Company and United Brands Continentaal BV* v. *Commission (United Brands)* [1978] ECR 207, para. 65.

[74] See A. Bavasso, 'The role of intent under Article 82 EC: From "flushing the Turkeys" to "spotting lionesses in Regent's Park"', *European Competition Law Review* 26 (2005), 616, 617; Jones and Sufrin (n. 67 above), pp. 253, 258. See also B. E. Hawk, *United States, Common Market and International Antitrust: A comparative guide*, 2nd edn (Aspen: Law & Business, 1990), pp. 788 *et seq.*

Article 102 TFEU may be especially helpful for third-sector providers to challenge established structures in health markets. For instance, the long-established NHS providers often have a very strong position due to their near monopoly before the turn to the market system in the 1990s. PCTs and LHBs have even complained about the limited power they have against such providers.[75] Third-sector providers could possibly challenge the conduct of such organisations under Article 102 TFEU if a particular contracting policy should constitute an abuse of their dominance.

In the Netherlands, healthcare providers have attempted to challenge the strong bargaining position of health insurers with the Dutch health-care authority and the Dutch competition authority.[76] The difficulty is, however, to demonstrate (an abuse of) a dominant position (with ulti-mately detrimental effects for patients). This could be the case where healthcare providers are subjected to anti-competitive tariffs or contract terms by the care-purchasing health insurers. According to the Dutch competition authority (*Nederlandse Mededingingsautoriteit*, NMa) this could, however, not be established in the existing market circumstances. It has to be assumed in particular that care services are purchased at conditions that allow a quantitatively and qualitatively predictable sup-ply in the interest of patients.[77] A similar line of reasoning is true where particular individual healthcare providers are not accepted for contract by health insurers. In these circumstances, Article 102 TFEU therefore currently does not enhance the position of third-sector providers in the Netherlands.

D   Third-sector providers under Article 107 TFEU (ex Article 87 EC)

A further avenue under EU competition law potentially opening an opportunity for the third sector is provided by Article 107(1) TFEU (ex Article 87(1) EC). The provision prohibits any kind of state aid,

---

[75] See the case study by Abbott, Procter and Iacovou (n. 20 above), pp. 5 *et seq.*

[76] See NMa (n. 71 above), pp. 14, 29–33; and NZa Annual Report (2009), www.nzajaarverslag.nl.

[77] NMa (n. 71 above), pp. 32–3. The NMa so far has not found a case of a buying power abuse, despite a number of providers claiming that their bargaining position would be considerably weaker compared to that of the health insurers. See 'NMa wijst klachten zorgaanbieders tegen zorgverzekeraars af', NMa press release, 27 May 2005, www.nma net.nl/nederlands/home/Actueel/Nieuws_Persberichten/NMa_Persberichten/2005/05–16.asp.

unless exempted under Article 107(2) or (3) TFEU. The state may, however, buy services for its citizens. The Court established four conditions in its famous *Altmark*[78] judgment which need to be fulfilled in order for such a transaction to fall outside the scope of state-aid rules. First, there must be clearly defined public service obligations. Secondly, the compensation must be calculated on transparent parameters established in advance. Thirdly, the compensation (including relevant revenue and reasonable profit) must not exceed what is necessary to cover the special obligation. Finally, the costs themselves must be reasonable; therefore a public procurement procedure should be undertaken or an analysis of what is normally paid for such a service in the sector has to be conducted. According to Hatzopoulos's analysis[79] of the General Court's *BUPA* judgment,[80] it might appear that in the field of politically sensitive areas, such as healthcare, the *Altmark* criteria are applied less strictly. Moreover, the European Commission has adopted Decision 2005/842/ EC, which sets out the conditions under which state aid in the form of public service compensation granted to small service providers, smaller transport providers, hospitals and social housing providers entrusted with the operation of services of general economic interest is compatible with the Common Market.[81]

Therefore hospitals providing medical services are excluded from EU rules on state aid. All other healthcare provision, however, has to respect the *Altmark* principles which require care providers to deliver their services according to prices covering full economic costs. Third-sector providers, however, used to dedicate profits made in other areas to develop their activities according to their particular ethos and their infrastructure further (e.g. in areas where they provide free services for the community). Under the *Altmark* principles, such cross-subsidy is not possible. Where applicable, competition law thus threatens this particular third-sector practice. In addition, grants that the third sector sometimes receives from the state (at least in Wales) could be regarded as state aid if those providers also compete with other providers in areas outside the grant-financed activities.

[78] See C-280/00 *Altmark* [2003] ECR I-7747.
[79] See Hatzopoulos (n. 5 above), pp. 236 *et seq.*   [80] See T-289/03 *BUPA* [2008] ECR II-81.
[81] See Arts. 1–2 of Decision 2005/842/EC, OJ EU 2005 L 312/67. See also A. Biondi and L. Rubini, 'Aims, effects and justifications: EC state aid law and its impact on national social policies' in E. Spaventa and M. Dougan (eds.), *Welfare and EU Law* (Oxford: Hart Publishing, 2005), pp. 89 *et seq.*, 94 *et seq.*; Hatzopoulos (n. 79 above), pp. 227 *et seq.*, 232 *et seq.*

On the other hand, state-aid rules might also offer possibilities for third-sector providers. In fact, they might be able to challenge public providers who use state facilities and resources that are not accessible for other competitors in the sector. If, for instance, in a competitive market no rent, or a rent below market rate, is being paid for the use of such resources, this could be challenged under state-aid rules by third-sector providers.

E   Third-sector providers under Article 106(2) TFEU (ex Article 86(2) EC)

Restrictions of competition in healthcare markets can be legitimised for services of general economic interest (SGEI) on the basis of Article 106(2) TFEU (ex Article 86(2) EC). It may seem counterintuitive to qualify public healthcare as a service of economic interest, as the provision of public healthcare is based on social interests. However, as in relation to the definition of an undertaking, the term 'economic' in SGEIs refers to the economic nature of the service in question, not to the underlying interest. Having said this, applying Article 106(2) TFEU is complex due to the difficulty in defining the concept of an SGEI.[82] It is safe to say, though, that insofar as comprehensive public healthcare for every citizen falls within the scope of application of EU competition law, it would also qualify as a SGEI. Therefore if an entity is deemed to infringe EU competition law rules, it may rely on Article 106(2) TFEU insofar as applying those rules would obstruct the performance, in law or fact, of providing the particular SGEI assigned to it.[83]

The relevance of Article 106(2) TFEU lies in the recognition of general interests to guarantee certain public services. The drafters of the Treaty acknowledged that the continuance of SGEIs should not be jeopardised

---

[82] The General Court recently stated 'there is no clear and precise regulatory definition of the concept of an SGEI mission and no established legal concept definitively fixing the conditions that must be satisfied' (T-298/03 *BUPA*, para. 165). For more detail on the interpretation and development of SGEIs, see Neergaard in ch. 7 of this volume.

[83] Obstruction in this sense means that it would not be possible for the undertaking to perform the particular tasks entrusted to it under economically acceptable conditions: C-157/94 *Commission* v. *The Netherlands (Dutch Electricity Monopoly)* [1997] ECR I-5899, para. 52. Moreover, the restriction in question has to be proportional and the development of trade may not be affected in a way as would be contrary to EU interests. The proportionality test especially safeguards that the exception from the competition rules is necessary in the light of the task assigned to the service provider. See Neergaard (n. 5 above), pp. 211 *et seq.*

by an indiscriminate application of the Treaty prohibitions. The objective of Article 106(2) TFEU therefore is the efficient provision of SGEIs which respects the balancing of the EU's interest in economic integration with the Member States' interest in using certain undertakings as an instrument of economic, fiscal or social policy.[84]

While Article 106(2) TFEU thus (potentially) recognises the autonomy of Member States to subject their public healthcare systems to strict regulation or other market intervention measures, the application of EU competition rules does not seem to generally obstruct the performance of the tasks of public, commercial or third-sector healthcare providers in the three countries under scrutiny here, as they are positioned in (managed) market systems where competition is wanted. Conversely, one may consider whether integrating third-sector providers in the healthcare systems pursues a public interest in itself that justifies an exception under Article 106(2) TFEU. The aim would be to guarantee an accessible and affordable system of secondary care through organisations bound not to seek profits, rooted in their community and providing especially socially responsible care. This would require, however, a clear government policy that satisfies the legal requirements under Article 106(2) TFEU that the operation of the SGEI has been entrusted to third-sector providers by an act of public authority.[85]

VI   Conclusion

The purpose of this case study was to examine whether the application of EU competition law predominantly constitutes an opportunity or a threat to the third sector in providing healthcare services as an alternative to state provision and commodification. To illustrate the point, three exemplary healthcare systems have been examined. It has been shown that the commodification processes in these systems, on the one hand, enables third-sector organisations to play a bigger role in healthcare provision. On the other hand, the introduction of more competition requires them to adapt to the changed (market) conditions. In particular,

[84] C-202/88 *French Republic* v. *Commission (Telecommunications Terminal Equipment)* [1991], para. 12; C-157/94 *Dutch Electricity Monopoly*, para. 39; Case C-67/96 *Albany* [1999] ECR I-5751, para. 103. See also Opinion of AG Jacobs in C-475/99 *Ambulanz Glöckner*, para. 184.

[85] No specific formal act is needed as long as it can be distilled from the combination of rules: see C-159/94 *Commission* v. *French Republic* [1997] ECR I-5815, para. 66; Commission Decision N 541/2004 and N 542/2004 (n. 36 above), para. 4.2.1.

they have to organise themselves in a professional and more cost-efficient way to be able to compete. As a consequence, public perception of their activities as mainly ethos-oriented might change. Where they adapt to the new environments successfully – inter alia, using their competitive advantage of public trust in them – they will in principle be subject to EU competition law as they compete in a market and thus provide an economic activity. Charitable activities without an appreciable effect on competition, however, are not subject to competition law.

The consequences of this are mixed. On the one hand, EU competition law can have an enabling function for third-sector providers. They can invoke Article 101 TFEU to gain access to markets closed by a collusion of public and/or private undertakings and they can challenge abusive behaviour of a dominant public or private undertaking under Article 102 TFEU. The latter seems to be especially valuable in the UK system where NHS providers are particularly strong. Third-sector providers might also be able to invoke state-aid rules against preferential treatment (use of state facilities) of NHS providers. These claims might be brought before the national courts or by raising a complaint to the relevant national competition authorities and/or the European Commission.

On the other hand, competition rules also put constraints on third-sector organisations. Many such organisations traditionally operate in co-operatives, which could be challenged under Article 101 TFEU. In addition, state-aid rules will prevent cross-subsidy within the organisation forcing third-sector providers to compartmentalise their various activities due to the relative concept of 'undertaking'. A system of grants, as partly still existent in Wales, may also constitute a competition law problem.

It appears, however, that the EU still partly recognises the primary responsibility of the Member States and the special function of healthcare as a SGEI. Decision 2005/842/EC excludes medical services provided in hospitals from the state-aid rules and Article 106(2) TFEU provides a justification ground for SGEIs. While the provision of healthcare services in a given system arguably may qualify as a SGEI, this is not self-evident and needs to be demonstrated in a given case.

Overall, the conclusions of this case study seem to confirm the general assumption, expressed in the first few chapters of this book, that economic integration is far ahead of social integration, which is adjacent to the former and keeps up only at a lower speed. At present the system of hard EU competition law appears to be generally flexible enough for third-sector providers, provided they either function in a completely charitable way or adopt an efficiency-driven way of operating in pursuing their social objectives. On balance, competition law provides both challenges to maintaining an essentially ethos-oriented healthcare activity and opportunities for providing alternative healthcare services of a particularly socially responsible character. In light of the social dimensions of European integration, it might be desirable to minimise the challenges by an overall interpretative approach offering broader justifications for third-sector providers in order to fully explore the benefits of not-for-profit-oriented service provision.

BIBLIOGRAPHY

Abbott, S., S. Procter and N. Iacovou, 'NHS purchaser–provider relationships in England and Wales: The view from primary care', *Social Policy & Administration* 43 (2009), 1

Ahlquist, J. A., and C. Breunig, 'Country clustering in comparative political economy', MPIfG Discussion Paper 5 (2009)

Albareda, L., 'The changing role of governments in corporate social responsibility: Drivers and responses', *Business Ethics: A European Review* 17 (2008), 347

Albareda, L., J. M. Lozana and T. Ysa, 'Public policies on corporate social responsibility: The role of governments in Europe', *Journal of Business Ethics* 74 (2007), 391

Alcock, P., 'A strategic unity: Defining the third sector in the UK', *Voluntary Sector Review* 1 (2010), 5

Allen, F., and D. Gale, 'A comparative theory of corporate governance', Wharten Working Paper Series 3 (2002), p. 1

Alston, P. (ed.), *The EU and Human Rights* (Oxford: Oxford University Press, 1999)
    Non-State Actors and Human Rights (Oxford: Oxford University Press, 2005)

Alter, K., 'Who are the masters of the Treaty?: European governments and the European Court of Justice' in K. Alter (ed.), *The European Court's Political Power – Selected essays* (Oxford: OUP, 2009) (first published in *International Organization* 52 (1998), 121
    The European Court's Political Power: Selected essays (Oxford: Oxford University Press, 2009)
    'The European Union's legal system and domestic policy: spillover or backlash' in K. Alter (ed.), *The European Court's Political Power: Selected essays* (Oxford: Oxford University Press, 2009)

Alter, K., and S. Meunier-Atsahalia, 'Judicial politics in the European Community', *CPS* 26 (1994), 316

Ammassari, S., and R. Black, 'Harnessing the potential of migration and return to promote development: Applying concepts to West Africa', IOM Migration Research Series 5 (2001)

Angenendt, S., 'Circular migration: A sustainable concept for migration policy?', SWP Comments No. 11 (2007)

Anheier, H. K., 'The third sector in Europe: Five theses', Civil Society Working Paper (2002)

Antoniadis, A., 'Social Europe and/or global Europe? Globalisation and flexicurity as debates on the future of Europe', *Cambridge Review of International Affairs* 21 (2008), 327

Apeldoorn, B. V., *Transnational Capitalism and the Struggle over European Integration* (London: Routledge, 2002)

Apostolakou, A., and G. Jackson, 'Corporate social responsibility in Western Europe: An institutional mirror or substitute?', University of Bath, School of Management, Working Paper Series 1 (2009)

Århammar, A., 'Migration och integration – om framtidens arbetsmarknad. Bilaga 4 till Långtidsutredningen 2003/04', *SOU* 73 (2004)

Armour, J., *et al.*, 'How do legal rules evolve? Evidence from a cross-country comparison of shareholder, creditor and worker protection', ECGI Working Paper 129 (2009)

Arnull, A., 'The Americanization of EU law scholarship' in A. Arnull, P. Eackhout and T. Tridimas (eds.), *Continuity and Change in EU Law: Essays in honour of Sir Francis Jacobs* (Oxford: Oxford University Press, 2008)

Ashiagbor, D., *The European Employment Strategy* (Oxford: Oxford University Press, 2005)

Atkinson, T. *et al.*, *The EU and Social Inclusion* (Oxford: Oxford University Press, 2002)

Axelrod, R., 'Review symposium: Beyond the tragedy of the commons', *Perspectives on Politics* 8 (2010)

Aylward, M., 'Health Commission Wales: A review', Wales Centre for Health, 2008, www.wales.nhs.uk/sites3/docopen.cfm?orgid=222&id=99810&uuid=BDD78622-1143-E756-5C584B471069B525

Baelz, K., and T. Baldwin, 'The end of the real seat theory (Sitztheorie): The European Court of Justice decision in Ueberseering of 5 November 2002 and its impact on German and European company law', *German Law Journal* 3 (2002)

Bakker, F. G. A., P. Groenewegen and F. Hond, 'A bibliometric analysis of 30 years of research and theory on corporate social responsibility and corporate social performance', *Business & Society* 44 (2005), 283

Balassa, B., *International Economic Integration* (Amsterdam: Elsevier, 1961)
The Theory of Economic Integration (Homewood, IL: R. D. Irwin, 1961)

Baldwin, R., and C. Wyplosz, *The Economics of European Integration* (London: McGraw Hill 2009)

Baquero Cruz, J., *Between Competition and Free Movement* (Oxford: Hart, 2002)
'Services of general interest and EC law' in G. de Búrca (ed.), *EU Law and the Welfare State: In search of solidarity* (Oxford: Oxford University Press, 2005)

Barkhuysen, T., and S. Lindenbergh (eds.), *Constitutionalisation of Private Law* (Leiden, Boston: Martinus Nijhoff, 2006)

Barnard, C., *EC Employment Law*, 2nd edn (Oxford: Oxford University Press, 2007)
'*Viking* and *Laval*: An introduction', *Cambridge Yearbook of European Legal Studies* 10 (2008), 463
Barnard, C. (ed.), *The Cambridge Yearbook of European Legal Studies* (Oxford: Hart Publishing, 2007/2008)
Barón Crespo, E., 'Economic governance and the Treaty of Lisbon', Contribution to Global Jean Monnet – ECSA-World Conference 2010
Bartholomée, Y., and H. Maarse, 'Empowering the Chronically Ill? Patient collectives in the new Dutch health insurance system', *Health Policy* 84 (2007), 163
Bavasso, A., 'The role of intent under Article 82 EC: From "flushing the turkeys" to "spotting lionesses in Regent's Park"', *European Competition Law Review* 26 (2005), 616
Bebchuk, L., A. Cohen and A. Farrell, 'What matters in corporate governance?', *Review of Financial Studies* 22 (2009), 783
Beckert, J., 'Wer zähmt den Kapitalismus' in J. Beckert *et al.* (eds.), *Transformation des Kapitalismus* (Frankfurt am Main: Campus, 2006)
Behrens, P., 'Public services and the internal market: An Analysis of the Commission's Communication on Services of General Interest in Europe', *European Business Organisation Law Review* 2 (2001), 469
'Centros and company law' in G. Ferrarini, K. J. Hopt and E. Wymeersch (eds.), *Capital Markets in the Age of the Euro: Cross-border transactions, listed companies and regulation* (Den Haag: Kluwer Law International, 2002)
'Europäische Gesellschaft' in M. A. Dauses (ed.), *EU-Wirtschaftsrecht* (Munich: Beck, 2010)
Bercusson, B., 'The trade union movement and the European Union: judgment day', *ELJ* 13 (2007), 279
European Labour Law (Cambridge: Cambridge University Press, 2009)
'The Lisbon Treaty and Social Europe', *ERA Forum* 10 (2009), 87
Berg, E. M. van den, and T. Brandsen, 'The Dutch third sector and the European Union: Connecting citizens to the EU?', Scientific Council for Government Policy, 2007, www.wrr.nl/content.jsp?objectid=4039
Bertelsmann Stiftung (ed.), *Die gesellschaftliche Verantwortung von Unternehmen* (Gütersloh, 2005)
Berwick, D. M., 'Improvement, trust, and the healthcare workforce', *Qual Saf Health Care* 12 (2003), 448
Besselink, L., 'Integration and immigration: The vicissitudes of the Dutch "Inburgering"' in E. Guild, K. Groenendijk and S. Carrera (eds.), *Illiberal Liberal States: Immigration, citizenship and integration in the EU* (Aldershot: Ashgate, 2009)
Besson, S., 'Special issue on citizenship', *ELJ* 13 (2007), 573
Best, J., 'From the top-down: the new financial architecture and the re-embedding of global finance', *New Political Economy* 8 (2003), 363

Bieler, A., *The Struggle for a Social Europe: Trade unions and EMU in times of global restructuring* (Manchester: Manchester University Press, 2006)

Bihan, D. C. Le and A. Moriceau, 'Services d'intérêt économique general et valeurs communes', *Revue du Marché commun et de l'Union europénne*, 519 (Juin 2008), 358

Bilchitz, D., *Poverty and Fundamental Rights: The justification and enforcement of socio-economic rights* (Oxford: Oxford University Press, 2007)

Biondi, A., and L. Rubini, 'Aims, effects and justifications: EC state aid law and its impact on national social policies' in E. Spaventa and M. Dougan (eds.), *Welfare and EU Law* (Oxford: Hart Publishing, 2005)

Blanpain, R., and A. Świątkowski (eds.), *The Laval and Viking Cases: Freedom of services establishment v. Industrial conflict in the European Economic Area and Russia* (Deventer: Kluwer, 2009)

Block, F., 'Karl Polanyi and the writing of *The Great Transformation*', *Theory and Society* 32 (2003), 275

Bohle, D., and B. Greskovits, 'Neoliberalism, embedded neoliberalism and neo-corporatism: Towards transnational capitalism in Central-Eastern Europe', *West European Politics* 30 (2007), 443

Bolukbasi, T., 'On consensus, constraint and choice: Economic and monetary integration and Europe's welfare states', *JEPP* 16 (2009), 527

Bonoli, G., 'Classifying welfare states: A two-dimension approach', *JnlSoc.Pol.* 26 (1997), 351

Borrel, C., 'Enquêtes Annuelles de Recensement 2004 et 2005: Près de 5 million d'immigrés à la mide de 2004', Insee Première N° 1098 (2006)

Bovis, C., 'Financing services of general interest in the EU: How do public procurement and state aids interact to demarcate between market forces and protection?', *ELJ* 11 (2005), 75

Bowen, H., *Social Responsibilities of the Businessman* (New York: Harper & Row, 1953)

Brandsen, T., and W. van de Donk, 'The third sector and the policy process in the Netherlands: A study in invisible ink' in J. Kendall (ed.), *Handbook on Third Sector Policy in Europe: Multi level processes and organised civil society* (Cheltenham/Northampton, MA: Edward Elgar, 2009)

Bratton, W., J. McCahery and E. Vermeulen, 'How does corporate mobility affect lawmaking? A comparative analysis', ECGI Law Working Paper 91 (2008), p. 1

Braun, S., 'Gesellschaftliches Engagement von Unternehmen', *Politik und Zeitgeschichte* 31 (2008), 6
  Gesellschaftliches Engagement von Unternehmen. Der deutsche Weg im internationalen Kontext (Wiesbaden: VS-Verlag für Sozialwissenschaften, 2010)

Bronzini, G., 'The social dilemma of European integration', *Law and Critique* 19 (2008), 255

Brouwer, E., *Digital Borders and Real Rights: Effective remedies for third-country nationals in the Schengen information system* (Leiden: Martinus Nijhoff Publishers, 2007)

Browne, J., S. Deakin and F. Wilkinson, *Social Rights and European Market Integration* (University of Cambridge CBR WP 253, December 2002)

Bruce, M., *The Rise of the Welfare State* (London: Weidenfeld and Nicolson, 1973)

Bruun, N., and B. Hepple, 'Economic policy and labour law' in B. Hepple and B. Veneziani (eds.), *The Transformation of Labour Law in Europe* (Oxford/Portland: Hart Publishing, 2009)

Buchanan, J., 'Europe's constitutional opportunity' in J. Buchanan *et al.* (eds.), *Europe's Constitutional Future* (London: The Institute of Economic Affairs, 1990)

Buendia Sierra, J. L., *Exclusive Rights and State Monopolies under EC Law: Article 86 (formerly Article 90) of the EC Treaty* (Oxford: Oxford University Press, 1999)

Buendia Sierra, L., 'Article 86: Exclusive rights and other anti-competitive state measures' in J. Faull and A. Nikpay (eds.), *The EC Law of Competition* (Oxford: Oxford University Press, 2007)

Bundesamt für Migration und Flüchtlinge, *Konzept für einen bundesweiten Integrationskurs. Überarbeitete Neuauflage* (Bundesregierung, Berlin, 2009)

Búrca, G. de, *EU Law and the Welfare State* (Oxford: Oxford University Press, 2005)
   'Rethinking law in neofunctionalist theory', *JEPP* 12 (2005), 310
   'Towards European welfare' in G. de Búrca (ed.), *EU Law and the Welfare State* (Oxford: Oxford University Press, 2005)

Búrca, G. de, and J. Scott, *Law and Governance in the EU and the US* (Oxford *et al.*: Hart Publishing, 2006)

Burger, A., and V. Veldheer, 'The growth of the nonprofit sector in the Netherlands', *Non-profit and Voluntary Sector Quarterly* 30 (2001), 221

Burley, A.-M., 'Europe before the Court: A political theory of legal integration', *International Organization* 47 (1993), 41

Büschel, I., 'La constitution économique de l'Union européenne et l'environnement' in L. Giepi (ed.), *La Constitution économique de l'Union Européenne* (Brussels: Bruylant, 2008)

Bussler, C., 'Ergebnisse des EU-Konsultationsprozesses zu Rahmenbedingungen für die soziale Verantwortung von Unternehmen' in A. Fonari and C. Bussler (eds.), *Sozial- und Umweltstandards bei Unternehmen: Chancen und Grenzen* (Munich: Digitaldruck leibi.de, 2005)

Camara, H., *Spiral of Violence* (London: Sheed and Ward, 1971)

Campbell, D., 'What's in store for public services under the coalition – on health', *guardian.co.uk*, 19 May 2010, www.guardian.co.uk/society/2010/may/19/public-services-policy-coalition-government

Caporaso, J., and S. Tarrow, 'Polanyi in Brussels: Supranational institutions and the transnational embedding of markets', *International Organization* 63 (2009), 593

Cappelletti, M., M. Seccombe and J. Weiler (eds.), *Integration Through Law: Europe and the American federal experience* (Berlin and New York: Walter de Gruyter, 1985)

Care Quality Commission, 'How the NHS is structured' (2010), www.cqc.org.uk/usingcareservices/healthcare/makingdecisionsaboutnhshealthcare/howthenhsisstructured.cfm

Carrera, S., *A Comparison of Integration Programmes in the EU: Trends and Weaknesses*, CHALLENGE Research Paper (Brussels: CEPS, 2006)

  In Search Of The Perfect Citizen?: The intersection between integration, immigration and nationality in the EU (Leiden: Martinus Nijhoff Publishers, 2009)

Carroll, A. B., 'A three-dimensional conceptual model of corporate social performance', *Academy of Management Review* 4 (1979), 497

  'Corporate social responsibility: Evolution of a definitional construct', *Business & Society* 38 (1999), 268

Carrubba, C., 'Judicial behavior under political constraints: Evidence from the European Court of Justice', *American Political Science Review* 102 (2008), 435

Castles, S., 'The guest-worker in Western Europe: An obituary', *International Migration Review* 20 (1986), 761

  'Back to the future? Can Europe meet its labour needs through temporary migration?', International Migration Institute (IMI) Working Paper 1 (2006)

Cernat, L., 'The emerging European corporate governance model: Anglo-Saxon, Continental, or still the century of diversity?', *Journal of European Public Policy* 1 (2004), 147

Chalmers, D., G. Davies and G. Monti, *European Union Law*, 2nd edn (Cambridge: Cambridge University Press, 2010)

Checkel, J., 'Social construction and integration', *JEPP* 6 (1999), 268

Christiansen, T., K. Jørgensen and A. Wiener, *The Social Construction of Europe* (London *et al.*: Sage, 1999)

Chryssochoou, D., *Theorizing European Integration*, 2nd edn (Abingdon: Routledge, 2008)

Cichowski, R., 'Courts, rights and democratic participation', *Comparative Political Studies* 39 (2006), 50

Coase, R. H., 'The nature of the firm', *Economica* 3 (1937), 386

Cohen, J., and C. Sabel, 'Directly-deliberative polyarchy', *ELJ* 3 (1997), 343

Compa, L., 'Corporate social responsibility and workers' rights', *Comparative Labour Law and Policy Journal* 30 (2008), 1

Conant, L., *Justice Contained: Law and politics in the European Union* (Ithaca: Cornell University Press, 2002)

  'Individuals, courts and the development of European social rights', *Comparative Political Studies* 39 (2006), 76

Conseil Economique et Social, 'Analysis of the implications of the Lisbon Treaty on services of general interest and proposals for implementation', Discussion paper drawn up by European experts (2008)

Constantinesco, L. J., 'La Constitution économique de la CEE', *R.T.D.E.* 2 (1977), 249

Craig, P., *EU Administrative Law* (Oxford: Oxford University Press, 2006)

Craig, P. and G. de Búrca, *EU Law* (Oxford: Oxford University Press, 2007)
    EU Law: Text, cases and materials, 4th edn (Oxford: Oxford University Press, 2008)

Crouch, C., 'The state: Economic management and incomes policy' in P. Edwards (ed.), *Industrial Relations: Theory and evidence in Britain*, 2nd edn (Oxford: Blackwell Publishers, 2003)

Cuesta Gonzalez, M., and C. Valor Martinez, 'Fostering corporate social responsibility through public initiative: From the EU to the Spanish case', *Journal of Business Ethics* 55 (2004), 275

Curtin, D., 'European legal integration: Paradise lost' in D. Curtin (ed.), *European Integration and Law* (Antwerp/Oxford: Intersentia, 2006)

Cutler, C., *Private Power and Public Authority* (Cambridge: Cambridge University Press, 2003)

Dallas, G. S., *Governance and Risk: An analytical handbook for investors, managers, directors, and stakeholders* (New York: McGraw-Hill Companies, 2004)

Damjanovic, D., and B. de Witte, 'Welfare integration through EU law: The overall picture in the light of the Lisbon Treaty' in U. Neergaard, R. Nielsen and L. M. Roseberry (eds.), *Integrating Welfare Functions into EU Law: From Rome to Lisbon* (Copenhagen: DJØF, 2009)

Dani, M., 'Constitutionalism and dissonances: Has Europe paid off its debt to functionalism?', *ELI* 15 (2009), 324

Däubler, W., *Der Kampf um einen weltweiten Tarifvertrag* (Baden-Baden: Nomos, 2002)

Davis, D., 'Socioeconomic rights: Do they deliver the goods?', *ICON* 6 (2008), 687

Deak, D., 'Cartesio: A step forward in interpreting the EC freedom to emigrate', *Tax Notes International* 54 (2009), 493

Deakin, S., 'The capability concept and the evolution of the European Social Model' in M. Dougan, and E. Spayenta (eds.), *Social Welfare and EU Law* (Oxford: Hart, 2005)
    'Regulatory competition after *Laval*', *Cambridge Yearbook of European Legal Studies* 10 (2008), 581

Deakin, S., and A. Supiot, *Capacitas* (Oxford: Oxford University Press, 2009)

Delhey, J., 'European social integration: From convergence of countries to transnational relations between people', WZB Discussion Paper, Berlin, February 2004, http://skylla.wzb.eu/pdf/2004/i04–201.pdf

Department of Health, 'No excuses. Embrace partnership now: Step towards change!', Report on the Third Sector Commissioning Task Force, 2006

Department of Health, 'Primary care trust procurement guide for health services', 25 March 2010, www.dh.gov.uk/en/MediaCentre/DH_4015576

Deutsch, K., *The Analysis of International Relations* (Englewood Cliffs, NJ: Prentice Hall, 1971)

Devroe, W., 'Deugdelijk bestuur van overheidsondernemingen. (autonome overheidsbedrijven, publiekrechtelijke naamloze vennootschappen)' ['Corporate governance of publicly held undertakings'], *Tijdschrift voor Rechtspersoon en Vennootschap* (1998)

'Challenges for economic governance and economic law in Europe', *Maastricht Journal of European and Comparative Law* 10 (2003), 335–44

DGB, 'Stellungnahme zum Grünbuch der Europäischen Kommission Europäische Rahmenbedingungen für die soziale Verantwortung der Unternehmen', Berlin 2001, http://ec.europa.eu/comni/employment_social/soc-dial/csr/pdf/082-SP TUNAT_DGB_DE_01%20i23i_de.pdf

DGIS, *Verband tussen migratie en ontwikkeling* (Ministerie van Buitenlandse Zaken, 2004)

Doh, J. P., and T. R. Guay, 'Corporate social responsibility, public policy, and NGO activism in Europe and the United States: An institutional-stakeholder perspective', *Journal of Management Studies*, 47 (2005)

Dougan, M., 'The spatial restructuring of national welfare states within the European Union: The contribution of Union citizenship and the relevance of the Treaty of Lisbon' in U. Neergaard, R. Nielsen and L. M. Roseberry (eds.), *Integrating Welfare Functions into EU Law: From Rome to Lisbon* (Copenhagen: DJØF Forlag, 2009)

Drinoczi, T., 'Some elements of the economic constitution of the EU: Social market economy and relevant fundamental rights', *Free Law Journal* 1 (2005), 68

Duff, A., *The Treaty of Amsterdam. Text and Commentary* (London: Federal Trust/Sweet & Maxwell, 1997)

Dukes, R., 'Constitutionalising employment relations: Sinzheimer, Kahn-Freund, and the role of labour law', *J Law&Soc* 35 (2008), 341

Duperon, O., 'Service public ou service d'intérêt économique général?' in L. Giepi (ed.), *La Constitution économique de l'Union Européenne* (Brussels: Bruylant, 2008)

Dworkin, R., *Freedoms Law: The moral reading of the American Constitution* (Oxford: Oxford University Press, 1996)

Easterley, L., and P. Miesing, 'NGOs, social venturing and community citizenship behaviour', *Business & Society* 48 (2009), 538

Ebke, W. F., 'Centros: Some realities and some mysteries', *The American Journal of Comparative Law* 48 (2000), 623

Eichenhofer, E., *Sozialrecht*, 4th edn (Tübingen: Mohr-Siebeck, 2003)

Eidenmüller, H., 'Theorien zur Bestimmung des Gesellschaftsstatus und Wettbewerb der Gesellscahftsrechte' in H. Eidenmüller (ed.),

Ausländische Kapitalgesellschaften im deutschen Recht (Munich: Beck, 2004)

'Abuse of law in the context of European insolvency law', *European Company and Financial Law Review* (2009), http://ssrn.com/abstract=1353932

Eisele, K., 'Making Europe more competitive for highly-skilled immigration', Maastricht Graduate School of Governance Policy brief 2 (2010)

Ekenger, K., and F. Wallen, *Invandring för tillväxt och nya job* (Stockholm: Svenskt Näringsliv, 2002)

Eklund, R., 'A Swedish perspective on *Laval*', *Comparative Labour Law and Policy Journal* 29 (2008), 551

El-Agraa, A. M., *The European Union: Economics and policies* (Harlow: Prentice Hall, 2004)

Emiliou, N., *The Principle of Proportionality in European Law: A comparative study* (The Hague: Kluwer Law International, 1996)

Engert, A., 'Rechtslage nach dem Ende der Sitztheorie' in H. Eidenmüller (ed.), *Auslänische Kapitalgesellschaften* (Munich: Beck, 2004)

Enriques, L., and T. Tröger, 'Issuer choice in Europe', ECGI Working Paper 90 (2008), p. 1

Epstein, G., A. Hillman and A. Weiss, 'Creating illegal immigrants', *Journal of Population Economics* 12 (1999) 3

Esping-Andersen, G., *The Three Worlds of Welfare Capitalism* (Cambridge: Cambridge University Press, 1990)

Social Foundations of Post-Industrial Economies (Oxford: Oxford University Press, 1999)

Evers, A., 'Mixed welfare systems and hybrid organizations: Changes in the governance and provision of social services', *Intl Journal of Public Administration* 28 (2005), 737

Evers, A., and J.-L. Laville, 'Social services by social enterprises: On the possible contributions of hybrid organisations and a civil society' in A. Evers and J.-L. Laville (eds.), *The Third Sector in Europe* (Cheltenham: Edward Elgar, 2004)

Evers, A. *et al*, 'Defining the third sector in Europe' in A. Evers and J.-L. Laville (eds.), *The Third Sector in Europe* (Cheltenham: Edward Elgar, 2004)

Everson, M., 'The legacy of the market citizen' in J. Shaw and G. More (eds.), *New Legal Dynamics of European Union* (Oxford: Clarendon Press, 1995)

Farjat, G., 'La Constitution économique de l'Europe et le couplage droit – économie' in L. Giepi (ed.), *La Constitution économique de l'Union Européenne* (Brussels: Bruylant, 2008)

Ferrera, M., *The Boundaries of Welfare* (Oxford: Oxford University Press, 2005)

Fitoussi, J.-P., and F. K. Padoa Schioppa (eds.), *Report on the State of the European Union* (London: Palgrave Macmillan, 2005)

Flaesch-Mougin, C., 'Les aspect constitutionnels du budget de l'Union européenne' in L. Giepi (ed.), *La Constitution économique de l'Union Européenne* (Brussels: Bruylant, 2008)

Fligstein, N., *Euroclash: The EU, European identity, and the future of Europe* (Oxford: Oxford University Press, 2008)

Flynn, L., 'Competition policy and public services in EC law after the Maastricht and Amsterdam Treaties' in D. O'Keeffe and P. Tworney (eds.), *Legal Issues of the Amsterdam Treaty* (Oxford: Hart Publishing, 1999)

Follesdal, A., and S. Hix, 'Why there is a democratic deficit in the EU: A response to Majone and Moravcsik', *JCMS* 44 (2006), 533

FORSA/Gesellschaft für Sozialforschung und statistische Analysen, *Corporate Social Responsibility in Deutschland* (Berlin, 2005)

'Free business movement and the right to strike in the European Community: Two views', editorial, *Comparative Labor Law and Policy Journal* 29 (2008), 547

Freeman, R., 'People flows in globalization', National Bureau of Economic Research Working Paper 12315 (2006)

Freeman, R. E., *Strategic Management: A stakeholder approach* (Boston: Pitman, 1984)

Frenz, W., 'Dienste von algemeinem wirtschaftlichen Interesse', *Europarecht* 36 (2000), 901

Freshfields, 'Implementation of the EU cross-border merger directive in Germany' (2007), www.freshfields.com/publications/pdfs/2007/may21/18736.pdf

Friedman, M., 'The social responsibility of business is to increase its profits', *New York Times*, 13 September 1970

Gajewska, K., 'The emergence of a European labour protest movement?', *European Journal of Industrial Relations* 14 (2008), 104

Gänßler, G., '"Inspire Art": Briefkastengesellschaften "on the move"', *DStR* 50 (2003), 2167

Garrett, G., D. R. Kelemen and H. Schultz, 'The European Court of Justice, national governments, and legal integration in the European Union', *International Organization* 52 (1998), 149

Gelter, M., 'Tilting the balance between capital and labour? The effects of regulatory arbitrage in European corporate law on employees', *Fordham International Law Journal* 33 (2010)

Gemici, K., 'Karl Polanyi and the antinomies of embeddedness', *Socio-Economic Review* 6 (2008), 5

Gerber, D., 'Constitutionalising the economy: German neo-liberalism, competition law and the "new" Europe', *Am. J. Comp. L.* 42 (1994), 25
  'Re-imagining the story of European competition law', *OJLS* 20 (2000), 155

Gerven, D. van, and P. Storm, *The European Company* (Cambridge: Cambridge University Press, 2006)

Gerven, W. V., 'Schets van een Belgisch economisch grondslagenrecht', *SEW* (1971), 418

Giddens, A., *The Third Way and Its Critics* (Cambridge: Polity, 2000)
  'A social model for Europe?' in A. Giddens, P. Diamond and R. Liddle (eds.), *Global Europe, Social Europe* (Cambridge: Polity, 2006)
Giddens, A., P. Diamond and R. Liddle (eds.), *Global Europe, Social Europe* (Cambridge: Polity, 2006)
Gill, S., 'European governance and new constitutionalism: Economic and monetary union and alternatives to disciplinary neoliberalism in Europe', *New Political Economy*, 3(5) (1998), 5
  'New constitutionalism democratisation and global political economy', *Pacifica Review: Peace, Security & Global Change*, 10 (1998), 23
Ginsburg, T., *Judicial Review in New Democracies* (Cambridge: Cambridge University Press, 2003)
Global Commission on International Migration, *Migration in an Interconnected World: New directions for actions* (Global Commission on International Migration, Geneva, 2005)
Golbeck, C., 'Non-profit organisations & social service provision: Chances for new governance arrangements in the third sector?', Research Group European Civil Society & Multilevel Governance (2008)
Goldsmith, A. A., 'The state, the market and economic development: A second look at Adam Smith in theory and practice', *Development and Change* 26 (1995), 633
Greer, S. L., *Four Way Bet: How devolution has led to four different models for the NHS* (London, 2004)
Gribben, C., K. Pinnington and A. Wilson, *Governments as Partners: The role of the central government in developing new social partnerships* (Copenhagen: The Copenhagen Centre, 2001)
Grimm, D., 'Integration by constitution', *International Journal of Constitutional Law* 3 (2005), 193
Groenendijk, K., 'Citizens and third country nationals: Differential treatment or discrimination?' in J. Carlier and E. Guild (eds.), *The Future of Free Movement of Persons in the EU* (Brussels: Bruylant, 2006)
  'Family reunification as a right under Community law', *European Journal of Migration and Law* 8 (2006), 215
  'The Long-Term Residents Directive, denizenship and integration' in A. Baldaccini, E. Guild and H. Toner (eds.), *Whose Freedom, Security and Justice? EU immigration and asylum law and policy* (Oxford: Hart Publishing, 2007)
Groot, G.-R. de, J. Kuipers and F. Weber, 'Passing citizenship tests as a requirement for naturalization: A comparative perspective' in E. Guild, K. Groenendijk and S. Carrera (eds.), *Illiberal Liberal States: Immigration, citizenship and integration in the EU* (Aldershot: Ashgate, 2007)

Grosser, K., and J. Moon, 'Best practice reporting on gender equality in the UK: Data, drivers and reporting choices', University of Nottingham, ICCSR Research Paper Series 35 (2006)

Grundmann, S., 'Ausbau des Informationsmodells im Europäischen Gesellschaftsrecht', *DStR* 6 (2004), 232

Guibboni, S., *Social Rights and Market Freedom in the European Constitution* (Cambridge: Cambridge University Press, 2006)

Guild, E., 'Fundamental rights and EU citizenship', Global Jean Monnet – ECSA-World Conference 2010, http://ec.europa.eu/education/jean-monnet/doc/ecsa10/guild_en.pdf

Guild, E., K. Groenendijk and S. Carrera (eds.), *Illiberal Liberal States: Immigration, citizenship and integration in the EU* (Aldershot: Ashgate, 2009)

Guimezanes, N., 'Loi de 24 juillet 2006 relative à l'immigration et à l'intégration', *La Semaine Juridique – Édition Générale* 36 (2006), 1623

Haagsma, A., 'The EU citizen between the market and the state', *Web JCLI* 5 (2005)

Haas, E., 'Introduction' in E. Haas and D. Dinan (eds.), *The Uniting of Europe: Political, social and economic forces 1950–1957* (Indiana: University of Notre Dame Press, 2004)

Haas, H. de, 'International migration, remittances and development: myths and facts', *Third World Quarterly* 26 (2005), 1243

'Statement', Conference on migration and development 2006, www.thehague process.org/News/news/Documenten/Migranten%20als%20bruggenbouw ers2006–1.pdf

Habermas, J., *Between Facts and Norms* (Cambridge: Polity Press, 1996)

'The post-national constellation and the future of democracy' in J. Habermas (ed.), *The Postnational Constellation* (Cambridge: Polity, 2001)

'Why Europe needs a constitution', *New Left Review* 11 (2001), 5

Hailbronner, K., 'Union citizenship and access to social benefits', *CMLR* 42 (2005), 1245

Hall, P., 'The role of interests, institutions, and ideas in the comparative political economy of the industrialized nations' in M. I. Lichbach and A. S. Zuckerman (eds.), *Comparative Politics: Rationality, culture, and structure* (Cambridge: Cambridge University Press, 1997)

Hall, P. A., and D. W. Soskice, 'An introduction to varieties of capitalism' in P. A. Hall and D. W. Soskice (eds.), *Varieties of Capitalism: The institutional foundations of comparative advantage* (Oxford: Oxford University Press, 2001)

Haltern, U., 'Integration through law' in A. Wiener and T. Diez (eds.), *European Integration Theory*, 1st edn (Oxford: Oxford University Press, 2004)

Hancher, L., 'Case C-320/91 P, Procureur du Roi v. Paul Corbeau, Judgment of the full Court, 19 May 1993', *CML Rev* 31 (1994), 105

Hardin, G., 'The tragedy of the commons', *Science* 162 (1968), 1243

Hart, H. L. A., *The Concept of Law*, 2nd edn (Oxford: Clarendon Press, 1994)

Hart, S. M., 'Self-regulation, corporate social responsibility, and the business case: Do they work in achieving workplace equality and safety?', *Journal of Business Ethics* 92 (2009), 23

Hartley, T., *EU Law in a Global Context* (Cambridge: Cambridge University Press, 2004)

Hatje, A., 'The economic constitution' in A. von Bogdandy and J. Bast (eds.), *Principles of European Constitutional Law* (Oxford: Hart Publishing, 2006)

Hatzopoulos, V., 'Services of general interest in healthcare: An exercise in deconstruction?' in U. Neergaard, R. Nielsen and L. Roseberry (eds.), *Integrating Welfare Functions into EU Law: From Rome to Lisbon* (Kopenhagen: DJØF, 2009)

Hauser-Ditz, A., and P. Wilke, 'Corporate social responsibility: Soziale und ökologische Verantwortung von Unternehmen. Eine Betriebsrätebefragung zu den Handlungsfeldern für Arbeitnehmervertretungen', Diskussionspapier (2005)

Hawk, B. E., *United States, Common Market and International Antitrust: A comparative guide*, 2nd edn (Aspen: Law & Business, 1990)

Hayek, F., *The Constitution of Liberty* (London: Routledge & Kegan Paul PCL, 1960)
    Law, Legislation, and Liberty, I: *Rules and Order* (London: Routledge & Kegan Paul PCL, 1973)

Hayek, F. A., *The Road to Serfdom* (Chicago: University of Chicago Press, 1944)

Hees, R. B. van, 'Het Cartesio-arrest en re-incorporatie binnen de Europese Unie', *V&O* 1 (2009), 5

Heijke, J., *Migratie van Mediterranen: economie en arbeidsmarkt* (Leiden: Stenfert Kroese, 1986)

Heller, H., 'Political democracy and social homogeneity' in A. Jacobsen and B. Schlink (eds.), *Weimar: A jurisprudence of crisis* (Berkeley *et al.*: University of California Press, 2000)

Hemerijck, A., 'The self-transformation of the European Social Model(s)' in G. Esping-Andersen (ed.), *Why We Need a New Welfare State* (Oxford: Oxford University Press, 2002)

Herbert, U., *Geschichte der Ausländerpolitik in Deutschland: Saisonarbeiter, Zwangsarbeiter, Gastarbeiter, Flüchtlinge* (Munich: Beck, 2001)

Hirschl, R., *Towards Juristocracy* (Cambridge, MA: Harvard University Press, 2004)

Hofmann, R., and H. Hoffmann, *Ausländerrecht. Handkommentar* (Baden-Baden: Nomos, 2008)

Hogg, C., *Citizens, Consumers & the NHS: Capturing voices* (Basingstoke/New York: Palgrave Macmillan, 2009)

Holmwood, J., 'Three pillars of welfare state theory: T. H. Marshall, Karl Polanyi and Alva Myrdal in defence of the national welfare state', *European Journal of Social Theory* 3 (2000), 23

Höpner, M., 'Corporate governance reform and the German party paradox', *Comparative Politics* 39 (2007), 401

Höpner, M., and A. Schäfer, 'A new phase of European integration: Organized capitalism in post-Ricardian Europe', *West European Politics* 33 (2010), 344

Höpner, M. S., *et al.*, 'Kampf um Souveränität? Eine Kontroverse zur europäischen Integration nach dem Lissabon-Urteil des Bundesverfassungsgerichts', *Politische Vierteljahresschrift* 51 (2010), 323

Hopt, K. J., 'Internationales Gesellschaftsrecht und europäische Einflüsse' in A. Baumbach, K. J. Hopt and H. Merkt (eds.), *Handelsgesetzbuch* (Munich: Beck, 2010)

Horn, L., *The Transformation of Corporate Governance Regulation in the European Union: Towards a marketisation of corporate control* (Amsterdam: University of Amsterdam, 2008)

Hughes, D., and P. Vincent-Jones, 'Schism in the church: National Health Service systems and institutional divergence in England and Wales', *Journal of Health and Social Behaviour* 49 (2008), 400

Hugo, G., '*Circular Migration: Keeping development rolling? Migration information source*' (Migration Policy Institute, 2003)

Huijstee, M. V. and P. Glasbergen, 'The practice of stakeholder dialogue between multinationals and NGOs', *Corporate Social Responsibility and Environmental Management* 15 (2007), 289

Human Rights Watch, *The Netherlands: Discrimination in the name of integration* (2008), www.hrw.org/backgrounder/2008/netherlands

Hyman, R., 'Trade unions and the politics of the European Social Model', *Economic and Industrial Democracy* 26 (2005), 9

'Britain and the European Social Model: Capitalism against capitalism?' IES Working Paper 19 (2008), p. 1

IOM, *World Migration 2005: Costs and benefits of international migration* (IOM: Geneva, 2005)

Permanent or Circular Migration? Policy choices to address demographic decline and labour shortages in Europe (Geneva: IOM, 2008)

Ireland, P., *Becoming Europe: Immigration, integration and the welfare state* (Pittsburgh: University of Pittsburgh Press, 2004)

Israel, J., *European Cross-Border Insolvency Regulation* (Antwerp: Intersentia, 2005)

Jachtenfuchs, M., and B. Kohler-Koch, 'Multi-level governance' in A. Wiener and T. Diez (eds.), *European Integration Theory* (Oxford: Oxford University Press, 2004)

Jacobs, A. T. J. M., 'The social Janus head of the European Union: The social market economy versus ultraliberal policies' in J. Wouters, L. Verhey and P. Kiiver (eds.), *European Constitutionalism beyond Lisbon* (Antwerp: Intersentia, 2009)

Jacobsoon, C., 'Baxläxa för Sverige i EU domston', *Dagens Nyheter* (19 December 2007)

Jederlund, L., 'In transition: From immigration policy to integration policy in Sweden', *Scandinavian Review* 87 (1999), 1

Jensen, M., and W. Meckling, 'Theory of the firm: Managerial behavior, agency costs and ownership structure', *Journal of Financial Economics* 3 (1976), 305

Jewell, T., and J. Wilkinson, 'Health and social care regulation in Wales: An integrated system of political, corporate and professional governance for improving public health', *JRSH* 128 (2008), 306

Joerges, C., 'States without a market? Comments on the German Constitutional Court's Maastricht judgment and a plea for interdisciplinary discourses', *EIOP* 1(20) (1997), http://papers.ssrn.com/sol3/papers.cfm?abstract_id=302713.

'The social market economy as Europe's social model?' in L. Magnusson and B. Strath (eds.), *A European Social Citizenship? Pre-conditions for future policies in historical light* (Brussels: Peter Lang, 2005)

'What is Left of the European Economic Constitution? A melancholic eulogy', *ELRev* 30 (2005), 470

'European challenges to private law: On false dichotomies, true conflicts and the need for a constitutional perspective', *LSI* 18 (2006), 146

'Rethinking European law's supremacy: A plea for a supranational conflict of laws' in B. Kohler-Koch and B. Rittberger (eds.), *Debating the Democratic Legitimacy of the European Union* (Lanham: Rowman & Littlefield Publishers, 2007)

'A new alliance of de-legalisation and legal formalism? Reflections on response to the social deficit of the European integration project', *Law and Critique* 19 (2008), 225

'The Lisbon judgment, Germany's "Sozialstaat", the ECJ's labour law jurisprudence and the reconceptualisation of European law as a new type of conflicts law' in A. Fischer-Lescano, C. Joerges and A. Wonka (eds.), 'The German Constitutional Court's Lisbon ruling: Legal and political science perspectives', ZERP Discussion Paper 1 (2010)

Joerges, C., and F. Rödl, 'Social market economy as Europe's "social model"', EUI Working Paper 8 (2004)

'On the "social deficit" of the European integration project and its perpetuation through the ECJ-judgements in *Viking* and *Laval*', RECON Online Working Paper 6 (2008)

'Informal politics, formalized law and the "social deficit" of European integration: Reflections after the judgments of the ECJ in *Viking* and *Laval*', *ELJ* 15 (2009), 1

Joerges, C., and E. Vos (eds.), *EU Committees: Social regulation, law and politics* (Oxford: Hart, 1999)

Johansson, J., 'Så gör vi inte här i Sverige. Vi brukar göra så här. Retorik och praktik i LO:s invandrarpolitik 1945–1981', *Historic tidskift* (2008)

Jones, A., and B. E. Suffrin, *EC Competition Law*, 2nd edn (Oxford: Oxford University Press, 2004)

Kabinet, 'Kabinetsreactie op advies ACVZ, Regulering en facilitering van arbeids-migratie' (Dutch Cabinet, 2004)

Kang, N., 'A critique of the "varieties of capitalism"', University of Nottingham, ICCSR Research Paper Series 45 (2006)

Kaufmann, F.-X., *Herausforderungen des Sozialstaates* (Frankfurt am Main: Suhrkamp, 1997)

Keller, B., 'The European Company Statute: Employee involvement – and beyond', *Industrial Relations Journal* 33 (2002), 424

Kendall, J., 'The third sector and the development of European public policy: Framework for analysis?', Civil Society Working Paper 19 (2001)

'Terra incognita: Third sectors and European policy processes' in J. Kendall (ed.), *Handbook on Third Sector Policy in Europe: Multi-level processes and organized civil society* (Cheltenham/Northampton, MA: Edward Elgar, 2009)

Keohane, R. O., 'Beyond the tragedy of the commons: A discussion of governing the commons: The evolution of institutions for collective action', *Perspectives on Politics* 8 (2010), 577

Ker, S., and I. Anderson, 'Service innovations: Developing a specialised (tertiary) service for the treatment of affective disorders', *Psychiatric Bulletin* 30 (2006), 103

Kieninger, E., 'Aktuelle Entwicklungen des Wettbewerbs der Gesellschaften', German Working Papers in Law and Economics 14 (2007)

Kilpatrick, C., 'New EU employment governance and constitutionalism' in G. de Búrca and J. Scott (eds.), *Law and Governance in the EU and the US* (Oxford et al.: Hart Publishing, 2006)

Kinderman, D., 'The political economy of corporate responsibility in Germany 1995–2008', Mario Einaudi Center for International Studies, Working Paper Series 5 (October 2008)

'Why do some countries get CSR sooner, and in greater quantity, than others? The political economy of corporate responsibility and the rise of market liberalism across the OECD 1977–2007', WZB Discussion Paper SP III 301 (2009)

Kostakopoulou, D., 'The evolution of European Union citizenship', *EPS* 7 (2008), 285

Kostakopoulou, D., S. Carrera and M. Jesse, 'Doing and deserving: Competing frames of integration in the EU' in E. Guild, K. Groenendijk and S. Carrera (eds.), *Illiberal Liberal States: Immigration, citizenship and integration in the EU* (Aldershot: Ashgate, 2009)

Koutnatzis, S., 'Social rights as a constitutional compromise: Lessons from comparative experience', *Columbia JTL* 44 (2005), 74

Kraakman, R., *The Anatomy of Corporate Law* (Oxford: Oxford University Press, 2006)

Krajewski, M., 'Providing legal clarity and securing policy space for public services through a legal framework for services of general economic interest: Squaring the circle', *EPL* 14 (2008), 377

Kröger, S., *Soft Governance in Hard Politics: European coordination of anti-poverty policies in France and Germany* (Wiesbaden: Verlag fuer Sozialwissenschaften, 2008)

   'The open method of coordination: Underconceptualisation, overdetermination, depoliticisation and beyond' in S. Kröger (ed.), 'What we have learnt: Advances, pitfalls and remaining questions in OMC research', *EIOP* 13 (2009)

   'What we have learnt: Advances, pitfalls and remaining questions in OMC research', *EIOP* special issue 13 (2009)

Kruse, V., *Sitzverlegung von Kapitalgesellschaften innerhalb der EG* (Köln: Carl Heymanns Verlag, 1996)

Kühling, J., 'Staatliche Handlungspflicht zur Sicherung der Grundfreiheiten', *NJW* (1999), 403

La Porta, R., F. Lopez-de-Silanes and A. Shleifer, *Investor Protection: Origins, consequences, reform* (Cambridge, MA: National Bureau of Economic Research, 1999)

Laborde, C., 'The culture(s) of the Republic: Nationalism and multiculturalism in French Republican thought', *Political Theory* 29 (2001), 716

Labour/Plaid Cymru, 'One Wales: A progressive agenda for the government of Wales' (2007), http://wales.gov.uk/about/programmeforgovernment/strategy/publications/onewales/?lang=en

Lakemann, P., *Binnen zonder kloppen: Nederlandse immigratiepolitiek en de economische gevolgen* (Amsterdam: Meulenhoff, 1999)

Lamassoure, A., 'Mission report for President Sarkozy' (2008), http://www.alain lamassoure.eu/liens/975.pdf

Laurent, E., and J. Le Cacheux, 'What (economic) constitution does the EU need?', de Travail OFCE, Sciences-Po 4 (2007), p. 18

Laursen, F., *Comparative Regional Integration: Theoretical perspectives* (Aldershot: Ashgate, 2003)

   Comparative Regional Integration: Europe and beyond (Aldershot: Ashgate, 2010)

Law Society of England and Wales, 'Consultation on the results of the study on the operation and the impact of the statute for a European Company (SE)', http://circa.europa.eu/Public/irc/markt/markt_consultations/library?I=/company_law/statute_european/registered_organisations/40law_wales-enpdf/_EN_1.0_&a=d

Lebessis, N., and J. Paterson, 'Evolution in governance: What lessons for the Commission? A first assessment', European Commission Forward Studies Unit Working Paper (Brussels, 1997)

Leibfried, S., 'Social policy? Left to the judges and the markets?' in H. Wallace, M. A. Pollack and A. R. Young (eds.), *Policy-Making in the European Union*, 6th edn (Oxford: Oxford University Press, 2010)

Leibfried, S., and P. Pierson, 'Social policy: Left to courts and markets?' in H. Wallace and W. Wallace (eds.), *Policy-Making in the European Union* (Oxford: Oxford University Press, 2000)

Lenaerts, K., and P. van Nuffel, *Constitutional Law of the European Union* (London: Sweet & Maxwell, 2005)

Lewis, J., 'The state and the third sector in modern welfare states: Independence, instrumentality, partnership' in A. Evers and J.-L. Laville (eds.), *The Third Sector in Europe* (Cheltenham/Northampton, MA: Edward Elgar, 2004)

Liebert, U., 'European social citizenship. Preconditions for promoting inclusion' in L. Magnusson and B. Strath (eds.), *A European Social Citizenship: Preconditions for future policies from a historical perspective* (Brussels: Peter Lang, 2004)

  'The politics for a Social Europe and the Lisbon process' in L. Magnusson and B. Strath (eds.), *European Solidarities: Tensions and contentions of a concept* (Brussels: Peter Lang, 2007)

Liebert, U., J. Falke and A. Maurer (eds.), *Postnational Constitutionalism in the New Europe* (Baden-Baden: Nomos, 2006)

Liebert, U. with S. Sifft (eds.), *Gendering Europeanization (Public Discourses on EC Equal Treatment and Equal Opportunity Norms in Six Member States)* (Brussels: Peter Lang, 2003)

Lombardo, S., 'Conflict of law rules in company law after Überseering: An economic and comparative analysis of the allocation of policy competence in the European Union', *European Business Organization Law Review* 4 (2003), 301

Longley, M., 'Health care systems in transition: The Welsh report', WHO Regional Office for Europe on behalf of the European Observatory on Health Systems and Policies (2004)

Lucassen, J., and R. Penninx, *Nieuwkomers, Nakomelingen, Nederlanders. Immigranten in Nederland 1950–1993* (Amsterdam: Het Spinhuis, 1994)

Lundborg, P., 'Invandringspolitik för cirkulär migration', *Swedish Institute for European Policy Studies* 9 (2009)

Lundh, C., 'Invandrarna i den svenska modellen – hot eller reserv? Fackligt program på 1960-talet', *Arbetarhistoria* 2 (1994)

Lutter, N., 'Konzepte, Erfolge und Zukunftsaufgaben Europäischer Gesellschaftsrechtsharmonisierung' in S. Grundmann (ed.), *Systembildung und Systemlücken in Kerngebieten des Europäischen Privatrechts* (Tübingen: Mohr Siebeck, 2000)

Lynch-Fannon, I., *Working within Two Kinds of Capitalism* (Portland: Hart Publishing, 2003)

Maaß, F., and R. Clemens, 'Corporate Citizenship. Das Unternehmen als guter Bürger', *Institut für Mittelstandsforschung Bonn, Jahrbuch zur Mittelstandsforschung* (2002)

Mabbett, D., 'The development of rights-based social policy in the European Union: The example of disability rights', *JCMS* 43 (2005), 645

McGowan, L., 'Theorising European integration: Revisiting neo-functionalism and testing its suitability for explaining the development of EC competition policy?', *EIOP* 11 (2007)

McKay, S., 'European Court gives preliminary ruling on union cases over conflicting rights', *EIROnline* (2007)

McWilliams, A., and D. Siegel, 'Corporate social responsibility: A theory of the firm perspective', *Academy of Management Review* 26 (2001), 117

McWilliams, A., D, Siegel and P. Wright, 'Corporate social responsibility: Strategic implications', *Journal of Management Studies* 43 (2006), 1

Maduro, M., *We the Court: The European Court of Justice and the European economic constitution: A critical reading of Article 30 of the EC Treaty* (Oxford: Hart, 2000)
  'European constitutionalism and three models of Social Europe' in M. Hesselink (ed.), *The Politics of a European Civil Code* (Kluwer International, 2006)

Magnusson, L., '*After Lisbon: Social Europe at the crossroads?*', ETUI Working Paper 1 (2010)

Maher, I., 'Re-imagining the story of European competition law', *OJLS* 20 (2000), 163

Maillo, J., 'Services of general interest and EC competition law' in G. Amato and D. Ehlermann (eds.), *EC Competition Law: A critical assessment* (Oxford: Hart Publishing, 2007)

Maisto, G., *Residence of Companies under Tax Treaties and EC Law* (Amsterdam: IBFD, 2009)

Majone, G., *Dilemmas of European Integration: The ambiguities and pitfalls of integration by stealth* (Oxford: Oxford University Press, 2005)
  'The common sense of European integration', *JEPP* 13 (2006), 607

Malaret, E., 'Public service, public services, public functions, and guarantees of the rights of citizens: Unchanging needs in a changed context' in M. Freedland and S. Sciarra (eds.), *Public Services and Citizenship in European Law: Public and labour law perspectives* (London: Clarendon Press, 1998)

Mäntysaari, P., *Comparative Corporate Governance: Shareholders as a rule-maker* (Heidelberg: Springer, 2005)

Mantzavinos, C., *Individuals, Institutions and Markets* (Cambridge: Cambridge University Press, 2001)

Marshall, T., 'Citizenship and social class (1950)' in T. Marshall and T. Bottomore (eds.), *Citizenship and Social Class* (London: Pluto Press, 1992)

Marshall, T. H., *Citizenship and Social Class* (Oxford: Oxford University Press, 1950)

Martinez, B., 'Structure, power, and discourses of development in Spanish NGOs', *Nonprofit Management & Leadership* 20(2) (2009), 203

Mäsch, G., 'EGBGB Art. 12: Begriff, Aufgabe und Ziele des IPR' in H. G. Bamberger and H. Roth (eds.), *Beck'scher Online-Kommentar* (2009)

Matten, D. A. and J. Moon, 'Implicit and explicit CSR: A conceptual framework for the understanding of corporate social responsibility', *Academy of Management Review* 33 (2008), 404

Mattli, W., 'Revisiting the European Court of Justice', *International Organization* 52 (1998), 177

Maurer, A., 'Consumer protection and social models of Continental and Anglo-American contract law and the transnational outlook', *IJGLS* 14 (2007), 135

Maydell, B. von, *et al.*, *Enabling Social Europe* (Vienna: Springer, 2006)

Mei, A. P. van der, 'Cross-border access to health care within the European Union: Recent developments in law and policy', *European Journal of Health Law* 10 (2003), 369

Meijer, S., R. Douven and B. van den Berg, 'Recent developments in Dutch hospitals', CP Memorandum, CPB Netherlands Bureau for Economic Policy Analysis (2010), http://www.cpb.nl/sites/default/files/publicaties/download/memo239.pdf

Méndez de Vigo, I., 'La Unión Europea después del Tratado de Lisboa y los Derechos Fundamentales de la Unión Europea', Global Jean Monnet – ESCA-World Conference 2010, http://ec.europa.eu/education/jean-monnet/doc/ecsa10/vigo_en.pdf

Menendez, A. J., 'European citizenship after Martínez Sala and Baumbast: Has European law become more human but less social?' RECON Online Working Paper 5 (2009)

Meyer, J. W., 'Reflections: Institutional theory and world society' in G. Krücken and G. S. Drori (eds.), *World Society. The writings of John W. Meyer* (Oxford: Oxford University Press, 2009)

Michalowski, I., 'Liberal states: Privatized integration policies?' in E. Guild, K. Groenendijk and S. Carrera (eds.), *Illiberal Liberal States: Immigration, citizenship and integration in the EU* (Aldershot: Ashgate, 2009)

Mitchell, R. K., B. R. Agle and D. J. Wood, 'Toward a theory of stakeholder identification and salience: Defining the principle of who and what really counts', *Academy of Management Review* 22 (1997), 853

Moeller, K., 'Two conceptions of positive liberty: Towards an autonomy-based theory of constitutional rights', *OJLS* 29 (2009), 757

Molle, W., *The Economics of European Integration: Theory, practice, policy*, 5th edn (Aldershot: Ashgate, 2006)

Monar, J., 'The institutional balance after the Treaty of Lisbon', Global Jean Monnet – ECSA-World Conference 2010, http://ec.europa.eu/education/jean-monnet/doc/ecsa10/monar_en.pdf

Monks, J., 'European Court of Justice and Social Europe: A divorce based on irreconcilable differences?', *Social Europe Journal* 4 (2008), 22

Monnet, J., *Mémoires* (Paris: Fayard, 1976)

Moon, J., 'Government as a driver of corporate social responsibility', University of Nottingham, ICCSR Research Paper Series 2 (2004)

Moon, J., and D. Vogel, 'Corporate social responsibility, government, and civil society' in A. Crane (ed.), *The Oxford Handbook of Corporate Social Responsibility* (Oxford: Oxford University Press, 2004)

Moravcsik, A., *The Choice for Europe: Social purpose and state power from Messina to Maastricht* (Ithaca: Cornell University Press, 1998)

'Reassessing legitimacy in the European Union', *JCMS* 40 (2002), 419

Möschel, W., 'Competition as a basic element of the social market economy', *European Business Organisation Law Review* 2 (2001), 713

Mossialos, E., *et al.* (eds.), *Health Systems Governance in Europe: The role of EU law and policy* (Cambridge: Cambridge University Press, 2010)

Mucciarelli, F. M., 'Company "emigration" and EC freedom of establishment: *Daily Mail* revisited', *European Business Organization Law Review* 9 (2008), 267

Mühleisen, M., and K. F. Zimmermann, 'A panel analysis of job changes and unemployment', *European Economic Review* 38 (1994), 793

Müller-Graff, P. C., 'Der Vertrag von Lissabon auf der Systemspur des Europäischen Primärrechts', *Integration* 2 (2008), 123

Münch, R., 'Constructing a European society by jurisdiction', *ELJ* 14 (2008), 519

Munck, R., 'Globalization and contestation: A Polanyian problematic', *Globalizations* 3 (2006), 175

Mutz, G., and J. Egbringhoff, *Gesellschaftliche Verantwortung von Unternehmen. Die Rolle der Arbeitnehmervertretung* (Berlin: Hans Bockler Stiftung, 2006)

Muylle, K., 'Angry farmers and passive policemen: Private conduct and the free movement of goods', *ELRev* 23 (1998), 467

Naborn, E. M., 'Gezinshereniging. De overkomst van gezinsleden van migranten en Nederlanders', Ministerie van Justitie, Wetenschappelijk onderzoek- en documentatie centrum (1992)

Neal, A. C., 'Corporate social responsibility: Governance gain or laissez-faire figleaf?', *Comparative Labor Law and Policy Journal* 29 (2008), 593

Neergaard, U., 'Modernising Article 82 EC: With particular focus on public and otherwise privileged undertakings', *Europarättslig Tidskrift* 54 (2007)

'Service concessions and related concepts: The increased pressure from Community law on Member States' use of concessions', *Public Procurement Law Review* (2007), 387

'Services of general economic interest: The nature of the beast' in M. Krajewski, U. Neergaard and J. van der Gronden (eds.), *The Changing Legal Framework of Services of General Interest in Europe: Between competition and solidarity* (Cambridge: T. M. C. Asser Press, 2009)

Neergaard, U., 'Services of general (economic) interest: What aims and values count' in U. Neergaard, R. Nielsen and L. M. Roseberry (eds.), *Integrating Welfare Functions into EU Law: From Rome to Lisbon* (Copenhagen: DJØF, 2009)

Neergaard, U., and R. Nielsen, *EU Ret*, 5th edn (Copenhagen: Thomson, 2009) 'Blurring boundaries: From the Danish welfare state to the European Social Model?' (Copenhagen 2010), http://papers.ssrn.com/sol3/papers.cfm? abstract_id=1618758

Neergaard, U., R. Nielsen and L. Roseberry (eds.), *The Services Directive: Consequences for the welfare state and the European Social Model* (Copenhagen: DJØF, 2008)

Integrating Welfare Functions into EU Law: From Rome to Lisbon (Copenhagen: DJØF, 2009)

The Role of Courts in Developing a European Social Model (Copenhagen: DJØF, 2010)

Nello, S., *The European Union: Economics, policies and history*, 2nd edn (London: McGraw Hill, 2009)

Nelson, J., and S. Zadek, *Partnership Alchemy: New social partnerships in Europe* (Copenhagen: The Copenhagen Centre, 2000)

Nergelius, J., 'Between collectivism and constitutionalism: The Nordic countries and constitutionalism' in J. Nergelius (ed.), *Constitutionalism: New challenges* (Leiden/Boston: Martinus Nijhoff, 2008)

Newdick, C., 'Charities in the health care market: Can trust survive NHS competition?', *The King's College Law Journal* 18 (2007)

Newland, K., 'Learning by doing: Experiences of circular migration', *MPI Insight* (September 2008)

Ngo, D. *et al.*, *Supervising the Quality of Care in Changing Healthcare Systems: An international comparison* (Rotterdam: University of Rotterdam (Rotterdam 2008), http://oldwww.bmg.eur.nl/personal/r.bal/Supervising%20the%20qu ality%20of%20care.pdf

NHS, 'NHS structure' (2010), www.nhs.uk/NHSEngland/thenhs/about/Pages/ nhsstructure.aspx

Nicolaas, H., and A. H. Sprangers, 'De nieuwe gastarbeider: manager uit de VS of informaticus uit India', *Maandstatistiek van de bevolking* 9 (2000)

Niechoj, T., 'Does supranational coordination erode its national basis? The case of European labour market policy and German industrial relations', in S. Kröger (ed.), 'What we have learnt: Advances, pitfalls and remaining questions of OMC research', *EIOP* special issue 1(13) (2009)

Niemann, A., and P. Schmitter, 'Neo-functionalism' in A. Wiener and T. Diez (eds.), *Theories of European Integration* (Oxford: Oxford University Press, 2009)

NMa, 'NMa wijst klachetb zorgaanbieders tegen zorverzekeres af', NMa press release, 27 May 2005, http://www.nmanet.nl/nederlands/home/Actueel/ Nieuws_Persberichten/NMa_Persberichten/2005/05-6.asp

'*Richtsnoeren voor de zorgsector*' (2010), http://www.nmanet.nl/Images/Richt
    snoeren%20voor%20de%20zorgsector_tcm16–135479.pdf
Nolke, A., 'Private governance in international affairs and the erosion of coordi-
    nated market economies in the European Union', Cornell University, Mario
    Einaudi Center for International Studies, Working Paper Series 3 (2008)
Noordam, F., *Hoofdzaken sociale-zekerheidrechts*, 3rd edn (Deventer: Kluwer,
    2004)
Novitz, T., 'Human rights analysis of the *Viking* and *Laval* judgments', *The
    Cambridge Yearbook of European Legal Studies* 10 (2007), 357
Nyberg, P., *Emigration, ekonomisk tillväxt och stabilitet: en teoretisk undersökning
    kring emigrationens orsaker och effekter på medellång sikt* (Helsingfors:
    Finlands bank, 1980)
Offe, C., 'The European model of "social" capitalism: Can it survive European
    integration?', *Journal of Political Philosophy* 11 (2003), 437
Ohlsson, R., *Ekonomisk strukturförändring och invandring: en undersökning av
    invandrare i Malmö under perioden 1945–1967* (Lund: Skrifter utgivna av
    ekonomisk, 1978)
Okoye, A., 'Theorising corporate social responsibility as an essentially contested
    concept: Is a definition necessary?', *Journal of Business Ethics* 89 (2009), 613
O'Neill, M., *The Struggle for the European Constitution: A past and future history*
    (London/New York: Routledge, 2008)
    The Struggle for the European Constitution (London: Routledge, 2009)
Oosterom-Staples, H., 'The Family Reunification Directive: A tool preserving Member
    State interest or conducive to family reunification unity?' in A. Baldaccini,
    E. Guild and H. Toner (eds.), *Whose Freedom, Security and Justice? EU immi-
    gration and asylum law and policy* (Oxford: Hart Publishing, 2007)
Oplustil, K., and C. Teichmann, *The European Company: All over Europe* (Berlin:
    De Gruyter, 2004)
Orlandini, G., 'The free movement of goods as a possible "Community" limitation
    on industrial conflict', *ELJ* 6 (2000), 341
    'Trade union rights and market freedoms: The European Court of Justice sets
    out the rules', *Comparative Labor Law & Policy Journal* 29 (2008), 573
Ostrom, E., *Governing the Commons* (Cambridge: Cambridge University Press,
    1990)
    'The comparative study of public economies: Acceptance paper for the Frank
    E. Seidman Distinguished Award in Political Economy', *The American
    Economist* 42 (1998)
    Understanding Institutional Diversity (Princeton: Princeton University Press,
    2005)
    'Gemeingütermanagement – eine Perspektive fuer bürgerschaftliches
    Engagement' in S. Helfrich and Heinrich Böll-Stiftung (eds.), *Wem gehört
    die Welt? Zur Wiederentdeckung der Gemeingüter* (Munich: Oekom, 2009)

Ostrom, E., and S. Crawford, 'Classifying rules' in E. Ostrom (ed.), *Understanding Institutional Diversity* (Princeton: Princeton University Press, 2005)

Outhwaite, W., *European Society* (Oxford: Oxford University Press, 2008)

Palier, B., 'Is there a social route to welfare reforms in Europe?', APSA Annual Meeting, Philadelphia (2006)

Pallis, A., and G. Tsiotsis, 'Maritime interests and the EU port services directive', *European Transport* 38 (2008), 17

Papademetriou, D., 'Reflections on restoring integrity to the United States immigration system: A personal vision', *Insight* 5 (2005)

Pastore, F., 'Circular migration: Background note for the Meeting of Experts on Legal Migration' (Rabat, 2008)

PatientPlus, 'Community care' (2008), www.patient.co.uk/doctor/Community-Care.htm

Pestoff, V. and T. Brandson (eds.), *Co-production: The third sector and the delivery of public services* (London: Routledge, 2007)

Petersmann, E., 'Multilevel trade governance in the WTO requires multilevel constitutionalism' in C. Joerges and E. Petersmann (eds.), *Constitutionalism, Multilevel Trade Governance and Social Regulation* (Oxford: Hart, 2006)

Pierson, C., *Beyond the Welfare State* (Cambridge: Polity, 1998)

Piris, J.-C., *The Lisbon Treaty: A legal and political analysis* (Cambridge: Cambridge University Press, 2010)

Pisani-Ferry, J., and A. Sapir, 'Last exit to Lisbon' (Brussels/Bruegel 2006), www.bruegel.org/uploads/tx_btbbreugel/pc_march2006_exitlisbon.pdf

Pistor, K., 'Co-determination in Germany: A socio-political model with governance externalities' in M. Blair and M. Roe (eds.), *Employees and Corporate Governance* (Washington: Brookings Institution Press, 1999)

Pluskat, S., 'Die Arbeitnehmerbeteiligung in der geplanten Europäischen AG', *DStR* 35 (2001), 1483

Poiares Maduro, M., and L. Azoulai (eds.), *Past and Future of European Law. The classics of EU law revisited on the 50th anniversary of the Rome Treaty* (Portland: Hart Publishing, 2010)

Polanyi, K., *The Great Transformation* (Boston: Beacon Press, 1957)
    The Great Transformation, 2nd edn (Boston: Beacon Press, 2001)

Pontusson, J., and P. Swenson, 'Labor markets, production strategies and wage bargaining institutions', *Comparative Political Studies* 29 (1996), 223

Prechal, S., 'Fundamental rights and the liberalization of service markets' in J. van de Grouden (ed.), *EU and WTO Law on Services Limits to the realization of general interest policies within the services markets?* (Alphen aan der Rijn: Kluwer, 2009)

Preuss, L., A. Haunschild and D. Matten, 'Trade unions and CSR: A European research agenda', *Journal of Public Affairs* 6 (2006), 256

Ptak, R., 'Neoliberalism in Germany: Revisiting the ordoliberal foundations of the social market economy' in P. Mirowski and D. Plehwe (eds.), *The Road from*

Mont Pélérin: The making of neoliberal thought (Cambridge, MA: Harvard University Press, 2009)

Pütter, U., *Die Wirtschafts- und Sozialpolitik der EU* (Wien: Facultas, 2009)

Rammeloo, S., *Corporations in Private International Law: A European perspective* (Oxford: Oxford University Press, 2001)

Reh, C., 'The Convention on the Future of Europe and the Development of Integration Theory: A lasting impact?', *JEPP* 15 (2008), 781

    'The Lisbon Treaty: De-constitutionalising the European Union?', *JCMS* 47 (2009), 625

Rehder, B., 'What is political about jurisprudence? Courts, politics and political science in Europe and the United States', MPIfG Discussion Paper 5 (2007)

Reibling, N., 'Healthcare systems in Europe: Towards an incorporation of patient access', *Journal of European Social Policy* 20 (2010), 5

Reichert, J., 'Experience with the SE in Germany', *Utrecht Law Review* 4 (2008), 28

Rhodes, M., and B. van Apeldoom, 'Capital unbound? The transformation of European corporate governance', *Journal of European Public Policy* 5 (1998), 406

Ringe, W., 'No freedom of emigration for companies?', *European Business Law Review* 3 (2005), 1

    'Forum shopping under the EU insolvency regulation', Oxford University Legal Research Paper 33 (2008), p. 1

Risse, T., 'Social constructivism and European integration' in A. Wiener and T. Diez (eds.), *European Integration Theory* (Oxford: Oxford University Press, 2004)

Rodrigues, S., 'Vers une loi européenne des services publics', *Revue du Marché commun et de l'Union européenne* (2003), 503

Roe, M. J., *Political Determinants of Corporate Governance: Political context, corporate impact* (Oxford: Oxford University Press, 2003)

Rohwer, A., 'Bismarck versus Beveridge: Ein Vergleich von Sozialversicherungssystemen in Europa', *Ifo Schnelldienst* 61 (2008)

Röpke, W., 'Zwischenbilanz der Europäischen Wirtschaftsintegration. Kritische Nachlese', *ORDO Jahrbuch* (1959) 87

Ross, M., 'Article 16 E.C. and services of general interest: from derogation to obligation?', *ELRev* 30 (2000), 22

Ross, M., and Y. Borgmann-Prebil (eds.), *Promoting Solidarity in the European Union* (Oxford: Oxford University Press, 2010)

Rothgang, H. *et al.*, 'The changing role of the state in healthcare systems', *European Review* 13 (2005), 187

Rousseva, E., 'The concept of "objective justification" of an abuse of a dominant position: Can it help to modernise the analysis under Article 82 EC?', *The Competition Law Review* 2 (2006), 27

Ruggie, J., 'International regimes, transactions, and change: Embedded liberalism in the postwar economic order', *International Organization* 36 (1982), 379

Sanders, P., *Naar een Europese N.V.?* (Zwolle: W. E. J. Tjeenk Willink, 1959)

Sauter, W., *Competition Law and Industrial Policy in the EU* (Oxford: Oxford University Press, 1997)

'The economic constitution of the European Union', *Columbia JEL* 4 (1998), 28

'Services of general economic interest and universal service in EU law', *ELRev*, 38 (2008), 172

Sbragia, A. M., 'Governance, the state, and the market: What is going on', *Governance* 13 (2000), 243

Schaal, G., *Integration durch Verfassung und Verfassungsrechtsprechung?* (Berlin: Duncker & Humblot, 2000)

'Integration durch Verfassung und Verfassungsrechtssprechung?', *ÖPZ* 30 (2001), 221

Schäfer, A., and S. Leiber, 'The double voluntarism in EU social dialogue and employment policy', *EIOP* 13 (2009)

Scharpf, F., *Governing Europe: Effective and democratic?* (Oxford: Oxford University Press, 1999)

Regieren in Europa. Effektiv und demokratisch? (Frankfurt am Main: Campus, 1999)

'The European Social Model: Coping with the challenges of diversity', *JCMS* 40 (2002), 645

'Reflections on multi-level legitimacy', MPIfG Working Paper 7 (2003)

'Legitimacy in the multilevel European polity', MPIfG Working Paper 1 (2009), http://www.mpifg.de/pu/workpap/wp09-1.pdf

'The double asymmetry of European integration', MPIfG Working Paper 12 (2009)

'Weshalb die EU nicht zur sozialen Marktwirtschaft werden kann', *Zeitschrift für Staats- und Europawissenschaaften* 7 (2009), 419

'The asymmetry of European integration, or why the EU cannot be a "social market economy"', *Socio-Economic Review* 8 (2010), 211

Schepel, H., *The Constitution of Private Governance: Product standards in the regulation of integrating markets* (Oxford: Hart, 2005)

Schiek, D., 'Sozialstaat' in E. Denninger (ed.), *Alternative Kommentar zum Grundgesetz 2* (Neuwied: Luchterhand, 2001)

'Autonomous collective agreements as a regulatory device in European Labour Law: How to read Article 139 EC', *ILJ* 34 (2005), 23

'Private rule-making and European governance: Issues of legitimacy', *ELRev* 32 (2007), 443

'The European Social Model and the Services Directive' in U. Neergaard, R. Nielsen and L. Roseberry (eds.), *The Services Directive: Consequences for the welfare state and the European Social Model* (Copenhagen: DJØF, 2008)

Schmidt, R. H., and S. Grohs, 'Angleichung der Unternehmensverfassungin Europa aus ökonom. Perspektive' in S. Grundmann (ed.), *Systembildung und Systemlücken in Gerngebieten des Euroäischen Privatrechts* (Tübingen: Mohr Siebeck, 2000)

Schmidt, S., 'Mutual recognition as a new mode of governance', *JEPP* 14 (2007), 713

Schmidt, V., 'EU economic solidarity: A great leap forward or a bridge too far?', *Neue Gesellschaft – Frankfurter Hefte* 7 (2010), 18

Schneidermann, D., 'Investment rules and the new constitutionalism', *LSI* 25 (2000), 762

Schön, W., 'The mobility of companies in Europe and the organizational freedom of company founders', *European Company and Financial Law Review* 3 (2006), 122

Schutter, O. de, 'Corporate social responsibility European style', *ELJ* 14 (2008), 203

Schwarze, J., *European Administrative Law* (London: Sweet and Maxwell, 1992)

Schwimbersky, S., 'Worker participation in Europe: Current developments and its impact on employees outside the EU', *AIRAANZ* (2005), 189

Scott, S., 'Corporate social responsibility and the fetter of profitability', *Social Responsibility Journal* 3 (2007), 31

Shaw, J., 'Introduction' in J. Shaw and G. More (eds.), *New Legal Dynamics of European Union* (Oxford: Clarendon Press, 1995)

'Post-national constitutionalism in the European Union', *Journal of European Public Policy* 6 (1999), 579

Social Law and Policy in an Evolving European Union (Oxford: Hart, 2000)

'Process, responsibility and inclusion in EU Constitutionalism', *ELJ* 9 (2003)

Sick, S., 'Mitbestimmungsrelevante Unternehmen mit ausländischen/kombiniert ausländischen Rechtsformen' (2010), www.boeckler.de/pdf/mbf_2010_01_20_sick.pdf

Sierra, J. L. B., 'Article 86: Exclusive rights and other anti-competitive state measures' in J. Faull and A. Nikpay (eds.), *The EC Law of Competition* (Oxford: Oxford University Press, 2007)

Silver, B., and G. Arrighi, 'Double movement: The *belle époques* of British and U.S. hegemony compared', *Politics & Society* 31 (2003), 325

Smend, R., 'Verfassungslehre und Verfassungsrecht (1928)' in R. Smend (ed.), *Gesammelte Schriften*, repr. edn (Berlin: Duncker & Humblot, 1968)

Snyder, F., 'Soft law and institutional practice in the European Community' in S. Martin (ed.), *The Construction of Europe: Essays in honour of Emile Noel* (Dordrecht: Kluwer Academic Publishers, 1993)

Social and Economic Council, 'Ontwerpadvies Arbeidsmigratiebeleid' (Dutch Social and Economic Council, 2007)

Sousa Santos, B. de, *Towards a New Legal Common Sense*, 2nd edn (Elsevier: Reed, 2002)

Spaventa, E., 'Seeing the wood despite the trees? On the scope of Union citizenship and its constitutional effectiveness', *CMLR* 45 (2008), 13

Steurer, R., 'The role of governments in corporate social responsibility: Characterising public policies on CSR in Europe', *Policy Sciences*, 15 (2009)

Stiglitz, J. E., A. Sen and J.-P. Fitoussi, *Mis-measuring our Lives: Why GDP doesn't add up: The Report by the Commission on the Measurement of Economic Performance and Social Progress* (New York/London: The New Press, 2010)

Storm, P., 'The Societas Europaea: A new opportunity?' in D. van Gerven and P. Storm (eds.), *The European Company* (Cambridge: Cambridge University Press, 2006)

Strath, B., 'The monetary issue and European economic policy in historical perspective' in C. Joerges, B. Strath and P. Wagner (eds.), *The Economy as a Polity: The political constitution of contemporary capitalism* (London et al.: UCL Press, 2005)

Stratton, A., 'Burnham faces private healthcare sector challenge over NHS "bias"', *guardian.co.uk*, 6 January 2010, www.guardian.co.uk/society/2010/jan/06/nhs-challenge-private-healthcare-sector-competition

Streeck, W., 'Competitive solidarity: Re-thinking the European Social Model', MPIfG Working Paper 8 (1999)

　　Korporatismus in Deutschland. Zwischen Nationalstaat und Europäischer Union (Frankfurt am Main: Campus, 1999)

Streit, M. E. and W. Mussler, 'The economic constitution of the European Community: From "Rome" to "Maastricht"', *ELJ* 1 (1995), 10

Sweet, A. and W. Sandelholtz, 'Integration, supranational governance and institutionalization of the European polity' in A. Sweet and W. Sandelholtz (eds.), *European Integration and Supranational Governance* (Oxford: Oxford University Press, 1998)

Syrpis, P., *EU Intervention in Domestic Labour Law* (Oxford: Oxford University Press, 2007)

Szczekalla, P., 'Grundfreiheitliche Schutzpflichten', *Deutsches Verwaltungsblatt* (1998), 219

Szyszczak, E., 'Public service provision in competitive markets', *Yearbook of European Law* (2001), 35

　　'Legal tools in the liberalisation of welfare markets' in U. Neergaard, R. Nielsen and L. M. Roseberry (eds.), *Integrating Welfare Functions into EU Law: From Rome to Lisbon* (Copenhagen: DJØF, 2009)

Teichmann, C., *Binnenmarktkonformes Gesellschaftsrecht* (Berlin: De Gruyter, 2006)

The King's Fund, 'Primary and community care' (2009), www.kingsfund.org.uk/topics/primary_and_community_care/

Timmermans, C. W. A., *Company Law as Ius Commune?* (Antwerp: Intersentia, 2002)

Tinbergen, J., *International Economic Integration* (Amsterdam: Elsevier, 1954)

Trachtman, J., 'The international law of economic integration: Towards the fourth freedom', W. E. Upjohn Institute for Employment Research, Kalamazoo (2009)

Trachtman, J. P., 'The role of international law in economic migration', *Society of International Economic Law Working Paper* 24 (2008)

Tränhardt, D., 'Inclusie of exclusie: discoursen over migratie in Duitsland', *Migrantenstudies* 18 (2002), 225

Trebek, K., 'Exploring the responsiveness of companies: Corporate social responsibility to stakeholders', *Social Responsibility Journal* 4(3) (2008), 351

Trenz, H.-J., 'Elements of a sociology of European integration', ARENA Working Paper 11 (2008), www.arena.uio.no/publications/working-papers2008/papers/wp08_11.pdf

Triggle, N., 'NHS "to undergo radical overhaul"', BBC News, 12 July 2010, www.bbc.co.uk/news/10557996

Trimidas, T., *The General Principles of EU Law* (Oxford: Oxford University Press, 2006)

Tröger, T H., '*Choice of Jurisdiction in European Corporate Law: Perspectives of European corporate governance*' (2004, rev. 2007), http://www.ssrn.com/abstract=568782

Trubek, D., and L. Trubek, 'Hard and soft law in the construction of Social Europe: The open method of coordination', *ELJ* 11(3) (2005), 343

Tsagouris, N., *Transnational Constitutionalism* (Cambridge: Cambridge University Press, 2007)

Turnbull, P., 'The war on Europe's waterfront: Repertoires of power in the port transport industry', *British Journal of Industrial Relations* 44 (2005), 305

Tweede Kamer, 'Verbanden tussen ontwikkeling en migratie', Vergarderjaar 2003–2004, 29 693, nr. 1 (2004), p. 30

UK House of Commons, *Migration and Development: How to make migration work for poverty reduction* (London: The Stationery Office, 2004)

United Nations, *International Migration and Development*, United Nations, Report of the Secretary General (New York, 2006)

Urth, H., 'Building a momentum for the integration of third-country nationals in the European Union', *European Journal of Migration and Law* 7 (2005), 163

Valk, O., 'Increasing corporate mobility through outbound establishment', *Utrecht Law Review* 6 (2010), 151

Vanberg, V. J., 'The Freiburg School: Walter Eucken and ordoliberalism', Freiburg Discussion Papers on Constitutional Economics (2004)

Vauchez, A., 'The transnational politics of judicialization. Van Gend en Loos and the making of EU polity', *ELJ* 16 (2010), 1

Verdun, A., 'Ten years EMU: An assessment of ten critical claims', *International Journal of Economics and Business Research* 2 (2010), 144

Verloren van Themaat, P., 'Recht en Economische Orde. Een oud probleem in een nieuw gewaad', *SEW* (1977), 262

Verloren van Themaat, P., 'Het Economisch grondslagenrecht van de Europese Gemeenschappen' in X. (ed.), *Liber Amicorum J. Mertens de Wilmars* (Antwerp: Kluwer, 1982)

'They also guide the division of competences between the legislative and the judiciary' in E. J. Estmäcker, H. Möller and H.-P. Schwarz (eds.), *Eine Ordnungspolitik für Europa. Festschrift für Hans von der Groeben zu seinem 80. Geburtstag* (Baden Baden: Nomos, 1987)

Vertovec, S., 'Circular migration: The way forward in global policy?', IMI Working Papers 4 (2007)

Vincent-Jones, P., and C. Mullen, 'From collaborative to genetic governance: The example of healthcare services in England' in O. de Schutter and J. Lenoble (eds.), *Reflexive Governance* (Oxford: Hart Publishing, 2010)

Vis, B., 'The importance of socio-economic and political losses and gains in welfare state reform', *Journal of European Social Policy* 19 (2009), 395

Voigt, R. (ed.), *Abschied vom Staat – Rückkehr zum Staat?* (Munich: IfS-Werkstatt, Universitätsdruckerei der Universität der Bundeswehr München, 2000)

Voss, C. J. J. H. van, *Inleiding sociaal recht*, 4th edn (Den Haag: Boom Juridische uitgevers, 2005)

Vossestein, G. J., 'Grensoverschrijdende zetelverplaatsing en omzetting van vennotschappen', *NTER* 5 (2009), 184

Vries, S. de, *Tensions within the Internal Market: The functioning of the internal market and the development of horizontal and flanking policies* (Europa Law Publishing, 2006)

Walker, N., 'The idea of constitutional pluralism', *MLR* 65 (2002), 317

'Constitutionalism and pluralism in a global context', RECON Online Working Paper 3 (2010)

Waltermann, R., *Sozialrecht*, 4th edn (Heidelberg: Müller, 2004)

Ward, H., and C. Smith, *Corporate Social Responsibility at a Crossroads: Futures to CSR in the UK to 2015* (London: International Institute for Environment and Development, 2006)

Weiler, J., and M. Wind, *European Constitutionalism beyond the State* (Cambridge: Cambridge University Press, 2003)

Welsh Assembly Government, 'Procurement and the third sector: Guidance for the Public Sector in Wales' (2008), www.buy4wales.co.uk/PRP/10693.file.dld

Wiener, A., 'Contested meanings of norms', *CompEurPolit* 5 (2007), 1

Wiener, A., and T. Diez, 'Introducing the mosaic of integration theory' in A. Wiener and T. Diez (eds.), *European Integration Theory* (Oxford: Oxford University Press, 2004)

'Taking stock of integration theory' in A. Wiener and T. Diez (eds.), *European Integration Theory* (Oxford: Oxford University Press, 2004)

European Integration Theory, 2nd edn (Oxford: Oxford University Press, 2009)

Wiener, J., 'Better regulation in Europe', *Current Legal Problems* 59 (2006), 447

Wiesbrock, A., 'Discrimination instead of integration? Integration requirements in Denmark and Germany' in E. Guild, K. Groenendijk and S. Carrera (eds.), *Illiberal Liberal States: Immigration, citizenship and integration in the EU* (Aldershot: Ashgate, 2009)

Legal Migration to the European Union (The Hague: Martinus Nijhoff, 2010)

Williams, C. A. and R. V. Aguilera, 'Corporate social responsibility in a comparative perspective' in A. Crane *et al.* (eds.), *The Oxford Handbook of Corporate Social Responsibility* (Oxford: Oxford University Press, 2008)

Wils, G., *De bijdrage van het Hof van Justitie to de ontwikkeling van een Europese markteconomie [The Contribution of the Court of Justice to the Development of a European Market Economy]* (Leuven: University of Leuven, 1994)

Wils, W., 'The search for the rule in Article 30 EEC: Much ado about nothing?', *ELRev* 17 (1993), 478

Wincott, D., 'A Community of law? "European" law and judicial politics: The Court of Justice and beyond', *Government and Opposition* 35 (2000), 3

Witte, B. de, 'The past and future role of the European Court of Justice in the protection of human rights' in P. Alston (ed.), *The EU and Human Rights* (Oxford: Oxford University Press, 1999)

Woolfson, C., and J. Sommers, 'Labour mobility in construction: European Implications of the Laval un Partneri dispute with Swedish labour', *European Journal of Industrial Relations* 12 (2006), 49

World Bank, *International Labor Migration: Eastern Europe and the former Soviet Union* (Washington DC: World Bank, Europe and Central Asia Region, 2006)

Wouters, J., L. Verhey and P. Kiiver (eds.), *European Constitutionalism Beyond Lisbon* (Antwerp: Intersentia, 2009)

Wymeersch, W., 'Company law in Europe and European company law', Financial Law Institute Working Paper 6 (2001), p. 1

Yalden, R., *Business Organizations: Principles, policies and practices* (Toronto: Emond Montgomery Publication, 2008)

Zmirak, J., *Wilhelm Röpke. Swiss localist, global economist* (Wilmington: ISI Books, 2001)

INDEX

qualified majority voting (QMV),
     increased use of 54–6, 57

real-seat theory
     adherence to 157
     description 157–8, 161
     employee protection 157–8
RECON project, contribution to
     research 4–5
Rhenish capitalism 239
Romania, Societas Europaea,
     stakeholder protection 169

seat transfer *see* company law
secondary legislation
     enforcement as governance mode
          6–7
     impact on national policies 1–3
self-governance and socially embedded
     constitutionalism 39
services of general economic interest
     (SGEIs)
     analytical framework of ECJ
          185–91
     case law 182–94
     chapter summary 11
     development in Treaties 176–81
     exemption under TFEU 182–94,
          273–4
     healthcare *see* healthcare
     main issues 174–6
     protocol 106–7, 111
     state aid to 272
     summary of case law
          developments 194
     summary of issues 195
     summary of Treaty
          developments 181
shareholder protection, consequences
     of lack of 151
skilled migrants *see* highly skilled
     migrants
Slovakia, adherence to incorporation
     theory 157
Slovenia
     real-seat theory, adherence to 157
     Societas Europaea, stakeholder
          protection 169

social actors
     aims 75
     arbitrary rule emanating from 37–8
     constitutionalism constructed by
          9–10
     economic actors, interplay with 23–4
     and European Court of Justice 27
     and 'new governance' 43
     and open method of co-ordination
          32–3
     research focus on 19–20, 21–2
     response to ECJ rulings 75
     social embedding, role in 13
     social policy, role in 30
     social practice of law 42
     transnational actors
          emergence 14
          and European Court of Justice 9
     transnational mobilisation 79–80
     types 75, 81
     use of constitutional law 8
social capitalism
     survival 64, 71–2
     transformation 8
'social Europe' policy *see* social
     integration
social exclusion, social integration
     becoming instrument of 3
social integration *see also* socially
     embedded constitutionalism
     approaches to 29–33
     balancing of competences 54–6
     and companies *see* company law;
          corporate social responsibility
          (CSR)
     development lacking 3–4, 5
     and economic integration
          case analysis *see Laval* case;
               Viking case
          company law *see* company law
          decoupling 5
          divergence in decision making 48
          'flux' between 9–10
          integration possibilities 5–6
          interrelation in actuality 13
          interrelation under Treaties 33–6
          multilayered polycentric
               self-governance model 68–9